W9-BMN-440

Includes 1 CD-ROM

WITHDRAWN

CREATING YOUR WORLD

CREATING YOUR WORLD
THE OFFICIAL GUIDE TO ADVANCED
CONTENT CREATION FOR SECOND LIFE

AIMEE WEBER
KIMBERLY RUFER-BACH
RICHARD PLATEL

Wiley Publishing, Inc.

ACQUISITIONS EDITOR: WILLEM KNIBBE
DEVELOPMENT EDITOR: CANDACE ENGLISH
PRODUCTION EDITOR: PATRICK CUNNINGHAM
COPY EDITOR: CANDACE ENGLISH
PRODUCTION MANAGER: TIM TATE
VICE PRESIDENT AND EXECUTIVE GROUP PUBLISHER: RICHARD SWADLEY
VICE PRESIDENT AND EXECUTIVE PUBLISHER: JOSEPH B. WIKERT
VICE PRESIDENT AND PUBLISHER: NEIL EDDE
MEDIA ASSOCIATE PROJECT MANAGER: LAURA ATKINSON
MEDIA ASSISTANT PRODUCER: JOSH FRANK
MEDIA QUALITY ASSURANCE: ANGIE DENNY
BOOK DESIGNER AND COMPOSITOR: PATRICK CUNNINGHAM
PROOFREADER: JEN LARSEN, WORD ONE
INDEXER: TED LAUX
ANNIVERSARY LOGO DESIGN: RICHARD PACIFICO
COVER DESIGNER: RYAN SNEED
COVER IMAGE: AIMEE WEBER

■ DEAR READER

Thank you for choosing *Creating Your World: The Official Guide to Advanced Content Creation for Second Life.* This book is part of a family of premium quality Sybex books, all written by outstanding authors who combine practical experience with a gift for teaching.

Sybex was founded in 1976. More than thirty years later, we're still committed to producing consistently exceptional books. With each of our titles we're working hard to set a new standard for the industry. From the paper we print on, to the authors we work with, our goal is to bring you the best books available.

I hope you see all that reflected in these pages. I'd be very interested to hear your comments and get your feedback on how we're doing. Feel free to let me know what you think about this or any other Sybex book by sending me an email at nedde@wiley.com, or if you think you've found a technical error in this book, please visit http://sybex.custhelp.com. Customer feedback is critical to our efforts at Sybex.

Best regards,

Neil Edde
Vice President and Publisher
Sybex, an Imprint of Wiley

ABOUT THE AUTHORS

Aimee Weber is the founder and CEO of Aimee Weber Studio (`www.AimeeWeber.com`). Aimee Weber Studio is one of the largest content-creation companies in *SL* and has worked with such organizations as PR Newswire, NBC, The United Nations, Save the Children, The National Oceanic and Atmospheric Administration, American Cancer Society Relay for Life, American Apparel, Warner Music, and the Exploratorium. Aimee graduated from Columbia University with a bachelor's degree in English and a minor in computer science. She is also a member of The International Academy of Digital Arts and Sciences, writes for AOL's *Second Life* Insider (`www.secondlifeinsider.com`) and is a frequent speaker on virtual worlds.

Kimberly Rufer-Bach, a.k.a. Kim Anubis in *Second Life*, is owner, designer, and producer of The Magicians (`www.themagicians.us`), one of the oldest, most innovative content-development companies in *Second Life*. Clients include the British Council, University of California Davis Medical Center, Global Kids, NASA, and New York Law School.

Richard Platel, a.k.a. Wednesday Grimm, has been a resident of *Second Life* and an LSL scripter since before the public beta and has been a professional software developer for over seven years. Richard organized and help create the very first *Second Life* group build and community, Lindenberg. He has created many popular builds and scripts, and recently scripted the marine life in sim Meteroa.

■ INTRODUCTION

In the beginning *Second Life* was a mere technical curiosity, devoid of rich content and filled with questions about the future. Back then we always suspected we were sitting on something enormous, something bigger than ourselves, but we didn't have the luxury of a roadmap. We were in uncharted territory.

You, my dear reader, come to *Second Life* during a golden age. *Second Life* sports a booming population, enormous interest from the outside world, and an economy that permits hard-working and creative residents to quit their day jobs and earn a living in a 3D world. Unlike us, you don't have to grope around in the dark for answers. You can get started quickly and easily using active forums, wikis, tutorials . . . and this book!

Creating Your World is ideal for the budding content creator who is already well versed in using *Second Life*. If you are brand-new to the platform, I recommend starting with *Second Life: The Official Guide*, also by Wiley. Once you feel comfortable moving around the grid and interacting with others, then you will have the prerequisites to get started on this book.

We start with a refresher course in **Chapter 1**. This chapter covers all the introductory material you will need before you get started with serious content creation. There may be some overlap with *Second Life: The Official Guide*, but be warned: this is not a complete introduction, so if this is your first time using *Second Life*, you would be better off starting with *The Official Guide*.

Chapter 2 introduces you to the process of building and goes over the details of the user interface in preparation for **Chapter 3**, where we go into extreme detail as to how prims work and how to get them to do what you want. **Chapter 4** explains how to texture your objects to simulate materials, lighting, and shadows. This is an important chapter, as quality textures can spell the difference between good work and highly polished professional work. **Chapter 5** is where we depart from the abstract building theory and apply our knowledge to joining the booming business of virtual clothing and accessories.

In **Chapter 6** we give you a foundation in LSL programming, allowing you to move to on to advanced programming in **Chapter 7**. Once you are familiar with the basics, we go on to work on full scripting projects in **Chapter 8**.

In **Chapter 9** we take a step back from the nitty-gritty of content creation to talk about creating a good overall user experience. This subject is often overlooked, but it's critical. In **Chapter 10** we discuss land-management features and the art of terraforming so you can transform undistinguished terrain into exciting locations. In **Chapter 11** we provide instructions on creating animations and poses. In **Chapter 12** we discuss the balance between elaborate, wasteful builds and efficient, light-weight builds. **Chapter 13** covers the ins and outs of directing winning virtual movies, known as *machinima*. Finally, in **Chapter 14** we wrap it all up with a final tutorial for creating an airplane.

NOTE

Be sure to check out the CD for templates, tools, tutorial files, great machinima, and more.

So what does *Creating Your World* offer? As you can see, we cover all the definitions and techniques associated with content creation, but that alone would not be enough to transform our readers into top virtual builders. To speed your journey from competent builder to *Second Life* guru, we immerse you the mechanics behind the scenes. We don't just tell you how a prim looks and what it does; we tell you exactly why things work they way they do. Armed with this deeper understanding, you'll be able to accomplish things well beyond the scope of this book, and possibly beyond anything we could have imagined.

CONTENTS AT A GLANCE

CONTENTS

■ CHAPTER 12: PERFORMANCE AND FIGHTING THE LAG MONSTER 304

■ CHAPTER 13: ACTION! CREATING MACHINIMA 318

■ CHAPTER 14: CREATING AN AIRPLANE 328

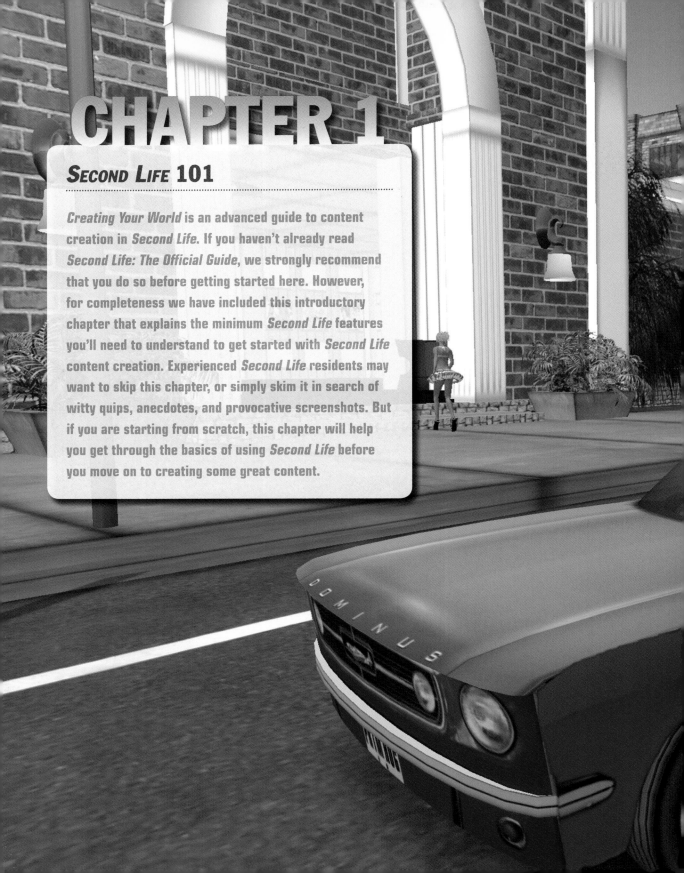

CHAPTER 1

SECOND LIFE 101

Creating Your World is an advanced guide to content creation in *Second Life*. If you haven't already read *Second Life: The Official Guide*, we strongly recommend that you do so before getting started here. However, for completeness we have included this introductory chapter that explains the minimum *Second Life* features you'll need to understand to get started with *Second Life* content creation. Experienced *Second Life* residents may want to skip this chapter, or simply skim it in search of witty quips, anecdotes, and provocative screenshots. But if you are starting from scratch, this chapter will help you get through the basics of using *Second Life* before you move on to creating some great content.

CONTENTS

CHAPTER 1

SECOND LIFE
AND YOUR
CHARACTER

MOVING
AROUND

LOOKING
AROUND

UNDER-
STANDING
YOUR
INVENTORY

NAVIGATING
THE
INVENTORY
MENUS

ORGANIZING
YOUR
INVENTORY

USING THE
DEBUG MENUS

SECOND LIFE AND YOUR COMPUTER

Second Life has a well-deserved reputation for needing to run on a pretty powerful computer. It's true; you really do need a decent computer to run *Second Life* well. In fact, *Second Life* can take advantage of the greatest amount of RAM or CPU capacity you throw at it.

That said, most of us aren't going to run out and sink $7,000 on a new machine. *Second Life* will run reasonably well on even a $1,000 computer. However, we do recommend at least the following:

 **1GB of RAM**

An ATI or NVIDIA video card with at least 128MB of video RAM

Additionally, a dual-core CPU gives you a lot more resources. If you can afford it, it's great to have.

Obviously, you can create *SL* content on a less powerful computer, so what's the fuss? If you're doing more than just basic scripting or building, you'll want to be able to run more than just *Second Life*. Those other programs will compete with *Second Life* for your system resources and make it slow to switch between them.

TIP

If Second Life *is running too slowly for you, it might be time for a computer upgrade. If you don't have much experience buying computers for specific features—and especially if you're shopping on a budget—try talking to other* Second Life *users to get an idea of what you'll need and how to get the most bang for your buck.*

If you already have a fast enough computer to run *SL*, you might be interested in other, less necessary hardware such as graphics tablets, extra monitors, surround-sound speakers, or any number of other devices or upgrades. Just don't rush out and buy things you're not sure you'll use. Try running *Second Life* on your existing computer until you know what you want and need.

■ MACINTOSH, WINDOWS, OR LINUX?

The "platform wars" are irrelevant when it comes to *Second Life*. *SL* looks and performs virtually the same on Macintosh and Windows. (Running *Second Life* on Linux can be a bit trickier, but if you use Linux, you probably expected that.) However, you will want to use a multibutton mouse no matter which operating system you use. (See the sidebar, "Working with a One-Button Mouse.")

NOTE

This book is written with the assumption that you're using a PC as the portal to your second life. If you're using a Mac, please refer to `http://secondlife.com/corporate/sysreqs.php`.

CHAPTER 1
CHAPTER 2
CHAPTER 3
CHAPTER 4
CHAPTER 5
CHAPTER 6
CHAPTER 7
CHAPTER 8
CHAPTER 9
CHAPTER 10
CHAPTER 11
CHAPTER 12
CHAPTER 13
CHAPTER 14
APPENDICES
INDEX

MORE INFO

WORKING WITH A ONE-BUTTON MOUSE

As a longtime Mac user, I've found the most annoying thing about the Macintosh is Apple's refusal to equip their computers with mice that have more than one button. That just doesn't work for building in *Second Life*. Luckily, OS X does support multibutton mice—all you have to do is plug them in. So what should you get? Basically, any USB mouse with more than one button will do. I'd recommend a mouse made by Logitech or Microsoft—both are excellent brands. If you'd like to stick with Apple hardware, try Apple's Mighty Mouse.

That said, if you *must* build with a one-button mouse or on a laptop, there are ways you can fake a right-click: holding down your Control key and clicking your mouse button (Control-click) will replicate a right-click in most OS X applications, but in *Second Life* you'll want to use Command-click instead. Alternatively, if you're using a MacBook or MacBook Pro without a mouse, simply place two fingers on your trackpad and click the button with your thumb.

■ THE NETWORK

Many users report trouble when running *Second Life* over a wireless network. If you find your objects aren't staying put when you move them around or if you're getting chat messages out of order, we recommend you stay plugged in. But as long as you have a fast and high-bandwidth Internet connection, you should be alright. However, you will likely run into trouble if you try running *Second Life* over the following:

- **Dial-up modem**
- **ISDN**
- **Cellular modem**
- **Satellite connection**

TIP

I prefer using Second Life *on a computer with more than one monitor. I can put* Second Life *on one and my scripting editor, Photoshop, or my Web browser on the other. This obviously isn't necessary; it's just something I find easier. And this way there's no switching between* Second Life *and your other programs—you just move your mouse over to the second display. Most new computers support at least two monitors—and those that don't are usually easy to upgrade.*

CHAPTER 1

SECOND LIFE
AND YOUR
CHARACTER

MOVING
AROUND

LOOKING
AROUND

UNDER-
STANDING
YOUR
INVENTORY

NAVIGATING
THE
INVENTORY
MENUS

ORGANIZING
YOUR
INVENTORY

USING THE
DEBUG MENUS

MOVING AROUND

In *Second Life*, as in your first life, you must learn to crawl before you can learn to walk. The good news is, in *Second Life* you don't have to stop there. You can fly, teleport, and bring entire worlds into existence simply by moving your fingers around.

Figure 1.1: The flight-control window

Second Life uses the standard WASD key configuration for moving around. (What's WASD? If you have a QWERTY keyboard, look for those keys: they form an arrow.) Alternatively, you can use the actual arrow keys. If you really want to punish yourself, right-click on your avatar and select Go . . . This will bring up the movement control panel, allowing you to move by pressing arrow buttons with your mouse (Figure 1.1). It's a tedious process but could prove handy if you're using your left hand to clutch this valuable tome.

Flying is just as easy as walking. Here is a complete list of basic movements and their associated keys:

Move forward: W or up arrow

Move backward: S or down arrow

Turn left: A or left arrow

Turn right: D or right arrow

Move left: Shift+A or Shift+Left arrow

Move right: Shift+D or Shift+Right arrow

Jump or fly up: E or Page Up

Crouch or fly down: C or Page Down

Begin flying: F or Home

Gravity is no obstacle for the majestic *SL* avatar, so if you stop moving around, your avatar will just float in the air.

NOTE

At around cloud-layer altitude it becomes difficult to gain more altitude. If you want to fly higher you will need to use some kind of vehicle. See Chapter 8, "Scripting the Fun Stuff," for details on vehicles.

LOOKING AROUND

CHAPTER 1

CHAPTER 2
CHAPTER 3
CHAPTER 4
CHAPTER 5
CHAPTER 6
CHAPTER 7
CHAPTER 8
CHAPTER 9
CHAPTER 10
CHAPTER 11
CHAPTER 12
CHAPTER 13
CHAPTER 14
APPENDICES
INDEX

Once you've mastered movement in *Second Life*, you should become familiar with ways to look around. You may have already noticed that your point of view, referred to as your *camera*, is located about three meters behind and slightly above your avatar (Figure 1.2). When you turn your avatar, your camera moves with it so that the camera is always behind you. Certain obstacles may cause your camera to move closer to you—for example if you back up against a wall. This is to prevent your camera being forced through the wall, which would make it impossible to see your avatar.

You don't have to move your avatar to look around. If you hold down the Alt key and left-click any object around your avatar (or the avatar itself) any movement of the mouse will cause your camera to rotate horizontally or zoom into or away from the object you selected. If you hold down the Alt key and the Control key, you'll be able to rotate the camera vertically around your selected object. These camera controls are called *Alt-zooming*.

Alt-zooming is one of the most important skills to master in *Second Life* as it gives you the ability to examine objects around you more closely from all angles, to view locations too small for your avatar to explore, to zoom out and get a bird's-eye view of the terrain, and to look up ladies' skirts (but don't let us catch you doing that!).

TIP

There are various techniques for handling Alt-zoom. While some people use their pinky finger for Control and their middle finger for Alt, others prefer to use their thumb for Alt and the side of their left hand for Control. You will have to find a position that feels right for you, but remember that you will likely be Alt-zooming more often than you'll do anything else in SL, so shoot for maximum performance.

Figure 1.2: (left) In third-person mode, the camera sits three meters behind your avatar. (right) In mouselook mode, the camera is positioned near your avatar's eyes.

Another important way of looking at our world is called *mouselook*. Pressing M causes your camera view to change such that you are looking through the eyes of your avatar (Figure 1.2). While in mouselook your mouse determines the direction you are looking. Left-clicking causes you to touch objects or use equipped items. Most movement controls function normally, but the A and D keys cause you to move sideways rather than turn. Mouselook can be very useful when operating in small spaces and in playing first-person-shooter-style games. To exit mouselook mode, simply press M or Esc.

CHAPTER 1

SECOND LIFE
AND YOUR
CHARACTER

MOVING
AROUND

LOOKING
AROUND

UNDER-
STANDING
YOUR
INVENTORY

NAVIGATING
THE
INVENTORY
MENUS

ORGANIZING
YOUR
INVENTORY

USING THE
DEBUG MENUS

■ TELEPORTING

With unaided flight, it takes the average user approximately 17 seconds to fly from one end of a 255-meter region to the other (we timed it!). If your destination lies 40 regions away, you're in for a bit of a commute. Fortunately, there is an easier way. The age of teleportation is upon us!

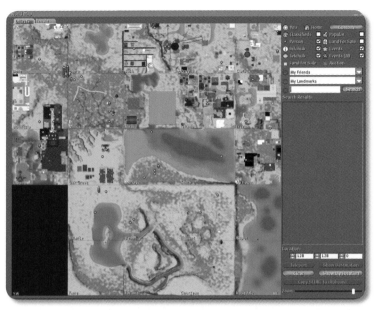

Figure 1.3: You can teleport to any location simply by double-clicking the map, by choosing a location from a pull-down menu, or by entering coordinates.

There is a variety of ways to teleport in *Second Life*, but the most basic way is to use the map button on the lower-right corner of your screen to display a map of the entire *Second Life* grid, including the mainland and all the islands. By dragging the map with your mouse and zooming in and out with the zoom slider or the mouse wheel, you can locate your intended destination. When you click on the map a red circle appears with the name of the region and the coordinates where you clicked. When you double-click you are instantly transported to your destination. It's as simple as that.

Pull-down menus on the right side of the screen provide you with instant access to the locations of friends and landmarks. More importantly, there is a search feature that helps you find any sim you're looking for simply by entering the sim's name. If you need to fine-tune your arrival location in a sim, you can do this by entering the location coordinates on the lower-right side of the map screen (Figure 1.3).

You can find a friend at his location, but there are also several ways you can invite a friend to visit you at your location:

> Create a landmark at your location by going to World ▸ Create Landmark Here and then passing that landmark to your friend. Landmarks come with their own Teleport button, so your friend needs only click the button to join you instantly.

> Teleport your friend to your location directly via your friend's user profile. To find someone's user profile, press the Search button and enter a name in the Find field. Your friend's profile has an Offer Teleport button, which allows you to send an invitation, with a short message to join you with a single mouseclick.

> Direct friends who are outside of *Second Life* to your location by giving them a SLURL (*Second Life* URL.) To do this, press the Copy SLURL to Clipboard button on the lower-right side of your map, then paste the SLURL into an email or an instant message to your friend.

UNDERSTANDING YOUR INVENTORY

CHAPTER 1

CHAPTER 2
CHAPTER 3
CHAPTER 4
CHAPTER 5
CHAPTER 6
CHAPTER 7
CHAPTER 8
CHAPTER 9
CHAPTER 10
CHAPTER 11
CHAPTER 12
CHAPTER 13
CHAPTER 14
APPENDICES
INDEX

One side effect of becoming a content creator in *Second Life* is that you end up with stuff. An unfathomable plethora of stuff! And it all resides in your Inventory! It's therefore very important that you understand how the *Second Life* Inventory system works, and how make the best use of it.

Figure 1.4: The Inventory window

To get started, take a look at your Inventory by pressing the Inventory button on the lower-right side of your screen. This opens the Inventory window (Figure 1.4). If you haven't been in *SL* long, your Inventory is probably pretty empty. If you've been in *SL* for a while, your Inventory is likely to be much more crowded. Even casual *Second Life* users can get thousands of items in just a few weeks.

In your Inventory you can see folders and Inventory items, which are the *Second Life* equivalent of a file. *Second Life* items behave much in the same way as files do, but they exist somewhat differently on the server than they would if you were viewing them on the client.

In general, objects can exist in *Second Life* in two ways: as an actual object in the world itself (you can interact with it, push it, walk over it, even ride around on it—it all depends on what the object's creator has decided it's for) or as a "frozen" copy in your Inventory. An object item in your Inventory doesn't exist as anything more than data, and you can't modify it beyond its name and a few item properties. Likewise, textures, sounds, and other nonobject items cannot be moved from Inventory into the world, because they don't exist in a format that the world can recognize unless applied to or contained within an object.

However, there are three exceptions to this rule—body parts, clothing, and attachments—that, when worn, exist on your avatar and in your Inventory at the same time. *Attachments* are otherwise-normal objects attached to your avatar just like clothing and body parts. We'll talk more about Attachments in Chapter 5, "Clothing and Accessories."

TIP

A tidy Inventory is essential for any content creator. Items in Inventory subfolders will not be downloaded until the subfolder is opened, so a well-organized Inventory is faster than one that is not. Also, if your Inventory (or login) is slow, empty your trash.

ITEMS (AKA ASSETS)

There are several different types of Inventory item: objects, textures, scripts, clothing, animations, calling cards, gestures, sounds, snapshots, body parts, landmarks, and notecards. Some behave similarly: Textures and snapshots are effectively the same; they just have different icons in your Inventory. Clothing and body parts both affect your avatar's shape, though they're still distinct item types.

■ FOLDERS

Items prefer to make their homes within folders. They tend not to actually communicate this desire, but believe us—they like it. Conveniently, folders are a very handy way of sorting items so you don't get them mixed up. It's a win-win!

By default, your Inventory will have folders with names like Animations, Body Parts, or Sounds. These default folders are good guidelines to organizing your Inventory: clothing goes in the Clothing folder, objects go in your Objects folder, and so on. You can also create your own folders alongside and within existing folders by right clicking and selecting New Folder from the pull down menu. For instance, you can create separate folders for each of your own projects or sort clothes you get from other users into subfolders such as Marching Band Uniforms or Swimwear.

For more detail on using folders, see the section "Using Inventory Folders" later in this chapter.

■ TRASH

When you delete items from your Inventory, they go into your Trash folder. Objects you delete from the world will also show up there. You can open items inside your Trash folder, but don't think of your trash as a place to put things; there are regular folders for that!

If you pull an object out of your trash then take it back into your Inventory, it will appear in your Objects folder. This ensures you don't accidentally use your Trash folder for storing things and risk losing them by mistake. Those "Oh no—what did I just do?" moments can be a pain.

■ LIBRARY

The Library folder is special. It's a Linden Lab-approved set of default avatar outfits, textures, scripts, and other Inventory items that all users have in their inventories. You can't add to or delete from it, and it changes only when the Lindens decide to change it. When you're getting started, some of the items in the Library folder are useful, but you can find better items elsewhere.

NAVIGATING THE INVENTORY MENUS

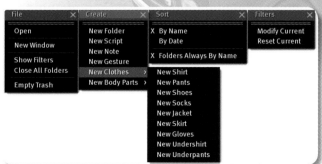

The *Second Life* Inventory has many familiar features and options that allow you to sort, filter, open, and manipulate your Inventory just as you would in any standard operating system (Figure 1.5). In this section we will take a detailed look at the Inventory menus and see what each option does for us.

Figure 1.5: The Inventory window's File, Create, Sort, and Filters menus

THE FILE MENU

The File menu contains Open, New Window, Show Filters, Close All Folders, and Empty Trash options. Each option is detailed here.

CHAPTER 1

CHAPTER 2
CHAPTER 3
CHAPTER 4
CHAPTER 5
CHAPTER 6
CHAPTER 7
CHAPTER 8
CHAPTER 9
CHAPTER 10
CHAPTER 11
CHAPTER 12
CHAPTER 13
CHAPTER 14
APPENDICES
INDEX

- **Open is the same as double-clicking any Inventory item (except in the case of folders— rather than opening the selected folder, File ▸ Open won't do anything). File ▸ Open produces the following item-specific results:**
  - **Clothing items and body parts will be worn on your avatar.**
  - **Scripts and notecards will be opened in their respective editors.**
  - **Textures will be opened in the texture viewer.**
  - **Objects will have their Inventory Item Properties window opened.**
  - **Animations will be opened in the animation player.**
  - **Gestures will be opened in the gesture editor.**
  - **Sounds will be opened in the audio player.**
  - **Landmarks will be opened in the landmark viewer.**

- **New Window opens a new Inventory window. This is handy because it lets you drag and drop Inventory items and folders from one Inventory window to another without having to navigate your entire Inventory in a single window.**

- **Show Filters toggles the Modify Filters window on and off. We'll talk a little more about searching your Inventory in a moment.**

- **Close All Folders closes all open folders. If you've been searching your Inventory or moving a lot of items around, you'll likely have a bunch of folders open. It can be annoying to have to close them all individually.**

- **Empty Trash permanently deletes everything inside your Trash folder. Remember, there's no way to get these items back once you've deleted them!**

THE CREATE MENU

The Create menu is pretty straightforward. You can create new folders or a variety of Inventory items. Each new Inventory item type will create a new, blank Inventory item for that type, then open it in the appropriate editor: body parts and clothes in the Appearance window, Gestures in the gestures editor, and so forth.

THE SORT MENU

The Sort menu lets you choose how to view your Inventory's folders and items: by name or date. You can see the date or time your items were created by right-clicking them and selecting Properties.

THE FILTERS MENU

Filters are a great way to make your Inventory easier to navigate. They allow you choose exactly what kind of Inventory items you want to look at a from what time period. The filters menu contains the Modify Current and Reset Current options.

All Items ✕

✗ ☑ Animation
📇 ☑ Calling Cards
👕 ☑ Clothing
👐 ☑ Gestures
✎ ☑ Landmarks
◆ ☑ Notecards
📦 ☑ Objects
📜 ☑ Scripts
🔈 ☑ Sounds
▦ ☑ Textures
🖼 ☑ Snapshots

[All]
[None]

☐ Always show folders
☐ Since Logoff
— OR —
Hours Ago ⇕ 0.000
Days Ago ⇕ 0.000
[Close]

- Modify Current opens the search-filters menu for the given tab (Figure 1.6). This is the same as selecting File ▸ Show Filters.

- Reset Current resets the current search filters to their original settings for that tab.

■ THE ALL ITEMS AND RECENT ITEMS TABS

Immediately above the actual folders and items of the Inventory window are two tabs: All Items and Recent Items. By default, these tabs are presorted in two ways: All Items shows all items in your Inventory; Recent Items shows all items since last logoff by default; however, you can specify a different time period in days or hours.

There's no way to create new tabs, which is kind of annoying. They are easy to reset, but they won't retain their filter settings between sessions. This means that if you close *Second Life*, your carefully crafted "only show animations and snapshots from the last week" search filter will be lost. That may not the biggest tragedy ever, but it can be a pain if you find that you need to sort using such a system.

Figure 1.6: The screen that appears when you click the Modify Current selection in the Filters menu

You can have as many items in your Inventory as you want, but the larger your Inventory is the longer it'll take to download and the harder it'll be to find things if you don't clean it out once in a while. You shouldn't expect to be able to keep your Inventory almost empty, so don't agonize over whether something is worth deleting. If there's a chance you want to keep it around, keep it! However, you should keep your Inventory organized. A tidy Inventory is essential for any content creator. Additionally, items in subfolders will not be downloaded until the subfolder is opened, so a well-organized Inventory will operate faster than a disorganized one.

■ SEARCHING YOUR INVENTORY

The search bar allows you to search your Inventory. When typing something into it, your Inventory will automatically adjust to display the search results as you type. To clear your search results, click the X that appears to the right of the search field when performing a search.

You can narrow your search by clicking Filters ▸ Modify Current at the top of the Inventory window; for instance, you can choose to restrict your search on "jeans" to clothing items only. You can't restrict your search to pants only, which would be more helpful—*Second Life* isn't that specific about Inventory items.

A handy way to see everything you've got on at a glance is to just search your Inventory for "worn" items. This will show you all the body parts, clothing items, and attachments you've got on, though it'll also show items with "worn" in the name, like Worn Sneakers. If you have a lot of "worn" clothes, that can pose a problem. All the items you're actually wearing will still show up with their names in bold, Try searching for *(worn*, without the closing parenthesis. Leaving off the closing parenthesis will allow you to see body parts and clothing marked *(worn)* as well as attachments marked something like *(worn on scalp)*.

GIVING DESCRIPTIVE NAMES

Rather than naming your new pair of jeans My Pants, why not make it something more unique, like Blue Jeans with Red Heart Pocket Detail? You don't have to be that specific, but doing so lets you and any potential customers search for things like *blue jeans*, *jeans*, *heart*, or *pocket* and find it quickly. By naming Inventory items as accurately as possible, you can make it easier to find what you're looking for.

If you search for the word *jean* in your Inventory search bar, the search will return things like *jean jacket* or *jean vest*, and even calling cards from people you've met named Jean. However, if you type in *denim*, you'll get a completely different result. It's good to think about how people will search for things you've created when they want to find them and name them accordingly. There's no reason not to put keywords in an Inventory item's name if it makes it easier to find.

For instance, you could go all out and name your new scarf Red-and-White Striped Woolen Scarf - Woolen Scarves Scarfs Neck. That might seem a little excessive and confusing out of context, but there aren't a lot of people who could miss it in their inventories!

That said, you don't have to be overly descriptive; it's just something to think about. There's nothing stopping you from naming your pants Outfit 4 - Pants, but that can get pretty confusing for both your customers and yourself! A little descriptive naming makes your Inventory far easier to search.

SETTING UP A FOLDER STRUCTURE

If you just put all your items in an existing folder or the root of your My Inventory folder, you'll very quickly create a tremendous, innavigable mess. You don't want that—trust us. By putting all the Inventory items associated with a project in one folder and organizing subfolders within that folder, you can keep your Inventory neat and tidy, making it easy to find things.

For instance, you could have a project that depicts a turn-of-the-century circus. You could have one master folder called Circus, with subfolders inside it: Animals, Big Top, Trapeze, and Costumes. You could then further sort the Animals folder into Lion, Elephant, and so on. These would let you contain each little part of the project in a separate folder, better allowing you to find individual parts of the project as well as collaborate on them with other creators.

Sometimes you'll end up with items in your Inventory that haven't been named to your satisfaction. Perhaps there's a typo in an item's name, or maybe it just doesn't mesh well with the organizational system you've come up with. If the object creator has granted you permission to modify the object, it's easy: you can just rename it. However, if the object is set as no-modify, you'll be stuck with its name forever.

CHAPTER 1

🌿 SECOND LIFE
AND YOUR
CHARACTER

🌿 MOVING
AROUND

🌿 LOOKING
AROUND

🌿 UNDER-
STANDING
YOUR
INVENTORY

🌿 NAVIGATING
THE
INVENTORY
MENUS

🌿 ORGANIZING
YOUR
INVENTORY

🌿 USING THE
DEBUG MENUS

For example, suppose you've been given a sand castle. It looks pretty cool and you'd like to rez it! (See the following note on *rezzing*.) Unfortunately, there's a problem: it's named scastle1, a really, really unhelpful name. You'll find it quickly if you remember to search for *castle*, but you'll also find every other Inventory item that contains the word *castle*. If you've spent a few weeks building a castle, you could have dozens, even hundreds of textures and objects and scripts, all with *castle* somewhere in their names.

NOTE

We use the term rez to describe the process of creating an object or pulling an object out of Inventory. This term was borrowed from the 1982 film Tron, where the term de-rez was used to describe killing somebody inside the computer. Tron's use of the term is a reference to the mainframe console command DS, which discontinues or "kills" a running program.

What's a *Second Life* user to do? By placing scastle1 in a folder named Sand Castle, you'll be able to find it easily. To get at the object inside your folder, select the folder in the list of results from your "sand castle" search, then click the X in the search bar. That will both clear your search and keep the Sand Castle folder selected and open, showing its contents: scastle1. You can now rez to your heart's content!

■ USING OBJECT INVENTORIES

Objects can contain Inventory items, but objects' inventories cannot contain folders, nor can they contain two Inventory items with the same name, regardless of Inventory-item type. This means that if you have an object containing a script named New Script and you drag a script also named New Script into the object, the second script will be renamed New Script 1. Likewise, if you drag a notecard named New Script—which is a very confusing name for a notecard, incidentally!—into your object, its name will be changed.

When taking an object from the world into Inventory, the object's Inventory contents will be saved along with the object itself. Placing the object back in the world will not harm any of the Inventory items inside.

WARNING

Unlike items in your personal Inventory, deleting an Inventory contained within an object will not send it to your personal Inventory's Trash folder; it'll just delete it. More than one content creator has lost work after forgetting this!

We'll talk more later about putting Inventory items in objects in Chapter 2, "Mastering *Second Life*'s Building Blocks."

USING THE DEBUG MENUS

Like most programs, *Second Life* contains hidden features used for testing purposes. Most of them won't mean a lot if you don't work for Linden Lab, but some are useful to content creators as well. You can tell your client to display the world in wireframe mode or not to draw water, objects, or avatars, and you can visualize how your scripts are affecting the world. You can even choose where to put the sun to make it easier to see what you're doing.

Figure 1.7: The Client menu

The features we care about when building and scripting are mostly under the Client menu (Figure 1.7). A few features also reside under the View and World menus (though they all originated in what is now the Client menu).

NOTE

By default, the Client and Server menus aren't visible to users. To toggle them on and off, use Control+Alt+Shift+D. This will add Client and Server to the right of Help at the top of your *Second Life* window.

THE CLIENT MENU

The Client menu is filled with a plethora of options tools, and effects that you will undoubtedly find helpful. These effects appear locally on your client so they will only be visible by you. You can move the sun and the moon, zoom your camera great distances, and make facets of your world appear and vanish at will.

By default, the Client menus aren't visible to users. To toggle them on and off, use Control+Alt+Shift+D. This will add the Client and Server items to appear on the far right at the top of your *Second Life* window (Figure 1.7).

CLIENT ▶ RENDERING ▶ TYPES

These features allow you to select which types of geometry will be rendered on your client. What does that mean? Easy: they let you view the world without things like clouds, water, or objects. Table 1.1 shows the types of items you can toggle on or off and the shortcuts that give you instant access to this power.

CHAPTER 1

● SECOND LIFE
  AND YOUR
  CHARACTER

● MOVING
  AROUND

● LOOKING
  AROUND

● UNDER-
  STANDING
  YOUR
  INVENTORY

● NAVIGATING
  THE
  INVENTORY
  MENUS

● ORGANIZING
  YOUR
  INVENTORY

● USING THE
  DEBUG MENUS

Table 1.1: Item Types, Keyboard Shortcuts, and Toggles

TYPE	SHORTCUT	TOGGLES
Simple	Control+Shift+Alt+1	All prims with a normal texture, including attachments.
Alpha	Control+Shift+Alt+2	All prims with a transparent (alpha-mapped) texture.
Tree	Control+Shift+Alt+3	Trees—though not ones made of prims!
Character	Control+Shift+Alt+4	Avatars, including all their attachments.
SurfacePatch	Control+Shift+Alt+5	The terrain you can walk on within a sim.
Sky	Control+Shift+Alt+6	The sky. It'll be replaced by a black void.
Water	Control+Shift+Alt+7	The water plane.
Ground	Control+Shift+Alt+8	The inaccessible plane that exists outside the sim to the horizon line.
Volume	Control+Shift+Alt+9	All prims, however they're textured.
Grass	Control+Shift+Alt+0	Grass objects.
Clouds	Control+Shift+Alt+hyphen (-)	Clouds in the sky.
Particles	Control+Shift+Alt+equals sign (=)	Particles.
Bump	Control+Shift+Alt+\	Bump-mapped and reflective objects—however, they'll just appear to be ordinary prims; this simply toggles their bump and reflection maps.

NOTE

Remember—just because you've created a plant object, it doesn't mean it'll be turned off when you turn off grass or trees. Because it's made from prims, it'll be turned off and on with Simple or Alpha.

■ CLIENT ► RENDERING ► WIREFRAME

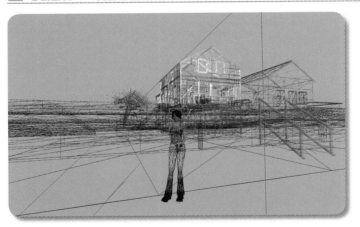

Wireframe mode lets you see the world in a way that's more familiar to 3D modelers than to the average *Second Life* user: without textures (Figure 1.8). By viewing the world as your video card sees it, made up of its component triangles, you can better gauge how costly your prims are to render. Remember that everything in *Second Life* must be drawn on your computer. Complex objects take longer to draw.

Figure 1.8: Wireframe mode

■ CLIENT ► LIMIT SELECT DISTANCE

Most users keep this feature turned on because it means that when you drag-select objects, you'll select only objects closer than around 50 meters. This is handy because it means that if you have a low draw distance or you're building in a crowded area, you'll select only nearby objects and won't risk grabbing something that you didn't mean to.

CHAPTER 1

CHAPTER 2
CHAPTER 3
CHAPTER 4
CHAPTER 5
CHAPTER 6
CHAPTER 7
CHAPTER 8
CHAPTER 9
CHAPTER 10
CHAPTER 11
CHAPTER 12
CHAPTER 13
CHAPTER 14
APPENDICES
INDEX

NOTE

In the world Edit ▸ Preferences ▸ Graphics menu you can set a draw distance, the minimum distance your avatar must be from an object for it to rez.

■ CLIENT ▸ DISABLE CAMERA CONSTRAINTS

For *Second Life*'s first three years of existence, this nifty little feature was hidden away in the God menu, accessible only by Lindens for testing purposes. Fortunately, it's now available for all users. So what is it? By default, you can Alt-zoom only about 50 meters away from your avatar. That sounds like a decent distance, but if you have to build a large structure or do much terraforming, it can be very annoying to deal with. Disable Camera Constraints allows you to break past that limit and zoom in on land and objects anywhere in the sim.

WARNING

The farther you Alt-zoom away from your avatar, the fewer objects will have loaded. Object loading and rendering isn't tied to your camera position, but rather to your avatar. If you try to Alt-zoom more than a sim away, you won't even see land load.

■ CLIENT ▸ SHOW UPDATES

Figure 1.9: Show Updates indicating a partially updated prim

Show Updates presents a quick indicator of which objects are being updated, causing their parametric data to be resent to the client. When Show Updates is turned on, you'll see colored, triangular halos (Figure 1.9) appear within an object then rise out of the object.

Red halos appear when a prim is fully updated. This happens when the object is rezzed or edited. Blue halos appear when a prim is partially updated: when it changes in some way. Green halos appear when a prim is deleted. This can be caused by a script, an object return, or by a user deleting the object or taking the object into Inventory.

So why is Show Updates useful? Suppose you have a script that's updating an object needlessly. Show Updates allows you to see what's going on.

CHAPTER 1

● SECOND LIFE
   AND YOUR
   CHARACTER

● MOVING
   AROUND

● LOOKING
   AROUND

● UNDER-
   STANDING
   YOUR
   INVENTORY

● NAVIGATING
   THE
   INVENTORY
   MENUS

● ORGANIZING
   YOUR
   INVENTORY

● USING THE
   DEBUG MENUS

TIP

A common complaint about Show Updates is that you can't see updates for attachments on your own avatar. The only way to view them is to use an alternate account on a second Second Life client, and put both your avatars in the same location. You'll be able to see the updates for each avatar on the other's viewer.

THE WORLD AND VIEW MENUS

Figure 1.10: The View and World menus

Not all of the helpful extra features are hidden away inside the Client menu. Some are in the View and World menus (Figure 1.10), where anyone can find them. Longtime *SL* users will note that all these features were originally found within the Debug menus.

WORLD ▶ FORCE SUN

Depending on your computer, your eyes, and the lighting around you in *SL*, it can be really hard to build when it's dark out. How do you know if everything is lining up right? Move the sun! You can choose to set the sun's position to Sunrise, Noon, Sunset, or Midnight. However, this will allow you to change the sun's position only on your own client. Other users will see the sun position change only if it's changed in the Region/Estate settings—and the Estate owner can make that change. To reset the sun to the same position that everyone else in the region sees, select Revert to Region Default.

CLIENT ▶ WORLD ▶ MOUSE MOVES SUN

When the debug mode is active, you can move the sun's position, enter mouselook mode, and simply look around. The sun will reposition itself in the sky to wherever you point. To reset it, simply go back to the World menu.

VIEW ▶ ALT SHOWS PHYSICAL

With this feature toggled on, you'll see all physical objects—anything that can move through the world instead of just sitting there—tinted red. This lets you identify items that might have escaped your clutches: monster trucks, basketballs, parakeets. We'll talk more about physical objects in Chapter 2, but for now, believe us: they can run off on you if you're not careful.

■ VIEW ▸ HIGHLIGHT TRANSPARENT

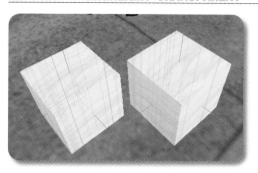

Much like Alt Shows Physical, this toggle will put a red tint on any texture that's even partly transparent (Figure 1.11). If you've lost something invisible or you're unsure where one transparent object ends and another begins, this is an invaluable tool.

Figure 1.11: Highlighted transparent objects and object beacons

■ VIEW ▸ BEACONS

The features under the View ▸ Beacons menu let you see at a glance which objects have something special about them. Objects can contain scripts that affect what they do, how they look, and how they move. They can be physical (as mentioned previously) or they can spew forth particles or play sounds, both of which can be annoying if you forget which object is doing it!

CHAPTER 2

MASTERING SECOND LIFE'S BUILDING BLOCKS

This chapter will provide you with the foundations of basic building. We will start by explaining how to manipulate objects and then go on to describe everything you need to know about prims and how they behave. We will examine the Edit window and explore every option and feature. Finally, we will finish up with a tutorial that lets you solidify what you have learned by creating a snowman.

CONTENTS

CHAPTER 2

◆ MAKING
   YOUR PRIMS
   OBEY YOU

◆ MEET THE
   PRIM FAMILY

◆ MAKING THE
   MOST OF THE
   EDIT WINDOW

◆ LINKED PRIMS

◆ TUTORIAL:
   BUILDING A
   SNOWMAN

MAKING PRIMS OBEY YOU

The word *prim* is short for *primitive* and refers to the most basic building blocks for all *Second Life* objects. Before you really dig into the nitty-gritty of the nature of prims, you'll need a solid understanding of how to create, move, rotate, stretch, copy, and otherwise enforce your all-powerful will over the stuff that makes up our virtual world.

■ LET THERE BE PRIMS!

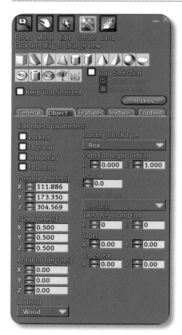

Figure 2.1: The Edit window provides a view of your prim options.

What better way to start learning about prim manipulation than by creating the very prims we will be torturing in the next few sections? To create a prim, you can either click the Build button on the bottom right of your screen or press Control+4. Alternatively, you can right-click on the ground and choose Create from the pie menu. This will bring up the Build menu and place you in Create mode, indicated by a magic-wand pointer. In Create mode (Figure 2.1), a prim will appear wherever you left-click—as long as you aren't clicking on the sky or on people! The Build menu provides a graphical list of prims to choose from (including plants and grass). We'll discuss all of these options in greater depth later, but for now we'll work just with boxes.

Click on the ground with your magic-wand tool. With a thunderous rumble, a plywood box will appear out of nowhere. Feeling powerful yet?

When creating prims, be mindful of the resources each prim consumes. The parcels of land upon which you are standing allow a limited number of prims—the more land, the more prims you're allowed. This cap prevents the terrible performance problems that would occur if you rezzed millions of prims in one place. One region can support a maximum of 15,000 prims, so use them wisely in your builds.

■ MOVING STUFF AROUND

When you first create a prim you will switch from Create mode to Edit mode, and your mouse pointer will turn into an arrow. If you wish to edit a prim that has already been created, right-click on it and select Edit from the pie menu or press Control+3. The first things you will notice are the colorful *object handles* extending outward from the prim along each axis. Red represents the x-axis, green represents the y-axis, and the vertical blue arrow represents the z-axis. If you're coming to *Second Life* from another 3D-rendering environment, such as Maya, this may throw you off since the y- and z-axes are reversed from the industry standard.

To move your prim along the desired axis, hover your pointer over the appropriate object handle until it glows, then left-click and drag the prim along the axis (Figure 2.2). The little colored triangles

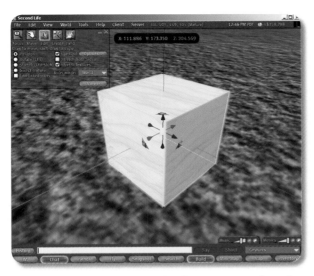

Figure 2.2: The object handles let you move the prim along the color-coded axis. The triangles snap the prim to the grid.

CHAPTER 1
CHAPTER 2

CHAPTER 3
CHAPTER 4
CHAPTER 5
CHAPTER 6
CHAPTER 7
CHAPTER 8
CHAPTER 9
CHAPTER 10
CHAPTER 11
CHAPTER 12
CHAPTER 13
CHAPTER 14
APPENDICES
INDEX

near the arrows will snap the prim to the nearest grid unit if the Snap to Grid option is turned on (Tools ▶ Snap to Grid or simply press the G key.)

An alternative method of moving an object is called Move mode, and is indicated by a little hand as a mouse pointer. To enter Move mode, click on the Move button in the Build menu or press Control+2. Then when you left-click and drag an object, it will move freely (albeit imprecisely) along the x- and y-axes. Holding down the Control key while you move the prim will permit the object to also move along the z-axis.

The Move-mode method of moving prims may feel a bit more comfortable to newer users because it simulates the way we move things in the real world, but don't get used to it! If you want to do serious content creation in *Second Life*, you really should stick to working with the single-axis object handles. You're going to need the precision!

MORE INFO

GETTING A GRIP ON PERSPECTIVE

One major challenge to the new builder is getting a grip on perspective. Take for example the two boxes shown here (from two different perspectives).

Although it appears that both boxes are the same size, and are right next to each other, in fact one is very small and close to your camera. The other is very large and far away! Until you straighten out your perspective, you're going to make a lot of clumsy mistakes.

The solution? Keep alt-zooming, baby! I stressed the importance of alt-zoom in Chapter 1 and I'm going to reiterate it here. The more you keep that camera scanning around, the more accurate information your brain will have to work with when trying to figure out where things are. Always look at your building situation from every angle before messing with your objects.

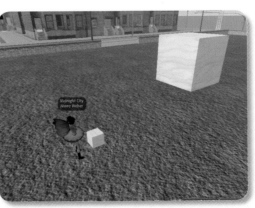

■ ROTATING PRIMS

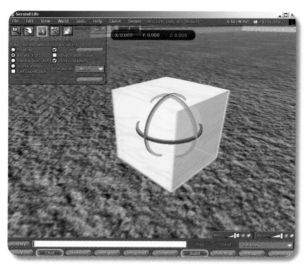

Figure 2.3: The Rotate Handles allow you to rotate the object around the color-coded axis.

Now that you're moving prims all over the map, it's time to learn to rotate. Simply edit the prim like you did earlier to move it, but this time hold down the Control key. The movement arrows turn into colorful circles known as *rotate handles*. Like the arrows, each circle represents an axis, only rather than moving your prim *along* an axis, you are now rotating the prim *around* the axis (Figure 2.3). With the Control button pressed, drag one of the rotate handles. You're now rotating the prim. You can achieve the same effect by pressing the Rotate radio button on the Edit window.

You can also rotate the prim while in Move mode by holding down the Control and Shift keys, left-clicking, and dragging the prim in different directions. As mentioned in the previous section, this method is not recommended for serious building because it lacks the precision and single-axis movement and rotation available in Edit mode.

■ SIZE MATTERS

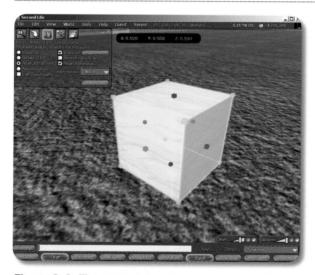

Figure 2.4: The stretch handles allow you to stretch the object along the color-coded axis. The white handles allow you to stretch the object uniformly along all axes.

To change the fundamental size and shape of a prim, simply go into Edit mode, select the prim, and hold down Control+Shift. Small white boxes called *stretch handles* appear in each corner of the prim; you can drag them to resize the whole object proportionately. You will also notice small colored stretch handles on the sides of the prim. As you might suspect, each color corresponds to an axis. Dragging these colored stretch handles will resize the prim along only one axis (Figure 2.4). This is great for stretching and distorting a prim into nonstandard shapes and sizes. You can achieve the same effect with the Stretch radio button on the Edit window.

The Stretch Both Sides option on the Edit window determines if both sides stretch while the center of the prim remains stationary (checked), or if only one side of the prim stretches while the opposite side remains stationary (checked). The Stretch Textures option will control whether textures are stretched when you resize, or if they remain the same and repeat or get cropped. We will discuss this option in greater detail in Chapter 4, "Let There Be Texture (and Light)!".

You should know a few particulars about resizing prims. First, the largest a prim can be on any axis is 10 meters, and the smallest is 0.010 meters. If you wish to create larger objects you will have to combine multiple prims by linking (discussed later in this chapter). There are also tricks to get sizes smaller than 0.010, but we will discuss that in the next chapter.

NOTE

At some point you may run into a prim larger than the aforementioned 10-meter limit, and think, "That Aimee is a filthy liar!" But wait—there's an explanation! These "mega prims" are the creation of famous SL hacker Gene Replacement, aka Plastic Duck. Some time ago it was discovered that the 10-meter limit was enforced entirely by the Second Life client, but if you could circumvent the client, Second Life's server was perfectly happy handling your overstuffed prim. So Gene created a makeshift client that permitted him to rez prims of any size he wished. This hack has since been fixed, putting the kibosh on any new mega prims. But the old ones are still floating around and are considered treasured tools by serious SL builders.

■ COPYING AND DELETING PRIMS

One easy way to copy a prim is to select it in Edit mode, hold Shift, and then move the prim along one of the move handles. This will leave behind a brand-new object that is identical to the one you are currently working with. The fact that we are moving the original prim and leaving a new one behind is a small but important detail. It may not appear to make a difference in this simple example, but it impacts object ownership and group tags in more-complex examples.

A second method is to go into Edit mode and select the prim you wish to copy. Then click Create on the Build menu's Edit window (Control+4) and check the Copy Selection option. When you click on a surface to create a prim, the prim created will be identical to the one you had selected. If you intend to make multiple copies, you may want to select the Keep Tool Selected option.

When you are finished you can delete a prim simply by selecting it and pressing the Delete key or going to File ▸ Delete. The prim will be de-rezzed and will appear in your inventory's Trash folder. It's a trivial matter—unless you have become overly fond of your prim.

MEET THE PRIM FAMILY

While atoms are the building blocks of our universe, prims are the building blocks of our virtual world. In your travels you'll discover all kinds of wonderful, complex shapes and designs. The nature of some shapes will be obvious, but other shapes will seem a mystery. If you hope to become a proficient builder in *Second Life* you need to understand the nature and characteristics of each shape, just as a chemist understands the periodic table of elements.

One of my fondest childhood memories involved a Play-Doh extruder. The idea was simple; you had plastic dies with cut-outs of fancy shapes through which a mass of Play-Doh was forced. The result was a three-dimensional version of the two-dimensional shape (which I immediately rolled into a ball and threw at my sister). This extrusion process is pretty much what's going on behind the scenes of every prim; the question is how the extrusion is handled. We have two options:

CHAPTER 1
CHAPTER 2

CHAPTER 3
CHAPTER 4
CHAPTER 5
CHAPTER 6
CHAPTER 7
CHAPTER 8
CHAPTER 9
CHAPTER 10
CHAPTER 11
CHAPTER 12
CHAPTER 13
CHAPTER 14
APPENDICES
INDEX

Figure 2.5: Linearly extruded prims include the box, cylinder, and prism.

Figure 2.6: Radially extruded prims include the torus, tube, and ring.

Linear extrusion: A linearly extruded prim (Figure 2.5) can be best visualized as a simple two-dimensional shape that has been extruded into the third dimension along the z-axis (usually upward). For example, imagine drawing a square on a piece of paper. If you could grab that square and stretch it upward, you would have an extruded shape consisting of the bottom face, the top face you just grabbed, and the four sides that fill in the space between the top and the bottom. In other words, a box! Now imagine cutting a hole from the middle of that two-dimensional square before extruding it. The 3D shape you end up with will look like a hollow box. That's how linear extrusion works.

Radial extrusion: Not all of the basic prim shapes follow a simple path along the z-axis. Another kind of prim extrudes a two-dimensional shape along a circular path around the z-axis (Figure 2.6). For example, if you start with a two-dimensional circle and extrude it around the z-axis, the resultant shape will look much like a donut. A delicious, delectable donut (pros call it a torus, largely to dissuade us from eating it).

Sculpted: The newest addition to the prim family is the sculpted prim, which is an entirely different animal. Rather than deriving its shape from geometric processes performed on two-dimensional shapes, the sculpted prim receives its shape from a specially created image that has all of the geometry data encoded in the pixels.

Next I'll describe the fundamental prim types, including each one's two-dimensional base shape and the extrusion method used to produce it. These two pieces of information will give you the foundation to understand how prims work, to differentiate between otherwise identical-looking prims, and to understand how a prim will react to twists, tapers, and flexible paths.

**Figure 2.7:
The box prim**

■ THE BOX

The box is, without a doubt, the most frequently used building block in *Second Life* construction (Figure 2.7). The shape features a linearly extruded square base extruded along the z-axis. In its natural state the box has six sides, but it can be reduced to a five-sided pyramid by tapering one of the base sides to zero (discussed in Chapter 3, "Advanced Building Techniques").

**Figure 2.8:
The prism prim**

■ THE PRISM

The prism prim is very similar to the box prim, except that it features a linearly extruded triangular base rather than a square one (Figure 2.8). In its natural state the prism is a five-sided object, but by adjusting the taper you can transform the prism into a tetrahedron (a four-sided object, just like those cute little dice used in Dungeons & Dragons).

CHAPTER 1
CHAPTER 2

CHAPTER 3
CHAPTER 4
CHAPTER 5
CHAPTER 6
CHAPTER 7
CHAPTER 8
CHAPTER 9
CHAPTER 10
CHAPTER 11
CHAPTER 12
CHAPTER 13
CHAPTER 14
APPENDICES
INDEX

NOTE

You can make a box prim look like a prism by adjusting its taper. But don't be fooled into thinking the prism is another kind of box! Remember that the prim "path" is extruded from the base—which is a triangle, not a square. This means features that function along the path, such as hollow and twist, will do so between the two triangles of a prism, whereas on a box they function between the two squares that form the two sides. These are two very different prims.

■ THE CYLINDER

A cylinder is a circle linearly extruded along the z-axis and will therefore behave a lot like the box and the prism (Figure 2.9). By adjusting the taper you can transform a cylinder into a cone.

Figure 2.9: The cylinder prim

■ THE TUBE

A tube is a radially extruded rectangle. Imagine taking some Play-Doh that has been extruded through a rectangle shape, and then curling it around so the head touches the tail. It ends up looking like a hollow cylinder (Figure 2.10)! You can always see the rectangle shape buried inside the tube by doing a Path Cut of around 0.500. (Path cuts are described in more detail in Chapter 3.)

Figure 2.10: The tube prim

Because radially extruded prims do not follow the standard z-axis path, you will not be able to set the object to be flexible. (We will discuss flexible objects more under "The Features Tab" later in this chapter.)

TIP

It's very easy to confuse the tube prim for a hollowed-out cylinder since they look identical in their default state. However, it's important to put aside any preconceived notions about the tube prim and remember the nature of radially extruded prims. Otherwise your confusion will likely make the object-transformation behavior (see "A Remarkable Transformation" later in this chapter) seem mysterious, if not completely random!

■ THE TORUS

Now that you understand how tubes work, the torus prim will be a piece of cake—tori are handled almost identically. A torus is a radially extruded circle (Figure 2.11). This forms the donut shape mentioned earlier. As with the tube, you can view this circle by doing a path cut of .500. Also like the tube, the lack of a z-axis path means this prim can never be flexible.

Figure 2.11: The torus prim

Figure 2.12:
The ring prim

THE RING

Ring may not be an ideal name for this object, but once you understand the torus and the tube, you pretty much understand the ring (Figure 2.12). Rather than a circle or a rectangle, the ring prim uses a triangle shape extruded 360 degrees around the z-axis. Once again, the unusual handling of the path means this prim cannot be made flexible.

Figure 2.13:
The sphere
prim

THE SPHERE

The sphere is a bit of an oddball. Fundamentally, a sphere is a two-dimensional half-circle that is radially extruded around the z-axis (Figure 2.13). Like the tube, torus, and ring, the sphere cannot be flexible. But the sphere also doesn't feature many of the transformation functions available to the other prims, and it's the only prim that provides a special kind of cut, called a *dimple* (a cone-shaped hole around the z-axis of the sphere). The sphere is not a complex object, but its unique set of features makes it hard to categorize.

THE SCULPTED PRIM

The sculpted prim fits in its own category. To create a sculpted prim you must use a third-party modeling tool such as Maya, Blender, or 3ds Max to create a NURB—a shape that you can easily mold into soft, rounded forms such as fruit, trees, or great-big bean-bag chairs. You then export this shape from your third-party modeling tool to a bitmap (.BMP) file, which will probably look like a rainbow of pretty tie-dye colors. (Those colors actually have the geometry data encoded in them!)

Once you have your bitmap file, all you have to do is upload it into *Second Life* by going to File ▸ Upload Image. You can then create a prim (any prim type is fine) and edit it by selecting Sculpted from Building Block Type in the Object Edit window. Drag and drop your newly uploaded bitmap into the Sculpt Texture window and immediately your prim will take on the shape of the NURB you created in the third-party modeling tool. Unlike other prims, the characteristics of sculpted prims are fixed. You can't cut them or twist them—anything like that. The most you can do is resize, rotate, and reposition them.

MAKING THE MOST OF THE EDIT WINDOW

Now that you know the fundamentals behind every basic prim type, we will take a detailed look at all the Edit window's options to modify these prims. You will learn how to yank, pull, cut, poke, and prod prims until they beg for mercy. But there will be no mercy here—we have an important job to do!

THE GENERAL TAB

The General tab (Figure 2.14) covers some of the basic characteristic of the prim, such as name, creator, and privileges.

Figure 2.14: The General tab

CHAPTER 1
CHAPTER 2

CHAPTER 3
CHAPTER 4
CHAPTER 5
CHAPTER 6
CHAPTER 7
CHAPTER 8
CHAPTER 9
CHAPTER 10
CHAPTER 11
CHAPTER 12
CHAPTER 13
CHAPTER 14
APPENDICES
INDEX

Name: You can name a prim anything you wish, but it's best to select something descriptive. The default is Object, but if left unchanged, that name will make your object nearly impossible to locate in an inventory brimming with items that also contain the word *Object* in their names.

Description: You can use this field to communicate more details about your object, to provide quick instructions as to how to use the object, or (in some cases) as a parameter field for scripts contained inside the prim.

Creator: This provides the name of the person who created the prim. The creator value will never change. A Profile button allows you to get more information about the creator.

Owner: This displays the current owner of the prim, which may be different from the creator.

Group: Objects may be associated with certain user groups. (And a group can be set without the group owning the object—so that the individual still owns it.) This becomes important when the object exists in a parcel of land that permits only builds that belong to a certain group. Group association is often necessary for collaborative projects.

Share with Group: If your prim is associated with a group, this option will allow any member of that group to manipulate the object. The object may be deeded with the Deed button, transferring ownership of the object to the group. Any money paid to the group-owned object is shared amongst the entire group. This can be very helpful for group projects.

Allow Anyone to Move: As the name implies, this option allows anybody to freely move the prim.

Allow Anyone to Copy: Also self-explanatory.

For Sale: This option allows you to put the object up for sale for any price you name. If your object catches the interest of a shopper, that shopper can purchase it by right-clicking on the object and selecting Buy from the pie menu. The purchase money will be transferred into your account instantly.

There are three different ways a user can purchase a prim: They could buy the original, which means they take ownership of it and you will no longer own it. They can purchase a copy that appears in their inventory while your copy remains under your ownership. Finally, they can buy the contents of the prim. We will discuss object contents later in this chapter.

Next Owner Can: This option allows you to control what rights the future owner of your object will have over the object.

Checking the Modify checkbox allows the next owner to make modifications to your object such as resizing it, or taking it apart completely. This can be handy for the next user to customize your products to their exact needs, but may prefer to keep this option turned off if you wish to preserve the integrity of your original design. The copy option allows the next owner to make as many copies of your object as they please. Resell/Give Away allows the next owner to transfer the object to another user.

The combination of these settings is referred to as the permissions, or "perms" for short. For example, some content creators like to set their perms to "Copy/No Transfer," which means they allow the next owner to copy but not resell or give away the item. Other content creators like to set their products as "No Copy/Transfer" which means the next owner can transfer the object to another user, but like giving objects away in the real world, they will no longer have a copy of their own! This setting is useful for objects intended to be gifts and collectables.

CHAPTER 2

🟤 MAKING
YOUR PRIMS
OBEY YOU

🟤 MEET THE
PRIM FAMILY

🟤 MAKING THE
MOST OF THE
EDIT WINDOW

🟤 LINKED PRIMS

🟤 TUTORIAL:
BUILDING A
SNOWMAN

Finally there is "Full Perms" which means the next owner can copy, transfer, and modify. Remember that as soon as you hand an object set with full perms to another user, that object can be freely distributed to anybody and everybody.

Think carefully about the permissions before you pass an object to another user.

■ THE OBJECT TAB

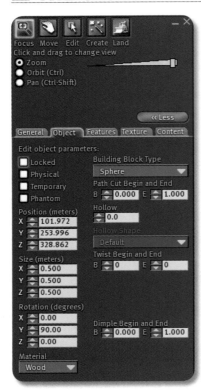

Figure 2.15: The Object tab

Let's switch to the Object tab (Figure 2.14), where you can perform most of your prim transformations. This may be the most powerful tool a builder will ever have, so read it, learn it, and love it.

> **NOTE**
>
> Some elements of the Object tab appear only when working with certain prim shapes.

Locked: This option allows you to lock a prim into its position and shape until the option is unchecked. I highly recommend locking any objects that are part of a completed stationary project. Accidentally moving a prim or two on a finished build is easier than you might think.

Physical: When this option is turned on, the prim will become subject to the laws of *Second Life* physics. It can be pushed, pulled, dropped, and bounced like a ball. We will discuss more about the *Second Life* Physics engine in Chapter 8.

Temporary: Objects marked as temporary will vanish shortly after creation, and they do so with minimum impact on performance. Temporary objects are perfect for bullets or exploding debris because they disappear automatically when they are no longer needed. The time it takes for objects to disappear depends on variables such as parcel limits.

Phantom: When an object is set to Phantom, avatars and objects can pass freely through them. This is handy for creating bushes, lighting, and water effects using prims. For example, users could walk through a waterfall to find a hidden cave if the water were set to Phantom.

■ POSITION, SIZE, AND ROTATION

Using the number values on the Object tab to adjust position, size, and rotation is sometimes called *building by the numbers*. Although this technique may require some simple math and additional time to finish a project, the perfection of the seamless build that results often makes it worth the effort.

Position: This section allows you to view and set the position of an object within the sim boundaries. Those boundaries, measured in meters, are 0 to 256 in the x and y direction and 0 to 768 in the z direction.

Size: This allows you to view and set the size of the prim along the x-, y-, and z-axes. The maximum size of a prim is 10 meters and the minimum is 0.010 meter.

Rotation: This allows you to view and set the rotation in degrees around the x-, y-, and z-axes.

Building Block Type: This pull-down menu allows you to select from the seven basic prim types: box, prism, cylinder, torus, ring, tube, and sphere.

Path Cut Begin and End: The path cut allows us to take a pie-like slice out of our prim with the object's z-axis as the center of the proverbial pie. Therefore, this feature can best be seen when viewing the prim from above. The slice starts at the center of the prim at the z-axis and extends to the outside corner of the prim. The size of the cut ranges from 0.0 to 1.0. Therefore, a Path Cut value of 0.5 cuts the prim exactly in half.

Figure 2.16: You can hollow prims with squares, circles, or triangles.

Hollow and Hollow Shape: As mentioned earlier, prims are created by extruding two-dimensional shapes into three-dimensional objects. The Hollow feature works by cutting a hole in the original 2D base shape. The hole then follows the path used to create the prim. For linear extrusion, this hole moves in a straight line, while for radial extrusion the hole hollows out the resultant donut shape. The Hollow Shape option allows you to select the shape of the hole, which means you can have square shapes with round hollows, round shapes with triangular hollows, and many other combinations to suit your building needs (Figure 2.16).

Figure 2.17: A torus with skew values of 0.0, 0.25, 0.50, and 0.95

Skew: The Skew feature is available only for radially extruded prims and allows you to resize the starting and ending base shapes in opposite directions along the z-axis. The shape that results is, well, skewed! One good use of this feature would be to turn a tube into a spiral ramp (Figure 2.17).

Figure 2.18: A box and a torus with twist values of 0, 90, and 180

Twist Begin and End: The Twist feature rotates either the beginning side (B) or the end side (E) of the path that forms the prim. When twisting a linearly extruded prim such as a cube, prism, or cylinder, the twist occurs along the z-axis, forming a shape not unlike a Dunkin' Donuts cruller (Figure 2.18).

When applying Twist to radially extruded prims like tori, tubes, rings, and spheres, remember that the path circles the z-axis. Therefore, twists will take effect all the way around the prim.

Hole Size: This curious feature is available only for radially extruded prims. One could easily confuse Hole Size with Hollow, but remember that Hollow bores a hole through the extruded base shape, not the "donut hole" in the middle. If you want to make the donut hole bigger or smaller, you have to use Hole Size.

In reality, Hole Size affects the hole only indirectly as you adjust the size of the two-dimensional base shape from which the object is extruded. The X value makes the shape shorter or taller. The Y value makes the shape wider or narrower. By making the Y value larger the width of the shape begins to close off the "donut hole" in the center of the object. This may be confusing to new builders who puzzle over why larger Y values create smaller holes (and why X values do nothing to the hole size at all!). But if you keep firmly in mind that Hole Size X and Y really means base prim size X and Y, you will never go wrong.

Figure 2.19: A box with Top Shear values of 0.0 and 0.5

Top Shear: The Top Shear feature allows you to change the object shape by sliding the parallel two-dimensional base prims so they are no longer directly in line with each other. The effect is a shape that is slanted, or *sheared* (Figure 2.19). You might use this feature for the bow of a ship.

For tori, tubes, and rings, the beginning shape is located in the same position as the end shape; therefore, shear functions slightly differently. The two parallel shapes that are moved in relation to each other are located opposite each other halfway along the circular route around the z-axis.

Profile Cut: This feature is available only for radially extruded prims. Profile Cut takes a pie-shaped slice out of the base two-dimensional shapes that form the object. The result of the cut is passed all the way around the prim. You can use this feature if you wish to have a groove in your prim, perhaps to make a yo-yo.

Taper: Taper allows you to resize one of the two ends of a path along the x- or y-axis, which translates into a slope along the path. This allows you to turn boxes into pyramids and cylinders into cones. When applied to radially extruded shapes, you can make curls taper to sharp ends, which is ideal for making curly prim hair.

Radius Delta: This feature is available only for radially extruded prims. Radius Delta adjusts the distance from the center of the prim of just one of the shapes. The result is a one-revolution turn ideal for creating scrolls.

Figure 2.20: A torus with 0 and 4 revolutions

Revolutions: Revolutions are another feature unique to tori, rings, and tubes. The moment you make any change in the Revolution value, the skew of the object will also change (Figure 2.20). Revolved objects are always skewed. In Revolution mode, the 2D start and end shapes are positioned away from each other along the z-axis. As you increase revolutions, the circular path around the z-axis repeats a maximum of four times. This shape is ideal for hair or curly telephone cords.

Dimple Begin and End: The sphere is the only shape that allows dimples. This feature cuts a cone-shaped hole in the beginning (usually the bottom) or the end (usually the top) of the prim. The larger the value, the wider the cone. Dimples combined with path cuts can create many useful spherical shapes, such as low prim chairs.

Material: This option lets you select the kind of material you would like your prim to simulate. Options include stone, metal, glass, wood, flesh, plastic, and rubber. These settings affect the sound produced when a body collides with the material, the friction the material produces when it slides against another material, and the elasticity of the object. The material does not affect the prim's mass, but it does change how the object bounces.

■ THE FEATURES TAB

We now move to the Features tab (Figure 2.21), which displays two special features: flexibility and light. Flexible prims allow for flexible behavior along the path of a linearly extruded prim such as a box, prism, or cylinder. Radially extruded prims cannot be flexible. The base of the flexible prim (the extreme Z surface) acts as a stationary anchor while the rest of the prim moves about like a whip or a tree in the wind. When an object is set to Flexible it will automatically become phantom. You control the flexible behavior with the following parameters.

Figure 2.21: The Features tab

Softness: This value controls the rigidity of the flexible object. Values of 0.0 are not at all soft, and will mostly cause the prim to hinge stiffly at the base. A value of 3.0 is very soft, causing the object to flop with the slightest touch.

Gravity: While you cannot change the effects of gravity globally, you can make local changes to individual flexible prims. Gravity values range from 10.0 to –10.0. A value of 10.0 causes your prim to be pulled to the ground with relentless force, a value of 0.0 causes it to float without regard to gravity, and a value of -10.0 causes the prim to flex upward as though gravity has been reversed completely.

Drag: This value controls the speed at which a flexible prim changes velocity as a result of some force. The greater the drag the slower and more hindered the prim's motion will appear. A value of 0.0 simulates a drag-free state in which the flexible prim can react instantly to any exerted force.

Wind: Keen observers may have noticed that trees and other plants in *Second Life* will sway in response an unseen breeze. Wind is a measurable quantity in *Second Life* that you can view via Client ▶ HUD Info ▶ Wind. The higher you set the Wind value of your flexible prim, the more the prim will sway and react to the current wind conditions.

Tension: This value sets the force at which a flexible prim will straighten itself out after being displaced. A value of 10 will cause the prim to snap into a straightened position right away, whereas a value of 0 will cause the prim to make no effort to straighten out—it will come to rest however it was displaced.

Force X, Y, Z: These values exert a constant force along the selected axis. This force behaves much like the wind force, but rather than being at the mercy of the weather as you are with the Wind setting, you get to determine the strength and direction of this force.

▣ LIGHTING EFFECTS

Figure 2.22: A lighted prim illuminates this dark street but casts no shadows.

Second Life offers powerful tools to create attractive real-time lighting effects with minimal impact on your computer's performance. The graphics cards in most home computers prevent perfect shadows from being generated in real time. As a result, lighting effects in *Second Life* function without any awareness of opaque obstacles. Therefore, objects do not cast shadows (Figure 2.22) and light cannot be contained by the walls of a room. Additionally, the *Second Life* client renders only six light sources, based on their intensity and proximity to the user.

These limitations hardly prohibit attractive, realistic builds, though—with frugal, well-thought-out designs, the results can be stunning. Here are the parameters that control the way we illuminate our world.

CHAPTER 1
CHAPTER 2
CHAPTER 3
CHAPTER 4
CHAPTER 5
CHAPTER 6
CHAPTER 7
CHAPTER 8
CHAPTER 9
CHAPTER 10
CHAPTER 11
CHAPTER 12
CHAPTER 13
CHAPTER 14
APPENDICES
INDEX

Color: This is the color of the light the prim is casting. Generally speaking, wide-spectrum colors like those of sunshine feel natural, while monochromatic selections provide powerful emotional reactions. Electric blue is ideal for a rock concert, bright green for an alien spaceship, and deep red to simulate the fiery pit of Hell!

MORE INFO

ACHIEVING THE CORRECT LIGHTING EFFECTS

People have a natural familiarity with real-world lighting conditions, so it's very important that you achieve the correct lighting for your setting. While the bluish-green hue of fluorescent lighting adds a perfect touch to an office scene, it will feel wrong around a campfire. Here are some suggested RGB values to simulate real-world light sources:

- Sunlight: (255, 255, 255)
- Cloudy-day light: (200, 225, 255)
- Wood-fire light: (255, 166, 41)
- Incandescent light: (255, 215, 170)
- Halogen light: (255, 243, 220)
- Fluorescent light: (244, 255, 250)

Intensity: This value ranges from 0 (which casts no light) to 1.0 (which is the brightest intensity).

Radius: This value sets the maximum range that light travels from the casting prim.

Falloff: The Falloff value sets how abruptly or gradually light will fade from bright to dark. A value of 0.0 will cause the light to mostly fill its radius (see the Radius value) before quickly falling off to darkness, much like a spotlight. Higher values will create a gentler, moody lighting effect.

■ THE TEXTURE TAB

The addition of textures can transform a good build into a breathtaking build. In Chapter 4 we will go into detail about creating beautiful textures and using them to overcome limitations in the *Second Life* engine, to help conserve resources, and to aid performance. But for now we'll simply cover the basics of applying textures, tint, and bumpiness to prims (Figure 2.23).

TIP

It's not obvious on the Texture tab, but there is another, very useful way to update a texture. You can drag a texture from your inventory onto the prim itself. This will make the texture appear only on the side of the prim you dragged the texture onto, rather than all surfaces. If you want the texture applied to all surfaces, you can Shift-drag instead.

CHAPTER 1
CHAPTER 2
CHAPTER 3
CHAPTER 4
CHAPTER 5
CHAPTER 6
CHAPTER 7
CHAPTER 8
CHAPTER 9
CHAPTER 10
CHAPTER 11
CHAPTER 12
CHAPTER 13
CHAPTER 14
APPENDICES
INDEX

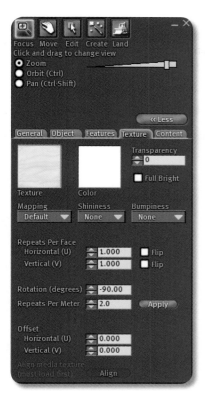

Figure 2.23: The Texture tab

Texture: Clicking on the Texture box brings up the Texture Picker window, which allows you to search your inventory for the perfect image. You can also use the Eyedropper tool to click on other prims in your area to select textures from them; however, the Eyedropper will only work only on textures you actually own. Alternatively, you can press the Blank button to start with a blank texture, or the Default button to get a plywood texture. Finally, if you find a texture in your inventory window or if you have a certain texture open, you can drag and drop it onto the texture preview. When you press the Select button your texture will appear on all surfaces of the prim.

Color: Clicking on the color box brings up a Color Picker (Figure 2.24) that provides you with a number of ways to select color. You can click on the color display to select a color visually and then play with the brightness by using the vertical brightness bar to the right. You can enter precise RGB or Hue, Sat (Saturation), and Lum (Luminosity) values, which is good if you need to emulate a specific color from an outside source. You can also use the Eyedropper tool to select an exact color from a nearby prim.

If you use the same set of colors frequently in a project, consider using the color palette to save time. Simply drag the current color onto one of the colors in the palette; it will be there if you need it in the future.

Transparency: Setting this value allows you to make a prim partially or almost completely invisible. This is useful for creating windows or water effects.

Figure 2.24: The Color Picker

NOTE

You cannot use the Edit window to set a prim higher than 90% transparent. If you need complete invisibility, you can set the object's texture to a full alpha texture (discussed in Chapter 4) or write a script that uses the llSetAlpha command (which is beyond the scope of this book). If you lose an invisible object, you can toggle to View Transparent mode by pressing Control+Alt+T.

Full Bright: This feature is sometimes confused with lighting, but it functions in a very different way. Whereas the Light feature (discussed earlier) causes a prim to illuminate the surrounding objects and avatars, Full Bright casts no light at all. Instead, it causes the prim to become "unshaded" by ambient lighting conditions, making it appear to be illuminated fully by a bright light source. This handy feature can be used to create the illusion of light without any of the aforementioned lighting limitations or impacts on performance.

Mapping: This pull-down menu lets you choose between the Default and Planar mapping modes. The Default mode distorts the texture to follow the contours of the prim. In most situations this creates the most desirable results, but occasionally it can introduce unwanted distortion.

CHAPTER 2

MAKING
YOUR PRIMS
OBEY YOU

MEET THE
PRIM FAMILY

MAKING THE
MOST OF THE
EDIT WINDOW

LINKED PRIMS

TUTORIAL:
BUILDING A
SNOWMAN

Planar mapping, on the other hand, is a simple, undistorted mapping system that can be used to overcome texture distortion on tapered surfaces and prisms.

Shininess: This feature creates the look of a shiny object by reflecting the appearance of the horizon. You have four degrees of shininess to choose from, but you cannot combine shininess with transparency. Keep in mind that not everybody has their clients set to display shiny objects. It's important for you to occasionally look at your builds with Shininess turned off to ensure it still looks good! If it doesn't, tinker with the color and textures before you declare the project complete.

Bumpiness: Bumpiness or *bump-mapping* uses a texture to simulate a rich, detailed surface that reacts to the ambient lighting conditions. You have 17 bump maps to choose from, including Stone and Brick, many of which create a stunning visual effect when combined with textures.

Repeats per Face: This allows you to set the number of times a texture is repeated on the face of a prim. You can do this in two different directions (referred to as u and v). Selecting values of less than 1 lets you show partial sections of a texture on an object face, which is handy for using texture sheets. Finally, you can flip the texture on either the u- or v-axis (or both).

Rotation: As the name implies, this allows you to rotate the texture on the prim face. Most frequently you will need to shift a texture 90 degrees.

Repeats per Meter: This allows you to set the repeats based on a global measurement (meters) rather than the object size. This is very handy if you have a build consisting of multiple objects of various sizes and you wish to have textures with a consistent appearance.

Offset: This allows you to slide the texture along the u- or v-axis until it is positioned to your liking. Normally you will use this along with Repeats per Face to align textures with the textures of other prims.

■ THE CONTENT TAB

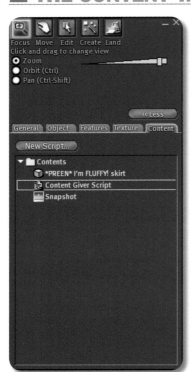

Each *Second Life* prim is capable of holding content such as other prims, objects, notecards, textures, animations, or any other inventory item you can think of (Figure 2.25). To add an asset to an object's contents, drag it from your inventory into the box where the Contents folder is. One of the most common uses for this feature is to add scripts that will operate on a prim and on prims that interact with it. The New Script button instantly sets you up with a "hello avatar" template script, but you can also drag scripts into the prim contents from your inventory.

Figure 2.25: The Content tab

CHAPTER 1
CHAPTER 2
CHAPTER 3
CHAPTER 4
CHAPTER 5
CHAPTER 6
CHAPTER 7
CHAPTER 8
CHAPTER 9
CHAPTER 10
CHAPTER 11
CHAPTER 12
CHAPTER 13
CHAPTER 14
APPENDICES
INDEX

LINKED PRIMS

By now you must be a master of twisting and shaping individual prims. But just about all your greatest builds will consist of multiple prims masterfully arranged to take on the shape of your creative vision. In this section you will learn about linking multiple prims and working with these linked objects.

LINKING AND UNLINKING PRIMS

Up until now, we have been using the terms *prims* and *objects* interchangeably, but it's time to get specific about these terms. A prim, as you know, is the basic building block in *Second Life.* An object, on the other hand is a discrete inventory item that may be just one prim or a linked set of many prims.

To link multiple objects, you must have them all selected. You can do this by holding Shift while individually selecting (and deselecting) prims, or by dragging the marquee around your group of prims. Once all are selected, go to Tools ▸ Link in the menu bar, or press Control+L. A group of linked objects will behave as one single object. You can move them, resize them, script them, and inventory them as one discrete unit. You can add more prims and other linked objects to the current linked object by performing the exact same procedure.

However, there are some limitations to linking: You cannot link objects that are too far apart. For example, if you create 10-meter prims and place them end-to-end, you will be able to link only four of them before the *Second Life* client refuses to link more. Additionally, you cannot link more than 256 prims. If you intend to make your object physical, like a vehicle, you are limited to 31 prims. Finally, while you may resize a linked object, you must do so on all three axes such that the object is resized in proportion.

To unlink, select the object and go to Tools ▸ Unlink or press Shift+Control+L.

EDITING LINKED OBJECTS

Once a set of prims is linked you may want to edit individual prims in the linked set. One obvious way to do this is to unlink the set, make your modifications, and then relink. But for smaller jobs it's much easier to go to your Edit ▸ Edit Linked Parts, then select the individual prim you would like to edit. You'll then be able to move and resize the prim as you wish. You can even remove a single prim from the linked set by unlinking it individually without affecting the rest of the set. (As you will discover later in this book, it is sometimes necessary to modify scripts contained in the individual pieces of a linked set, and this is the method you will use to do that.)

LINK ORDER AND ROOT PRIMS

When you select a linked set, you may notice that most of the selected prims glow blue while one prim glows yellow. The yellow prim is the *root prim*; it carries most of the characteristics of the linked set, such as name, description, and scripts.

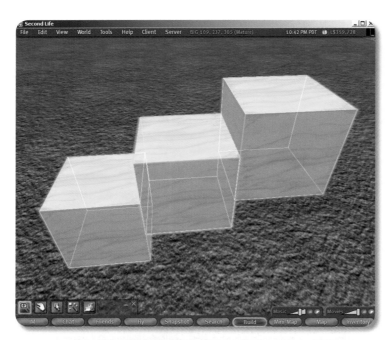

For some of your projects, it may be necessary to control which prim gets to be the root prim. The last prim selected before you link becomes the root prim. If you are Shift-selecting your prims, simply make sure the last prim you select is the one you wish to be the root. However, the procedure is different if you are selecting a large group of prims by dragging. Once all your prims are selected, find your root prim, Shift-select it to remove it from your selection, and Shift-select it again to add it as the last selected prim. When you relink you will find that your last selected prim is the yellow-glowing root prim (Figure 2.26).

Figure 2.26: The root prim in this linked set glows yellow when selected, while the others glow blue.

TUTORIAL: BUILDING A SNOWMAN

Now it's time to put your nose to the grindstone with a serious, no-nonsense demonstration of what you have learned so far. Let's build a snowman!

▧ CREATING THE BASIC SHAPE

1. To start out, click the Build button and select a sphere. Left-click on the ground to rez the base of the snowman.

2. While editing the sphere, hold Shift and Control and drag the white boxes to resize the base of the snowman. The sphere, while resting on the ground, should come to about the waist of your avatar.

3. Hold Shift and then drag the blue arrow upward to create a second sphere.

4. Now we want to resize the second sphere so it's smaller than the first, but we don't want the act of resizing to make the sphere move off-center. So before we resize, we will select Stretch Both Sides while in Edit mode.

5. Hold Shift and Control and resize the second sphere until it's a little smaller than the base sphere.

6. Drag the blue arrow until the second sphere sits nicely on top of the base sphere.

7. Repeat steps 3–6 on the second sphere to produce a third sphere, which will be the snowman's head (Figure 2.27).

CHAPTER 1
CHAPTER 2

CHAPTER 3
CHAPTER 4
CHAPTER 5
CHAPTER 6
CHAPTER 7
CHAPTER 8
CHAPTER 9
CHAPTER 10
CHAPTER 11
CHAPTER 12
CHAPTER 13
CHAPTER 14
APPENDICES
INDEX

Figure 2.27: Our snowman is off to a great start.

■ PUTTING THE *SNOW* IN SNOWMAN

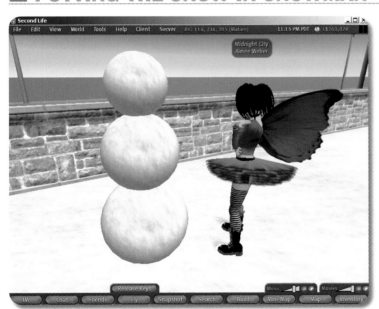

Figure 2.28: Textures make a more convincing snowman.

We now have a plywood model of a snowman, and that's not going to impress anybody! So let's texture our snowman with snow (Figure 2.28)! Linden Lab provides us with a wonderfully rich set of default textures, one of which is snow.

1. While in Edit mode, hold Shift and select all three spheres.

2. Go to the Texture tab on the Edit window and select Texture.

3. In the Texture Picker window, go to Library ▸ Textures ▸ Terrain Textures ▸ Terrain Textures - Winter ▸ Primitive Island - Snow 1, then click the Select button.

■ MAKING THE SNOWMAN'S OLD SILK HAT

1. Rez a cylinder on top of the snowman's head.

2. Resize the hat until it looks in proportion to the snowman's head (about two-thirds the diameter).

3. Drag the arrows until the cylinder appears to be well centered and sitting on top of the snowman's head.

4. To make the hat rim we will Shift+drag the hat upward to create another cylinder that we can work on.

5. Press Control+Shift and resize the second cylinder using the white squares so that it's larger than the original cylinder.

6. Press Control+Shift and resize the second cylinder along the z-axis until it looks about the thickness of the brim of a hat.

7. Drag the blue arrow to place the brim of the hat at the bottom of the original cylinder.

Now we can change the texture so that it looks like an old silk hat rather than a plywood hat (Figure 2.29).

8. Shift-select the hat and the brim.

9. Set Texture to Blank.

10. Set Color to Black.

11. Set Shininess to High.

Figure 2.29: A hat to add charm

■ SCULPTING THE SNOWMAN'S FACE

1. Rez a sphere; set its Texture to Blank and its Color to Black.

2. Resize the sphere such that it is much smaller than the snowman's head, about the size of a lump of coal.

3. Position the coal on the snowman's head to form an eye.

4. Shift-drag the coal across the snowman's face to form the second eye.

5. Next we will create a carrot nose. Rez a cone and set Texture to Blank and Color to Orange.

6. To simulate the rough texture of a carrot, set Bumpiness to Woodgrain.

7. Resize the cone so that it looks more like a carrot. The best way to do this is to make the cone much larger along the z-axis. This will make the carrot ridiculously large, but you can resize the whole thing on all axes (using the white blocks) until it's the size of a normal carrot.

8. Hold the Control key and rotate the carrot 90 degrees until it is pointing away from the snowman's face.

9. Position the carrot beneath the snowman's eyes (Figure 2.30).

Figure 2.30: Now that's a handsome snowman.

■ LINKING UP THE SNOWMAN'S PRIMS

To finish up, you need to link the snowman, give it a name, set it for sale, and then grab a copy for your inventory.

1. Go into Edit mode (Control+3) and drag the marquee to select all the prims in your snowman.

2. Press Shift+L to link them all.

3. Under Objects ▸ General give your snowman a more descriptive name, such as Snowman or Book Tutorial Chap 2.

4. Right-click on the snowman and select More ▸ Take Copy from the pie menu.

5. On the General tab of the Edit menu, check For Sale, set the price to L$20 and check Copy.

6. Under Next Owner Can, check Modify and Resell/Give Away, but keep Copy turned off. After all, you don't want just anybody muscling in on the snowman biz!

7. Wait for the cash to come pouring in!

CHAPTER 3

ADVANCED BUILDING TECHNIQUES

You're now intimately familiar with the inner workings of prims and all of the build options. With a little practice you should be able to construct just about anything. But now it's time you roll up your sleeves and really get dirty. In this chapter you are going to refine your building techniques and push the limits of what prims can do for you.

CONTENTS

CHAPTER 3

🔹 PRIM
   TORTURE

🔹 WORKING
   WITH TINY
   PRIMS

🔹 BUILDING
   BY THE
   NUMBERS

🔹 TUTORIAL:
   BUILDING A
   STAIRCASE

PRIM TORTURE

Prim torture is the phrase *Second Life* builders use to describe the sick, sadistic process of morphing prims into exotic new shapes that even Linden Lab may not have anticipated. The results can be useful, bizarre, artistic, and sometimes utterly paradoxical. This section will expand your understanding of how prims really work and arm you with some tips and tricks to get the most bang from your prim buck.

■ PATH CUT

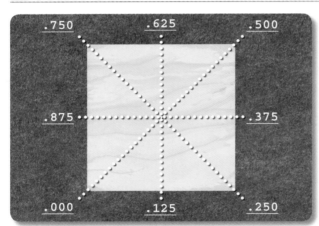

Figure 3.1: Commonly used cut values on a box prim

A *path cut* causes a wedge gap to appear in the prim such that the point of the wedge lines up with the prim's z-axis. An easy way to visualize this is to imagine the prim as a pie viewed from above, and the path cut as a slice taken away by a hungry kid. The cut will normally begin in the corner of the prim for those that have corners, such as boxes and prisms. You can choose any value between 0 and 1 but there are eight commonly used cuts you should commit to memory for frequent use (Figure 3.1). Cut values of 0.0, 0.25, 0.5, and 0.75 are used to create diagonal cuts from corner to corner while values of 0.125, 0.375, 0.625, and 0.875 create cuts from edge to edge.

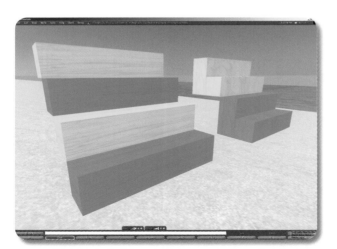

Figure 3.2: Four steps created using four prims (left), and the same number of steps created using just two prims (right)

Path cuts are essential for creating shapes that are more complex and detailed than the basic building blocks themselves. For example, to create a drawer handle you could use a hollow cylinder or torus and then cut it in half (cut value 0.5). However, path cuts can also be used to conserve prims. Let's say you're building a set of stairs, each step 0.25 meters tall. You might consider using one box for each step, but by using cuts you can halve the number of prims. Simply use a 0.5-meter box path cuts of 0.125 and 0.875, creating an L-shaped prim. Stacking these boxes corner to corner would give you the exact same steps but would consume only half the number of prims (Figure 3.2)!

■ HOLLOW

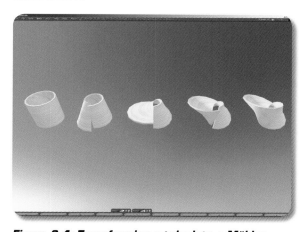

Figure 3.3: A room using four prims (left), and the same room using one prim (right)

Remember that the Hollow feature works along the path of an extruded 2D shape. This means that for linearly extruded objects a hollow will appear along the z-axis (much like with path cuts), but for radially extruded objects Hollow will hollow out a rounded shape. While most hollow shapes match the extruded 2D shape, you can also hollow out a circle, a square, or a triangle.

Like path cuts, Hollow can be used to help save prims. For example, if you want to create a room with four walls, you might use one box per wall, totaling four boxes. But the savvy builder could use one large hollowed box (Figure 3.3). That's four wall surfaces for the price of one! If you need to add a door, simply play with the cut values. (Unfortunately, the door will have to appear in the corner of the room since that's where box path cuts start.)

WARNING

Using a hollow prim as a room is a great way to save prims, but it has one drawback: When you try to alt-zoom inside the room, Second Life's camera will become confused and start behaving as though you are trying to look at the outside of the prim. This can be annoying, so using a hollow prim as a room is recommended only when prim conservation is your highest priority.

■ TWIST

Twists are the weapon of choice for many organic builds, such as trees and flowers. Like hollows, twists occur along the path of extrusion, so they behave quite differently for linearly extruded objects and radially extruded objects. Linearly extruded objects are fairly straightforward; for example, twisting a box can give it a cruller shape, and if tapered to a point it could make a convincing drill or unicorn horn.

Figure 3.4: Transforming a tube into a Möbius strip using twist

Radially extruded objects, on the other hand, cause one of the ends of the extruded loop to break continuity and flip around. If you enter a twist of 180 degrees on the beginning part of a tube it causes a half-twist, where it once again meshes up seamlessly with the end. This creates the famous shape known as a Möbius strip (Figure 3.4). Performing the same trick on a torus makes a pretty, lily-like flower shape.

Many prims become distorted when twisting. Here is a cool trick that takes advantage of this. As you know, there is a 10-meter limitation on prim sizes. But say you wanted a cylinder larger than 10 meters—perhaps for the foundation of a castle or for a landing pad for a spaceship.

CHAPTER 1
CHAPTER 2
CHAPTER 3
CHAPTER 4
CHAPTER 5
CHAPTER 6
CHAPTER 7
CHAPTER 8
CHAPTER 9
CHAPTER 10
CHAPTER 11
CHAPTER 12
CHAPTER 13
CHAPTER 14
APPENDICES
INDEX

CHAPTER 3

PRIM
TORTURE

WORKING
WITH TINY
PRIMS

BUILDING
BY THE
NUMBERS

TUTORIAL:
BUILDING A
STAIRCASE

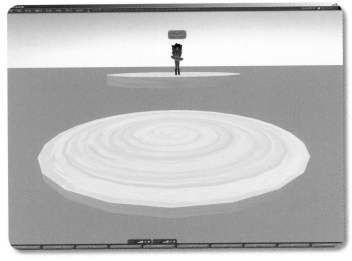

Figure 3.5: A 10m cylinder (background) and a 20m tube twisted to "cheat" the 10m size limit (foreground)

Impossible? Not if we torture the prims enough! Create a 10-meter tube and set the Y Hole Size (the hole size on the y-axis) to 0.05, which is the smallest possible value. Now enter a begin (B) twist of 90 and an end (E) twist of 90. I recommend starting at smaller Twist values and working up gradually to 90 so you can see how the prim becomes distorted and begins to spread out. By the time both values are set to 90, you're left with a cylinder that has a 20-meter diameter! It almost feels like cheating (Figure 3.5).

Twists can sometimes be used in compensating for lower mesh detail in cylinders. Remember that all prims, even round ones, are actually made up of flat, triangular polygons. People with lower-end graphics cards typically run with lower mesh-detail settings, and so cylinders may appear blocky. Adding just a little twist—maybe a value of 25 or so—creates a greater illusion of roundness.

Finally, twists behave very strangely on spheres, enabling the most abstract art designs. As you know, spheres are radially extruded semicircles. Adding twist to a sphere will cause these semicircles to rotate around the point that would be the circle's center. This causes some odd effects when part of the semicircle pulls away from the z–axis and leaves a section of the prim "undefined." This undefined area allows you to see right through the sphere!

MORE INFO

USING LEVEL OF DETAIL (LOD) TO YOUR ADVANTAGE

Level of detail (or LOD, as it is usually called) is a graphics trick used for processing management. Prims, when viewed from a distance, are rendered with fewer polygons. This has a number of annoying effects, along with a few useful ones.

Among the annoyances is the apparent shrinking of round prims—most notably the sphere, but also the tube, ring, torus, and cylinder—compared to rectangular prims and to each other. You can see this by creating two dissimilar prims next to each other, then using your camera controls to zoom back from them. When producing rounded-corner builds, the effect is quite apparent.

One of the most useful unintended aspects of LOD is the one-prim door called an *automatic iris* (because of the way the opening dilates and contracts like an iris). To produce this, rez a box and hollow it to 95.0. Now give it an end twist of 90 degrees and a z-axis height of 0.01. As you zoom your camera toward it, it will appear to open; it will seem to close as you zoom away. This is because *SL* is rendering it with fewer polygons as the distance from the camera increases. However, the effect will not be the same to each viewer—your friend standing back some distance may see you walk through a seemingly closed door.

◼ TAPER

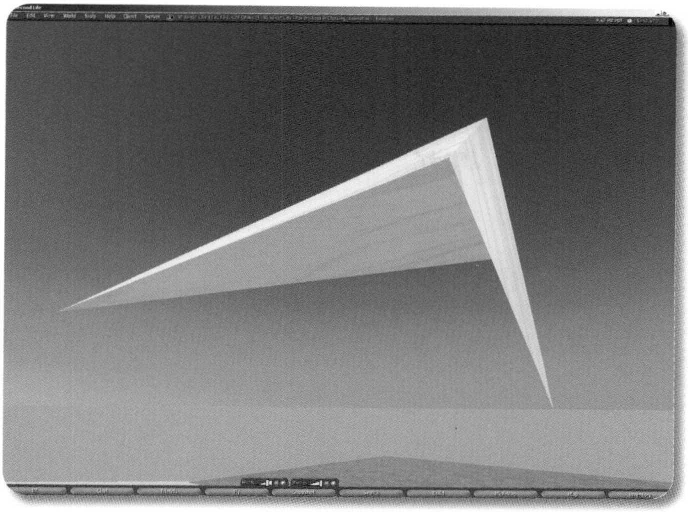

Figure 3.6: Tapering turns the prism into a mysterious shape with a two-dimensional side.

Taper is fairly straightforward with linearly extruded prims. It lets you transform a cylinder into a cone, and a box into pointy box. This is handy, especially when you want to create an obelisk or a monument. But tapering a prism is far more interesting. Let's try it. Rez a prism and set the begin (B) and end (E) taper values to 0.00. Now slowly increase the B taper value to 1.0 and watch the sides of the shape. You will notice that one side buckles outward while another side buckles inward. In fact, the inward-buckling side buckles so far that when you reach a taper of 1.0, part of the prim becomes two-dimensional (Figure 3.6). This is because all prims are made up of triangular polygons. Press Ctrl+Shift+R to see the wireframe of the prim so you can see how the prim distortion works.

As always, Taper is a different animal when applied to radially extruded objects. For tori, tubes, and rings, Taper works very much like the Hole Size option, except that the change in 2D base object size happens only on one end rather than on both.

◼ TOP SHEAR

Figure 3.7: Shear on a linearly extruded shape (left) versus a radially extruded shape (right)

For linearly extruded prims, Top Shear offsets the 2D base shapes along the x- and y-axis so they are no longer located directly on top of one another. This creates a slanted or *sheared* appearance. The maximum offset is 50 percent, so there will always be at least a 50 percent overlap between the top and bottom shapes.

For radially extruded prims, Top Shear is more like "side shear." The two parallel shapes that are moved in relation to each other are located opposite each other halfway along the circular route around the z-axis. This makes the prim slope from one side of the loop to another (Figure 3.7). This looks fairly natural and can be useful for organic builds such as statues of animals or people.

CHAPTER 3

PRIM
TORTURE

WORKING
WITH TINY
PRIMS

BUILDING
BY THE
NUMBERS

TUTORIAL:
BUILDING A
STAIRCASE

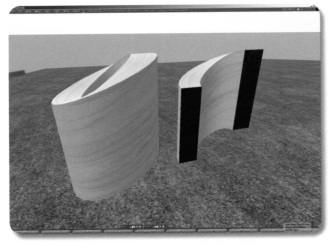

Figure 3.8: Shear applied to a tube looks odd. A cross-section of the prim shows that the rectangular base shapes are the reason.

Sheared tubes behave much like other radially extruded prims, but you may notice that the tube looks a little odd when Top Shear is applied to it. The top and the bottom seem to have a little distortion in the form of a bump. But when you look inside the prim by doing a path cut of B = 0.250 and E = 0.750 you can plainly see that the distortion is caused by the inside corners of the base 2D rectangle, which do not tilt when shear is applied (Figure 3.8).

HOLE SIZE

Hole Size exists only on radially extruded prims. As mentioned in Chapter 2, "Mastering *Second Life*'s Basic Building Blocks," this feature has a very confusing name since its values control the hole size only indirectly by adjusting the dimensions of the 2D base shape. The X value (which represents the x-axis) adjusts the hole depth, while the Y value (which pertains to the y-axis) makes the hole smaller by widening the base shape.

Hole Size is useful for fine-tuning tori destined to become vehicle tires or inner tubes. You can also use it to simulate the cylinder's hollow effect on a tube.

PROFILE CUT

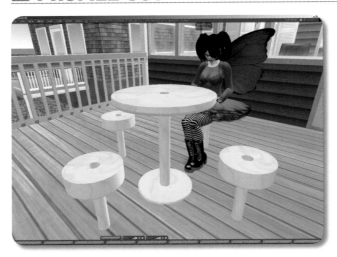

Figure 3.9: Aimee's five-prim patio-furniture set. The stools are minor variations on the table design.

Profile Cut is available only in radially extruded prims. This feature is extremely useful for creating a variety of complex shapes that look like they use many more prims than they actually do!

Let's explore the Profile Cut options by making a little lounge table out of a tube. Set Hollow to 95 and Hole Size Y = 0.45. Now do a profile cut of B = 0.25 and E = 0.90. As you can see, we now have a lovely restaurant table complete with base, a central stand, and a tabletop, all with one single prim! If you want to simulate a tablecloth, set the profile cut B = 0.20. By copying and reducing the size of the table, the same design can make for attractive low-prim chairs (Figure 3.9).

The torus is even more interesting with Profile Cut. Doing a profile cut of E = 0.65 will give you a shape with a round base. I like to stretch this shape along the z-axis and use it as a low-prim streetlamp. Now set Hollow to 95 and set Profile Cut to E = 0.55. You'll start to see an hourglass shape (Figure 3.10), which you can adjust using the Hole Size Y value.

Figure 3.10: This torus has some sexy curves!

■ RADIUS DELTA AND REVOLUTIONS

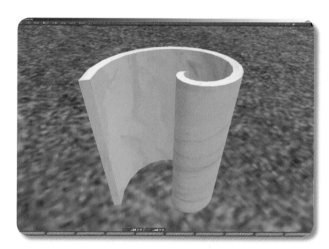

Radius Delta is available only for radially extruded prims. It lets you vary the distance for the 2D base shapes from the prim's z-axis. The result looks something like a scroll (Figure 3.11). To see this, rez a tube, set the Hole Size Y value to 0.05, and set the Radius Delta to 0.947.

This scroll is rolled up for only one revolution. If you want to roll the scroll up more, you will need to change the Revolutions setting; however, there are some catches. First, you're allowed a maximum of 4.00 revolutions. Second, the moment you change the revolutions, the Skew value for the prim is adjusted automatically to prevent any part of the prim from overlapping with itself. This creates a prim that looks more like a spring or a telephone cord than a scroll.

Figure 3.11: A scroll created by adjusting the Radius Delta of a tube

To see the effect of Revolutions on Skew, rez a tube and change the Revolutions value from 1.00 to 1.01. You will notice that the prim instantly sets its Skew to 0.50.

TIP

Although some edit features are available only for certain prims, you can sometimes carry those effects over to other kinds of prims. For example, if you apply a dimple to a sphere then change the prim type to box, you will be left with a box that is smaller than the size values indicate. (See the section "Building a Tiny Box" for details.) Feel free to experiment with different settings, and then switch prim type to get results that go beyond even Linden Lab's expectations.

CHAPTER 3

Figure 3.12: Aimee making cute banana curls using revolved, tapered tori. Plywood-colored hair is in fashion this season!

Using Revolutions values on a torus is the foundation of an entire *Second Life* industry known affectionately as *Hoochie Hair*. To make a single curl of hair, rez a torus, set Revolutions to 4.00, set the X and Y taper to 1.00, and set the skew to about 0.90. You now have a curly strand of hair. Copy this approximately eight thousand times, link, and apply to the head (Figure 3.12). You now have a 'doo that will slow anybody's client to a grinding halt (which obviously is undesirable, so use tori spraringly!). We will talk more about hair creation in Chapter 5, "Working with Clothing and Accessories."

WORKING WITH TINY PRIMS

As you recall, the minimum size for any prim is 0.010 meters, or one centimeter. This is fine for most builds, but some projects (such as jewelry) require far more intricate detail. This section will extend your knowledge of prim torture to whittle the little prims down to almost microscopic sizes.

■ BUILDING A TINY BOX

We will start by making a box that is 0.005 meters on all sides. To do this, we will "trick" the box into being smaller than advertised by adding a dimple.

1. Rez a box.

2. Change the box to a sphere under Object ▶ Building Block Type.

3. Set the Dimple Begin value to 0.50 (leave the End value as 1.00).

4. Change the prim type back to a box.

5. Set Path Cut B = 0.625 and E = 0.875.

6. Use Shift+Alt to size the prim as small as it can get.

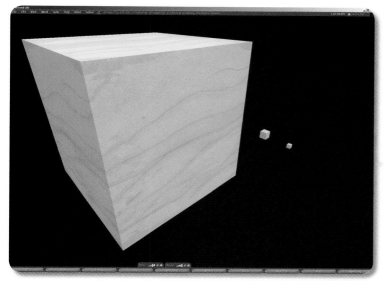

Technically this prim is still 1 centimeter in size, but by using Path Cut and Dimple we got the actual size to half a centimeter for any given side. Figure 3.13 should give you a feel for how much smaller things can get from the 0.01m minimum.

Figure 3.13: Three boxes of size 0.5m, 0.010m, and 0.005m

BUILDING AN EVEN TINIER BOX

Hollow, when combined with cuts and dimples, can also be used to overcome the 0.010-meter minimum prim size limit. Let's try it.

1. **Rez a sphere.**

2. **Set Hollow to 95 and set Dimple to B = 0.53 and E = 0.55.**

3. **Set the Path Cut to B = 0.620 and E = 0.640.**

4. **Shrink the whole prim using the size handles until it's a teeny-weenie prim.**

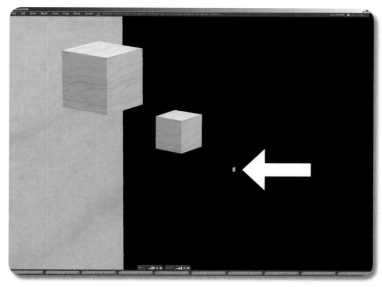

The prim is now a fraction of the size of the 1-centimeter box (Figure 3.14)! To make slight adjustments on the shape of the prim to get something closer to a cube, you may want to reduce the hollow or the dimple.

Figure 3.14: Even compared to the 0.005m prim (the third one from the left), the micro prim is barely a speck!

■ CONSTRUCTING A DELICATE CHAIN

Figure 3.15: Aimee examines her miniscule new bling bling made with hollow-cut tori.

Let's create the links of a very delicate chain (Figure 3.15).

1. Rez a torus and size it down to 0.010 on all sides.

2. Set Hollow to 95 and set Profile Cut values to B = 0.28 and E = 0.30. We now have a very tiny chain link that is about half a centimeter in diameter, but let's not stop there.

3. Set the hole size to value X = 0.25 and Y = 0.45. You could go even smaller, but the shape would no longer look like a chain link.

4. Now copy and rotate the teeny prims until you have a little chain.

5. Turn on Shiny for a pretty, metallic look.

TIP

You just learned how to make a tiny item, but after you have those skills, you can simplify things by working on a large scale when working with small prims, then resizing the item when it's complete. In most cases (especially for rings), I will work at 50× scale so that no dimension (x-, y-, or z-axis size) will be less than 0.5m. I use cuts and tapers to produce sizes smaller than my chosen minimum. When you must work with small prims, work on top of a larger prim with a contrasting color. It is very easy to lose tiny pieces.

When determining final size of your item (at least when it's intended to be sold or shared), consider that other people may want it a different size than how you made it. Allow for a little extra shrinking.

BUILDING BY THE NUMBERS

By now you must think you're quite the hotshot, using movement, size, and rotation handles like a pro. But don't get too smug—your work is going to be sloppy until you learn one more critical concept: *building by the numbers.*

The limitations of the prim handles become apparent when a project has little room for error. When adjacent prims are not positioned perfectly against each other, you may see a subtle line disrupting the smooth surface. When prims overlap improperly, the textures on the overlapping prims may "flicker" as they fight to decide which texture is on top. When you build by the numbers you use some simple math to position and size your prims perfectly.

CHAPTER 1
CHAPTER 2
CHAPTER 3
CHAPTER 4
CHAPTER 5
CHAPTER 6
CHAPTER 7
CHAPTER 8
CHAPTER 9
CHAPTER 10
CHAPTER 11
CHAPTER 12
CHAPTER 13
CHAPTER 14
APPENDICES
INDEX

■ THE *M* WORD (MATH)

For our first example, we'll build a 20-meter-long wall. As you know, the prim size limit is 10 meters, so we will have to use two prims.

1. **Rez two prims and enter the following size values: X = 10.000, Y = 0.500, and Z = 5.000.**

2. **Copy and paste the Y and Z position values of the first wall over to the second wall. This will line up the two wall segments on all but one axis.**

We don't want the same values for the X position on both wall segments; that would cause both wall segments to occupy the same exact space! Instead we will do a little math so both prims are precisely side by side.

3. **Find the length of the first prim (the x-axis size) and divide it by two. (That's 10 ÷ 2 = 5.)**

4. **Find the length of the second prim (the x-axis size) and divide it by two. (That's also 10 ÷ 2 = 5.)**

5. **Add the two together. (5 + 5 = 10.) You now have the offset.**

6. **Find the x-axis position for the first prim, add the offset of 10 to that value, and paste the result into the X position for the second prim.**

If you did everything correctly you should have two wall segments sitting side by side. There will be no gaps and no overlap. It's mathematically perfect!

■ USING SNAP TO GRID

Figure 3.16: The Grid Options window

Another way to build precisely is to use the grid and the Snap to Grid option. The Use Grid option is found in the Edit window along with an Options button that allows you to control the details. To use the grid, grab the planar drag handles (the little triangular move handles) for the axis along which you wish to move. A white grid will appear around your prim; the grid includes a solid white line that represents grid units, and finer lines that represent sub-units. You can toggle Snap to Grid mode by pressing G or going to Tools ▶ Snap to Grid. Snapping to the grid is a lifesaver when it comes to allowing you to set precise positions without having to do as much math.

By setting the Ruler mode in the Edit window, you can chose between using the global grid, which is based on global coordinates, and local grid, which adjusts the grid to fit the prim's current position. You can also elect to

CHAPTER 3

PRIM
TORTURE

WORKING
WITH TINY
PRIMS

BUILDING
BY THE
NUMBERS

TUTORIAL:
BUILDING A
STAIRCASE

snap one or more prims to the grid along the x- and y-axis using Tools ▶ Snap Object XY to Grid, or by pressing Shift+X. This can be handy because it works on multiple selected prims, saving you the trouble of having to snap each one individually to the grid.

For finer grid control, you can bring up the Grid Options window (Figure 3.16) by pressing the Options button in the Edit window, going to Tools ▶ Grid Options, or pressing Ctrl+Shift+B. This window allows you to set the grid units and the extents for the grid, and brings up a slider that lets you set the opacity for the grid. You can also get a finer level of detail by changing the grid units or enabling the Sub-Unit Snapping option. The Show Cross Sections option colors the area of the prim where it intersects the grid, making it easier to judge perspective.

Finally, you can change the characteristics of the grid itself by using the Use Selection for Grid option in the Tools menu or by pressing Shift+G. This feature will adjust the proportions for the grid units based on the dimensions and rotation of the currently selected prim.

TUTORIAL: BUILDING A STAIRCASE

Figure 3.17: Stairs made perfect by using grid features

One of the biggest pains in the virtual keister is making stairs. The problem is that very small errors from one step to the next eventually result in a sloppy overall appearance. Therefore, "eye-balling" stairs is not recommended (but give it a shot so you can see for yourself!). Instead, you should use the Grid Options menu to make perfect stairs in record time (Figure 3.17).

1. Make the first step. Rez a box and set its size to X = 1.500, Y = 0.400, and Z = 0.050. That's a fine-looking step.

2. Now bring up the Grid Options window and set Grid Units to 0.300 meters. This is a decent distance from one step to the next.

3. Now you must make sure the first step is aligned to the grid, so pull on the planar drag handles in all directions until the prim snaps into one of the grid spots.

4. Now Shift-drag the planar drag handles upward, creating a whole new step, and then drag the step in the Y direction.

5. Now do it again, 10 more times. Ta-da! Perfect steps.

■ BUILDING A SPIRAL STAIRCASE

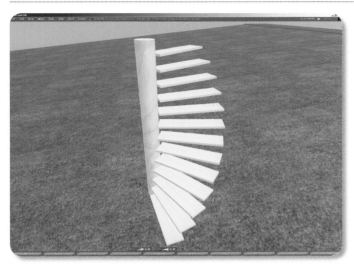

Figure 3.18: Perfect spiral stairs

Now let's make something a little more impressive—a spiral staircase (Figure 3.18). This time we're going to use a combination of grid-snapping and rotation.

1. **Rez a step with the same dimensions as the last step (X = 1.500, Y = 0.400, and Z = 0.050) and again, set Grid Units to 0.300.**

2. **We now want to link a pivot point into the step. Drag-copy another step in the X direction so both steps sit side by side, then resize this new prim so that it's a perfect square (set X = 0.400).**

Now we want to place the two prims perfectly side by side, so we are going to use the math we learned earlier.

3. **Take half the X size of the first prim (1.5 ÷ 2 = 0.75) and half the X size of the second prim (0.4 ÷ 2 = 0.200).**

4. **Add the two together (0.75 + 0.2 = 0.95).**

5. **Find the X position of the first prim, add 0.95 to it, and then use that as the X position value for the smaller pivot prim.**

You now have two prims set perfectly side by side. You may want to tint the smaller pivot prim to another color, such as red—you will be deleting the other pivot prims later, but for now we will be using them as a center point for rotation.

Now you need to link the two prims together. In the previous chapter I mentioned how the order in which you select prims prior to linking is very important. Well this will be your first real example as to why. When we link prims, the last prim selected becomes the root prim—the prim around which the whole build will rotate when we start to enter rotational values.

6. **Select the long step first, and then Shift-select the smaller pivot prim. Press Ctrl+L to link your prims. (The root prim glows yellow when selected, while all other prims glow blue.)**

7. **As we did with the regular staircase, we want to start out with our stair snapped to a spot on the grid. Go to Tools ▶ Snap Object XY to Grid (or use Shift+X), and then use the planar drag handles to snap the step on the z-axis.**

8. **Using the planar drag handles, Shift-drag the step upward to produce another step.**

9. **Do this several more times until you have a stack of steps with 0.300 meters between every step.**

Now we are going to rotate each step by entering incrementally larger numbers into the Z rotation axis. We can rotate each step at any increment as long as we use the same increment for each step. I think 10 degrees of rotation per step will look nice.

10. Leave the first step alone (z-axis rotation of zero) and set the Z rotation for the second step to 10.00 degrees. (The next one will be 20.00 degrees, then 30.00, then 40.00, so on and so on.)

You should now see an attractive spiral staircase. The next step will be to remove the pivot points.

11. Select all the steps and press Shift+Ctrl+L to unlink them all.

12. Delete all but the first little pivot steps; the rest are no longer needed.

TIP

Why keep the first pivot point? Well, when you get used to building by the numbers, certain prims may become valuable simply because they hold position or size data that you may need later. In this case, we're going to place a cylinder down the center of the spiral staircase. You could rez a new cylinder and then go through the mathematical process of finding the exact center of the spiral, but why bother? The pivot prim contains that information already!

Now we'll build a column that will finish off the look of our spiral staircase.

13. Edit the first little pivot step.

14. Set the building-block type to Cylinder.

15. Stretch the cylinder along the z-axis until it becomes a mighty support pole, giving apparent strength to our beautiful creation.

CHAPTER 4

LET THERE BE TEXTURE (AND LIGHT)!

Outstanding builds are only half finished if you don't spice things up with quality texture work. *Textures*—images mapped to the surface of the 3D geometry—have multiple uses in *Second Life*. First, textures create the illusion of building materials. Textures help tell stories that prims alone struggle with. One simple box prim can tell many different stories depending on how it's textured. Is it a bomb? Is it a birthday present? Is it the mysterious Time Cube?

Textures can also help reduce prim usage. Just imagine the number of prims you would need to create all the little instruments and controls in a space shuttle's cockpit. But a few textured prims provide the same visual effect at a fraction of the performance penalty.

Finally, textures can enhance the feeling of light and depth in a build. On a city-street build, textures can mean the difference between a bright, busy metropolis and a dark, mysterious backstreet. In this chapter we will talk about using textures to add detail and feeling to your already-outstanding builds.

NOTE

Providing tutorials on specific software packages goes well beyond the scope of this book. To get the most out of this chapter, you should already be familiar with your graphics tools of choice. The examples here will focus largely on Photoshop, but the fundamental ideas can be translated into most software tools.

CONTENTS

TEXTURE SOURCES

Linden Lab provides us with a considerable collection of textures in our inventory library. This folder includes landscaping textures, wood, stone, fabrics, tiles, and many more. However, by no means are you limited to the default textures. There are many ways to create your own.

■ PHOTOGRAPHS

*Figure 4.1: Snapshots of everyday surfaces can make great **Second Life** textures.*

In real life, I carry a digital camera in my bag in case I come across a texture that is perfect for *Second Life* use. As you walk down a city street, you might find an attractive brick wall, a cobblestone road, a cool-looking door, or a rusty old mailbox. Snap whatever you can find (Figure 4.1) and keep the images in your own personal texture archive so they will be ready when you need them.

Remember that the best textures should be photographed at a high enough resolution that you will still have detail when you've finished distorting and resizing it. I would recommend at minimum 1024×1024 pixels. It's also best to photograph the subject as straight-on as possible. This usually results in a photo with poor composition as far as photography goes, but will make for a great source photo for textures. When photographing the ground (perhaps for pavement textures) it's best to get the camera as high as possible. You may need to stand on a bench and raise the camera over your head to get as much of the ground scene in the shot as you can. Remember not to get your shadow in the shot!

■ HAND-DRAWN TEXTURES

If you have the artistic inclination, you may consider hand-drawing textures. This technique can create a dramatic, stylish effect that will really stand out in a virtual world that strives for photographic realism (Figure 4.2). Some texture artists will start their creations on paper using conventional media such as colored pencil, watercolors, or ink. They then use a flatbed scanner to digitize the image for processing and upload. Alternatively, artists can use a drawing tablet to enter their work directly into a data format. I own a 6"×8" Wacom tablet and it is one of my most valued tools.

Figure 4.2: Hand-drawn textures can create a warm, friendly, almost surreal effect.

CHAPTER 1
CHAPTER 2
CHAPTER 3
CHAPTER 4

CHAPTER 5
CHAPTER 6
CHAPTER 7
CHAPTER 8
CHAPTER 9
CHAPTER 10
CHAPTER 11
CHAPTER 12
CHAPTER 13
CHAPTER 14
APPENDICES
INDEX

RESIDENTS SPEAK

NYLON PINKNEY ON THE BENEFITS OF HAND-DRAWN TEXTURES

When I first joined *Second Life*, the majority of textures and clothing were from photos. I'll admit, I probably would have gone that route too if I didn't find them so hard to create. All that warping and cloning was too much work for me. Instead I decided to draw all my textures and clothing for *Second Life* in Adobe Photoshop using a Wacom pen and tablet.

I feel like drawn textures have a lighter, more fun feel to them—they don't have to look realistic because that's part of the appeal. Drawing definitely helps make textures look as if they were made to fit your mesh perfectly, down to the last strategically placed wrinkle. You're creating the texture exactly how you want, so there's basically no limit like there would be if you were working with a photo of an already-made shirt.

I find it fun because you can add little details, like little stray threads or heart-shaped buttons. Simply figure out what you want to make, then start with a rough sketch and paint it. It definitely takes an artistic hand to paint and draw, but Photoshop does make the whole process a little easier.

■ PROCEDURAL TEXTURES

A variety of 3D rendering tools (see the sidebar "Tools of the Trade") allow you to generate textures using an algorithm. These are known as *procedural textures* and often require more programming skills than artistic skills. Procedural textures excel at creating an enormous amount of nonrepeating detail, a feat that would take ages to accomplish by hand.

MORE INFO

TOOLS OF THE TRADE

There is a variety of handy tools on the market for creating textures. Adobe Photoshop, Adobe Illustrator, and Corel Paint Shop Pro are the most popular commercial graphics software packages for creating textures for *Second Life*. If those tools are out of your price range, you can look to various inexpensive or free utilities on the market, including Paint.NET and GIMP (the GNU Image Manipulation Program). Additionally, the expensive 3ds Max and Maya both allow 3D rendering and procedural texture creation, but Bryce and LightWave are less-expensive options, and Blender is free.

■ THE WEB

Most Web search engines can be used to track down images and textures within seconds. If you're creating a model of the solar system, you could enter "solar system textures" into Google and quickly find textures from the NASA Jet Propulsion Laboratory (http://maps.jpl.nasa.gov/) that fit the bill exactly.

■ COMPOSITE TEXTURE

Figure 4.3: I like the front window in the photo on the left so I copied and pasted it onto the brick image to make a composite texture.

You may discover that you need only a tiny part of a photo, or that you need bits and pieces from multiple photos combined with additional hand-drawn detail to get the results you desire (Figure 4.3). When you master texturing in *Second Life*, you will find that nearly all of your textures will be composite in some way.

MORE INFO

CONSIDERING COPYRIGHT LAWS

Be mindful of the copyright laws in your jurisdiction when using any textures that you did not create yourself. Unless otherwise specified, assume that images you find on the Web are protected by copyright laws and you may not use them in your *Second Life* project without permission. However, there are some wonderful non-copyrighted resources. Most government agencies automatically grant permission for any third-party use, and there are a variety of free and royalty-free image archives on the Web.

Using a small portion or a derivative of a copyrighted work may be protected under the fair use doctrine. Unfortunately, there are no clear-cut rules to determine what is fair use and what is a violation. Judges take into consideration the amount of original work that was "borrowed," the purpose of the work, and the for-profit/nonprofit use of the derivative work. You can learn more about fair use from the Electronic Frontier Foundation (`http://www.eff.org/IP/eff_fair_use_faq.php`), but if in doubt, always ask permission before you use third-party works.

UPLOADING TEXTURES

Uploading an image into *Second Life* is very simple: go to File ▸ Upload Image. You can choose any .tga, .bmp, .jpg, or .jpeg file.

NOTE

Uploading an image will cost you 10 Linden dollars. This nominal fee helps reduce frivolous or unnecessary texture uploads, which consume server space at Linden Lab.

Once you've selected an image, you will see the image-preview window, which allows you to select a different name and enter an optional description. You can also preview the image wrapped around different avatar body types (more on that in Chapter 5, "Working with Clothing and Accessories." Once you've uploaded the texture it will appear on your screen and in the Texture folder in your inventory, ready for use.

CHAPTER 1
CHAPTER 2
CHAPTER 3
CHAPTER 4

CHAPTER 5
CHAPTER 6
CHAPTER 7
CHAPTER 8
CHAPTER 9
CHAPTER 10
CHAPTER 11
CHAPTER 12
CHAPTER 13
CHAPTER 14
APPENDICES
INDEX

TIP

Second Life *stores all textures in resolutions that are a power of 2 across the width and height (32, 64, 128, 256, 512, and 1024.) Any texture uploaded to* Second Life *that doesn't follow this rule will be "clamped" down to the nearest power of 2 automatically. For example, if you upload a texture that is 300×300 pixels in size, it will be converted to a 256×256-pixel image.*

To maintain better control of your texture resolutions, make a habit of sizing your images to powers of 2 before uploading. This will help reduce any surprises you may run into when it comes to texture size or resample quality.

WORKING WITH TEXTURED PRIMS

Now that we have the basics squared away, let's get our hands dirty with some textured prims! In this section you will learn about all the texture-related options available on the prim Edit window and how they are used.

UTILIZING REPEATS AND OFFSETS

When you slap a texture onto the side of a prim, normally the whole texture is displayed as if it were a painting ready to be hung on a museum wall. This may be good for paintings, but *Second Life* also provides the ability to change the repeats and offsets, allowing you to tile an image multiple times, view only a part of the image, or slide the image around the prim face. In this section we will show you how and why repeats and offsets are used.

TILING WITH REPEATS

Let's start with tiling—specifically, floor tiling!

1. **Rez a box that is sized to 10m×10m×0.5m. This is going to be a floor.**

2. **Go into your inventory library and find a texture under Library ▸ Textures ▸ Floor Tile. I'm going to go with Floor Tile13.**

3. **Drag the texture onto your floor; you will notice that the "tile" isn't tiled at all.**

4. **To fix this, edit the floor prim, go to the Texture tab, and set Repeats per Face to Horizontal (U) = 13, Vertical (V) = 13. (See Figure 4.4.)**

CHAPTER 4

TEXTURE
SOURCES

UPLOADING
TEXTURES

WORKING
WITH
TEXTURED
PRIMS

DISTORTING
TEXTURES

CREATING
DEPTH WITH
TINTS AND
TEXTURES

TUTORIAL:
BAKING A
SPOTLIGHT
ONTO A WALL

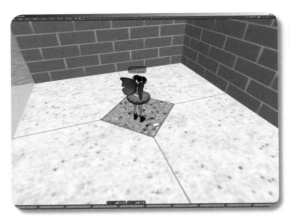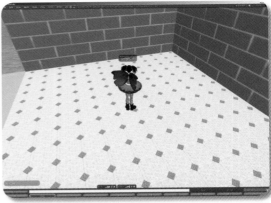

Figure 4.4: (a) A floor with no tiling and (b) a floor tiled with settings of U = 13, V = 13

ZOOMING WITH REPEATS

If you'd like to get a closer look at a certain subject matter, zooming in on an image is helpful. Entering a Repeat value less than 1.0 will cause the image to stretch (or *zoom*). In Figure 4.5, I changed the zoom value from U = 1.0, V = 1.0 to U = 0.4, V = 0.4. This gives you a much better view of two very pretty chickies.

Figure 4.5: The left image is unadjusted; the right image is zoomed in.

SPANNING PRIMS WITH REPEATS AND OFFSETS

What if you want to display an image on a surface larger than 10 meters? Naturally, you would have to use multiple prims, but what about the texture? One solution would be to load the texture into Photoshop and then cut it in half so that you can display half a texture on each prim. An easy alternative is to use Repeat values and Offset values to make the texture span multiple prims. Let's try it.

1. Rez a box whose size is X = 10.0, Y = 0.5, Z = 10.0.

2. Shift-drag the box along the x-axis, creating a copy that is side by side with the original. (Refer to Chapter 3, "Advanced Building Techniques," for details on this procedure.)

3. Drag the American Flag texture from the Linden texture library at Library ▸ Textures ▸ American Flag. You now have two American flags sitting side by side (Figure 4.6). Let's make one big one.

CHAPTER 1
CHAPTER 2
CHAPTER 3
CHAPTER 4

CHAPTER 5
CHAPTER 6
CHAPTER 7
CHAPTER 8
CHAPTER 9
CHAPTER 10
CHAPTER 11
CHAPTER 12
CHAPTER 13
CHAPTER 14
APPENDICES
INDEX

4. Edit the first prim, and on the Texture tab, set Horizontal (U) repeats to 0.5. This basically cuts the image in half along the U direction. Then set Horizontal Offset to 0.75 so that we see the left side of the flag. Note that −0.25 would also work.

5. On the second prim, set the Horizontal repeats to 0.5 and set Horizontal Offset to 0.25. You now have one big American flag (Figure 4.7)!

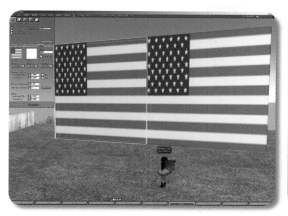

Figure 4.6: Two prims, each with the American flag, but we want one big flag!

Figure 4.7: Much better.

TIP

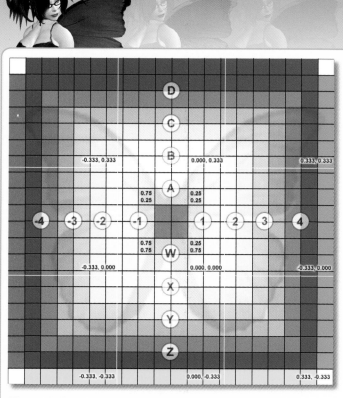

When attempting to line up a complex array of repeated prims and textures, it can be handy to start with a reference grid texture (Figure 4.8). This texture provides numbered grid lines and orientation so you can easily line up textures.

I'm including my favorite reference grid on the CD in the back of this book. The reference grid also includes the offset values for spanning 2×2 textures, and 3×3 textures. Enjoy!

Figure 4.8: A reference grid is handy for lining up textures.

■ CREATING SHINY HAPPY PRIMS

When new *Second Life* users discover the Shininess option (often called shiny for short), you can almost taste their unmitigated glee. This is because shiny looks really cool. You can bring instant dazzle to any build with the flick of a pull-down menu, but be careful not to use shiny as a crutch. Builds that overuse or misuse the effect tend to look amateurish. Take a moment to look around your environment and see what is shiny and what is not. Here are some typical Shininess settings for common material types.

Low: **Unpolished metals, polished wood, plastic**

Medium: **Porcelain, teeth**

High: **Highly polished metals, chrome**

Unfortunately, shiny doesn't work on any surface that is set as transparent using the Transparency option or a transparent texture (generally known as an *alpha surface*). So if you are using a texture with an alpha layer or if you have Transparency set to anything but 0%, Shiny turns off automatically.

■ UTILIZING THE FULL BRIGHT SETTINGS

As you know from Chapter 2, "Mastering *Second Life*'s Building Blocks," the Full Bright feature renders a prim as though it were being illuminated to maximum brightness. A full-bright prim is different from a light object because it doesn't cast light onto surrounding prims, you are not limited to just six of them, and they do not cause any reduction in client performance. Full-bright prims are ideal for creating the illusion of lighting, especially when it's dark. As a fun example, let's create a city building that has illuminated windows.

1. First grab a copy of the brick texture from the Linden library. Go to Library ▸ Textures ▸ Buildings and copy the Bricks texture by right-clicking on it and selecting Copy from the menu.

2. Find a folder in your own inventory and select Paste. You now have your own copy of the brick texture.

3. Double-click on the brick texture to bring it up, and then go to File ▸ Save Texture As to save the texture on your hard drive.

4. Load up the brick texture in your graphics editor. I will use Photoshop in this example.

5. We want to see more contrast between light and dark, so let's darken the brick a little. In Photoshop, go to Image ▸ Adjustments ▸ Brightness/Contrast and set Brightness to –40 and contrast to –30. Now it looks like brick at night.

6. Create a new layer and fill it with RGB values of 146, 116, 81 to simulate interior lighting. Make sure the new layer is under the brick layer.

7. Using the marquee tool, select a square in the center of the brick texture and cut a hole for a window.

8. Right-click on the brick layer, select Blending Options, add a drop shadow, and adjust opacity and distance until the window appears to have a little depth (Figure 4.9).

9. Save it all as a 24-bit .tga file and upload the image into *Second Life*. Now apply the texture to a 10×10×10 prim and set Repeats to 3 on each axis.

10. View your new building in the dark (Figure 4.10). If it's not nighttime, you can force night by going to Client ▸ World ▸ Mouse Moves Sun and then look directly down in mouselook.

Figure 4.9: A brick wall with a window in it

Figure 4.10: A full-bright building at night

■ BUMPY!

Second Life's Bumpiness feature uses a special kind of texture known as a *bump map* to create rudimentary highlights and shadow effects. These shadows are achieved by dynamically interacting with the sun's position. So, depending on the orientation of the prim and the position of the sun, you will see different highlights and shadows. You can change the repeats, offsets, and rotation of the selected bump map by using the surface's texture controls. You have 17 bump maps to choose from, but unfortunately you cannot upload your own.

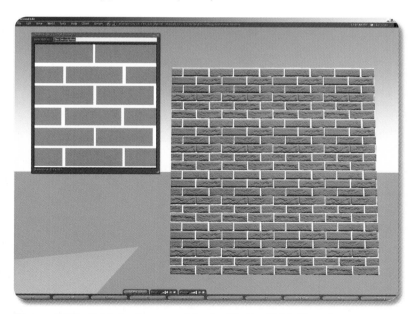

Figure 4.11: Brick texture combined with the Brick Bumpiness Feature

Bumpiness can create an overpowering visual effect, so don't overuse it unless your project calls for deep, pronounced grooves. The Woodgrain bump map, for example, is too harsh to use on a piece of plywood, but it's perfect for an old gnarled tree trunk. You can also use bump maps in conjunction with textures to create an even more realistic look. In Figure 4.11 you can see where I combine a simple flat brick texture with the Brick bump map to create a wall that looks like you could feel all the grooves.

CHAPTER 4

TEXTURE
SOURCES

UPLOADING
TEXTURES

WORKING
WITH
TEXTURED
PRIMS

DISTORTING
TEXTURES

CREATING
DEPTH WITH
TINTS AND
TEXTURES

TUTORIAL:
BAKING A
SPOTLIGHT
ONTO A WALL

DISTORTING TEXTURES

Say you're walking down the street and you see a fabulous brick wall that would make a great texture in *Second Life*. So you grab your trusty digital camera and take a shot. But when you apply your texture to a wall in *Second Life*, it looks all wrong. The problem is perspective. You need to lose it!

Photoshop has a marvelous tool under the Edit menu called Free Transform. It lets you morph and distort a texture until it fits the shape you are looking for. Let's try it on the following photo.

The wall in Figure 4.12 is perfect for *Second Life*, but if you apply it to a texture as is, the perspective will make it look all wrong.

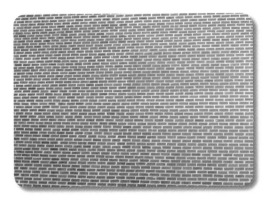

Figure 4.12: A photo of a brick wall, taken at an angle

1. The first thing we will do is grab some guides. (Press Control+R in Photoshop if the rulers aren't already visible, then drag the guides from the rulers.) Place vertical guides near the top and bottom of the image, and place horizontal guides near the left and right of the image. Leave a little room between the guides and the edge of the image.

2. Now select the whole image by pressing Control+A and go into transform mode by pressing Control+T.

3. We want to do a special kind of transform called a *distort*, so right-click anywhere in the selection and pick the Distort option from the drop down menu. Now we are ready to work.

4. Using the marquee handles, align the rows of brick with your guides. Also make sure the vertical gaps between the bricks line up with the vertical guides. This will take a bit of practice, but eventually it will come naturally.

5. When you are finished, press Enter and presto—you distorted the perspective out of your image (Figure 4.13).

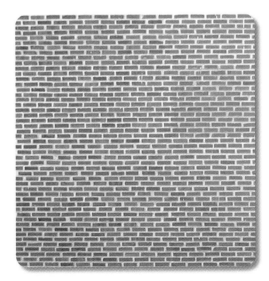

Figure 4.13: The brick wall ready to be used as a texture after transformation

CHAPTER 1
CHAPTER 2
CHAPTER 3
CHAPTER 4
CHAPTER 5
CHAPTER 6
CHAPTER 7
CHAPTER 8
CHAPTER 9
CHAPTER 10
CHAPTER 11
CHAPTER 12
CHAPTER 13
CHAPTER 14
APPENDICES
INDEX

NOTE

You may find that the edges of the distorted image have gaps, and some of the brick gets pushed off the image edge. This is to be expected. Simply crop the image so that all you can see is brick.

This little trick will come in very handy because you won't always be able to photograph textures at an ideal angle. When you photograph buildings you are typically standing on the ground looking up at them (which makes the bottom part look much larger than the top). When taking a photo of a street or a sidewalk, you normally have to take the photo at an angle because you cannot raise your camera high enough to get a bird's-eye view.

CREATING DEPTH WITH TINTS AND TEXTURES

In this section you will learn how to use tints and textures to emphasize depth and simulate dramatic lighting effects. These techniques have a tremendous impact on the visual appeal of your builds and can transform a good build into an exciting user experience.

■ TINTING

Before you touch a single texture, consider your tinting options. Tinting is a great way to add depth without the performance penalties of using textures.

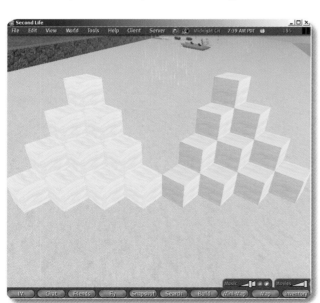

First let's consider Luminance (*Lum* for short) which is largely a measure of the prim's brightness. Freshly rezzed prims start out with a plywood texture, but they also start out white with a Lum value of 100%. This allows you to view the texture on the prim in its purest, brightest form, but it can also wash out and mute the shadow effects provided by sun and moonlight. Reducing the Lum value to 75–80% can help create contrast between different sides of the prim and instill a sense of depth for your audience (Figure 4.14).

Figure 4.14: The left pile has Lum set to 100%; the right pile has it set to 75%.

CHAPTER 4

TEXTURE
SOURCES

UPLOADING
TEXTURES

WORKING
WITH
TEXTURED
PRIMS

DISTORTING
TEXTURES

CREATING
DEPTH WITH
TINTS AND
TEXTURES

TUTORIAL:
BAKING A
SPOTLIGHT
ONTO A WALL

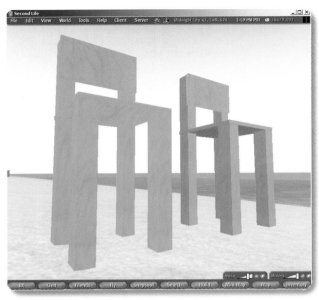

In some cases you may not want your build to be at the mercy of the ever-moving sun and moon. You might prefer that your builds respond to lighting of your own creation. A good start is to use a local light object (described Chapter 2), which, like a light bulb, will brighten up one side of your build, and accentuate the effect by tinting the surfaces that face away from the light source with lower Lum values. Figure 4.15 shows an example of this technique with two simple chairs, one tinted to accentuate the dark underside facing away from the sun.

Figure 4.15: Tinting the underside of the chair on the right makes the sunlight seem more real.

USING SHADOW PRIMS

Tinting can go a long way in creating builds with dramatic depth, but eventually you're going to want your objects to cast a shadow on the ground and on surrounding objects. There are multiple ways to accomplish this, but one of the most flexible and easiest ways is to use a *shadow prim*.

CREATING BASIC REUSABLE SHADOW PRIMS

The vast majority of objects that cast shadows will be served well with simple square or circular shadows applied to an otherwise-invisible prim. Reusing these shadow prims means fewer textures that users will have to download, which means quicker load times overall. This benefit comes at the cost of increased prim usage and increased alpha prim usage. When creating your shadow, it's best to use white on an alpha background. (The white will become the shadow. This is sometimes referred to as an *alpha shadow*.) When it's applied to a prim, you will be able to change the white color to black or any other color, depending on your needs.

Creating alpha shadows is very simple:

1. **Start with a small texture (around 128×128 pixels) with an alpha background. Draw a white square in the center, leaving ample room around the edges.**

2. **Blur the edges. In Photoshop the best way to do this is to go to Filter ▸ Blur ▸ Gaussian Blur and adjust until the edges are blurred the way you like them.**

3. **Save your shadow to a 32-bit .tga file, which will allow *Second Life* to render the alpha layer as transparent.**

4. **In *Second Life*, simply apply the shadow texture to the top of an invisible box and then reshape the box until your shadow matches the shadowed subject.**

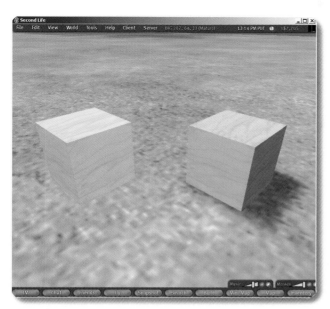

Figure 4.16: The box on the right has tinting and a shadow prim.

In Figure 4.16 I added tint and a prim shadow to the box to create a more realistic visual. The shadow prim is set with 50% transparency so the darkness doesn't appear too harsh. Note how the tinted side of the box falls on the side of the shadow, which is the side opposite the light source.

■ CREATING CUSTOM SHADOW PRIMS

Sometimes one size does not fit all, and you may find it useful to create a custom shadow that better fits the shape of your subject. One obvious way to do this is to hand-draw the alpha shadow. There's a clever trick you can use to create perfect shadows every time.

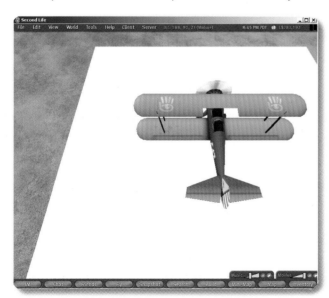

Figure 4.17: Look down at the airplane as if your camera were the light source.

1. Determine the direction the light is coming from, and set your camera looking in the direction the light is being cast. If the light is coming from the sun, stick your camera in the direction of the sun, looking down on your subject— an airplane, for example (Figure 4.17).

2. Since the light is coming from above, rez an untextured, full-bright prim under your subject. Use a color that creates the most contrast between your subject and the background. Normally I use white, but if your subject is mostly white you may consider using bright green or some other color that is easy to pick out of the image.

3. Take a snapshot of the subject.

4. Load the image into Photoshop and select the background color. Delete the background, leaving only the alpha (invisible) layer behind it.

Figure 4.18: The airplane's shadow makes the aircraft look more natural in the scene.

5. Set Brightness to –100 and Contrast to –100. This will create a black silhouette of the object on an alpha background.

6. Go to Filter ▸ Blur ▸ Gaussian Blur and adjust until the edges are blurred the way you like them.

7. Crop the image and resize to a power of two. 128×128 pixels is recommended, but remember that shadows are typically blurry, so high resolution is not critical here.

8. Save the image as a 32-bit .tga, upload it to *Second Life*, and apply your shadow to a prim. After some resizing and transparency adjustments, you will have a perfect shadow (Figure 4.18).

TIP

When creating shadows it's important to be conscious of the location of your imaginary light source for every part of the build. It's not uncommon to see lovely lighting and shadows cast in conflicting directions! This creates a confusing and uncomfortable visual. I recommend placing a big red prim at the location of your imaginary light, and using it as a reference for all the lighting effects you create in a scene.

■ TEXTURE BAKING

Texture baking is the term used when shadows are drawn directly onto the textures to be used in a model. This technique has a variety of pros and cons. Texture baking reduces the number of prims necessary for a shadowed scene since shadow prims are not used. It also lets you create much more beautiful and complex lighting effects than would be possible with shadow prims alone. On the downside, texture baking requires larger textures and more of them, which results in increased load times.

WARNING

If you bake a shadow directly into a floor texture—for example, for a shadow cast by a chair—the shadow will not follow the chair if it is ever moved!

CHAPTER 1
CHAPTER 2
CHAPTER 3
CHAPTER 4

CHAPTER 5
CHAPTER 6
CHAPTER 7
CHAPTER 8
CHAPTER 9
CHAPTER 10
CHAPTER 11
CHAPTER 12
CHAPTER 13
CHAPTER 14
APPENDICES
INDEX

■ MAKING GRADIENT SHADOWS WITH TEXTURE BAKING

Let's start with a simple example of baking a shadow into a prim. We are going to shadow a concrete pole.

Figure 4.19: Concrete texture with a shadow

Figure 4.20: This column has a dark side!

1. Grab the Concrete texture from Library ▸ Textures ▸ Concrete and copy it to your local *Second Life* inventory. Download a copy locally to your system, and load it in Photoshop.

2. Create a new layer on top of the concrete layer and move a guide to the exact halfway point along the Concrete texture.

3. Select the Reflected gradient tool and add a black-and-white gradient from the center of the image to the edge.

4. Change your new gradient into a *multiply layer* in the Layers window; doing so will cause the layer to act as a shadow cast upon the layer below it. You can now see how the concrete image moves from light to dark and then back to light again (Figure 4.19). If you want to fine-tune how the shadow looks, adjust the brightness and contrast on the multiply layer.

5. Upload the image as a 24-bit .tga file to *Second Life* and apply it to a cylinder. For added spice, place a shadow prim on the dark side of the column (Figure 4.20). The lower the light source, the longer the shadow should be.

This technique is good for any rounded objects that wrap around onto themselves, such as cylinders and spheres. You may use it on the fuselage of an aircraft to make the underbelly darker than the top, or on a chair cushion to accentuate soft curves.

TUTORIAL: BAKING A SPOTLIGHT ONTO A WALL

Now that you're an expert at textures and shadows, let's put it all together and see how these skills can turn a very simple scene into a stunning masterpiece. In this tutorial you'll create a very simple museum display and use texture baking to cast a spotlight on an art object. This will cause both light and shadow to be cast onto the wall and the floor.

■ SETTING UP THE SCENE

1. Rez a floor prim with dimensions of X = 5, Y = 10, Z = 0.5.

2. Shift-drag that prim along the x-axis and rotate it upright by 90 degrees. Position the prim so it makes an *L* shape with the other prim.

Figure 4.21: Two walls and a donut on a pedestal

3. Rez a box on the center of the floor (it will be our pedestal) with the dimensions X = 0.5, Y = 0.5, Z = 2.0.

4. On top of that box, rez a torus, reshape it so it looks a bit like a donut, and place it on its side. This will be our art object and the hole in the torus will make for a more-detailed shadow.

5. Finally, make the box and the donut black, make the wall white, and make the floor green. This is so we can get high contrast when we work with the image in Photoshop. You should end up with something like Figure 4.21.

6. Take a snapshot just like Figure 4.18. Avoid clipping the corners of the room; we want all of it in the scene. Load the snapshot in Photoshop.

Now we'll create our multiple shadow layers based on our snapshot.

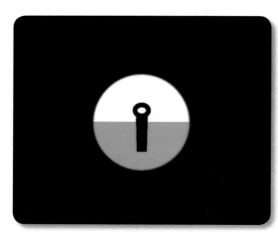

Figure 4.22: A very simple spotlight

7. Grab a copy of our art object. (This will be easy since the contrasting black will make it easy to select using Photoshop's Magic Wand tool. Select the black area, right-click on the selection, and choose Layer via Copy. You now have a layer consisting of the art object's silhouette.

8. Create a new layer and fill it with pure black. Set the opacity for that layer to about 50% so you can see the snapshot under the image.

9. Using the Elliptical Marquee tool, select a circle around the art object and delete that circle from the black layer. You should now have an image in that looks like a spotlight on the art object, as in Figure 4.22.

10. Set Opacity to 100%, Shift-select the black layer and the art object's shadow, and press Control+E to combine the two layers.

11. Use Filter ▸ Blur ▸ Gaussian Blur to add a little blur to your new shadow layer, but not too much! Remember that spotlights cast harsh light, and that usually means sharp shadows (Figure 4.23).

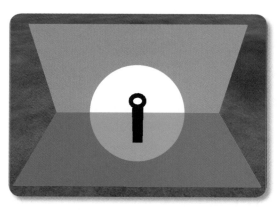

Figure 4.23: Our spotlight layer shows us how light will fall onto the floor and wall.

EXTRACTING THE SHADOW

We now want to cut out two different shadow textures from our scene—one for the floor and one for the wall.

1. Hide the shadow layer (by clicking the little eyeball) and use the Magic Wand tool to select the white wall. Notice the art object isn't included in the selection, and that's bad.

2. Using the Rectangular Marquee tool, hold the Shift key and select an area that spans from immediately over the art object all the way to the edge of the white wall section.

3. With the whole white wall selected, enable the shadow texture and select it. Now press Control+C to copy. Open a new image using File ▸ New (the correct image size will already be there!) and press Control+V to paste.

TEXTURE-BAKING THE WALL

We're almost there! Notice the shadow features perspective—that is, it's bigger at the top than on the bottom. This won't translate well when we apply it to a prim, so we need to adjust it using the Transform tool until it makes a perfect square.

1. Press Control+T to use the Transform tool. Right-click on the selection and choose Distort. Drag the bottom handles until the edge of the shadow perfectly matches the edge of the Photoshop canvas.

2. Create a new layer under the shadow. If you want white walls, you can simply fill it with white. If you have a nice plaster texture, you can use that instead.

3. Set the shadow layer to Multiply on the Layers window. You will want to adjust the brightness and contrast to your liking. Dark shadows usually imply that your spotlight is the only light source around. Light shadows imply that the shadowed area is being illuminated by soft ambient light from other sources. I decided to set brightness +100. (See the sidebar "Lighting from Multiple Sources for a discussion on that topic.)

MORE INFO

LIGHTING FROM MULTIPLE SOURCES

Photoshop's light-rendering feature (found under Filter ▸ Render ▸ Lighting Effects) is incredibly handy. I'm particularly fond of this feature because it provides a quick and easy way to simulate spotlights on a texture and does a beautiful job of mixing lighting effects. Try playing around with this to place a spotlight on a wall, or multicolored lights on the stage of a rock concert.

4. Now simply resize the image to, say, 256×128 pixels, save it as a 24-bit .tga file, upload it to *Second Life*, and apply the texture to the wall.

TEXTURE-BAKING THE FLOOR

1. For the floor we are going to do the exact same steps as for the wall, with one exception: we are going to cast this shadow onto a wood floor! Grab the WoodFloor texture from Library ▸ Textures ▸ Buildings ▸ WoodFloor and load up a copy in Photoshop.

2. Create a shadow multiply layer for the floor just as we did for the wall, only instead of using a white background layer, paste the WoodFloor texture. Repeat the WoodFloor texture horizontally three times so it won't look stretched out.

3. Add +100 to the shadow's brightness and +41 to the contrast to make for a realistic shadow.

4. Since the wood grain in the floor texture carries more detail than the wall does, I save this texture as 512×256 pixels.

5. Finally, set your art object to white and use the tinting tricks discussed earlier in this chapter so the back side of the art object matches the shadow it's casting. Figure 4.24 shows the final product.

Figure 4.24: This piece really speaks to me.

CHAPTER 5

WORKING WITH CLOTHING AND ACCESSORIES

One of the most precious and celebrated aspects of *Second Life* is the endless array of modifications and customizations for our avatars. People receive a deep satisfaction in projecting their personality and individuality to the rest of the world by how they appear. This fact has not escaped the booming fashion market in *Second Life*. *SL* users have an endless selection of pants, tops, skirts, dresses, hats, shoes, belts, bags, accessories, and even hair to choose from. And despite the cornucopia of options, users still demand more choices, more selection, and better-quality goods. In this chapter you will learn how to create clothing and accessories to make your avatar and the avatars of your customers look stunning.

CONTENTS

SLIDER CLOTHING VS. ATTACHMENTS

First let's discuss the two different methods used to create clothing: *slider clothing* and *attachments* (Figure 5.1). Slider clothing is a built-in function of the *Second Life* engine and can be accessed by editing your avatar's appearance. Using slider controls, you can create shirts, pants, shoes, socks, jackets, gloves, undershirts, underpants, and skirts. You can then apply images to those items; the images will become *composited*, or "*baked*" onto your avatar to create the illusion of texture.

Figure 5.1: Items like Aimee's hoodie and the stockings are slider clothing, while the tutu and the choker are attachment clothing

Attachments are geometry attached to your avatar. An attachment is made of primitives, just as you would make any other item discussed in previous chapters of this book. You can then attach the item to one of many attachment points on your avatar. The most common uses for attachments are for shoes, bags, hair, and belts. Some folks like to create avatars in the likenesses of their favorite animals (called "furries") and create "furry" attachments. I'm partial to blue butterfly wings myself, but your options are limitless.

GETTING STARTED WITH SLIDER CLOTHING

Let's look at our clothing-creation options. Right-click on your own avatar and select Appearance. Your avatar turns around and enters an edit pose, and you are presented with the Appearance edit window (Figure 5.2). From this window you can edit body parts and clothing. We will focus mostly on clothing.

The tabs on the left side of the Appearance window allow you to create or modify your shirt, pants, shoes, socks, jacket, gloves, undershirt, underpants, and skirt. Each item represents various layers that are baked on top of each other: Jackets are baked on top of your shirt and pants are baked on top of your undergarments. Socks are baked under your pants while gloves are baked under your shirt. Finally, skirts appear over pants but under jackets.

Let's create a shirt so we can see the different slider options.

1. If you are currently wearing a shirt, click the Take Off button, but make sure you are in a private location as you may attract crowds!

2. Press the Create New Shirt button. You will notice a wide selection of sliders that allow you to adjust the sleeve length, the shirt length and collar, the fit, the looseness, and wrinkles. Feel free to tinker with these options to see how they look on your body. Most of the other clothing offers similar features.

Figure 5.2: The Appearance window

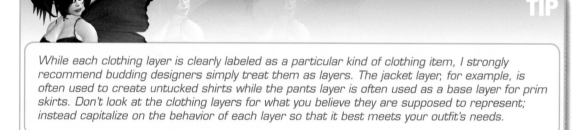

TIP

While each clothing layer is clearly labeled as a particular kind of clothing item, I strongly recommend budding designers simply treat them as layers. The jacket layer, for example, is often used to create untucked shirts while the pants layer is often used as a base layer for prim skirts. Don't look at the clothing layers for what you believe they are supposed to represent; instead capitalize on the behavior of each layer so that it best meets your outfit's needs.

GOING FROM 2D TO 3D

Each clothing layer includes a place to submit a fabric texture and a place to change the color or tint. These additional details are critical for creating realistic, attractive clothing items. The complex part is in taking a two-dimensional texture and wrapping it around a three-dimensional body avatar.

■ USING THE CLOTHING TEMPLATES

Templates are available for the upper body, lower body, and skirts for those wishing to create clothing and skins. (Templates for eyes, face, and hair are also available for makeup and body modifications.) The templates look like paper dolls (Figure 5.3), but remember that whatever appears on the

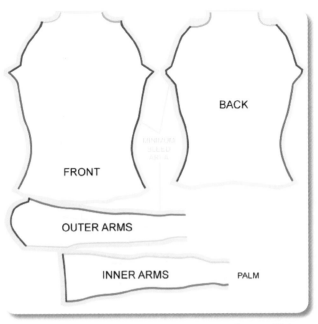

BACK

FRONT

OUTER ARMS

INNER ARMS   PALM

Figure 5.3: An example of a clothing template, which we will use in this chapter's tutorial

template must be stretched around a three-dimensional body form. You may recall in grade school how projecting a map of the earth from the 3D globe will cause distortion at the poles. While land around the equator appears normal in size, the Arctic Circle and Antarctica are stretched to unrealistically enormous proportions. Well, to a lesser extent this same effect happens to clothing textures.

NOTE

Most clothing items will cause a slight adjustment to your avatar, such as a jacket that add bulkiness to your torso or shoes that add a heel to your foot. Skirts, however, are the only clothing item that behaves like an entirely new body part. When your avatar wears a skirt in Second Life a skirt object appears almost like a flexible attachment. Unlike attachments, however, the skirt will move naturally with your body as it walks, runs, or sits.

The confusion comes when you look at the template as though you are looking at a person in a photo. Take for example a picture of an avatar wearing a T-shirt that says *AIMEE* in big letters on the front. When you look at that person, the letters *A* and *E* seem to go all the way across his chest right up to the area where the torso meets the arm. What you don't see is that the shirt continues to curve out of sight under his armpit.

TIP

Any texture can be used as a fabric, but for more compelling clothing you need to conform to the avatar mesh UV Map. This can be done using standard templates provided on the Linden Lab website (http://secondlife.com/community/templates.php).

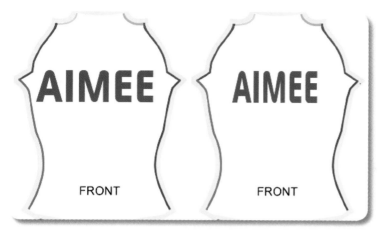

CHAPTER 1
CHAPTER 2
CHAPTER 3
CHAPTER 4
CHAPTER 5

CHAPTER 6
CHAPTER 7
CHAPTER 8
CHAPTER 9
CHAPTER 10
CHAPTER 11
CHAPTER 12
CHAPTER 13
CHAPTER 14
APPENDICES
INDEX

Figure 5.4: The writing on the left shirt looks normal in this view but the ends would disappear into the armpits of the wearer. The writing on the right shirt is narrowed and centered to appear normally when worn.

That unseen curvature is actually the area on the outside of the clothing template. This means if you try to write *AIMEE* all the way across the template, when the texture is applied to a body the *A* and the *E* will disappear into the man's underarm area. The solution? Simply be mindful of the fact that the outer portion of the template represents the sides of the body. In this case, make the word *AIMEE* narrow enough that it fits nicely in the center of the template (Figure 5.4).

The feet are another area that will give you untold trouble—the ankles in particular. There is one area around the ankles that stretches one or two pixels wider than the rest of the leg. This means that detail, such as shoe laces, may never look right around this area. Many designers simply make this area a solid color with no intended detail to avoid the blurring distortion. Others use prim attachments (discussed in the "Using Prim Attachments" section of this chapter) in lieu of texture detail.

■ WORKING WITH THE TEXTURE PREVIEW AND THOSE @#%& SEAMS

Next is one of the biggest challenges in *SL* clothing design: seams! Typing the word actually causes nightmarish flashbacks for me. As you can see, the clothing templates are divided into a front and back, which means every clothing item has a seam that runs along the sides of the avatar's legs, up their torsos, around the arms and fingers, up to the shoulders, and finally to the sides of the neck. Making the front of a shirt blue and the back of that shirt red would clearly show the clownish seam, but more insidious is if the texture and details on the front don't match the ones on the back in some small way. The difference will look unintentional and sloppy.

Let's say, for example, you wanted to place a blue stripe under the AIMEE logo that extends across the chest and all the way around the shirt. On the template you have to draw two different stripes, one for the front and one for the back. When you apply the texture to the shirt, chances are the front and the back won't line up properly and will make the shirt look sloppy. There is a variety of methods to help get seams lined up properly.

First try uploading the basic wireframe clothing template and wearing it as the clothing item. Aside from giving you a cool wireframe look, this method can give you a close look at the way individual guide lines fall across the avatar and line up front to back. You can then use these guides to estimate how you need to change details on your clothing item. I will often place the guide template on top of my clothing with 50 percent transparency so I can more easily estimate how things should be laid out.

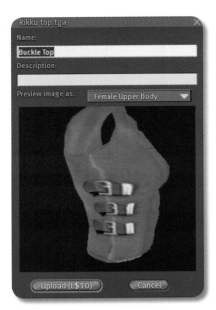

Figure 5.5: The preview feature is handy for viewing detail that resides along seams, like the buckles on this top.

Of course, uploading textures in a process of trial and error costs both time and money. Therefore, it's good to use the preview feature available when you upload any texture (Figure 5.5). You may have already noticed that right after selecting a texture to upload from your inventory you are presented with a preview of the image before you confirm the upload. What you may not have noticed is the pull-down menu that allows you to view that texture wrapped around a variety of surfaces, including the avatar face, torso, legs, and skirt. By zooming in on your seams you can tinker with the final product without spending a fortune on failed attempts.

Finally, it's sometimes worth the effort to adjust your design so that details do not fall across tricky seam lines. Of course, you should never compromise your creative vision to avoid complex work, but if a bow on the hip of a dress can be nudged over just a little bit to avoid the four seams where the top, bottom, front, and back meet, you could save yourself hours of work.

TEXTURING CLOTHING

While creating virtual clothing is quite different from making the real thing, there are some striking similarities. The clothing template itself looks a bit like the patterns used to indicate how to cut a swath of fabric in real life, and in fact you will use it to cut out your pattern images. In this section you'll learn how to make a clothing item using various techniques.

■ PHOTOSOURCING CLOTHING

In Chapter 4, "Let There Be Texture (and Light)!" we discussed the various sources where one could find textures, including hand-drawing, taking photographs, and sourcing images from the Web. All the same rules apply for clothing; however, there is an added level of complexity when you use photographs of clothing, especially if the clothing is being worn. Images of worn clothing have the advantage of providing a natural look and feel of fabric fitting the contour of a human body. This source also comes complete with shadows and highlights, making the texture more realistic (Figure 5.6).

The drawback, aside from the fact that you aren't actually creating a new item directly from your imagination, is the complex stretching and morphing a photo needs to properly fit the template. You now know that the sides of the templates represent the sides of the outfit. A photograph of a person wearing an outfit does not display the sides, which curve away from view. You have no choice but to fill in the blanks yourself.

1. **A good start is to cut out everything unrelated to the clothing item in Photoshop so you are left with nothing but the item. If you're creating a shirt, the sleeves will have to be separated into their own layer as well.**

2. **Center the front and back images onto the appropriate template and resize to fill the space appropriately.**

CHAPTER 1
CHAPTER 2
CHAPTER 3
CHAPTER 4
CHAPTER 5
CHAPTER 6
CHAPTER 7
CHAPTER 8
CHAPTER 9
CHAPTER 10
CHAPTER 11
CHAPTER 12
CHAPTER 13
CHAPTER 14
APPENDICES
INDEX

Figure 5.6: A sweatshirt sourced from a family photo

Remember that the edges of your item should not reach the sides of the template! That area is reserved for the side fabric, which doesn't appear in your photo. Visual cues such as a woman's bust or a neckline will sometimes be helpful in matching the image to the template properly.

3. **Next you will have to fill in the gaps on the sides and possibly the bottom of the outfit. Photoshop's Cloning Stamp tool allows you to copy fabric sections from one part of the item to your gaps. Just remember to copy from regions that have the same shading and few wrinkles or details; otherwise you will have little hope of matching the seams with the back side of the item.**

Some outfits may have enough unique details that the Cloning Stamp tool won't do the trick. In those cases you can stretch some section of fabric so that it covers your gaps. Photoshop's Liquify tool (Filter ▸ Liquify) allows you to drag and pull various-sized sections of an image, almost as if it were soft, stretchy cotton!

WARNING

Remember that Photoshop's Liquify tool will often cause small degradations in image quality, so use it sparingly and carefully, and if possible work with a large image (which will eventually be reduced to 512×512).

■ CREATING COMPOSITE-PATTERN CLOTHING

You're likely dreaming of creating truly unique outfits from scratch, and this section will help you get started on that process.

Just as designers do in the real-world fashion industry, you will likely want to start with a pattern. You may consider hand-drawing a lovely repeating floral pattern or scanning in a section of denim on a flatbed scanner. Whatever the source, you will want to start with a smooth, unwrinkled pattern with no shading or shadowing. Imagine your texture as a bolt of fabric ready to be cut into the shapes necessary to create your garment.

1. Place the texture under the template, which will be set to 50 percent transparency. This allows you to see both the template and the work you are doing on the fabric.

2. Using the Lasso tool, begin selecting the regions around the template that will make up your garment. Remember to use the template guide lines to ensure sleeve cuts and necklines match up front to back.

3. When you have your pattern selected, delete the area of the fabric that is not a part of your pattern.

The next step is to create well-defined seams. Remember that you want to create the feeling that the clothing is sitting on top of the avatar's skin. If the fabric ends abruptly, for example on a sleeve cuff, it may create the appearance that the skin was tattooed with your fabric!

4. I like is to use a multiply layer to draw a darkened line where the fabric ends. Use the Blur tool to blend the line into the fabric, but remember to erase any blur that spills off the sleeve; you don't want that part to appear on the avatar's skin.

Another method of making the item feel more finished is to include stitching along a seam. The kind of stitching depends on the kind of clothing. A denim jacket, for example, would look nice double-stitched with gold thread. I often keep a hand-drawn line of stitching in another window so that I can copy and paste onto my garment whenever needed.

5. Use the Liquify tool and the Transform options to make the stitch follow the contour of the seam. I recommend that you keep this stitching on its own layer so you can change the transparency level.

TIP

It may be tempting to use the slider controls to determine the length of sleeves, pant legs, collars, and other aspects of an item's cut. However, I strongly recommend that you set these kinds of sliders to their maximum value and then use your texture to shape the item. Slider cutoffs tend to create blurry and ill-defined lines that detract from the overall appeal of the item.

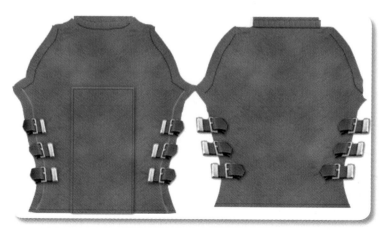

Figure 5.7: This vest started with a basic leather fabric. Photosourced buckles were added, along with hand-drawn seams.

We now have an item with an attractive pattern and a well-defined cut. It's time to add accessories. I like to collect images of clothing accessories, including buttons, ties, bows, hooks, buckles, and anything else I find online or on the streets (Figure 5.7). If you do this for a while your collection can really grow and provide you with a wide selection of options to spice up your outfits. You should also consider adding a drop shadow on your accessories using Photoshop's layer-blending options. Set the shadow to be illuminated from a 90-degree light source, and make the distance value very small and the shadow very light. This will give your accessories a hint of depth as though they were rising above your fabric.

You may consider adding pockets for extra detail. Returning to our real-world pattern analogy, we can make pockets by cutting the shape of the pocket from the same pattern used to create the original garment. You'd simply position the pocket cut-outs over the item as a separate layer and then outline it with stitching as we did for the cuffs and other seams. Like the buttons, adding a drop shadow from the layer-blending options will provide a feeling of depth. I would use zero distance and very light shading, as the effect should be very subtle.

One final step to transform a good clothing item into a fantastic one is to add highlights and shading. You will want to create a topmost multiply layer in Photoshop and begin painting black shadows on the underside of the arm, on the sides of the outfit, between the legs, under the buttocks, and under the calves. Then apply a Gaussian Blur (Filter ▸ Blur ▸ Gaussian Blur) until the shadow appears natural. By adjusting the layer's lightness and contrast you can change the intensity of the shadow.

MORE INFO

USING SKINS TO SHADOW CLOTHING

If you have difficulty drawing the shadows onto the outfit by hand, find a public-domain avatar skin that will fit the clothing templates perfectly.

1. Desaturate the skin by going to Images ▸ Adjustments ▸ Desaturate.

2. Use Image ▸ Adjustments ▸ Brightness/Contrast to set the contrast of the skin very high. This will cause the highlights to stand out and the shadows to deepen.

3. The result will look a bit pixelated, so add a little Gaussian Blur to create a smooth look.

4. Simply copy this image into a multiply layer on top of your outfit and adjust the brightness until it looks natural. Be sure to delete the parts of this multiply layer that do not appear over your clothing, or your avatar could appear unnaturally shadowed and cuffs will look blurred.

USING PRIM ATTACHMENTS

As you become more comfortable with slider clothing, you will come to know its limitations: Skirts expose an annoying gap around the waist between the avatar and the skirt. Clothing with defined bulk, such as protruding pockets, large cuffs on pants or shirts, or oversized belts are not possible using slider clothing. Slider shoes tend to look ill-formed and slider hats, handbags, and backpacks are nonexistent. The answer is to create these fashion details out of prims and attach them to your avatar.

CHAPTER 1
CHAPTER 2
CHAPTER 3
CHAPTER 4
CHAPTER 5

CHAPTER 6
CHAPTER 7
CHAPTER 8
CHAPTER 9
CHAPTER 10
CHAPTER 11
CHAPTER 12
CHAPTER 13
CHAPTER 14
APPENDICES
INDEX

Avatars have numerous *attachment points* where you can attach objects simply by right-clicking on them in your inventory or on the ground and selecting Attach To. These attachments are perfect for adding extra details to your outfits. You are permitted only one object per attachment point, however, which can cause problems when you're attempting to work with other outfits (my wings, for example, are often displaced by outfits that use the Spine attachment point!) Once an object has been attached to a particular area, you can simply right-click and select Wear; the object will attach to the last known attachment point. This is very helpful as it allows you to set up your accessories for your customers to attach without a complex fitting and adjustment process.

Creating fashion attachments uses the exact same process described in earlier chapters. You should, however, take position and texturing into consideration to ensure the item meshes properly with your outfit. Prim skirts, for example, often come in the form of multiple flexible prims attached in a circle around the waist. Under the skirt is normally a pants layer that features the same exact texture used on the flexible prims. This fills in any gaps that may appear between prims as you walk, and it utilizes the shape of the avatar buttocks, which would be difficult to simulate with the prim skirt. Using the same texture allows the attachment and the slider clothing to blend together to create a single great look.

TIP

Don't hesitate to add shadows to the slider clothing under locations that will feature prim accessories. Using the same shadow techniques described in Chapter 4, draw a subtle shadow onto the leg layers that will appear under a prim skirt, on the lower back under a backpack, or around the chest under a prim scarf. Just remember to include a nonshadowed version in case your customer decides to remove the prim accessory.

TUTORIAL: CREATING A HOODIE

It's time to take the threads of what we have learned in this chapter and knit them into a single learning experience. We are going to make a unisex hoodie.

Figure 5.8: Green fabric found in the Library section of your Inventory.

1. **In Photoshop, open the Upper Body template available at** `http://secondlife.com/community/templates.php`.

   Now you need to select a fabric. As we discussed under "Texturing Clothing," you have a few choices. You can find a photo online, you can take a photo with a digital camera, or you can draw something by hand. For simplicity's sake, let's use a texture from the *Second Life* texture library (Figure 5.8).

2. Go to Library ▸ Textures ▸ Fabric ▸ Fabric-Green. Right-click the item and select Copy.

3. In your own Inventory locate the texture folder, right-click, and select Paste.

4. Double-click on Fabric-Green in your own Inventory and then go to File ▸ Save Texture As and save a copy of the texture someplace on your hard drive.

5. Load Fabric-Green into Photoshop.

At this point our patch of fabric is smaller than our template, and we would like to cover the template entirely. You can copy the patch of fabric by hand fairly easily, or you can do a pattern fill like this:

6. In Photoshop, select the green fabric and then go to Edit ▸ Define Pattern and click OK in the dialog box.

7. Select the Upper Body template and create a new layer beneath the pattern layer.

8. With the new layer selected, go to Edit ▸ Fill.

9. Select Pattern from the Use pull-down menu.

10. Select your green fabric from the Custom Pattern pull-down menu. It will likely be the last pattern in the list.

■ CUTTING OUT THE PATTERN

Now you now have a bolt of raw fabric ready to be cut into the shape of a sweater. There are numerous ways you can do this.

1. Select the Upper Body Template layer (which should be on top of the green fabric layer) and give it a transparency of 50%. You can now see the template on top of the fabric.

2. Select the fabric layer and, using Photoshop's Polygonal Lasso tool, select and delete sections that lie outside the template's bleed line (the light-blue line that surrounds all the patterns). You now have a cut-out pattern that looks very much like a shirt (Figure 5.9)!

Figure 5.9: Cut the fabric according to the pattern, much like making clothing in real life.

ADDING A ZIPPER

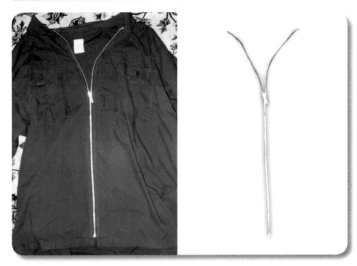

Figure 5.10: The zipper from this old jacket will look nice on our hoodie.

Let's add a zipper right down the front of the shirt. As with the fabric, you need to get ahold of a zipper texture. Drawing one by hand is very simple, but for this example I took a digital photo of an old jacket I had around the house (Figure 5.10).

1. **Load the photo of the jacket into Photoshop and using the Lasso tool, select and delete everything that is not part of the zipper. (Or simply use your own drawing of a zipper.)**

2. **Copy the zipper onto your hoodie as a separate layer.**

3. **Perform a Free Transform (Ctrl+T) on the zipper and resize it so that it fits nicely on the front of the hoodie, as in Figure 5.11. (The left side of the template is the front of the hoodie.)**

Figure 5.11: The zipper placed on the garment

4. Next we must make an open neck by cutting away the fabric located above the V-neck portion of the zipper (Figure 5.12).

Figure 5.12: The removed fabric from the neckline makes the hoodie look partially unzipped.

CREATING CUFFS

Let's add one more bit of detail: cuffs. Since I already demonstrated composite imaging with the zipper, let's draw the cuffs on by hand.

1. Create a new layer on top of the fabric.

2. Using the Paintbrush tool, draw black ridges at the cuffs.

When you are finished you'll want to ensure that your lines do not extend past the fabric onto the avatar's wrists! Here is a really quick and simple way to eliminate stray lines.

3. Select the fabric layer.

4. Using the Magic Wand tool, click in a region outside of the fabric area. This will select everything that is not part of your hoodie.

5. Switch back to your cuffs layer and hit Delete.

6. Make the cuffs layer a Multiply layer.

7. Go to Image ▸ Adjustments ▸ Brightness/ Contrast, and set Brightness to +100 and Contrast to +35. Feel free to adjust these values to make the cuffs more subtle or pronounced (Figure 5.13).

Figure 5.13: Hand drawn ridges create the appearance of elastic cuffs.

■ ADDING SHADOW

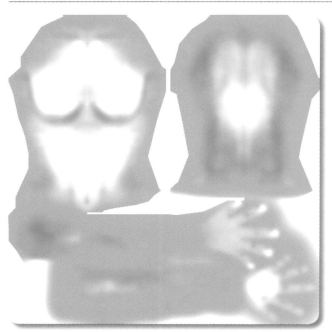

Figure 5.14: This high-contrast desaturated skin works great to add subtle shadows to clothing items.

We are now going to add shadowing to the item. Again, you can do this by drawing on a Multiply layer on top of all other layers and then adjusting the contrast and brightness. Remember to make the areas under the arms and around the lower back darker while making the chest and shoulders brighter.

In this section we are going to add shadows using the technique mentioned in the "Using Skins to Shadow Clothing" sidebar. Be sure you have a high-contrast desaturated skin texture ready, as described in the sidebar.

1. Copy your high-contrast desaturated skin image onto the topmost layer and set the layer to Multiply (Figures 5.14 and 5.15).

2. Adjust the brightness and contrast until the shadow is visually appealing. In this example I used a Brightness of +9 and a Contrast of +22, but it's mostly a matter of personal preference.

Figure 5.15: You can see the impact the multiply layer has on the garment.

CHAPTER 1
CHAPTER 2
CHAPTER 3
CHAPTER 4
CHAPTER 5

CHAPTER 6
CHAPTER 7
CHAPTER 8
CHAPTER 9
CHAPTER 10
CHAPTER 11
CHAPTER 12
CHAPTER 13
CHAPTER 14
APPENDICES
INDEX

We now need to trim the area around the garment to remove excess shadow (Figure 5.16). We can do this using the same trick we used to trim the cuffs.

3. **Select the fabric layer.**

4. **Using the Magic Wand tool, click in a region outside of the fabric area. This will select everything that is not part of your hoodie.**

5. **Switch back to your cuffs layer and hit Delete.**

Figure 5.16: The item is now nicely shadowed and neatly trimmed.

SAVING AND IMPORTING INTO *SECOND LIFE*

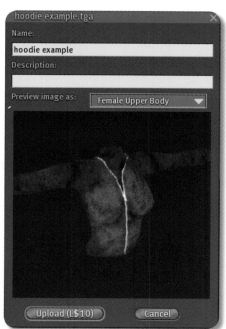

Figure 5.17: The preview allows you to inspect the item before you upload.

The area surrounding your hoodie is what is known as an *alpha*, or invisible, layer. If that area weren't invisible your hoodie would texture your avatar's hands and the open neck area when you wore it. To preserve this alpha layer it is important that we save the texture as a 32-bit TGA.

1. **Go to File ▸ Save As and select a location for your hoodie texture.**

2. **When Photoshop prompts you with the Targa options, be sure to select 32 bits/pixel.**

3. **In *Second Life* go to File ▸ Upload Image (L$10) and locate your hoodie texture.**

You will then be prompted with the image-preview window. The default mode for this window previews the flat image itself, but using the Preview Image As pull-down you can wrap your image around different parts of an avatar. This is very handy because it allows you to view the garment before spending the fee to upload the texture. So let's try it.

4. **In the Preview Image As pull-down menu, select Female Upper Body. (Since this is a unisex item, feel free to select the male version if you prefer.)**

5. Just as you would zoom in *Second Life*, zoom around the preview torso and examine the seams to ensure the texture meets with your satisfaction (Figure 5.17). If so, go ahead and upload. If not, then go back to the drawing board and fix the problem.

Once you've uploaded the texture, you need to create the clothing item itself.

6. **Click on your avatar and select Appearance. Select the Shirt tab on the left side of the Appearance window.**

7. **If you are wearing a shirt already, remove it by pushing the Take Off button. When that layer is clear, press the Create New Shirt button. You are now wearing a spiffy white shirt.**

8. **Set the Sleeve Length, Collar Front, and Collar Back to their highest settings.**

9. **Click the Fabric section and select your hoodie texture from your Inventory.**

10. **Save.**

■ PUTTING THE *HOOD* IN HOODIE

We now have a decent-looking top, but it's not a hoodie without a hood. Unfortunately, you cannot add complex shapes such as hoods and accessories to texture clothing, so we are going to make our hood out of prims!

1. **Rez a sphere.**

2. **Set the sphere hollow to 95.0.**

3. **Set the dimple to E = 0.70.**

4. **Set the Path Cut E = 0.50.**

5. **On the Texture tab, set the texture for the item to Fabric-Green (which you copied into your Inventory at the start of this tutorial).**

6. **Resize until X = 0.30, Y = 0.190, and Z = 0.255 meters.**

7. **Right-click on the prim and select More ▸ Attach ▸ Torso ▸ Spine.**

At this point the prim hood will be sticking out uncomfortably from your back at some awkward angle. It's very simple to fix that.

8. **Right-click on the attached hood and select Edit.**

9. **Holding the Shift key, rotate the hood until the dimple is facing up and the cut is facing your avatar's back. Adjust the position until the hood meshes nicely with your avatar's body.**

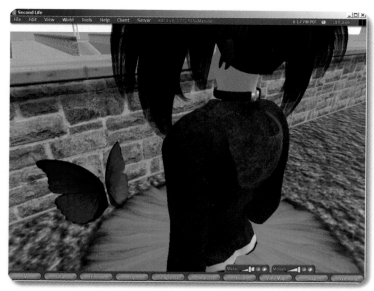

Now that you have the hood situated, you will not have to reposition it again, nor will your customers. Simply selecting Wear will forever position the hood in the correct place and at the correct orientation (Figure 5.18).

Figure 5.18: A prim hoodie adds the final finishing touch.

CHAPTER 6

GETTING YOUR FEET WET WITH SCRIPTING

An object in *Second Life* can be elaborately created, beautifully designed, and perfectly textured, but without scripting it's going to just sit there, not doing anything, forever. Scripting allows objects to move and to communicate with avatars, other objects and the Internet, and can give objects a rich and complicated set of behaviors.

Scripts in *Second Life* are written in LSL, the Linden Scripting Language, a powerful and full-featured programming language. LSL is similar to the C programming language, but it uses an event-driven state-based model (don't panic—it's not as scary as it sounds).

The syntax and semantics of LSL have remained basically unchanged since the beginnings of *Second Life*, but as new features have been added to the *Second Life* world, LSL has been updated to support them.

In this chapter you'll learn how to create LSL scripts and the parts that make up a script, and then see how to construct an interactive script from beginning to end. If you have any experience with another programming language, or even basic HTML authoring, you'll have no problems with LSL. And even if you have no experience, remember that many of *Second Life*'s best scripters had no scripting knowledge before they learned LSL.

CONTENTS

CHAPTER 6

BASIC
SCRIPTING
CONCEPTS

CONSTANTS

VARIABLES

DATA TYPES

FLOW-
CONTROL
STATEMENTS

STATES

FUNCTIONS

EVENTS
AND EVENT
HANDLERS

TUTORIAL:
THE AMAZING
FORTUNE-
TELLING
MAGIC
ANSWER BALL

BASIC SCRIPTING CONCEPTS

Let's jump right in and look at the basic default script that is created when the New Script button in the Content tab of the Object Editor dialog is clicked. This script says "Hello, Avatar!" when it's created, and "Touched." whenever it's touched. Listing 6.1 shows the basic script.

Listing 6.1: The Basic Script

```
default
{
    state_entry()
    {
        llSay(0, "Hello, Avatar!");
    }

    touch_start(integer total_number)
    {
        llSay(0, "Touched.");
    }
}
```

This script consists of one *state*, named `default`. The default state contains two *events*, `state_entry` and `touch_start`. Both events call a built-in *function*, `llSay`. The `llSay` function takes two arguments: the number of a chat channel to speak on and some text to say.

> **NOTE**
>
> *All scripts consist of at least one state; states consist of at least one event. Events consist of a series of statements. Scripts may also contain* functions, *chunks of script that events and other functions can use over and over again.*

Notice that all the parts of a script have the same structure: a name followed by a left curly brace, the content of the part and then a right curly brace. Also notice that all the statements in the script that are not part names end in a semicolon. Semicolons are used to indicate where a statement ends.

LSL ignores new lines and extra white space (spaces and tabs); the default script functions exactly the same way if it's written with all the extra spaces and new lines removed:

```
default{state_entry(){llSay(0,"Hello, Avatar!");}touch_start(integer
total_number){llSay(0,"Touched.");}}
```

Obviously this is much harder to read. White space and formatting are used to make scripts easier to read and more comprehensible.

WHAT HAPPENS WHEN A SCRIPT RUNS?

When a script is running, it's either sitting around waiting for something to happen, or it's responding to something that has happened. In LSL the term for "something happening" is *event*, and the chunk of LSL that deals with an event is called an *event handler*. (We'll explore event handlers in more detail later in the chapter.) A state is a set of event handlers that define how a script will behave in response to events.

All scripts must have a state named `default` because this is the state *SL* puts the script in when it is first compiled and whenever it is reset. *SL* tells the script that it has started running by calling the default state's `state_entry` event. In the basic script, the `state_entry` event contains one statement, a call to a built-in function: `llSay`. A *function* is a chunk of code defined somewhere else that can be called over and over again, with different arguments. Later in this chapter you'll learn how to define and use your own functions. Once the script has done everything in the `state_entry` event handler, it goes back to waiting for something to happen. The only other event that the basic script cares about is a user clicking on the object that contains the script. When this happens, the `touch_start` event handler is called. The `touch_start` event also calls the `llSay` function. Once that's done the script goes back to waiting. This is the key concept for LSL scripts: the waiting, event-handler, waiting cycle.

NOTE

Since a script can be doing only one thing at a time, it's important to write your event handlers so that they perform their function and then finish. If the script gets stuck inside one event handler, it won't be able to deal with other events when they occur.

EDITING, SAVING, AND DEBUGGING

Create an object, open the Build dialog for your object, select the Content tab, and click the New Script button. A script named New Script appears in the object's inventory and the object says `Hello, Avatar!`. Double-clicking on the script in the object's inventory brings up the script editor (Figure 6.1).

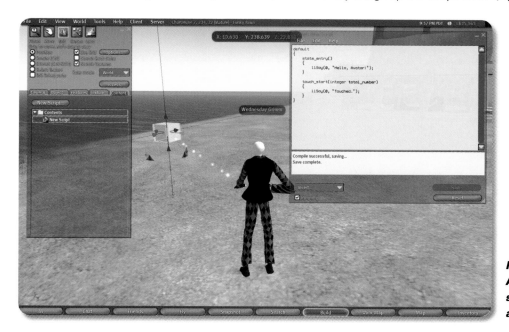

**Figure 6.1:
Adding a
script to
an object**

Let's improve this script slightly. Change the line in the state_entry event from llSay(0, "Hello, Avatar!"); to llSay(0, "Hello, "Mighty" Scripter!");. Then click the Save button. The *Second Life* client saves your script to the server and then tries to *compile* it. Compilation converts your LSL script to a form that the server can run.

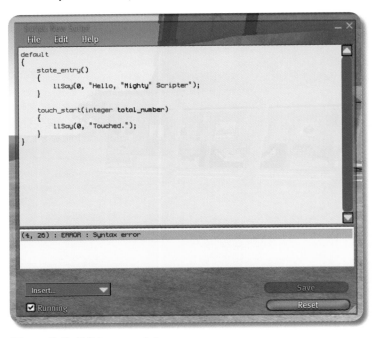

Figure 6.2: Editing a script

It seems there was a problem compiling our script. In Figure 6.2 the script editor is telling us that it has found a problem on line 4, character 26. We can't use double quotes inside a string, because double quotes are used to indicate the beginning and ending of a string. It's a sad fact of life for a scripter: most of the time your scripts won't compile on the first try. You will find your errors faster if write your script in small incremental parts, each adding a little bit of functionality.

The error in this script can be fixed by using the special backslash character to tell LSL that these double quotes are part of the string. Change the line to llSay(0, "Hello, \"Mighty\" Scripter!"); and click the Save button again. Now the script should compile and your object will greet you in a more appropriate manner. Listing 6.2 shows the modified script.

Listing 6.2: The Basic Script, Modified

```
default
{
    state_entry()
    {
        llSay(0, "Hello, \"Mighty\" Scripter!");
    }

    touch_start(integer total_number)
    {
        llSay(0, "Touched.");
    }
}
```

■ COMMENTS

Comments are annotations in a script to help a reader understand the script. Comments have absolutely no effect on how the script behaves, but they can be critically important in helping others (and even yourself) understand your script. Comments can be used to identify a script's author and creation date, and can provide notes for the script's usage, behavior, and options. Comments can also be used to annotate variables (describing for the user how the variable will be used), to describe events and functions, and to explain a tricky piece of scripting.

CHAPTER 1
CHAPTER 2
CHAPTER 3
CHAPTER 4
CHAPTER 5
CHAPTER 6
CHAPTER 7
CHAPTER 8
CHAPTER 9
CHAPTER 10
CHAPTER 11
CHAPTER 12
CHAPTER 13
CHAPTER 14
APPENDICES
INDEX

TIP

It's easy for a script to have too few comments, but it's hard for one to have too many.

Comments in LSL start with two slashes (//). The script ignores the two slashes and everything following them until the end of the line. A comment can take up a whole line by itself, or follow a line of script. Both approaches are shown in the following code snippet:

Listing 6.3: The Basic Script with Comments

```
// A basic script
//
// This is the basic script, with some modifications and comments.
// The script says something on the public chat channel when it is
// compiled or reset, and something else whenever it's touched.

default
{
    state_entry() // called whenever the script is called or reset
    {
        // script orginally said "Hello, Avatar!"
        llSay(0, "Hello, \"Mighty\" Scripter!");
    }

    // called when an avatar touches this object
    touch_start(integer total_number)
    {
        llSay(0, "Touched.");
    }
}
```

CONSTANTS

LSL provides a number of pre-defined *constants* for scripts. These are convenient names that can be used in place of a value in a script. As the name implies, a script cannot change the value of a constant.

Some constants are mathematical—for example PI, TWO_PI, and PI_BY_TWO can be used in trigonometric calculations and other instances where pi is used. DEG_TO_RAD and RAD_TO_DEG are values by which you multiply an angle in degrees to convert it to radians and vice versa. Mathematical

CHAPTER 6

Basic
Scripting
Concepts

Constants

Variables

Data

Flow-
Control
Statements

States

Functions

Events
and Event
Handlers

Tutorial:
The Amazing
Fortune-
Telling
Magic
Answer Ball

constants are useful when working with rotations, particles, and sensors. The following commented code shows mathematical scripts in use.

```
float radius = 5.0; // a float is a floating-point (decimal) number
float area = PI * radius * radius; // PI r squared
```

Other constants represent special values for built-in functions; for example, the function used to count the items in an object's inventory, llGetInventoryNumber, if passed the value 7 will return the number of notecards in the object's inventory. If it's passed the value 1 it will return the number of sounds in the object's inventory. Of course, remembering which value is associated with which type of inventory item is inconvenient, and using these values in the script makes the script more difficult to read. Therefore, the constants INVENTORY_TEXTURE and INVENTORY_SOUND (and constants for all other inventory types) are provided. All the constants available in LSL can be inserted via the Insert drop-down in the LSL editor. As this code sample demonstrates, a constant used in place of a literal value makes the code easier to read and understand:

```
integer nNotecards = llGetInventoryNumber(INVENTORY_NOTECARD);
```

Constants can also be used for checking the value a function returns. For example, the built-in function llGetInventoryType takes the name of an inventory item and returns its type, using the same values that llGetInventoryNumber does. For example, calling llGetInventoryType(0), to get the type of the first item in the object's inventory may return INVENTORY_OBJECT if the item is an object or INVENTORY_CLOTHING if the item is a piece of avatar clothing.

Yet more constants exist simply for convenience, to make the script easier to read. For example, TRUE with a value of 1 and FALSE with a value of 0 (See "Working with True and False: Boolean Operators").

VARIABLES

A *variable* is used in a script to hold a piece of data. As the name implies, a variable's value can change as the script runs. A variable has a specific type that defines what kind of data it can hold, but it can be used anywhere a literal value of the same type could be. There are seven data types in LSL: integers, strings, floats, keys, vectors, rotations, and lists (each of which is detailed in the following sections).

A variable is declared by giving the type and name of the variable, and then (optionally) assigning an initial value to the variable using the equals (=) sign. Variable names may consist of letters, numbers, and underscores but must not start with a number. The following line declares a *string* (a piece of text) variable named my_string and assigns it the value abc.

```
string my_string = "abc";
```

Where a variable can be used depends on where it is declared in the script. The part of a script where a variable can be used is known as the variable's *scope*. Variables declared outside of any state are called *global variables* and can be used anywhere. Variables declared inside of an event handler or a function can be used only inside that event handler or function. A variable can be used in the script only after it has been declared.

TIP

It's good scripting practice to declare variables so that they have the smallest possible scope. If a variable is used only in one event handler, for instance, it should be declared inside that event handler, not defined globally.

Listing 6.4 shows the basic script with variables in place.

Listing 6.4: The Basic Script with Variables

```
// A basic script
//
// This is the basic script, with some modifications and comments.
// The script says something on the public chat channel when it is
// compiled or reset, and something else whenever it's touched.

integer chat_channel = 0;  // the channel script will speak on

default
{
    // called whenever the script is called or reset
    state_entry()
    {
        string my_text = "Hello, \"Mighty\" Scripter";
        llSay(chat_channel, my_text);
    }

    // called when an avatar touches this object
    touch_start(integer total_number)
    {
        string my_text = "Touched.";
        llSay(chat_channel, my_text);
    }
}
```

Here a global variable named `chat_channel` is used to hold the chat channel number the script uses. This variable is global because it is used in both the `state_entry` and the `touch_start` event handlers. Each event handler now has a local string variable that holds the text that event will use. Note that both events can have a variable with the same name. Because the variables are in different scopes, there is no confusion about which one to use. This script behaves identically to the previous example, which did not use variables.

CHAPTER 6

BASIC
SCRIPTING
CONCEPTS

CONSTANTS

VARIABLES

DATA TYPES

FLOW-
CONTROL
STATEMENTS

STATES

FUNCTIONS

EVENTS
AND EVENT
HANDLERS

TUTORIAL:
THE AMAZING
FORTUNE-
TELLING
MAGIC
ANSWER BALL

DATA TYPES

Every constant, variable, and literal value in an LSL script is of specific type. LSL needs to know the type of a piece of data so it knows how much space in memory it can take up, and to ensure that it is being used correctly.

■ INTEGER

An integer is used to hold a whole number between –2,147,483,648 and 2,147,483,647. An integer might be used to hold the cost of an item in L$ or to indicate a specific face of a prim, or it could be completely internal to the script, keeping a count that the user of the object never sees. Integers can be specified with or without commas, and may appear in hexadecimal notation (see the sidebar "Understanding Hexadecimal Notation").

MORE INFO

UNDERSTANDING HEXADECIMAL NOTATION

Hexadecimal notation is a way of representing the binary-code (base-2 numbers) that computers use in a way that's easier for humans (well, some humans!) to understand. Hexadecimal notation uses base-16, meaning there are 16 characters used in the notation—the digits 0 through 9 plus six letters: a, b, c, d, e, and f. To indicate that an integer is in hexadecimal notation, start it with 0x, for example 0x9 or 0xa22e34.

You can find the usual decimal value of a number in hexadecimal notation simply by having your script output the number, like this:

```
llSay(0,(string)0xff);
```

the result is

```
Object: 255
```

Hexadecimal notation can be useful when you want to define your own flags. If this is confusing to you, don't worry—you can get by quite well in LSL without ever using hexadecimal notation, but if you see numbers starting with 0x in a script, be aware that they're just integers written a different way.

The following are some examples of how integers may be used in code:

```
0

-5  // negative 5

23

200234

0xff // hexadecimal notation, same as 255
```

CHAPTER 1
CHAPTER 2
CHAPTER 3
CHAPTER 4
CHAPTER 5
CHAPTER 6

CHAPTER 7
CHAPTER 8
CHAPTER 9
CHAPTER 10
CHAPTER 11
CHAPTER 12
CHAPTER 13
CHAPTER 14
APPENDICES
INDEX

■ USING ARITHMETIC WITH INTEGERS

Integers allow all the usual arithmetic operations: addition with the plus sign (+), subtraction with the minus sign (–), multiplication with the asterisk (*), and division with the slash character (/). The following code shows examples of each of these operators in use:

```
integer result;


result = 2 + 2;
// result is 4


result = result - 3;
// result is 1


result = 2 * 6;
// result is 12


result = result / 3;
// result is 4


result = 11 / 3;
// result is 3
```

Note the result in the final line of the example. It states that 11 divided by 3 equals 3; integer arithmetic does not round the result. Because 11 divided by 3 is 3.67, you might expect the result to be rounded up to 4, but with integer arithmetic any fractional part is thrown out. You must use the percent sign (%)to get the remainder, as in the following example:

```
result = 11 % 3;
// result is 2
```

There are two more arithmetic operators: shift left, which uses double less-than symbols (<<) and shift right, which uses double greater-than symbols (>>). x << y is equivalent to multiplying x by 2 *y* number of times. x >> y is equivalent to dividing *x* by 2 *y* number of times. The remainder is thrown out, according to the usual rules of integer division.

```
result = 10 << 2;
// result is 40 (10 * 2) * 2


result = 256 >> 2;
// result is 64, (256 / 2) / 2


result = 5 >> 1;
// result is 2
```

WORKING WITH TRUE AND FALSE: BOOLEAN OPERATORS

An operation that produces a true or false value returns an integer, with 0 meaning false and anything else meaning true. LSL provides some operators for dealing with true and false values, otherwise known as *Boolean operators*.

TIP

The built-in LSL constant FALSE has a value of 0, and the constant TRUE has a value of 1, but in LSL anything that's not 0 is true. It's important to be aware of this when comparing Boolean values. For example, if you have a variable with the value named z *that has a value of 0, then the expression* z == FALSE *(is* z *equal to* FALSE*?) is true. But if you have a variable* x *with a value of 10, then while* x *would evaluate to true,* x == TRUE *would be false because* x *is 10 and* TRUE *has a value of 1. In practice, you should never have to compare a variable to the constants* TRUE *and* FALSE*; these constants are useful for passing as arguments to functions, though.*

Two ampersands (&&) signify the "and" operator, which returns `true` if both of its arguments are true, as shown here:

```
integer result;


result = TRUE && TRUE;
// result is true


result = FALSE && TRUE;
// result is false
```

CHAPTER 1
CHAPTER 2
CHAPTER 3
CHAPTER 4
CHAPTER 5
CHAPTER 6
CHAPTER 7
CHAPTER 8
CHAPTER 9
CHAPTER 10
CHAPTER 11
CHAPTER 12
CHAPTER 13
CHAPTER 14
APPENDICES
INDEX

```
result = FALSE && FALSE;

// result is false
```

Two bars (||) signify the "or" operator, which returns `true` if one or both of its arguments are true, as shown here:

```
result = TRUE || FALSE;

// result is true
```

```
result = FALSE || FALSE;

// result is false
```

There is one more Boolean operator: the exclamation point (!)or "not" operator. While all the other operators take two arguments, one on the left and one on the right, the "not" operator takes only one, on its right. It returns `true` if its argument is false, and `false` if its argument is true, as in the following examples:

```
result = !TRUE;

// result is false
```

```
result = !FALSE;

// result is true
```

Boolean values and operators are important when your script needs to make a decision—for example, the answer to the question "Is this number larger than this number?" is a Boolean value, `true` or `false`. For more information see the "Flow-Control Statements" section later in this chapter.

■ COMPARING INTEGERS

There are six operators for comparing one integer to another: equality (==), inequality (!=), less than (<), greater than (>), less than or equal to (<=), and greater than or equal to (>=). They work pretty much as you would expect:

```
result = 4 == 4; // result is true
result = 4 != 4; // result is false
result = 4 < 3;  // result is false
result = 4 > 3;  // rsult is true
result = 4 <= 4; // result is true
result = 4 >= 3; // result is true
```

■ WORKING WITH FLAGS

Some built-in functions take an argument, sometimes called a *flag*, that encodes multiple options to the function in one integer. For example, the function `llSensor` takes a type argument that specifies the types of things to look for. This argument can be one or more of the following constants: AGENT, ACTIVE, PASSIVE, or SCRIPTED. These *mask arguments* are created using the *bitwise operators* on integers. (See the sidebar "Understanding Bitwise Operators" for details.)

The bitwise "or" operator—a single bar (|)—is used to create a set of flags. The following line creates a mask containing the AGENT, SCRIPTED, and ACTIVE flags, but not the PASSIVE flag.

```
integer mask = AGENT | SCRIPTED | ACTIVE;
```

The bitwise "and" operator—a single ampersand (&)—is used to check a mask for a value. For example, using the mask from the previous example, you'd write this code:

```
integer result;

result = mask & AGENT;   // result is TRUE

result = mask & PASSIVE; // result is FALSE;
```

MORE INFO

UNDERSTANDING BITWISE OPERATORS

Bitwise operators work on the binary representation of integers. One way to look at an integer in LSL is as a list of 32 1s and 0s. The bitwise operators combine each binary digit of an integer with the corresponding binary digit in another number using the same logic as the Boolean operators. In addition to the bitwise **and** and **or** operators, LSL has the bitwise XOR operator—a single caret character (^). LSL also has the bitwise "not" operator—a tilde (~) that changes all the 1s in a number to 0s and vice versa.

Setting a flag in a mask is actually just setting one of the binary digits in an integer to 1. For example, if the value of the constant AGENT is 00000[...]0001 and the value of the constant PASSIVE is 00000[...]0100, then the value of AGENT | PASSIVE is 00000[...]0101.

The "not" operator can be used to invert a set of flags; for example, the value of ~(AGENT | PASSIVE) is 11111[...]1010, or all the flags that are not AGENT and PASSIVE.

■ USING INCREMENT AND DECREMENT OPERATORS

There are two operators that can be used only on variables (not on literal values): the increment operator (++) that increases the value of a variable by 1, and the decrement operator (--) that decreases the value of a variable by 1. Writing `x--;` is equivalent to writing `x = x - 1;` while `x++;` is the same as `x = x + 1;`.

STRING

CHAPTER 1
CHAPTER 2
CHAPTER 3
CHAPTER 4
CHAPTER 5
CHAPTER 6

CHAPTER 7
CHAPTER 8
CHAPTER 9
CHAPTER 10
CHAPTER 11
CHAPTER 12
CHAPTER 13
CHAPTER 14
APPENDICES
INDEX

A string holds text data, letters, numbers, or punctuation, enclosed in double quotes. A string could hold text that a script wants to say to a user, or instructions, or data to be passed to another object. A double quote character can be used in a string by prefixing it with a backslash character. A new line can be placed in a string either by using the special sequence \n or by putting the new line directly in the string. The following code shows some examples:

```
"Hello, Avatar!"

""

"abc 123"

"line one \n line two"


"The sky above the port was the color of television, tuned to a dead
channel.

\"It's not like I'm using,\" Case heard someone say as he

shouldered his way through the crowd around the door of the

Chat."
```

■ OPERATIONS ON STRINGS

The only operations defined for strings are addition, equality, and inequality. Strings can be added together to join them:

```
string s1 = "abc";

string s2 = "123";

string s3 = s1 + s2;

// s3 is now "abc123";
```

Note that adding s1 to s2 does not change s1 or s2; adding s1 to s2 produces a new string that we store in s3. We can change a string by adding another string to it and storing that result in the same string:

```
s3 = s3 + " that's how easy love can be!";

// s3 is now "abc123 that's how easy love can be!"
```

The new value created by adding s3 to another string completely overwrites the old value in s3.

Strings can also be checked for equality by using the equality operator, (==) or for inequality using the inequality operator (!=). The result of comparing two strings is true or false, as described earlier. The following examples show the various string comparisons:

CHAPTER 6

BASIC
SCRIPTING
CONCEPTS

CONSTANTS

VARIABLES

DATA TYPES

FLOW-
CONTROL
STATEMENTS

STATES

FUNCTIONS

EVENTS
AND EVENT
HANDLERS

TUTORIAL:
THE AMAZING
FORTUNE-
TELLING
MAGIC
ANSWER BALL

```
integer t;  // an "integer" is a number, see below
string s1 = "abc";
string s2 = "abc";
string s3 = "123";


t = s1 == s2;
// t is true


t = s1 != s2
// t is false


t = s1 == s3;
// t is false


t = s1 == "abc";
// t is true


t = s1 == "ABC";
// t is false (upper and lower case matter)
```

■ FLOAT

A float can hold a floating-point number (a number with a fractional part); for example, 1.0, 0.5, –27.985, 3.141968, and 2.71828 can be stored in a float. A float may hold an angle of rotation or an absolute distance or a speed. The range for floats is between approximately -3.4×10^{38} to 3.4×10^{38}, which is to say, –34 or 34 followed by 37 zeros.

While integers are exact whole numbers, floats are approximate. They are more accurate with numbers that are close to zero, and less accurate with numbers in the millions or billions. This is fairly intuitive; a difference of, say, 0.0005 is important when dealing with very small numbers like 0.0004 and 0.0006 but less important when dealing with numbers like 7,000,000,000,000.

Floats can use the usual decimal notation or scientific notation, as shown here:

```
float temperature = 37.5;
float avogadro = 6.0221415E23;
```

Floats support all the same arithmetic and comparison operators as integers, but neither the modulus operator nor the shift and bitwise operators.

■ KEY

All the items in *Second Life*, including primitives, textures, notecards and even avatars are assigned a unique key when created, also known as a *UUID* (*universal unique identifier*). Scripts can use these keys to identify items, get information about them, and affect them. The special constant NULL_KEY can be used to represent no key, which is to say there will never be an object with a key that is the same as NULL_KEY. It is not possible for a script to change an item's key. A script can contain a literal key, but it is far more common to get the value of a key from a function, as shown here:

```
key nokey = NULL_KEY;

key owner = llGetOwner(); // owner of the object this script is in

key k = "3e1dea17-502c-c9fe-37b6-de7519d618cf";
```

There are no operations defined on keys.

■ VECTOR

A vector consists of three floats, named x, y, and z respectively, separated by commas and enclosed in angle brackets (<>). The x, y, and z components of a vector can be accessed and changed by placing .x, .y, or .z after the variable name.

A vector can represent the position of an object in the sim, giving its x-, y-, and z-axis coordinates each between 0 and 256 meters. A vector can also represent a direction, a velocity, or a color.

When vectors are used to represent colors, x, y, and z represent the red, green, and blue components of the color, respectively. The vector <0.0, 0.0, 0.0> represents the color black; <1.0, 1.0, 1.0> is white.

The special constant ZERO_VECTOR can be used for <0.0, 0.0, 0.0>. The following code shows some examples of vector declarations.

```
vector p = llGetPos(); // Get the object's position in the sim

vector up = <0.0, 0.0, 1.0>;


vector red = <1.0, 0.0, 0.0>;

vector purple = <1.0, 0.0, 1.0>;

vector pt292 = <0.44, 0.61, 0.84>;


vector v = ZERO_VECTOR; // v is <0.0, 0.0, 0.0>

v.x = 73.5; // v is now <73.5, 0.0, 0.0>

v.y = v.x + 0.5; // v is now <73.5, 74.0, 0.0>
```

■ OPERATIONS ON VECTORS

Vectors can be added or subtracted to produce a new vector, as shown here:

```
vector pos1 = <5.0, 2.0, 1.0>;

vector pos2 = <4.5, 3.0, 0.5>;

llOwnerSay ("pos1 to pos2: " + (string)(pos2 - pos1));
```

The operator for the vector dot-product is the asterisk (*); for the vector cross-product the operator is the percent sign (%).

NOTE

The dot-product and cross-product operations on vectors are concepts from geometry.

The dot-product of two vectors is a float: the length of the first vector times the length of the second vector times the cosine of the angle between the two vectors. This means that you can calculate the angle between two vectors a and b with **llAcos((a × b) ÷ (llVecMag(a) × llVecMag(b)))**.

The cross-product of two vectors is a vector that is perpendicular to both of the argument vectors.

A vector can be multiplied by a float to scale the vector:

```
vector direction = <0.707, 0.707, 0.0>;

float speed = 2.0;

vector newPos = speed * direction;
```

■ ROTATION

A rotation is declared similarly to a vector; it consists of four floats named x, y, z, and s, separated by commas and enclosed in angle brackets. All objects in *Second Life* have a natural zero-rotation when created; for example, when a cube is created it is aligned with the x-, y-, and z-axes of the sim. A rotation represents a change in the orientation (but not the position) of an object. This method of representing a rotation with four floating-point numbers is known as a *quaternion*. Quaternions are a mathematically efficient but difficult-to-visualize way of representing rotations. An easier-to-understand method is the *Euler* rotation (Figure 6.3), which uses a vector to store the object's rotation around the x-, y-, and z-axes respectively (this is the representation in the Edit window). Built-in functions can be used to convert between Euler rotations and quaternions.

The special constant ZERO_ROTATION with the value <0.0, 0.0, 0.0, 1.0> can be used to represent "no rotation," as shown here:

```
Rotation zero = ZERO_ROTATION;

Rotation r = llGetRot(); // Get the object's rotation
```

CHAPTER 1
CHAPTER 2
CHAPTER 3
CHAPTER 4
CHAPTER 5
CHAPTER 6
CHAPTER 7
CHAPTER 8
CHAPTER 9
CHAPTER 10
CHAPTER 11
CHAPTER 12
CHAPTER 13
CHAPTER 14
APPENDICES
INDEX

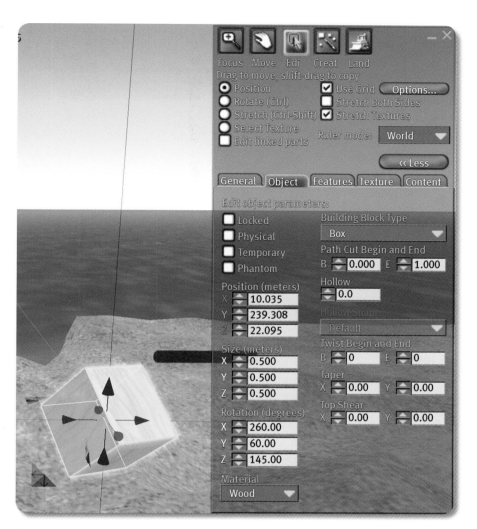

Figure 6.3: Euler rotations in the Edit window

LIST

A list is a special variable that holds an ordered set of values of any type (except another list). One list can hold different types of values. A list is declared by an opening square bracket ([ ), a list of values separated by commas, and then a closing square bracket ( ]).

```
[] // the empty list
[0, 5, 6, 9, -45, 10] // a list containing only integers
[<1.0, 0.0, 5.0>, "apple"] // a list containing a vector and a string
```

Note that if a variable is used to create a list, it is the value of the variable that goes in to the list; the list and the variable are not connected.

```
integer i = 5;

string s = "orange";

list l = [i, s];  // list is [5, "orange"]

s = "lemon";

i = 17;

// list is still [5, "orange"]
```

■ ACCESSING ITEMS INSIDE A LIST

Items in lists are accessed using the built-in functions `llList2Integer`, `llList2String`, `llList2Float`, and so on—one function for each data type. Items in lists are indexed starting at 0:

```
list clothes = ["shirt", "hat", "coat", "pants", "socks"];

string s;

s = llList2String(clothes, 0); // s is "shirt"

s = llList2String(clothes, 4); // s is "socks"

s = llList2String(clothes, 2); // s is "coat"
```

It is possible to grow a list by adding another list to it and assigning the result back to the original list:

```
list clothes = ["shirt", "hat", "coat", "pants", "socks"];

clothes =  clothes + ["shoes"];

// clothes is now ["shirt", "hat", "coat", "pants", "socks", "shoes"];
```

Lists are *immutable*, meaning once created the values in a list can't be changed. It is impossible, for example, to change the value "hat" in the previous example to "belt". The same effect can be achieved, however, by using the built-in function `llList2List` to build a new list out of slices of the old list. `llList2List` takes three arguments—the list, a start index, and an end index—and will return a list consisting of the items between start and end:

```
list clothes = ["shirt", "hat", "coat", "pants", "socks"];

clothes =
    llList2List(clothes, 0, 0) +
    ["belt"] +
    llList2List(clothes, 2, 4);

// clothes is now ["shirt", "belt", "coat", "pants", "socks"]
```

■ CASTING VARIABLES TO OTHER DATA TYPES

CHAPTER 1
CHAPTER 2
CHAPTER 3
CHAPTER 4
CHAPTER 5
CHAPTER 6

CHAPTER 7
CHAPTER 8
CHAPTER 9
CHAPTER 10
CHAPTER 11
CHAPTER 12
CHAPTER 13
CHAPTER 14
APPENDICES
INDEX

It is possible to covert some data types into other data types using a *cast*. Placing the desired data type in parentheses before the variable or value to be converted performs a cast. For example, any data type (except a list) can be cast to a string then passed to one of the chat functions:

```
llOwnerSay((string)<45.0, 10.0, 10.0>);  // vector cast to a string

float e = 2.71828183;

llOwnerSay("value of e: " + (string)e);  // float cast to a string
```

Conversely, a string can be cast to any data type (except a list). If the value of the string cannot be interpreted as a value of that type, the value is zero (or ZERO_VECTOR, or ZERO_ROTATION as appropriate):

```
rotation r = (rotation)"<0.70711, 0.00000, 0.00000, 0.70711>";

float f = (float)"qwerty";  // f is 0.0
```

Additionally, any data type (except a list) can be cast to a list. The result is a list containing one element, the original value:

```
list l = (list)"some string";  // l is ["some string"];
```

Finally LSL provides two *implicit casts*, meaning the value is automatically converted to a different type without the need for a data type in parentheses when the context requires it. LSL will implicitly cast an integer to a float and a string to a key. This means that anywhere a float is expected an integer can be used, and anywhere a key is expected a string can be used:

```
// get the square root.  2 is implicitly cast to 2.0
float root2 = llSqrt(2);

string k = "3e1dea17-502c-c9fe-37b6-de7519d618cf";
llOwnerSay(llKey2Name(k)); // string is cast to a key
```

FLOW-CONTROL STATEMENTS

If LSL scripts could execute only a series of lines of code in order, they could still accomplish a lot but they couldn't make decisions based on changing factors, and they would require a lot of typing from you, the scripter. Flow-control statements allow the script to jump around in the code, selectively executing some statements while skipping others, or repeating a set of statements a number of times. All the more-advanced flow-control constructs can be built out of the two basic ones, the if-else construct and the jump-label construct.

■ IF-ELSE

If-else statements allow a script to make decisions. They test some condition and execute different statements based on the result, as shown in Listing 6.5.

Listing 6.5: The If-Else Format

```
if (condition1)
{
    code-block1
}
else if (condition2)
{
    code-block2
}
else
{
    code-block3
}
other-statements
```

The conditions are integers or expressions that produce integers. The script will evaluate condition1. If it's true (not zero) then it will execute code-block1 then other-statements. If condition1 is false (zero) then the script will evaluate condition2. If condition2 is true, then it will execute code-block2. If neither condition1 nor condition2 is true, the script will execute code-block3, then other-statements. The else if and else parts are optional. Listing 6.6 provides an if-else example.

Listing 6.6: An If-Else Example

```
integer explicitTester(integer condition, string explanation)
{
    llOwnerSay(explanation);
    return condition;
}

default
{
    state_entry()
    {
        llOwnerSay("before if-else ");

        if (explicitTester(FALSE, "condition1"))
        {
            llOwnerSay("I'm in the if!");
        }
        else if (explicitTester(FALSE, "condition2"))
        {
            llOwnerSay("I'm in the else if!");
        }
        else
```

CHAPTER 1
CHAPTER 2
CHAPTER 3
CHAPTER 4
CHAPTER 5
CHAPTER 6

```
        {
            llOwnerSay("I'm in the else!");
        }
        llOwnerSay ("after the if-else");
    }
}
```

CHAPTER 7
CHAPTER 8
CHAPTER 9
CHAPTER 10
CHAPTER 11
CHAPTER 12
CHAPTER 13
CHAPTER 14
APPENDICES
INDEX

The first part of the script is a function named `explicitTester`. This function takes two arguments; the first is an integer named `condition` and the second is a string named `explanation`. When run, the script calls the built-in function `llOwnerSay`, which causes the script to say the contents string `explanation` to the object's owner. The function then returns `condition`, so the return result of this function will always be the same as `condition`.

When the script is compiled and run, the result is as follows:

```
Object: before if-else

Object: condition1

Object: condition2

Object: I'm in the else!

Object: after the if-else
```

When the script started, it ran the default state's `state_entry()` event. It performed the first `llOwnerSay`, then checked the `if` condition. Since this was false, it checked the `else` condition. Since this was false too, it ran the code in the `else` part, then ran the final `llOwnerSay` line.

If we change the if line to

```
if (explicitTester(TRUE, "condition1"))
```

then the result is

```
Object: before if-else

Object: condition1

Object: I'm in the if!

Object: after the if-else
```

The script checked the `if` condition, and because it was `TRUE`, it ran the code in the `if` part.

WARNING

Notice that `condition2` is never even checked. For this reason, it's important to be careful when using functions with side effects (changing things or performing actions) in `if` and `else` statements; conditions are not always evaluated.

■ JUMP

A jump (Listing 6.7) is a way of skipping over statements forward or backward. Jumps can go to a line only within the same event or function.

Listing 6.7: The Jump-Label Format

```
@label;
jump label;
```

When the script reaches the jump line, it skips forward or backward within the state or function to the specified label. The @label line has no effect in the script. Nothing happens when the statement is reached; it is simply a target for the jump line. Listing 6.8 shows a jump used to skip a line in a script.

Listing 6.8: A Jump Example

```
default
{
    state_entry()
    {
        llOwnerSay("I did this");

        jump jump_target;

        llOwnerSay("But not this");

        @jump_target;

        llOwnerSay("And this");

    }
}
```

When the script is run the result is as follows:

```
Object: I did this

Object: And this
```

The script performs the first llOwnerSay statement, then encounters the jump line, looks for the label jump_target, and starts running immediately after the label, skipping over any lines in between. Jumps tend to make scripts error-prone, difficult to read, and hard to change later. In most cases, a while loop, for loop, or function call can be used to achieve more-readable results.

■ WHILE LOOP

A while loop (Listing 6.9) is a way to execute the same series of statements over and over again as long as some condition is true.

Listing 6.9: The While Format

```
while (condition)

{

    statements

}
```

A while loop is shorthand for a combination of an `if`, a `jump`, and a `label`, as shown here:

```
@loop_top;
if (condition)
{
    statements
    jump loop_top;
}
```

Which is to say, the script will check the condition; if it's true, it will execute the statements then jump back up and check the condition again, over and over until the condition is false. Listing 6.10 demonstrates the use of a while loop:

Listing 6.10: A While Example

```
default
{
    state_entry()
    {
        integer x = 5;
        while (x > 0)
        {
            llOwnerSay("x is " + (string)x +
                " which is greater than 0");
            x = x - 1;
        }
        llOwnerSay("all done");
    }
}
```

Running this code results in the following:

```
Object: x is 5 which is greater than 0

Object: x is 4 which is greater than 0

Object: x is 3 which is greater than 0

Object: x is 2 which is greater than 0

Object: x is 1 which is greater than 0

Object: all done
```

CHAPTER 1
CHAPTER 2
CHAPTER 3
CHAPTER 4
CHAPTER 5
CHAPTER 6

CHAPTER 7
CHAPTER 8
CHAPTER 9
CHAPTER 10
CHAPTER 11
CHAPTER 12
CHAPTER 13
CHAPTER 14
APPENDICES
INDEX

This script declares an integer named x and sets its value to 5. The while loop checks to see if the value of x is greater than 0 and since it is, it executes the two statements inside the while loop, saying what the value of x is and then reducing it by 1. After the script has done this five times, the value of x is 0, which makes the condition false, and the script leaves the while loop. Note that the loop will run forever unless your condition checks something outside the script (for example, calling llGetPos() to check the position of the object containing the script) or the body of the loop changes the condition.

■ DO-WHILE

A do-while loop (Listing 6.11) is similar to a while loop except that a do-while loop will always execute its statements at least once.

Listing 6.11: The Do-While Format

```
do
{
    statements
} while (condition);

A do-while loop is shorthand for
@loop_top;
statements;
if (condition)
{
    jump loop_top;
}
```

Listing 6.12 shows a do-while loop in action:

Listing 6.12: A Do-While Example

```
default
{
    state_entry()
    {
        integer x = 6;
        do
        {
            llOwnerSay("x is " + (string)x);
        } while (x < 2);
        llOwnerSay("all done");
    }
}
```

The result is as follows:

```
Object: x is 6

Object: all done
```

The script declares a variable, x, and sets its value to 6. It then runs the statements inside the loop, checks the condition, and since it is false, exits the loop.

FOR

A for loop (Listing 6.13) is a way to perform an action a set number of times.

Listing 6.13: The For Format

```
for (initialization ; condition ; change)
{
    statements;
}
```

A for loop is also shorthand for a while loop with some extra statements:

```
initialization
while(condition)
{
    statements;
    change;
}
```

The for loop does the `initialization` statement once, then checks the `condition` and if it is true, performs the `statements` and then the `change`, then checks the `condition` again, looping until it is false. Listing 6.14 demonstrates a for loop that looks at every item in a list:

Listing 6.14: A For Example

```
default
{
    state_entry()
    {
        list items = ["orange", "apple", "banana"];
        string fruit;
        integer x;
        for (x = 0; x < llGetListLength(items); x = x + 1)
        {
            fruit = llList2String(items, x);
            llOwnerSay(fruit);
        }
        llOwnerSay("all done");
    }
}
```

The result of the code is as follows:

```
Object: orange

Object: apple

Object: banana

Object: all done
```

This script declares a list of three strings called items, a string called fruit, and an integer x. The for loop first does the initialization part, setting x to 0. It will then check the condition, to see if x is less than the length of the list. Since it is, the script performs the body of the loop, calling the built-in function llList2String to get an member from a list by its position in the list (in LSL, lists start counting at 0). This script is equivalent to the one in Listing 6.15.

Listing 6.15: A For Example, Unrolled

```
default
{
    state_entry()
    {
        list items = ["orange", "apple", "banana"];
        string fruit;
        fruit = llList2String(items, 0);
        llOwnerSay(fruit);
        fruit = llList2String(items, 1);
        llOwnerSay(fruit);
        fruit = llList2String(items, 2);
        llOwnerSay(fruit);
        llOwnerSay("all done");
    }
}
```

STATES

A state is a group of event handlers. All scripts have a state named default, and unsurprisingly, this is the default state for a script. When a script is first saved and whenever it is reset, it starts in the default state. A script can have additional states that can act as different modes of behavior, as Listing 6.16 demonstrates:

Listing 6.16: A State Example

CHAPTER 1
CHAPTER 2
CHAPTER 3
CHAPTER 4
CHAPTER 5
CHAPTER 6

CHAPTER 7
CHAPTER 8
CHAPTER 9
CHAPTER 10
CHAPTER 11
CHAPTER 12
CHAPTER 13
CHAPTER 14
APPENDICES
INDEX

```
vector color_default = <1.0, 1.0, 1.0>; // white
vector color_blue = <0.0, 0.0, 1.0>;

default
{
    state_entry()
    {
        llOwnerSay("state_entry() for default state");
        llSetColor(color_default, ALL_SIDES);
    }

    touch_start(integer total_number)
    {
        state blue;
    }

    state_exit()
    {
        llOwnerSay("state_exit() for default state");
        llSetTimerEvent(5.0);   // cause a timer() event every 5 seconds
    }
}

state blue
{
    state_entry()
    {
        llOwnerSay("state_entry() for blue state");
        llSetColor(color_blue, ALL_SIDES);
    }

    timer()
    {
        llSetTimerEvent(0.0); // turn off timer events
        state default;
    }

    state_exit()
    {
        llOwnerSay("state_exit() for blue state");
    }
}
```

The result of the code is as follows:

```
Object: state_entry() for default state
```

Then, when the object is touched, you get the following:

```
Object: state_exit() for default state
Object: state_entry() for blue state
```

Then, after five seconds, you get this:

```
Object: state_exit() for blue state

Object: state_entry() for default state
```

In this example, when the script starts the default state's `state_entry` event will be called. This event handler uses the built-in function `llSetColor` to change the color of all the sides of the scripts object to the default color. When the object is touched, the script changes to the state named `blue`. This causes the default state's `state_exit` event handler to run. This even handler uses the built-in function `llSetTimerEvent` to ask for a timer event in five seconds. Then the `blue` state's `state_entry` event is run. After five seconds the timer event the script asked for happens and the `blue` state's `timer` event is run, which sends the script back to the `default` state. This makes the `blue` state's `state_exit` event run, then the `default` state's `state_entry` event to run and the script is back where it started.

NOTE

Even though the timer is set in the **default** state, when the event happens the script is in the **blue** state, so it is the **blue** state's **timer** event handler that runs.

FUNCTIONS

A function (Listing 6.17) is a chunk of LSL that's given a name that can be used over and over again in different locations. A function can take a list of variables as arguments and can return a single value (which can be a list).

Listing 6.17: A Simple Function Example

```
sayOuch()
{
    llSay(0, "Ouch!");
}

default
{
    state_entry()
    {
        sayOuch();
    }

    touch_start(integer total_number)
    {
        sayOuch();
        sayOuch();
    }
}
```

The `sayOuch` function takes no arguments and returns no value; it just calls `llSay` to say `Ouch!` on the public chat channel. Notice that the function is defined outside of any state; the same function can be called from different states and from any event inside a state, as shown in Listing 6.18.

CHAPTER 1
CHAPTER 2
CHAPTER 3
CHAPTER 4
CHAPTER 5
CHAPTER 6

CHAPTER 7
CHAPTER 8
CHAPTER 9
CHAPTER 10
CHAPTER 11
CHAPTER 12
CHAPTER 13
CHAPTER 14
APPENDICES
INDEX

NOTE

The **sayOuch** *function is called the same way as the built-in LSL functions.*

Listing 6.18: A Function with an Argument

```
sayOuch()
{
    publicSay("Ouch!");
}

publicSay(string text)
{
    llSay(0, text);
}
```

The `publicSay` function takes one argument, a string, and then passes that to the `llSay` function. Notice that functions can call functions, and that the `sayOuch` function can call a function that's defined later in the script.

By using a `return` statement, a function can send a value back to the function or state that called it.

Listing 6.19: A Function with a Return Value

```
string getColor(string fruit)
{
    if (fruit == "apple")
    {
        return "red";
    }
    else if (fruit == "orange")
    {
        return "orange";
    }
    else if (fruit == "banana")
    {
        return "yellow";
    }
    else
    {
        return "don't know";
    }
}
```

The `return` statement immediately stops the function and returns the value to the caller. Functions that don't return a value can use a `return` statement with no value to bail out at any time, as in Listing 6.20.

Listing 6.20: A Function with Early Return

```
integer VOICE_ON = FALSE;

publicSay(string text)
{
    if (!VOICE_ON)
    {
        return;   // don't do anything
    }
    llSay(0, text);
}
```

EVENTS AND EVENT HANDLERS

Events are how an LSL script interacts with the world. Events can come from inside the script itself—for example a timer event or from the *SL* grid, for example, when a resident clicks on the object, or when the object hears chat messages or experiences physical collisions. Events can also come from the Internet in the form of emails or responses to XML-RPC requests the script has sent (see Chapter 8, "Scripting the Fun Stuff").

An event handler (Listing 6.21) has a specific predefined name relating to the event that causes the event handler to run. There are more than 30 event handlers in LSL, and a state can have any number of these 30. Event handlers can also have parameters, similar to a function's arguments, that can provide the script with the specific details of an event.

Listing 6.21: Using Event Handlers

```
default
{
    state_entry()
    {
        // ask for a timer event every 10 seconds
        llSetTimerEvent(10.0);
    }

    // this event has no parameters
    timer()
    {
        llOwnerSay("timer event raised");
    }

    // this event has one parameter, the number of avatars
    // clicking on this object
    touch(integer total_number)
    {
        llOwnerSay("There are " + (string)total_number + " people
touching me!");
    }
}
```

CHAPTER 1
CHAPTER 2
CHAPTER 3
CHAPTER 4
CHAPTER 5
CHAPTER 6

CHAPTER 7
CHAPTER 8
CHAPTER 9
CHAPTER 10
CHAPTER 11
CHAPTER 12
CHAPTER 13
CHAPTER 14
APPENDICES
INDEX

MORE INFO

PRODUCING READABLE CODE

Scripts should be written so that humans can read them. You will have to show your scripts to other scripters for collaboration, help, or just to show off, so it's in your best interests to make your code as easy to read and as easy to understand as possible. Furthermore, it's a safe bet that if you look at a script you wrote more than a month ago, you'll have no idea what you were thinking at the time; writing your scripts so others can understand them will help *you* understand them too. Here are some tips for achieving readable code:

- Pick an indentation style and use it consistently. Searching for "indentation style" on the Internet will give you pages and pages of long protracted discussions on the merits of one style over another, but it doesn't really matter what style you use as long as you stick to it.

- Write your code so that it reads well. Variable names should be nouns. If a function performs an action, its name should be a verb or verb phrase. If a function returns `true` or `false`, make its name a question.

- Never type the same thing twice. If you find yourself doing something twice, you'll probably have to do it additional times. Make a variable or function and use that instead. This way if you find a bug in your script, you have to fix it in only one place.

- Add comments—*lots* of comments. Don't describe what the code is doing; try to describe what it means. For example, don't say "add one to x." Say "done with this value; increment the index" instead. Comments will not only help you and others understand you code later, but forcing yourself to describe what the code is doing will help you write better, clearer code right now. For instance, as far as LSL is concerned, the following two blocks of code are exactly the same.

```
listen(integer a, string x, key k, string y)
{if (teststring(y){llSay(0, doIt() + x);}
}

listen(integer channel, string name, key id, string message)
{
// script heard something, if it's a question for this script,
    // answer it.
    if (isAQuestion(message))
    {
        llSay(0, generateAnswer() + name);
    }
}
```

It's up to you which you'd rather write and work with.

CHAPTER 6

- BASIC
  SCRIPTING
  CONCEPTS
- CONSTANTS
- VARIABLES
- DATA TYPES
- FLOW-
  CONTROL
  STATEMENTS
- STATES
- FUNCTIONS
- EVENTS
  AND EVENT
  HANDLERS
- TUTORIAL:
  THE AMAZING
  FORTUNE-
  TELLING
  MAGIC
  ANSWER BALL

TUTORIAL: THE AMAZING FORTUNE-TELLING MAGIC ANSWER BALL

Enough theory—let's make something. How about a ball that responds to yes or no questions spoken on the public chat channel?

PICKING A RANDOM ANSWER

Figure 6.4: Magic ball, version 1

The first version of our script (Listing 6.22 and Figure 6.4) contains the absolute bare minimum functionality: generating answers. It has a global list of answers and a function that picks a random entry from the list and returns it. It's a good idea to develop scripts incrementally, getting the most important bits first, then adding more slowly and testing every step of the way.

Listing 6.22: Magic Answer Ball, First Version

```
// Magic Answer Ball
// Version 1
//
// Provide a random answer when touched.


// The global variable holding all the answers
list answers = [
    // positive answers
    "Yes.",
    "It is certain.",
    "All signs point to yes.",
    "You may rely on it",
    "Without a doubt.",
```

CHAPTER 1
CHAPTER 2
CHAPTER 3
CHAPTER 4
CHAPTER 5
CHAPTER 6

CHAPTER 7
CHAPTER 8
CHAPTER 9
CHAPTER 10
CHAPTER 11
CHAPTER 12
CHAPTER 13
CHAPTER 14
APPENDICES
INDEX

```
        // negative answers
        "No.",
        "Absolutely not.",
        "Doubtful.",
        "Most assuredly not.",
        "My sources say no.",
        //non commital answers
        "Outlook hazy.",
        "Uncertain.",
        "The answer is unknowable.",
        "I'd better not tell you now.",
        "Cannot predict that at this time."
];

// pick a random answer from the list of answers and return it
string generateAnswer()
{
    // generate a random number between 0 and the length of the
        // list (but not exactly the length of the list), then cast it
        // to an integer. This will give us a random number betwen 0
        // and the length of the list - 1.
    integer answerIndex =
        (integer)llFrand(llGetListLength(answers));

    // return the answerIndex'th item of the list answers
    return llList2String(answers, answerIndex);
}

default
{
    touch_start(integer total_number)
    {
        llOwnerSay(generateAnswer());
    }
}
```

■ LISTENING TO RESIDENTS

The second version of the script (Listing 6.23 and Figure 6.5) listens for messages on the public channel and generates answers in response. In the state_entry event, the script calls the built-in function llListen and asks for a listen event to be raised whenever there is a message spoken on channel 0. In the listen event the script uses the name parameter to personalize its response.

Figure 6.5: Magic ball, version 2

CHAPTER 6

Basic
Scripting
Concepts

Constants

Variables

Data Types

Flow-
Control
Statements

States

Functions

Events
and Event
Handlers

Tutorial:
The Amazing
Fortune-
Telling
Magic
Answer Ball

Listing 6.23: Magic Answer Ball, Second Version

```
// Magic Answer Ball
// Version 2
//
// Provide a random personalized answer to anyone or anything speaks
// on the public channel

// The global variable holding all the answers
list answers = [
    // positive answers
    "Yes, ",
    "It is certain, ",
    "All signs point to yes, ",
    "You may rely on it, ",
    "Without a doubt, ",
    // negative answers
    "No, ",
    "Absolutely not, ",
    "Doubtful, ",
    "Most assuredly not, ",
    "My sources say no, ",
    //non commital answers
    "Outlook hazy, ",
    "Uncertain, ",
    "The answer is unknowable, ",
    "I'd better not tell you now, ",
    "Cannot predict that at this time, "
];

// pick a random answer from the list of answers and return it
string generateAnswer()
{
    // generate a random number between 0 and the length of the
        // list (but not exactly the length of the list), then cast it
        // to an integer. This will give us a random number betwen 0
        // and the length of the list - 1.
    integer answerIndex =
        (integer)llFrand(llGetListLength(answers));

    // return the answerIndex'th item of the list answers
    return llList2String(answers, answerIndex);
}

default
{
    state_entry()
    {
        // listen on the public chat channel for any text from
        // anyone or anything.
        llListen(0, "", NULL_KEY, "");
    }
```

```
        listen(integer channel, string name, key id, string message)
        {
            // script heard something, answer
            llSay(0, generateAnswer() + name);
        }
}
```

■ CLEANING UP AND POLISHING

Figure 6.6: Magic ball, version 3

CHAPTER 1
CHAPTER 2
CHAPTER 3
CHAPTER 4
CHAPTER 5
CHAPTER 6

CHAPTER 7
CHAPTER 8
CHAPTER 9
CHAPTER 10
CHAPTER 11
CHAPTER 12
CHAPTER 13
CHAPTER 14
APPENDICES
INDEX

The final version (Listing 6.24 and Figure 6.6) adds two new global variables, a question prefix, and some helpful instructions. This version also adds two new functions: isQuestion (which will return TRUE if it's argument is a question directed at the script) and startsWith (a utility function that takes two arguments and returns TRUE if the first argument starts with the second argument). In this code we add a new touch_start event handler that displays the help text when the object is touched.

Listing 6.24: Magic Answer Ball, Final Version

```
// Magic Answer Ball
// Version 3
//
// Provide a random personalized answer to anyone or anything speaks
// on the public channel

// Script will only answer qestions prefixed by this string
string questionPrefix = "Magic Ball, ";

// provide these instructions with touched
// script will add the questionPrefix string to this string
string instructions =
    "Ask me a yes or no question starting with ";
```

CHAPTER 6

BASIC
SCRIPTING
CONCEPTS

CONSTANTS

VARIABLES

DATA TYPES

FLOW-
CONTROL
STATEMENTS

STATES

FUNCTIONS

EVENTS
AND EVENT
HANDLERS

TUTORIAL:
THE AMAZING
FORTUNE-
TELLING
MAGIC
ANSWER BALL

```
// The global variable holding all the answers
list answers = [
    // positive answers
    "Yes, ",
    "It is certain, ",
    "All signs point to yes, ",
    "You may rely on it, ",
    "Without a doubt, ",
    // negative answers
    "No, ",
    "Absolutely not, ",
    "Doubtful, ",
    "Most assuredly not, ",
    "My sources say no, ",
    //non commital answers
    "Outlook hazy, ",
    "Uncertain, ",
    "The answer is unknowable, ",
    "I'd better not tell you now, ",
    "Cannot predict that at this time, "
];

// pick a random answer from the list of answers and return it
string generateAnswer()
{
    // generate a random number between 0 and the length of the
        // list (but not exactly the length of the list), then cast it
        // to an integer. This will give us a random number betwen 0
        // and the length of the list - 1.
    integer answerIndex =
        (integer)llFrand(llGetListLength(answers));

    // return the answerIndex'th item of the list answers
    return llList2String(answers, answerIndex);
}

// return TRUE if str starts with prefix.
integer startsWith(string str, string prefix)
{
    // get the substring of the string, from 0 to the length
    // of the prefix, and compare this substring to prefix
    return
        llGetSubString(str, 0, llStringLength(prefix) - 1) ==
                prefix;
}

// Return TRUE if candidate is a question, which is to say, if
    // the candidate begins with the question prefix.  This function
    // is case-insensitive (it ignores differences between upper and
    // lower case in the candidate and prefix)
integer isAQuestion(string candidate)
{
    return startsWith(llToUpper(candidate),
        llToUpper(questionPrefix));
}
```

```
default
{
    state_entry()
    {
        // listen on the public chat channel for any text
            // from anyone or anything.
        llListen(0, "", NULL_KEY, "");
    }

    touch_start(integer total_number)
    {
        // provide instructions
        llSay(0, instructions + "\"" + questionPrefix + "\"");
    }

    listen(integer channel, string name, key id, string message)
    {
        // script heard something, if it's a question for
            // this script, answer it.
        if (isAQuestion(message))
        {
            llSay(0, generateAnswer() + name);
        }
    }
}
```

Of course, there's really no such thing as the final version of a script, and there's always room for improvements. The following are some features that could be added to this script:

- Use the `id` parameter of the `listen` event to instant-message the question-asker instead of using the public chat channel.

- Remember the last question asked and provide an appropriately sarcastic response if someone asks the same question two times in a row.

- Add a `thinking` state that the ball goes into when it's thinking about an answer. Have the object spin or change color or perform other special effects to indicate to observers that the script is really thinking hard before providing an answer.

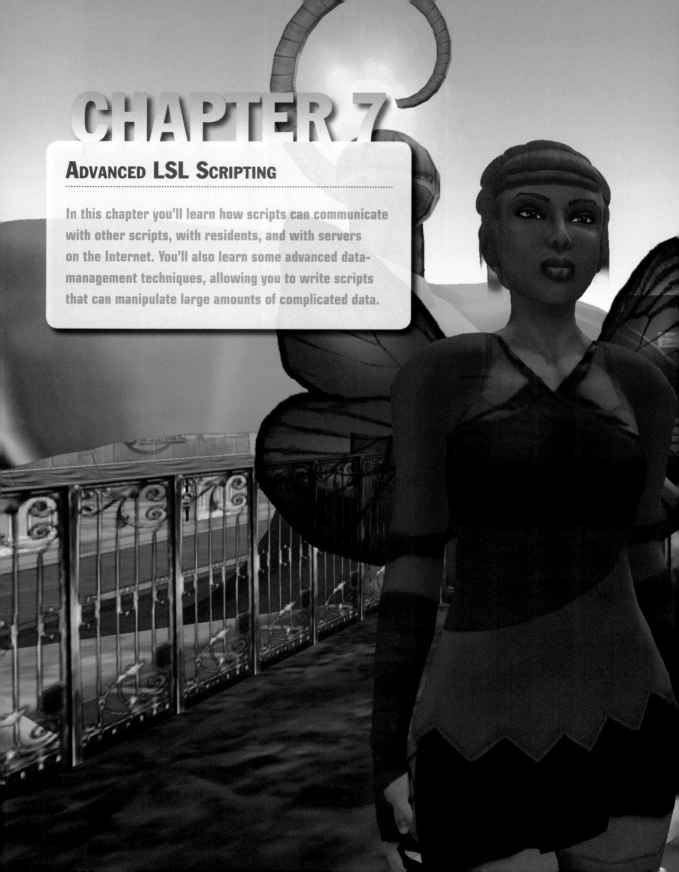

CHAPTER 7

ADVANCED LSL SCRIPTING

In this chapter you'll learn how scripts can communicate with other scripts, with residents, and with servers on the Internet. You'll also learn some advanced data-management techniques, allowing you to write scripts that can manipulate large amounts of complicated data.

CONTENTS

CHAPTER 7

● SENDING AND
  RECEIVING
  MESSAGES

● USER
  INTERFACES

● ADVANCED
  DATA
  MANAGEMENT

● INTERACTING
  WITH THE
  WORLD

● WORKING
  AROUND
  SCRIPT
  DELAYS

● SCRIPTING
  WITH THIRD-
  PARTY LSL
  EDITORS

SENDING AND RECEIVING MESSAGES

There are many ways for LSL scripts to communicate. Chat messages can be used to communicate with residents or other scripts that are nearby. Instant messages can be sent to residents anywhere in *SL*. Link messages can be sent between scripts in prims in a linked object. Scripts can send and receive regular email and access information from the Web by making HTTP requests. A script can also act as an XML-RPC server and field requests for client programs anywhere on the Internet, allowing you to interact with *SL* objects without being logged in to *SL*.

■ CHATTING

There are four functions a script can use to chat: `llWhisper`, `llSay`, `llShout`, and `llRegionSay`. Chat messages sent with `llWhisper` can be heard by objects and residents within 10 meters; messages sent with `llSay` travel 20 meters; those sent with `llShout` travel 100 meters. Messages sent with `llRegionSay` can be heard anywhere within the same region as the script; this function can send messages on any channel except channel 0, the chat channel used for regular resident chat. All of these built-in functions take the same arguments: an integer (the chat channel to broadcast on) and a string (the message to send).

There are two special channels: the constant `PUBLIC_CHANNEL`, with the value 0, and `DEBUG_CHANNEL`, with the hexadecimal value `0x7FFFFFFF`. Messages sent on the public channel are heard by residents and when residents chat, they chat on the public channel. Messages sent on the debug channel are displayed in the script console. When a debug message is heard, an icon will appear in the client's menu bar. Any other integer can be used as a chat channel, but only scripts that are specifically listening on that channel will receive those message (see the `llListen` call in Listing 7.3). Listing 7.1 demonstrates the use of the different chat functions.

Listing 7.1: Using the Chat Functions

```
default
{
    state_entry()
    {
        llWhisper(PUBLIC_CHANNEL,
            "this messages will be heard within 10 meters");

        llSay(PUBLIC_CHANNEL,
            "this message will be heard within 20 meters");

        llShout(PUBLIC_CHANNEL,
            "this message will be heard within 100 meters");

        llSay(23,
            "This message will be heard by scipts " +
            "listening on channel 23");
```

CHAPTER 1
CHAPTER 2
CHAPTER 3
CHAPTER 4
CHAPTER 5
CHAPTER 6
CHAPTER 7

CHAPTER 8
CHAPTER 9
CHAPTER 10
CHAPTER 11
CHAPTER 12
CHAPTER 13
CHAPTER 14
APPENDICES
INDEX

```
            llSay(DEBUG_CHANNEL, "This is a debug message");

            llRegionSay(23,
                "This message will be heard anywhere in this " +
                "region on channel 23");
        }
    }
```

Scripts can also use the function llOwnerSay to communicate. llOwnerSay sends messages that are similar to chat messages, but will be heard only by the object's owner, as long as the owner is in the same region as the object. llOwnerSay takes one argument, the string to say. Listing 7.2 shows a script that uses llOwnerSay to notify the object's owner of the object's position.

Listing 7.2: Using llOwnerSay

```
default
{
    state_entry()
    {
        // tell the owner this script's position
        llOwnerSay("Help, come get me, I'm at " + (string)llGetPos());
    }
}
```

Not only can scripts send chat messages; they can also receive them both from residents and other scripts. After calling llListen, the script will receive listen events for chat messages that conform to the filters passed to the llListen call. The llListen function takes four arguments, the chat channel to listen on, the name of the object or resident to listen for, the key of the object or resident to listen for, and the message to listen for. The name can be the empty string, the key can be NULL_KEY to receive messages from any source, and the message can be the empty string to receive any message.

The filters on the llListen call are additive, meaning, for example, that if a name and a message are passed to llListen, then the listen event handler will be called only when that exact message from a resident with that name is received.

NOTE

A script can have a maximum of 64 listeners. Listeners do not survive state changes; changing states in a script deletes all listeners created in the old state.

The listen event provides the same information in the same order as the arguments of the llListen function. Listing 7.3 shows a script that listens for all messages on channel 23 and passes those messages to the object's owner.

Listing 7.3: Listening to All Messages on a Channel

```
// Channel Listener
//
// This script listens for messages on a given channel, and passes
// them to the owner using llOwnerSay

integer myChannel = 23;

default
{
    state_entry()
    {
        // Listen on channel 23 for any message from anyone or anything
        llListen(myChannel, "", NULL_KEY, "");
    }

    listen(integer channel, string name, key id, string message)
    {
        llOwnerSay("Message on channel " + (string)myChannel +
            ": " + message);
    }
}
```

Listing 7.4 shows a script that listens for the message "activate" from its owner, using the owner's key.

Listing 7.4: Listening for a Specific Message from a Specific Key

```
default
{
    state_entry()
    {
        // Listen on the public channel for the message "activate!"
        // from scripts owner
        llListen(PUBLIC_CHANNEL, "", llGetOwner(), "activate!");
    }

    on_rez(integer param)
    {
        // Reset this script in case the owner has changed
        llResetScript();
    }

    listen(integer channel, string name, key id, string message)
    {
        // Got the message from the owner
        llOwnerSay("activated!");
    }
}
```

MORE INFO

CHAPTER 1
CHAPTER 2
CHAPTER 3
CHAPTER 4
CHAPTER 5
CHAPTER 6
CHAPTER 7

CHAPTER 8
CHAPTER 9
CHAPTER 10
CHAPTER 11
CHAPTER 12
CHAPTER 13
CHAPTER 14
APPENDICES
INDEX

WHAT'S THAT on_rez EVENT?

In the **state_entry** event, the script calls the **llGetOwner** function to get the key of the script's owner, and creates a listener that listens for messages from that key. If you create and save this script, it will be listening for messages from you. If you then give the object that contains this script to someone else, the script will still be listening for messages from you!

The **on_rez** event is called when the object is rezzed from inventory. The **llResetScript** function has the same effect as clicking the Reset button in the script editor; it completely resets the script and starts it in the default state again. So, with that event, if you give the object to someone else and they rez it, the script will be reset, the **state_entry** event will be called, and a listener listening for the new owner will be created.

Having a call to **llResetScript** in an **on_rez** event in every state in your script is a good way to ensure that the script always starts fresh with each new owner and each new instance of the script.

The llListen function returns an integer, an number that can be used to refer to the listener with the functions llListenRemove and llListenControl. The llListenRemove function deletes a listener. After calling it, the listen event handler will no longer be called for that listener. The llListenControl function temporarily turns on or off a listener. Listing 7.5 demonstrates the removal of a listener.

Listing 7.5: Removing a Listener

```
string  joeName = "Joe Avatar"; // the name of a resident
integer joeListener;  // id for listener for Joe
integer ownerListener;  // id for listener for owner

default
{
    state_entry()
    {
        // listen for
        joeListener = llListen(0, joeName, NULL_KEY, "");
        ownerListener = llListen(0, "", llGetOwner(),
            "stop listening to Joe");
    }

    on_rez(integer param)
    {
        // Reset this script in case the owner has changed
        llResetScript();
    }
```

CHAPTER 7

SENDING AND
RECEIVING
MESSAGES

USER
INTERFACES

ADVANCED
DATA
MANAGEMENT

INTERACTING
WITH THE
WORLD

WORKING
AROUND
SCRIPT
DELAYS

SCRIPTING
WITH THIRD-
PARTY LSL
EDITORS

```
listen(integer channel, string name, key id, string message)
{
    if (name == joeName)
    {
        llOwnerSay(joeName + " said: " + message);
    }
    else if (id == llGetOwner())
    {
        llOwnerSay("No longer listening to " + joeName);
        llListenRemove(joeListener);
    }
}
}
```

MORE INFO

KEYS ARE UNIQUE; NAMES ARE NOT!

Listing 7.5 creates a listener listening for messages from a resident or an object named Joe
Avatar. Anyone could create an object, rename the object to Joe Avatar, and put in a script
that calls llSay. The example script would hear these messages and act on them. If you want
to be sure where messages are coming from, use a key, not a name.

Listing 7.6 demonstrates how a script can turn a listener on or off using llListenControl.

Listing 7.6: Turning a Listener On and Off

```
integer ownerListener;   // id for listener
integer isListening = FALSE; // is the script listening or not?

default
{
    state_entry()
    {
        // listen for any message from the owner
        ownerListener = llListen(0, "", llGetOwner(), "");
        isListening = TRUE;
    }

    on_rez(integer param)
    {
        // Reset this script in case the owner has changed
        llResetScript();
    }

    listen(integer channel, string name, key id, string message)
    {
        llOwnerSay("Heard something");
    }
```

```
touch_start(integer num_detected)
{
    // if the owner of this object touched, toggle the listener
    if (llDetectedKey(0) == llGetOwner())
    {
        if (isListening)
        {
            //turn off the listener
            llOwnerSay("not listening");
            llListenControl(ownerListener, FALSE);
            isListening = FALSE;
        }
        else
        {
            //turn on the listener
            llOwnerSay("listening");
            llListenControl(ownerListener, TRUE);
            isListening = TRUE;
        }
    }
}
}
```

■ IMING

Scripts can also send *SL* instant messages. An IM sent by a script is the same as an IM sent by a resident; it will be delivered to the recipient if they're logged in, or stored and delivered later if not. Instant messages are sent with the function llInstantMessage. This function takes two arguments: the key of the resident to send the message to, and a string (the message). IMs can be sent only to residents. Calling llInstantMessage causes a two-second delay in the script. Listing 7.7 shows a script that sends an instant message to the object's owner whenever the object is touched.

Listing 7.7: Sending an Instant Message

```
default
{
    touch_start(integer n)
    {
        // Tell the owner of the script the name of the resident
        // that touched this object
        llInstantMessage(llGetOwner(),
            "Help, " + llDetectedName(0) + " is touching me!");
    }
}
```

■ SENDING LINK MESSAGES

Objects can be made of multiple prims, and each of those prims can contain multiple scripts. These scripts can send link messages to each other. Each prim in an object has a link number, starting at 1 for the root prim. llMessageLinked can send a message to all the scripts in a given object, or to a set of prims using special constants:

CHAPTER 7

SENDING AND
RECEIVING
MESSAGES

USER
INTERFACES

ADVANCED
DATA
MANAGEMENT

INTERACTING
WITH THE
WORLD

WORKING
AROUND
SCRIPT
DELAYS

SCRIPTING
WITH THIRD-
PARTY LSL
EDITORS

`LINK_SET` **sends the message to all scripts in all prims.**

`LINK_ALL_OTHERS` **sends the messages to all scripts in all other prims.**

`LINK_ALL_CHILDREN` **sends the message to all scripts in all prims except the root.**

`LINK_THIS` **sends the message to all scripts in the same prim.**

In addition to the link number (or special constant), `llMessageLinked` takes an integer, a string, and a key. These values make up the message. When the message is received by a script, the `link_message` event handler is called. This event handler is passed the link ID of the object that contains the script that sent the message, plus the number, string, and key. Listing 7.8 shows a script that both sends and receives link messages.

Listing 7.8: Sending and Receiving Link Messages

```
// if the script receives a link message with this as its integer
// part, it will send a link message to the next prim in this
// link set
integer LM_CONTINUE = 1;

// Send a message to the next prim in this linked object.
messageNextPrim()
{
    integer primToMessage = llGetLinkNumber() + 1;

    llMessageLinked(primToMessage, LM_CONTINUE,
        "Hello from prim number " + (string)llGetLinkNumber(),
        NULL_KEY);
}

// send a message to every linked object
messageAllPrims()
{
    llMessageLinked(LINK_SET, 0, "All done", NULL_KEY);
}


default
{
    touch_start(integer numDetected)
    {
        // if we are the root prim
        if (llGetLinkNumber() == 1)
        {
            messageNextPrim();
        }
    }

    link_message(integer from, integer n, string s, key k)
    {
        llOwnerSay(
            "Prim number " + (string)llGetLinkNumber() +
            " got a message from prim number " + (string)from +
            ": \"" + s + "\"");
```

```
        if (n == LM_CONTINUE)
        {
            // if this is the last prim in the set, message everyone
            if (llGetLinkNumber() == llGetNumberOfPrims())
            {
                messageAllPrims();
            }
            else
            {
                messageNextPrim();
            }
        }
    }
}
```

CHAPTER 1
CHAPTER 2
CHAPTER 3
CHAPTER 4
CHAPTER 5
CHAPTER 6
CHAPTER 7

CHAPTER 8
CHAPTER 9
CHAPTER 10
CHAPTER 11
CHAPTER 12
CHAPTER 13
CHAPTER 14
APPENDICES
INDEX

If this script is placed in every prim in a linked object, when the root prim is touched each prim will send a message to the next prim in the link set until the message reaches the last prim; then that prim will message all prims in the object. The script uses the integer part of the link message to specify what kind of action the recipient should take, uses the string part to carry a message, and does not use the key part at all. In a linked object made of three prims, the output is as follows:

```
Object: Prim number 2 got a message from prim number 1: "Hello from prim
number 1"

Object: Prim number 3 got a message from prim number 2: "Hello from prim
number 2"

Object: Prim number 2 got a message from prim number 3: "All done"

Object: Prim number 1 got a message from prim number 3: "All done"

Object: Prim number 3 got a message from prim number 3: "All done"
```

Notice the last line; when a link message is sent to LINK_SET or to the link number of the prim the script is in, the script will receive its own message. If your script has link messages that cause other link messages to be sent, it's important to be aware of this behavior so that you script doesn't get into an infinite loop.

■ EMAILING

Scripts can send and receive regular Internet email. An object's email address is [key]@lsl. secondlife.com. The function llEmail is used to send email. It takes an address, subject, and message body. When sent, the email body will contain some extra information about the object sending the message. Calling llEmail delays the script by 20 seconds. Listing 7.9 shows a script that sends a short email whenever the object is touched.

Listing 7.9: Sending an Email

```
string ownerEmail = "wednesday.grimm@gmail.com";

default
{
    touch_start(integer total_number)
    {
        llEmail(ownerEmail, "Touched!", "I was touched by " +
            llDetectedName(0));
    }
}
```

The email received is as follows:

```
Object-Name: Object

Region: Chartreuse (255744, 258048)

Local-Position: (8, 243, 21)


I was touched by Wednesday Grimm
```

To receive email, a script calls the function llGetNextEmail. This function takes two parameters, an address and a subject, and will get the next email that matches those strings. Either or both the address and subject can be blank to ignore that field and get any email. This function causes the email event handler to be raised. This event handler is passed the message details and the number of messages remaining to be retrieved.

llGetNextEmail retrieves an email only if there is already one waiting; if the script calls llGetNextEmail and there are not messages waiting but then later a message arrives, the event handler will not be raised. Listing 7.10 shows a script that periodically checks for email, retrieves the email, and communicates it to the object's owner.

Listing 7.10: Receiving Email

```
float mailCheckTimeout = 30.0; // how often to check for mail

default
{
    state_entry()
    {
        llSetTimerEvent(mailCheckTimeout);
        llOwnerSay((string)llGetKey());
    }

    timer()
    {
        llOwnerSay("Checking for messages");
        llGetNextEmail("", ""); // Get any message available
    }
```

```
email(string time, string address, string subject, string body,
    integer num_remaining)
{
    llOwnerSay("Got a message from: " + address);
    llOwnerSay("Subject: " + subject);
    llOwnerSay(body);

    // if there are any more messages, get the next one
    if (num_remaining > 0)
    {
        llGetNextEmail("", "");
    }
}
}
```

■ USING HTTP

An LSL script can fetch web pages from the Internet using the llHTTPRequest function. Calling this function causes the http_response event to be raised once the page is fetched. The llHTTPRequest function takes three parameters: a URL to fetch, a list of options, and a string (the body of the request). For most simple fetches, the last two options can be an empty list and an empty string. This request returns only the raw text of a web page, the HTML code that is seen when you "view source" in a web browser. The function llLoadURL can be used to open a web page in a separate web browser window. Listing 7.11 shows a script that retrieves an RSS feed from the Web and parses it.

NOTE

At present, **llHTTPRequest** *returns only the first 2048 characters of a page.*

Listing 7.11: Fetching a URL and Parsing the Result

```
// Get the first link in the first item in an RSS feed and open it in
// the user's web browser when the object is touched
//
// This script is very naive and not very robust. It expects only
// one user to be clicking on it at a time.

// URL for the RSS feed
string sourceURL=
    "http://blog.secondlife.com/feed/";

// The standard HTTP success response code
integer HTTP_OK = 200;

// Key of the resident that clicked on the object. Saved in the
// touch_start event so that it can be used in the http_response event.
key requestingResident = NULL_KEY;
```

CHAPTER 7

🔹 SENDING AND
RECEIVING
MESSAGES

🔹 USER
INTERFACES

🔹 ADVANCED
DATA
MANAGEMENT

🔹 INTERACTING
WITH THE
WORLD

🔹 WORKING
AROUND
SCRIPT
DELAYS

🔹 SCRIPTING
WITH THIRD-
PARTY LSL
EDITORS

```
// Parse an HTTP response that should be an RSS feed and return the
// first link from the first item, or "" if the link could not be found
//
// body is the response from an HTTP request. Since HTTP requests are
// currently limited to 2048 characters, and since this is unknown data
// from the outside world, the body may or may not actually contain the
// information we want.
//

string getFirstItemLink(string body)
{
    // Find the start of the "items" in the RSS feed
    string startItems = "<item>";
    if (llSubStringIndex(body, startItems) == -1)
    {
        return "";
    }

    // get the string from the beginning of the first item to the end
    // of the body
    string items =
        llGetSubString(body, llSubStringIndex(body, startItems), -1);

    // find the first link in the items
    string startLink = "<link>";
    string endLink = "</link>";
    integer startIndex = llSubStringIndex(items, startLink);
    integer endIndex = llSubStringIndex(items, endLink);

    // make sure startLink and endLink were found, and startLink is
    // before end link
    if (startIndex != -1 && endIndex != -1 && endIndex > startIndex)
    {
        string link =
            llGetSubString(
                items,
                startIndex +llStringLength(startLink),
                endIndex - 1);
        // Got it!
        return link;
    }
    else
    {
        return "";
    }
}

default
{
    touch_start(integer total_number)
    {
        // Save the requestor
        requestingResident = llDetectedKey(0);

        llSay(0, "Fetching: " + sourceURL);
        // Get the RSS feed
        llHTTPRequest(sourceURL, [], "");
    }
```

CHAPTER 1
CHAPTER 2
CHAPTER 3
CHAPTER 4
CHAPTER 5
CHAPTER 6
CHAPTER 7

CHAPTER 8
CHAPTER 9
CHAPTER 10
CHAPTER 11
CHAPTER 12
CHAPTER 13
CHAPTER 14
APPENDICES
INDEX

```
http_response(key id, integer status, list metadata, string body)
{
    // check if the page was successfully fetched
    if (status == HTTP_OK)
    {
        string link = getFirstItemLink(body);
        if (link != "")
        {
            // Got the link, load it in the user's browser
            llLoadURL(requestingResident, "", link);
        }
        else
        {
            // Got a response, but didn't get the link
            llSay(0, "Could not find link");
        }
    }
    else
    {
        llSay(0, "Couldn't fetch page, http status: " +
            (string)status);
    }

    // reset this variable
    requestingResident = NULL_KEY;
}
}
```

Using the options-list argument for llHTTPRequest, a script can do HTTP POST, PUT, and DELETE requests as well as GETs, can use SSL, and can post to an HTML form and perform other sophisticated HTTP operations. Extensive documentation on HTTP formatting, response codes, and message formatting can be found at http://www.w3c.org.

URLs cannot contain spaces and some other special characters. The function llEscapeURL can be used to convert a string to a form that is safe for use in a URL passed to llHTTPRequest or llLoadURL. llUnescapeURL reverses the conversion done by llEscapeURL, as shown in listing 7.12.

Listing 7.12: Escaping URLs

```
// URL to search digg.com, the search term is added to the end of this
string searchURLBase = "http://www.digg.com/search?section=news&s=";

searchDigg(string searchTerm)
{
    // build the URL
    string url =
        searchURLBase +
        llEscapeURL(searchTerm);
    llLoadURL(llGetOwner(), "", url);
}
```

CHAPTER 7

SENDING AND
RECEIVING
MESSAGES

USER
INTERFACES

ADVANCED
DATA
MANAGEMENT

INTERACTING
WITH THE
WORLD

WORKING
AROUND
SCRIPT
DELAYS

SCRIPTING
WITH THIRD-
PARTY LSL
EDITORS

```
default
{
    state_entry()
    {
        // search for stories about "second life" on digg.com
        searchDigg("\"second life\"");
    }
}
```

USING XML-RPC

XML-RPC is a standard protocol that programs in different languages on different platforms can use to exchange data. An LSL script can act as an XML-RPC server, and thus receive requests from and send replies to clients anywhere on the Internet. There are XML-RPC client implementations available for JavaScript, Java, Python, Ruby, Perl, and most other programming languages.

A script asks for an RPC channel to be created by calling llOpenRemoteDataChannel. When the channel is ready, the remote_data event is raised with the type REMOTE_DATA_CHANNEL and the channel set to the key of the newly created channel. Once the channel is open, XML-RPC clients that know this key can send requests to the script and receive replies. The URI (Uniform Resource Identifier) for RPC clients to send requests to LSL scripts is http://xmlrpc.secondlife.com/cgi-bin/xmlrpc.cgi.

Once the channel is open, an incoming RPC request will cause a remote_data event with the type REMOTE_DATA_REQUEST, the channel set to the ID of the channel (which will be the same as the channel key sent with the REMOTE_DATA_CHANNEL message), the message ID set to a new unique message ID, and the idata and sdata set to the integer and string parts of the request from the remote client. Listing 7.14 presents details of the XML request clients should send.

Scripts can reply to XML-RPC requests using llRemoteDataReply, passing the channel ID and message ID to the keys from the remote_data event, and passing arbitrary idata and sdata values to send back to the client. The length of the string data in sdata is limited to 254 characters.

Listing 7.13: Simple XML-RPC Server

```
// XML-RPC color setter and getter
//
// Allow XMl-RPC clients to get and set the color of this object
// remotely.
// This script accepts XML-RPC requests and interperts the integer part
// of the request as a command and the string part as an argument. Two
// commands are accepted: get the color of the object, and set the
// color of the object. There is no argument for the get color request.
// For the set color request, the string part is interperted as a
// vector, and is used as a color.
//
// The script sends an RPC reply, with the integer part set to the
//         // number of the command received. For the set color reply, the
//         string
// part is empty; for the get color request, the string part is the
// color of the object, as a vector.
//
// User must get the RPC channel key to the XML-RPC client manually.
```

```
// Constants for the commands
integer RPC_GET_COLOR = 1;
integer RPC_SET_COLOR = 2;

// Script has received a request, do the requested action and send
// the reply
dispatchRPCRequest(key channelid, key messageid, integer idata,
    string sdata)
{
    if (idata == RPC_SET_COLOR)
    {
        llSetColor((vector)sdata, ALL_SIDES);
        llRemoteDataReply(channelid, messageid, "", RPC_SET_COLOR);
    }
    else if (idata == RPC_GET_COLOR)
    {
        llRemoteDataReply(channelid, messageid, (string)llGetColor(0),
          RPC_GET_COLOR);
    }
    else
    {
        // Unknown request
        llRemoteDataReply(channelid, messageid, "unknown request",
          idata);
    }
}

default
{
    state_entry()
    {
        // ask for an XML-RPC channel
        llOpenRemoteDataChannel();
    }

    remote_data(integer event_type, key channel, key message_id,
        string sender, integer idata, string sdata)
    {
        if (event_type == REMOTE_DATA_CHANNEL)
        {
            // Channel is ready, tell the user the channel key so
            // the user can tell the RPC client
            llOwnerSay("XML-RPC channel key is: " + (string)channel);
        }
        else if (event_type == REMOTE_DATA_REQUEST)
        {
            // Got an RPC request, do it
            dispatchRPCRequest(channel, message_id, idata, sdata);
        }
    }
}
```

Listing 7.14 is a simple client for the XML-RPC example script written in the Perl programming language. This script can run on any computer on the Internet and interact with an object in *Second Life*!

The script takes the channel ID, a command number, and optionally an argument on the command line, sends the XML-RPC request to *Second Life*, and prints the response or error

CHAPTER 1
CHAPTER 2
CHAPTER 3
CHAPTER 4
CHAPTER 5
CHAPTER 6
CHAPTER 7

CHAPTER 8
CHAPTER 9
CHAPTER 10
CHAPTER 11
CHAPTER 12
CHAPTER 13
CHAPTER 14
APPENDICES
INDEX

CHAPTER 7

SENDING AND
RECEIVING
MESSAGES

USER
INTERFACES

ADVANCED
DATA
MANAGEMENT

INTERACTING
WITH THE
WORLD

WORKING
AROUND
SCRIPT
DELAYS

SCRIPTING
WITH THIRD-
PARTY LSL
EDITORS

received. This client could be written in any programming language that can perform XML-RPC calls. The script would be called as follows:

```
lslXML.pl 649798bf-17f8-9862-fac8-85cd096d1756 2 "<0.62, 1.0,  0.33>"
```

Listing 7.14: lslXML.pl, An XML-RPC Client Perl

```perl
#!/usr/bin/perl -w

use strict;

use LWP::UserAgent;
use HTTP::Request::Common;
use CGI;

my $LSL_RPC_URI = 'http://xmlrpc.secondlife.com/cgi-bin/xmlrpc.cgi';

# get the key command number and argument from the command line
# and escape them so they are safe to send over XML
my $LSLKey = CGI::escapeHTML(shift || "");
my $LSLCommand = CGI::escapeHTML(shift || "");
my $LSLArgument = CGI::escapeHTML(shift || "");

# we must have a key and a command
if (!$LSLKey or !$LSLCommand) {die "bad command line";}


# build the request. The method name is llRemoteData the parameters
# consist of a single struct:
#       Channel => the id of the RPC channel
#       IntValue => the integer data
#       StringValue => the string data
my $requestBody = "
<?xml version=\"1.0\"?>
<methodCall>
  <methodName>llRemoteData</methodName>
  <params>
    <param>
      <value>
        <struct>
          <member>
            <name>Channel</name>
              <value>
                <string>$LSLKey</string>
              </value>
          </member>
          <member>
            <name>IntValue</name>
              <value>
                <int>$LSLCommand</int>
              </value>
          </member>
```

CHAPTER 1
CHAPTER 2
CHAPTER 3
CHAPTER 4
CHAPTER 5
CHAPTER 6
CHAPTER 7
CHAPTER 8
CHAPTER 9
CHAPTER 10
CHAPTER 11
CHAPTER 12
CHAPTER 13
CHAPTER 14
APPENDICES
INDEX

```
        <member>
          <name>StringValue</name>
          <value>
            <string>$LSLArgument</string>
          </value>
        </member>
      </struct>
    </value>
  </param>
 </params>
</methodCall>
";

# create the user agent used to send the request
my $userAgent = LWP::UserAgent->new;
$userAgent->agent("Simple Perl RPC Demo 1.0");

# send the request and wait for the response
my $response = $userAgent->request(POST $LSL_RPC_URI,
        Content_Type => 'text/xml',
        Content => $requestBody);

# print the response or error received
print $response->error_as_HTML unless $response->is_success;

print $response->as_string;
```

There are a number of limitations in the current XML-RPC implementation in LSL. First and foremost, an XML-RPC channel can have only one reply at a time queued for sending. This means that if your script receives a number of requests in quick succession and sends replies, it is possible that a later reply will overwrite an earlier one, and the client waiting for the earlier reply will never receive it. One way to work around this limitation is to code your client such that it never sends a request until it has received a reply to the previous request.

Another limitation is that XML-RPC channels do not survive the object moving into a new sim. If your object is an attachment or is otherwise likely to move across a sim boundary, you can use the `changed` event to detect this and re-create the channel with another call to `llOpenRemoteDataChannel`. Finally, calling `llOpenRemoteDataChannel` delays the script by one second; calling `llRemoteDataReply` delays the script by three seconds.

USER INTERFACES

There are a lot of ways scripts can interact with users. In this section we'll cover a special kind of attachment called a HUD, as well as user-interface dialogs.

▪ HUDS

HUDs (heads-up displays) are special attachments that appear only to the resident they're attached to, and are locked to the *SL* user interface rather than the resident's avatar. HUDs behave and can be scripted exactly like other attachments, with the following exceptions: Sounds played with `llPlaySound` will be heard only by the object's wearer (sounds played with `llTriggerSound` will be heard normally). Particles do not work with HUDs.

The current position of a HUD on the user's display can be retrieved with `llGetLocalPos`; HUDs can be positioned with `llSetPos`. The coordinate system for HUDs is somewhat unintuitive. The y value controls the left-to-right position of the object, with the value decreasing further to the right, so `llSetPos(llGetLocalPos() - <0.0, 0.1, 0.0>)` will move the object to the right. The z value controls the top-to-bottom position of the object, with the value decreasing from top to bottom so `llSetPos(llGetLocalPos() - <0.0, 0.0, 0.1>)` will move the object down. The x value is used to determine the "stacking" order of HUDS, with smaller x-values being shown on top of larger values. So a HUD with an x coordinate of 1.0 will be on top of a HUD with an x coordinate of 2.0.

The position of a HUD is relative to the attachment point. In other words, `llSetPos(ZERO_VECTOR)` moves the object to the original position for the attachment point. The user's display is always one meter high, so if an object is attached to the bottom-left attachment point, calling `llSetPos(<0.0, 0.0, 1.0>)` will move the object to the top-left corner of the screen. It is impossible for a script to know how wide a user's display is. If the display is exactly square, it will be one meter wide; if it is taller than it is wide, it will be less than 1 meter wide; if it is wider than it is tall, it will be more than 1 meter wide.

HUDs can be resized using `llSetScale` or `llSetPrimitiveParams`. The scale is the same as the positioning scale, so a HUD attached to the center attachment point, at position <0, 0, 0>, with its z-size set to 1 will cover the user's screen from top to bottom (and be very annoying).

Since HUDs can be clicked on even when they're transparent, it's important for them to be either very small and unobtrusive or be scripted such that they can get out of the way. Listing 7.15 shows a script that positions and scales a HUD attachment.

Listing 7.15: HUD Positioning and Resizing

```
// Script for a HUD that doesn't do anything useful but get out of the
// way when clicked, and get back in the way when clicked again

default
{
    state_entry()
    {
        if(llGetAttached() == 0)  // see if object is attached
        {
            // this behavior could be scripted with llAttachToAvatar
            llOwnerSay("Attach me as a HUD to the bottom " +
                "left attachment point");
        }
        else
        {
            state inTheWay;
        }
    }
    on_rez(integer p)
    {
        llResetScript();
    }
```

```
attach(key id)
{
    if (id != NULL_KEY)
    {
        state inTheWay;
    }
}
}

state inTheWay
{
    state_entry()
    {
        // move to the middle-left of the screen
        llSetPos(<0.0, 0.0, 0.5>);
        llSetScale(<1.0, 1.0, 1.0>); // enlarge attachment
    }
    on_rez(integer p)
    {
        llResetScript();
    }
    touch_start(integer num)
    {
        state outOfTheWay;
    }
}

state outOfTheWay
{
    state_entry()
    {
        llSetPos(ZERO_VECTOR); // move back to original position
        llSetScale(<1.0, 0.1, 0.1>); // shrink attachment
    }
    on_rez(integer p)
    {
        llResetScript();
    }
    touch_start(integer num)
    {
        state inTheWay;
    }
}
```

■ DIALOGS

Scripts can interact with residents by accepting commands via chat, employing llListen, but this requires residents to remember commands and type them in exactly. An easier way accomplish this is using the llDialog command. This function presents a dialog to a resident (Figure 7.1) and then provides their selection on a chat channel. llDialog takes a key, the resident to show the dialog to, a string, the prompt for the resident, a list containing the choices that the resident will see as buttons on the dialog, and an integer—the chat channel to send the response on.

CHAPTER 7

SENDING AND
RECEIVING
MESSAGES

USER
INTERFACES

ADVANCED
DATA
MANAGEMENT

INTERACTING
WITH THE
WORLD

WORKING
AROUND
SCRIPT
DELAYS

SCRIPTING
WITH THIRD-
PARTY LSL
EDITORS

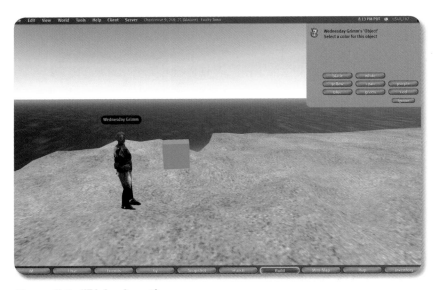

Figure 7.1: llDialog in action

There are some important things to be aware of when using llDialog. Any script listening on the right channel will hear the resident's response. It is impossible for a script to distinguish between chat messages sent because the resident clicked a button in a dialog, and messages sent on that chat channel via llSay or one of the other chat functions. Furthermore, it is possible for a resident to close the dialog without making a selection, so your script may never receive a response when you use llDialog. For these reasons, it's best to structure your scripts as if they are controlled by regular chat, then add llDialog functionality as a convenience feature. Listing 7.16 presents a color-picking dialog to residents.

Listing 7.16: Using llDialog

```
// Channel script will listen on and llDialog will use
integer dialogChannel = 1975;

// message to show user
string dialogMessage = "Select a color for this object";

// color options that will be presented to user
list colorNames = [
    "blue",
    "green",
    "red",
    "yellow",
    "cyan",
    "purple",
    "black",
    "white"
    ];
```

```
// color values. This color values in this list match the order of the
// color names in the colorNames list
list colorValues = [
    <0, 0, 1>,
    <0, 1, 0>,
    <1, 0, 0>,
    <1, 1, 0>,
    <0, 1, 1>,
    <1, 0, 1>,
    <0, 0, 0>,
    <1, 1, 1>
    ];


default
{
    state_entry()
    {
        // listen for any message from owner on dialogChannel
        llListen(dialogChannel, "", llGetOwner(), "");
    }

    on_rez(integer p)
    {
        // reset, incase owner has changed
        llResetScript();
    }

    touch_start(integer num_detected)
    {
        // if the owner is touching object, show dialog
        if (llDetectedKey(0) == llGetOwner())
        {
            llDialog(llGetOwner(), dialogMessage, colorNames,
                dialogChannel);
        }
    }

    listen(integer channel, string name, key id, string message)
    {
        // try to find the message in the list of color names
        integer colorIndex = llListFindList(colorNames, [message]);
        if (colorIndex != -1) // color name was found in the list
        {
            // get the color value that corresponds to the name
            vector newColor = llList2Vector(colorValues, colorIndex);
            llSetColor(newColor, ALL_SIDES);
        }
    }
}
```

■ OTHER USER INTERFACES

Any way that a script can receive input or sense something about the world can be used as a user interface. A script can detect that it was touched and act on that, or it can measure the time between touch_start and touch_end events and perform different functions based on how

CHAPTER 7

SENDING AND
RECEIVING
MESSAGES

USER
INTERFACES

ADVANCED
DATA
MANAGEMENT

INTERACTING
WITH THE
WORLD

WORKING
AROUND
SCRIPT
DELAYS

SCRIPTING
WITH THIRD-
PARTY LSL
EDITORS

long the user clicks and holds. An object could be made out of linked prims, and a script using `llDetectedLinkNumber` in a `touch_start` event could determine which prim the user clicked and act on that. Scripts can also detect physical collisions with an object, so users could jump on an object or bump into it to trigger some action. Sensors can be used (see "Interacting with the World") to detect nearby objects and avatars. The way your script interacts with residents is completely up to you.

ADVANCED DATA MANAGEMENT

In Listing 7.16, there are two lists: `colorNames` and `colorValues`; these are *parallel lists*. The item at index *n* of `colorNames` is related to the item at index *n* of `colorValues`. The name and value are two aspects of the same thing: a color. Another way to implement this kind of relation is in a *skip list*, a list in which the aspects of the thing appear in the list one after another. An item has a certain number of aspects; for our color example, there are two aspects: the value and the name. The size of the skip list will be the number of items multiplied by the number of aspects. Each aspect in an item has an offset, starting at 0. The index in the list of an aspect of element n is *n* × total number of aspects + aspect offset. Skip lists are a clearer, more readable way to store multifaceted data in your script. Listing 7.17 shows a skip list that holds color names and values.

Listing 7:17: Using a Skip List to Hold Data

```
// color options that will be presented to user
integer colorNameOffset = 0;
integer colorValueOffset = 1;
integer numColorAspects = 2;
list colors = [
    // name,      value
    "blue",       <0, 0, 1>,
    "green",      <0, 1, 0>,
    "red",        <1, 0, 0>,
    "yellow",     <1, 1, 0>,
    "cyan",       <0, 1, 1>,
    "purple",     <1, 0, 1>,
    "black",      <0, 0, 0>,
    "white",      <1, 1, 1>
    ];

string getColorName(integer idx)
{
    return llList2String(colors, idx * numColorAspects +
colorNameOffset);
}

vector getColorValue(integer idx)
{
    return llList2Vector(colors, idx * numColorAspects +
colorValueOffset);
}
```

```
vector getColorValueByName(string name)
{
    integer nameIdx = llListFindList(colors, [name]);
    if (nameIdx == -1) return ZERO_VECTOR; // name not found in list
    return llList2Vector(colors,
        nameIdx + colorValueOffset - colorNameOffset);
}
```

Notice that if we wanted to add another aspect to colors—say, mood—we would only have to change `numColorAspects` to 3, add a mood to each color, and add a function, `getColorMood`. None of the other functions or code that uses those functions would have to be changed.

CHAPTER 1
CHAPTER 2
CHAPTER 3
CHAPTER 4
CHAPTER 5
CHAPTER 6
CHAPTER 7

CHAPTER 8
CHAPTER 9
CHAPTER 10
CHAPTER 11
CHAPTER 12
CHAPTER 13
CHAPTER 14
APPENDICES
INDEX

INTERACTING WITH THE WORLD

In earlier sections in this chapter you learned how your scripts can interact with residents. In this section you'll learn how your script can get information about nearby objects and residents, and how your script can get and set land properties such as access lists and streaming media settings.

■ USING SENSORS

Sensors are used to detect objects or residents near the object that meet a set of criteria. The functions `llSensor` and `llSensorRepeat` create a sensor. The event handler `sensor` will be called if at least one object matching the criteria is found, the event handler `no_sensor` will be called if nothing is found. The function `llSensorRemove` removes a sensor created with `llSensorRepeat`.

WARNING

A script can have only one sensor at a time. Sensors can be hard on a sim, and excessive use of sensors can slow performance.

The arguments to `llSensor` are as follows:

A String: The name of objects or residents to search for. This can be "" to find things with any name.

A Key: The unique ID of an object or residents to search for. This can be NULL_KEY to find things with any key.

A Type: The AGENT, ACTIVE, PASSIVE and SCRIPTED arguments are used as follows:

- AGENT finds avatars (residents).
- ACTIVE finds objects that are being acted on by simulator physics or that have a script that is doing something right now.
- PASSIVE finds objects that are not ACTIVE.
- SCRIPTED finds objects that have a running script

At least one of these flags must be specified, and they can be combined with the bitwise or operator, " | " (but combining the SCRIPTED flag with other type flags can have unexpected effects (detecting objects erroneously), so it's best to use the SCRIPTED flag by itself).

Three Floats: The three floats are as follows:

- The range to look for objects in. The maximum range for a sensor is 96 meters. Ranges larger than 96 meters will be limited to 96 meters.

- The arc, in radians, to search.

- The rate, in seconds, to repeat the search.

These arguments are additive, so, for example, llSensor("Something", NULL_KEY, PASSIVE, 10.0, PI) will search for things named *Something* that are passive and within 10 meters and within pi radians.

The area searched by a sensor is a cone. The length of the cone is the range of the search. The angle of the cone is twice the arc argument. So a sensor with an arc of pi radians (or 180 degrees) will search the whole sphere around the object. An arc of PI_BY_TWO radians (90 degrees) will search the half sphere in front of the object. Try changing the values for arc and range in Listing 7.18 to visualize different sensor areas.

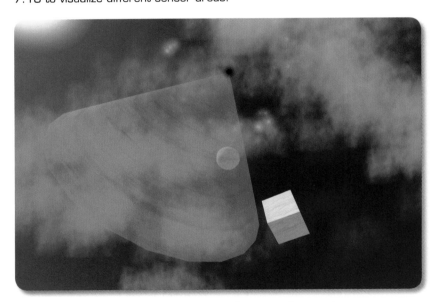

A sensor's search cone points out from the front of an object (Figure 7.2). The point of the cone is at the center of the object, meaning the point at the current position of the object. The "front" of an object is the direction along its positive x-axis. For sensors in attachments, the front is the direction the avatar is facing; in mouselook, it's the direction the avatar is looking.

Figure 7.2: Sensor sensing a sphere and not sensing a cube

The sensor event receives one parameter, the number of things matching the search criteria that were found by the sensor. Information about the objects found can be retrieved with the various llDetected functions—for example, llDetectedPosition, llDetectedName, llDetectedRot, etc. The no_sensor event receives no parameters.

A sensor will never detect the object it is in, and a sensor cannot detect attachments. Furthermore, a sensor in an attachment will not detect the avatar it is attached to. Listing 7.18 resizes and reshapes the object it is in so that it takes the shape of the area the sensor is scanning and reports objects it senses.

```
// Sensor visualizer
//
// This script turns the object into a transparent, phantom dimpled
// sphere that matches the area being searched by the sensor.

float senseRange = 3.0; // can be up to 96m for sensor,
                        // but should be <= 5m for this visualization
float senseArc = 0.7853981634 ; // == PI / 4.0, 45 degrees
float senseRate = 5.0;

// change the prim so it covers the area searched by the sensor, and is
// transparent and phantom
setupPrim()
{
    vector dimple = <0.0, senseArc / PI, 0.0>;
    llSetPrimitiveParams([
        PRIM_TYPE,
            PRIM_TYPE_SPHERE,    // type
                0,                       // hole shape
                <0.0, 1.0, 0.0>,         // cut
                0,                       // hollow
                ZERO_VECTOR,             // twist
                dimple,                  // dimple
        PRIM_SIZE,
            2 * <senseRange, senseRange, senseRange>,
        PRIM_PHANTOM,
            TRUE,
        PRIM_COLOR,
            ALL_SIDES,
            <1.0, 1.0, 1.0>,
            0.5
    ]);
}

default
{
    state_entry()
    {
        setupPrim();

        // search for PASSIVE (non-physical, unscripted) objects
        llSensorRepeat("", NULL_KEY, PASSIVE, senseRange, senseArc,
          senseRate);
    }

    no_sensor()
    {
        llOwnerSay("Nothing Sensed");
    }
```

```
    sensor(integer num_detected)
    {
        integer x;
        llOwnerSay("--------");
        for (x = 0; x < num_detected; x++)
        {
            llOwnerSay(
                "Sensed object " +
                llDetectedName(x) +
                " at " +
                (string)llDetectedPos(x)
            );
        }
    }
}
```

Listing 7.19 looks for its object's owner by key, and if the owner is found, sets its position and rotation to match the owner's.

Listing 7.19: Using A Sensor to Find the Owner's Position and Rotation

```
// Find object's owner, position this object in front of owner and
// point in the direction owner is looking

float senseRange = 20.0; // search within 20m
float senseArc = PI;     // search all around object
float senseRate = 5.0;   // search every 5 seconds

vector offsetFromOwner = <1.0, 0.0, 1.0>;

// turn object in to a small phantom cone
setupPrim()
{
    llSetPrimitiveParams([
        PRIM_TYPE,
            PRIM_TYPE_CYLINDER,      // type
                0,                   // hole shape
                <0.0, 1.0, 0.0>,     // cut
                0,                   // hollow
                ZERO_VECTOR,         // twist
                ZERO_VECTOR,         // taper
                ZERO_VECTOR,         // top shear
        PRIM_SIZE,
            <0.25, 0.25, 0.5>,
        PRIM_PHANTOM,
            TRUE
    ]);
}
```

```
        default
        {
            state_entry()
            {
                setupPrim();

                // search for owner by id
                llSensorRepeat("", llGetOwner(), AGENT, senseRange, senseArc,
                    senseRate);
            }
            on_rez(integer p)
            {
                llResetScript();
            }

            no_sensor()
            {
                // can't find owner, go away
                llDie();
            }

            sensor(integer num_detected)
            {
                // Since script is searching for owner by id, and since the
                // owner key is unique and the script sensed something, we
                // don't need to check num_detected; it will always be 1, and
                // the index of the owner sensed will always be 0

                // Point cone in direction owner is looking.
                // The extra rotation is becaue at zero rotation, cones point
                // along their z-axis, and we want this one to point along
                // the x-axis.
                llSetRot(llEuler2Rot(<0.0, PI_BY_TWO, 0.0>) *
                    llDetectedRot(0));

                // Place cone at offsetFromOwner, rotated so it is always in
                // the same position relative to the owner
                llSetPos(llDetectedPos(0) + offsetFromOwner *
                    llDetectedRot(0));
            }
        }
```

■ GETTING AND SETTING LAND PROPERTIES

Scripts can get and set the same properties that residents can access through the land information dialogs, which you'll learn about here.

■ PARCEL INFORMATION

LSL scripts can get information about a parcel of land in the same region as the script. The parcel, owner, and description, as well as the parcel flags, number of prims on the parcel and who owns those prims can be retrieved, as shown in Listing 7.20.

SENDING AND
RECEIVING
MESSAGES

USER
INTERFACES

ADVANCED
DATA
MANAGEMENT

INTERACTING
WITH THE
WORLD

WORKING
AROUND
SCRIPT
DELAYS

SCRIPTING
WITH THIRD-
PARTY LSL
EDITORS

Listing 7.20: Fetching Parcel Properties

```
sayFlag(integer does, string feature)
{
    if (does)
    {
        llOwnerSay("Parcel does " + feature);
    }
    else
    {
        llOwnerSay("Parcel does not " + feature);
    }
}

string keyOrName(key id)
{
    string name = llKey2Name(id);
    if (name == "")
    {
        return (string)id;
    }
    return name;
}

getLandInfo(vector at)
{
    llOwnerSay("Details of parcel containing " + (string)at);

    // parcel details
    list details = llGetParcelDetails(at,
        [PARCEL_DETAILS_NAME, PARCEL_DETAILS_DESC,
         PARCEL_DETAILS_OWNER, PARCEL_DETAILS_GROUP,
         PARCEL_DETAILS_AREA]);

    llOwnerSay("Parcel Name: " + llList2String(details, 0));
    llOwnerSay("Parcel Description: " + llList2String(details, 1));
    llOwnerSay("Parcel Owner: " + keyOrName(llList2Key(details, 2)));
    llOwnerSay("Parcel Group: " + keyOrName(llList2Key(details, 3)));
    llOwnerSay("Parcel Area: " + (string)llList2Integer(details, 4)
        +"sq meters");

    // parcel flags
    integer pFlags = llGetParcelFlags(at);
    sayFlag(pFlags & PARCEL_FLAG_ALLOW_FLY, "allow flying");
    sayFlag(pFlags & PARCEL_FLAG_ALLOW_SCRIPTS,
        "allow outside scripts");
    sayFlag(pFlags & PARCEL_FLAG_ALLOW_LANDMARK,
        "allow landmark creation");
    sayFlag(pFlags & PARCEL_FLAG_ALLOW_TERRAFORM,
        "allow anyone to terraform");
    sayFlag(pFlags & PARCEL_FLAG_ALLOW_DAMAGE, "allow damage");
    sayFlag(pFlags & PARCEL_FLAG_ALLOW_CREATE_OBJECTS,
        "allow anyone to create objects");
    sayFlag(pFlags & PARCEL_FLAG_USE_ACCESS_GROUP,
        "restrict access to a specific group");
    sayFlag(pFlags & PARCEL_FLAG_USE_ACCESS_LIST,
        "restrict access by an access list");
```

CHAPTER 1
CHAPTER 2
CHAPTER 3
CHAPTER 4
CHAPTER 5
CHAPTER 6
CHAPTER 7

CHAPTER 8
CHAPTER 9
CHAPTER 10
CHAPTER 11
CHAPTER 12
CHAPTER 13
CHAPTER 14
APPENDICES
INDEX

```
        sayFlag(pFlags & PARCEL_FLAG_USE_BAN_LIST, "use a ban list");
        sayFlag(pFlags & PARCEL_FLAG_USE_LAND_PASS_LIST,
            "allow land passes to be purchased");
        sayFlag(pFlags & PARCEL_FLAG_LOCAL_SOUND_ONLY,
            "restrict sounds to local sounds");
        sayFlag(pFlags & PARCEL_FLAG_RESTRICT_PUSHOBJECT,
            "restrict the use of llPushObject");

        // prim counts
        llOwnerSay("Parcel currently has " +
            (string)llGetParcelPrimCount(at, PARCEL_COUNT_TOTAL, FALSE) +
            " out of a maximum of " +
            (string)llGetParcelMaxPrims(at, FALSE) + "prims");

        // prim owners
        llOwnerSay("Prim owners:");
        list owners = llGetParcelPrimOwners(at);
        integer nOwners = llGetListLength(owners) / 2;
        integer x;
        for (x = 0; x < nOwners; x++)
        {
            llOwnerSay("  " + (string)llList2Integer(owners, x * 2 + 1) +
                " prims owned by " +
                keyOrName(llList2Key(owners, x * 2)));
        }
    }
}


default
{
    touch_start(integer total_number)
    {
        getLandInfo(llGetPos());
    }
}
```

STREAMING MEDIA

Scripts can get and set many of the land properties configurable in the About Land dialog. Parcel-streaming media properties can be queried with llParcelMediaQuery and, if the script's owner owns the land, set with llParcelMediaCommandList.

Listing 7.21: Controling Streaming Media for a Parcel

```
integer dialogChannel = 99;
string pauseCommand = "pause";
string changeCommand = "change";
string playCommand = "play";

list channels = [
 "http://images.apple.com/movies/wb/oceans_13/oceans_13-tsr-h.ref.mov",
 "http://images.apple.com/movies/lionsgate/fido/fido-h.ref.mov",
 "http://images.apple.com/movies/independent/paris_je_taime/paris_je_
taime-h.ref.mov"
    ];
```

CHAPTER 7

Sending and Receiving Messages

User Interfaces

Advanced Data Management

Interacting with the World

Working Around Script Delays

Scripting with Third-Party LSL Editors

```
integer currentChannel = 0;

// Change the streaming URL and start it playing in a loop
changeChannel()
{
    currentChannel = (currentChannel + 1) % llGetListLength(channels);
    llParcelMediaCommandList([
        PARCEL_MEDIA_COMMAND_URL,
          llList2String(channels, currentChannel),
        PARCEL_MEDIA_COMMAND_LOOP
        ]);
}

// pause stream
pause()
{
    llParcelMediaCommandList([
        PARCEL_MEDIA_COMMAND_PAUSE
        ]);
}

play()
{
    llParcelMediaCommandList([
        PARCEL_MEDIA_COMMAND_LOOP
        ]);
}

default
{
    state_entry()
    {
        // Get the parcel media texture and apply it;
        list media = llParcelMediaQuery([PARCEL_MEDIA_COMMAND_TEXTURE]);
        key mediaTexture = llList2Key(media, 0);
        if (mediaTexture != NULL_KEY)
        {
            llSetTexture(mediaTexture, ALL_SIDES);
        }

        // listen for commands
        llListen(dialogChannel, "", llGetOwner(), "");
    }

    touch_start(integer num_detected)
    {
        llDialog(llDetectedKey(0), "What would you like to do?",
            [changeCommand, pauseCommand, playCommand], dialogChannel);
    }
```

CHAPTER 1
CHAPTER 2
CHAPTER 3
CHAPTER 4
CHAPTER 5
CHAPTER 6
CHAPTER 7

```
listen(integer channel, string name, key id, string msg)
{
    if (msg == changeCommand)
    {
        changeChannel();
    }
    else if (msg == pauseCommand)
    {
        pause();
    }
    else if (msg == playCommand)
    {
        play();
    }
}

}
```

WORKING AROUND SCRIPT DELAYS

Many LSL functions have a built in delay. `llInstantMessage` delays a script for 2 seconds, whereas `llRemoteDataReply` delays for 3 seconds, and calling `llEmail` will pause your script for a whole 20 seconds. These script delays are there to prevent scripts from spamming residents and to prevent load on servers, but sometimes you need a script to perform one of these function yet stay responsive to user input. The easiest way to achieve this is to have two scripts in your object: the main script, and a script dedicated to the delaying function. When the main script wants to perform the action that causes the delay, it sends a link message to the dedicated script. Listing 7.22 shows a script that waits for link messages and sends emails in response.

Listing 7.22: A Dedicated Email Sender

```
// Dedicated email sender
// This script accepts link messages to set a to email address, message
// subject and message body, and a command to send an email with those
// parameters.

// These command codes must be the same in both scripts
integer SET_TO = 1;
integer SET_SUBJECT= 2;
integer SET_BODY = 3;
integer SEND = 4;

string to = "";
string subject = "";
string body = "";
```

CHAPTER 7

SENDING AND
RECEIVING
MESSAGES

USER
INTERFACES

ADVANCED
DATA
MANAGEMENT

INTERACTING
WITH THE
WORLD

WORKING
AROUND
SCRIPT
DELAYS

SCRIPTING
WITH THIRD-
PARTY LSL
EDITORS

```
default
{
    link_message(integer sender_num, integer num, string str, key id)
    {
        if (num == SET_TO)
        {
            to = str;
        }
        else if (num == SET_SUBJECT)
        {
            subject = str;
        }
        else if (num == SET_BODY)
        {
            body = str;
        }
        else if (num == SEND)
        {
            llEmail(to, subject, body);
        }
    }
}
```

Listing 7.23 sends link messages to the script in Listing 7.22, allowing the object to send emails and yet remain responsive to residents.

Listing 7.23: Using the Email Sender from Another Script

```
// Responsive Email sender
//
// This script will use link messages to send email via another script,
// so that it can continue to annoy the owner every 5 seconds.

// These command codes must be the same in both scripts
integer SET_TO = 1;
integer SET_SUBJECT= 2;
integer SET_BODY = 3;
integer SEND = 4;

sendEmailViaLink(string address, string subject, string body)
{
    // send the link messages to set the message parameters, then send
    // the message to send the email.
    llMessageLinked(LINK_THIS, SET_TO, address, NULL_KEY);
    llMessageLinked(LINK_THIS, SET_SUBJECT, subject, NULL_KEY);
    llMessageLinked(LINK_THIS, SET_BODY, body, NULL_KEY);
    llMessageLinked(LINK_THIS, SEND, "", NULL_KEY);

}
```

```
default
{
    state_entry()
    {
        llSetTimerEvent(5.0);
    }

    timer()
    {
        llOwnerSay("I'm a responsive script");
    }

    touch_start(integer total_number)
    {
        sendEmailViaLink(
            "wednesday.grimm@gmail.com",
            "TPS Report",
            "Everything's fine; how are things with you?"
            );
    }
}
```

SCRIPTING WITH THIRD-PARTY LSL EDITORS

The built-in LSL editor in the *Second Life* client is adequate for creating and editing short scripts like the examples in this chapter, but it lacks many of the features of most source-code editors, and creating, debugging, and revising a large script or series of scripts in the built-in editor can quickly become cumbersome. Fortunately, many residents have felt this pain, and some of them have developed and made available LSL plug-ins and configurations for some of the most popular source-code editors.

The Shill project, maintained by Adam Marker at http://adammarker.org/shill/ provides up-to-date files for and information about external LSL editors.

At present, there's no way to upload scripts directly to *Second Life*, other than copying them from your editor and pasting them into the LSL editor.

CHAPTER 8

SCRIPTING THE FUN STUFF

In this chapter we'll finally get to the good stuff: things that drive, smoke, play and move. In this chapter you'll learn how to use scripting to move objects, create vehicles with different characteristics and control schemes, script a board game from beginning to end, create particle effects, and manage an object's inventory.

CONTENTS

CHAPTER 8

MOVING
OBJECTS

SCRIPTING
VEHICLES

WORKING
WITH
PARTICLES

MANAGING
YOUR OBJECT'S
INVENTORY
WITH SCRIPTS

TUTORIAL:
BUILDING A
TIC-TAC-TOE
GAME

MOVING OBJECTS

Nothing's more eye-catching than something that moves. There are two types of object movement: nonphysics movement, and physics simulation movement. Physics simulation movement looks smoother and allows for a richer variety of motion, but places more load on the region and can be harder to control than nonphysics movement.

Objects without physics enabled can be moved with llSetPosition and rotated with llSetRot. The viewer will animate these movements, but as far as the region is concerned the object instantly moves from one location to the other. llTargetOmega (Listing 8.1) can be used to make a nonphysical object spin; this effect occurs entirely on the client side, which means that residents will not necessarily see the object at the same rotation.

Listing 8.1: Target Omega

```
default
{
    state_entry()
    {
        llSetRot(llEuler2Rot(<PI/4.0, PI/4.0, 0.0>));
        llTargetOmega(<0.0, 0.0, 1.0>, PI, 1.0);
    }
}
```

Physics-enabled objects can be pushed around with llApplyImpulse and turned with llApplyRotationalImpulse, a script can move another physical object with llPushObject. Listing 8.2 demonstrates a script that enables physics, then detects when something collides with its object and uses llApplyImpulse to shove it in the opposite direction.

Listing 8.2: Kick Box

```
default
{
    state_entry()
    {
        llSetStatus(STATUS_PHYSICS, TRUE);
    }

    collision_start(integer num_detected)
    {
        // Move away from the thing colliding with this object
        vector shove = llGetPos() - llDetectedPos(0);
        shove = llVecNorm(shove);
        shove = shove * 30.0;
        llApplyImpulse(shove, FALSE);
    }
}
```

SCRIPTING VEHICLES

Vehicles are special physical objects in *Second Life*. Turning an object into vehicle gives it the ability to drive around, swim, float, or fly. The characteristics of a vehicle are controlled by a series of parameters that are set using functions that take the name of the parameter and a value. `llSetVehicleFlags` and `llRemoveVehicleFlags` enable or disable an on/off vehicle parameter. `llSetVehicleFloatParam`, `llSetVehicleVectorParam`, and `llSetVehicleRotationParam` set values. Finally, `llSetVehicleType` sets the type of the vehicle.

WARNING

> It is generally not a good idea to mix regular SL physics applied by functions like `llApplyImpulse` and `llSetBuoyancy` with vehicle physics, as this can lead to unpredictable results.

The vehicle types are things like `VEHICLE_TYPE_CAR`, `VEHICLE_TYPE_BOAT`, and `VEHICLE_TYPE_AIRPLANE`. Setting a vehicle type makes the object a vehicle, whereas setting the vehicle type to `VEHICLE_TYPE_NONE` disables vehicle behavior. The vehicle types are really just shorthand for a set of vehicle parameters usual for that type of vehicle. Listing 8.3 turns on physics for its object and turns it in to a vehicle by calling `llSetVehicleType`.

Listing 8.3: Setting the Vehicle Type

```
default
{
    state_entry()
    {
        // A boring vehicle that doesn't do anything
        llSetStatus(STATUS_PHYSICS, TRUE);
        llSetVehicleType(VEHICLE_TYPE_CAR);
    }
}
```

■ MAKING A VEHICLE GO

Vehicles have a *linear motor* that makes the vehicle move. Setting the vector parameter `VEHICLE_LINEAR_MOTOR_DIRECTION` sets the velocity that the motor wants to achieve; thus, setting the linear motor direction to `<0,0,0>` does not turn off the motor, but rather slams on the breaks since the motor is now actively working to make the vehicle move at 0 m/s.

Real-world vehicles don't instantaneously accelerate and stop, so *Second Life* vehicles simulate this behavior with the `VEHICLE_LINEAR_MOTOR_TIMESCALE` parameter. This float parameter sets the number of seconds it takes the motor to get up to full speed.

The linear motor doesn't push the vehicle forever; the effectiveness of a motor decreases over time. The float parameter `VEHICLE_LINEAR_MOTOR_DECAY_TIMESCALE` indicates the number of seconds before the motor becomes ineffective. The maximum value for the decay timescale is 120 seconds, so in the absence of new input, the linear motor will become ineffective after a maximum of 2 minutes.

The combination of these parameters means that every time the vehicle motor is set, it's like a shove on the vehicle. The motor accelerates up to the velocity the linear motor is set to, then the motor slowly decays to nothing and the vehicle will coast in whatever direction it's going and slow down due to friction. Remember that the motor does not simply add to the vehicle's current velocity—it is the velocity that vehicle wants to have, so if the vehicle is going faster than this velocity, it will slow down and if the vehicle is going in a different direction than the velocity is pointing, the vehicle will go in the new direction. Listing 8.4 creates a vehicle with a linear motor that gets up to full speed in one second and decays after three seconds. It activates the linear motor when the vehicle is touched.

Listing 8.4: Setting Vehicle Motor Parameters

```
default
{
    state_entry()
    {
        llSetStatus(STATUS_PHYSICS, TRUE);
        llSetVehicleType(VEHICLE_TYPE_CAR);

        // The vehicle will get up to full speed in 1 second
        llSetVehicleFloatParam(VEHICLE_LINEAR_MOTOR_TIMESCALE, 1.0);

        // The motor will become ineffective after 3 seconds.
        llSetVehicleFloatParam(VEHICLE_LINEAR_MOTOR_DECAY_TIMESCALE,
            3.0);
    }

    touch_start(integer num_detected)
    {
        // Turn on the motor
        // Set to motor to go 20 meters/second forward
        // Note that the motor timescale and motor decay timescale are
        // parameters of the vehicle, and have to be set only once.
        llSetVehicleVectorParam(VEHICLE_LINEAR_MOTOR_DIRECTION,
            <20.0, 0.0, 0.0>);
    }
}
```

■ TAKING CONTROL

The easiest way for residents to control a vehicle is via the usual controls they use to control their avatar. A script can intercept these key presses by calling llTakeControls. To take control, a script must first request permission from the resident by calling llRequestPermissions then waiting for the run_time_permissions event.

Most of the time, when a script requests special permissions from a resident, the resident is presented with a dialog; however, when an avatar sits on an object the object is implicitly granted permission to take control from that avatar. The script must still call llRequestPermissions then llTakeControls, but no dialog is presented to the resident.

Once a script has taken over some or all of the viewer controls, the control event will be raised whenever one of the controls is pressed. When a script takes control, it has the option to pass on control events or not. If events are passed on, the script will receive the control inputs but the resident's avatar will behave normally. If control events are not passed on, only the script will receive the controls; the avatar will not move.

The `control` event passes the key of the avatar that the control event is from, and two sets of flags: the first flag, `level`, gives all the controls that are currently pressed; the second, `edge`, gives all the controls that have changed state, going from pressed to unpressed, or vice versa. So, a key that was just pressed will have both `level` and `edge` set, a key that is held down will have `level` set but not `edge`, and a key that was just released will have `edge` set, but not `level`. To get a set of flags for all keys that were just pressed, use `(level & edge)`; to get a list of keys that were just released, use `(~level & edge)`; for all keys held down, use `(level & ~edge)`; for all inactive keys use `(~level & ~edge)`.

CHAPTER 1
CHAPTER 2
CHAPTER 3
CHAPTER 4
CHAPTER 5
CHAPTER 6
CHAPTER 7
CHAPTER 8

CHAPTER 9
CHAPTER 10
CHAPTER 11
CHAPTER 12
CHAPTER 13
CHAPTER 14
APPENDICES
INDEX

MORE INFO

USING SIT TARGETS WITH VEHICLES

A *sit target* is the location where an avatar will sit on a prim, relative to the center of the prim, and the rotation of the avatar relative to the prim. Any object can have a sit target, set with `llSitTarget`, but with the exception of chairs, sit targets are most commonly used for vehicles. Note that setting the sit target to `ZERO_VECTOR` disables the sit target, so to set a sit target close to the object's center, use a very small vector such as `<0.0, 0.0, 0.1>`.

When an avatar chooses to sit on a linked object, the avatar will sit on the prim that has a sit target with the lowest link number that is unoccupied. If there are no unoccupied prims that have a sit target, the avatar will choose an unoccupied prim with the lowest link number.

Thus, it is useful to set the sit target for the driver of a vehicle in the root prim (link number 0), and then set any passenger-seat sit targets in linked prims. To limit the number of passengers, set a sit target in a high-numbered prim, and use `llUnSit` to eject any avatars that sit on this sit target.

The text for the sit option that appears in the viewer can be changed to "drive" or "fly" or "velocitize" or whatever you like with `llSetSitText`.

Listing 8.5 creates a sliding vehicle that goes in the direction of the driver's key presses. The script has two states; in the default state it is just a regular object that doesn't do anything interesting, but when an avatar sits on the object it goes to the vehicle state. In the vehicle state, it has vehicle parameters set and activates the linear motor based on the user's inputs. The friction and deflection parameters are set so that the vehicle has no preference for moving in a particular direction and has a strong tendency to not rotate in any direction.

Listing 8.5: Sliding Car

```
// set the vehicle parameters
setupVehicle()
{
    llSetStatus(STATUS_PHYSICS, TRUE);
    llSetVehicleType(VEHICLE_TYPE_CAR);

    // The vehicle will get up to full speed in 1 second
    llSetVehicleFloatParam(VEHICLE_LINEAR_MOTOR_TIMESCALE, 1.0);

    // The motor will become ineffective after 3 seconds.
    llSetVehicleFloatParam(VEHICLE_LINEAR_MOTOR_DECAY_TIMESCALE, 3.0);
```

```
    // Turn off angular and linear deflection
    llSetVehicleFloatParam(VEHICLE_ANGULAR_DEFLECTION_EFFICIENCY, 0.0);
    llSetVehicleFloatParam(VEHICLE_LINEAR_DEFLECTION_EFFICIENCY, 0.0);

    // Set low linear friction, equal in all directions
    llSetVehicleFloatParam(VEHICLE_LINEAR_FRICTION_TIMESCALE, 5000.0);

    // Set very high angular friction, this vehicle does not
    // like to turn
    llSetVehicleFloatParam(VEHICLE_ANGULAR_FRICTION_TIMESCALE, 0.1);
}

// stop this object from being a vehicle
noVehicle()
{
    // Turn off physics and vehicle params
    llSetVehicleType(VEHICLE_TYPE_NONE);
    llSetStatus(STATUS_PHYSICS, FALSE);
}

// give this prim a wedge shape and set it to about avatar size
setupObject()
{
    llSetPrimitiveParams([
    PRIM_TYPE,
        PRIM_TYPE_BOX,
        PRIM_HOLE_DEFAULT,
        <0.75, 1.0, 0.0>,
        0.0,
        <0.0, 0.0, 0.0>,
        <1.0, 1.0, 0.0>,
        <0.0, 0.0, 0.0>,
    PRIM_SIZE,
        <4.0, 1.5, 0.5>
        ]);
}

// default state, not a vehicle
default
{
    state_entry()
    {
        noVehicle();
        setupObject();

        // Set the location avatars will sit
        llSitTarget(<-1.0, 0.0, 0.5>, ZERO_ROTATION);
    }

    changed(integer change)
    {
        if (change & CHANGED_LINK)
        {
            if (llAvatarOnSitTarget() != NULL_KEY)
            {
```

```
                // someone is sitting on the object; request permission
                // to take controls
                llRequestPermissions(
                    llAvatarOnSitTarget(),
                    PERMISSION_TAKE_CONTROLS);
            }
        }
    }

    run_time_permissions(integer perm)
    {
        // the run time permissions have changed; if script can
        // take controls, do that and go to the vehicle state
        if (perm & PERMISSION_TAKE_CONTROLS)
        {
            llTakeControls(
                CONTROL_FWD | CONTROL_BACK |
                CONTROL_LEFT | CONTROL_RIGHT |
                CONTROL_ROT_LEFT |CONTROL_ROT_RIGHT,
                TRUE, FALSE);
            state vehicle;
        }
    }
}

state vehicle
{
    state_entry()
    {
        setupVehicle();
    }

    changed(integer change)
    {
        // If the avatar sitting on this object gets up, stop
        // being a vehicle
        if (change & CHANGED_LINK)
        {
            if (llAvatarOnSitTarget() == NULL_KEY)
            {
                // no one is sitting on the object; stop
                // being a vehicle
                llReleaseControls();
                state default;
            }
        }
    }

    control(key from, integer level, integer edge)
    {
        integer pressed = (level & edge);
        vector velocity = ZERO_VECTOR;
        float speed = 15.0;

        if (pressed & CONTROL_FWD)
        {
            velocity = <1.0, 0.0, 0.0>;
        }
```

```
        else if (pressed & CONTROL_BACK)
        {
            velocity = <-1.0, 0.0, 0.0>;
        }
        else if (pressed & CONTROL_LEFT ||
                pressed & CONTROL_ROT_LEFT)
        {
            velocity = <0.0, 1.0, 0.0>;
        }
        else if (pressed & CONTROL_RIGHT ||
                pressed & CONTROL_ROT_RIGHT)
        {
            velocity = <0.0, -1.0, 0.0>;
        }
        if (velocity != ZERO_VECTOR)
        {
            velocity = velocity * speed;
            llSetVehicleVectorParam(
                VEHICLE_LINEAR_MOTOR_DIRECTION,
                velocity);
        }
    }
}
```

MORE INFO

UNDERSTANDING VEHICLE DIRECTIONS

The direction a vehicle moves is linked to the rotation of the object. When the linear motor of a vehicle moves it forward, the vehicle moves in the direction of the positive x-axis of the root prim of the object. Thus the x-axis is called the *forward axis* for the vehicle. The y-axis is the left axis, and movement along this axis is called *slewing* or *sliding*. The z-axis is the upward axis, and movement along it is called *lift*. These axes are important because there are parameters that apply specifically to these directions; for example, the *vertical attractor*, a vehicle parameter that tries to keep the object's z-axis pointing up and doesn't have any counterpart for the x- or y-axes.

Rotations about each of the different axes have special names too: rotation about the x-axis is *roll*, rotation about the y-axis is *pitch*, and rotation about the z-axis is *yaw*. Rotations for vehicles follow the right-hand rule: to figure out which direction is positive rotation for an axis, point the thumb of your right hand in the positive direction of that axis and curl your fingers. The direction your fingers curl is the direction of positive rotation.

Once you've constructed the model for your vehicle, you may find that the root prim doesn't align with the axes you want to be forward and up. One option to fix this is to create a prim, make it transparent, align it with the axes you want for the vehicle, and link it to be the new root prim. A second option is to use the parameter **VEHICLE_REFERENCE_FRAME**. This parameter takes a rotation and rotates the vehicles axes. Suppose the root prim of a vehicle were a cone, and you wanted the point of the cone to be the forward axis of the vehicle. Without modification, the forward, x-axis points out of the side of the cone and the z-axis points through the tip. Calling

```
rotation Z_To_X = llEuler2Rot(<0.0, -1.0 * PI_BY_TWO, 0.0>);

llSetVehicleRotationParam(VEHICLE_REFERENCE_FRAME, Z_To_X);
```

will rotate the vehicle's frame of reference so that the x-axis points through the tip of the cone.

■ MAKING A VEHICLE TURN

CHAPTER 1
CHAPTER 2
CHAPTER 3
CHAPTER 4
CHAPTER 5
CHAPTER 6
CHAPTER 7
CHAPTER 8

CHAPTER 9
CHAPTER 10
CHAPTER 11
CHAPTER 12
CHAPTER 13
CHAPTER 14
APPENDICES
INDEX

Similar to the linear motor, vehicles have an *angular motor*. The angular motor tries to make the vehicle have the specified angular velocity, which is to say, be spinning at a specified number of radians per second around each axis. Like the linear motor, the angular motor has a timescale that controls how long it takes the motor to get up to full speed, and a decay timescale that controls how long it takes for the angular motor to shut off.

To add an angular motor, and thus rotation, to the car in the previous example, change the vehicle setup function to specify angular motor parameters, and change the friction parameters so that the vehicle likes to move only forward and backward, and likes to rotate only about the z-axis, as in Listing 8.6:

Listing 8.6: Vehicle Setup with Angular Motor Parameters

```
// set the vehicle parameters
setupVehicle()
{
    llSetStatus(STATUS_PHYSICS, TRUE);
    llSetVehicleType(VEHICLE_TYPE_CAR);

    // The vehicle will get up to full speed in 1 second
    llSetVehicleFloatParam(VEHICLE_LINEAR_MOTOR_TIMESCALE, 1.0);

    // The motor will become ineffective after 3 seconds.
    llSetVehicleFloatParam(VEHICLE_LINEAR_MOTOR_DECAY_TIMESCALE, 3.0);

    // The angular motor will quickly get up to speed, and
    // quickly decay
    llSetVehicleFloatParam(VEHICLE_ANGULAR_MOTOR_TIMESCALE, 0.1);
    llSetVehicleFloatParam(VEHICLE_ANGULAR_MOTOR_DECAY_TIMESCALE, 0.5);

    // Turn off angular and linear deflection
    llSetVehicleFloatParam(VEHICLE_ANGULAR_DEFLECTION_EFFICIENCY, 0.0);
    llSetVehicleFloatParam(VEHICLE_LINEAR_DEFLECTION_EFFICIENCY, 0.0);

    // Set high linear friction in all directions except forward
    llSetVehicleVectorParam(VEHICLE_LINEAR_FRICTION_TIMESCALE,
        <5000.0, 1.0, 1.0>);

    // Set very high angular friction around all axes except z
    llSetVehicleVectorParam(VEHICLE_ANGULAR_FRICTION_TIMESCALE,
        <0.1, 0.1, 5000.0>);
}
```

Note that in the previous example VEHICLE_LINEAR_FRICTION_TIMESCALE was set with llSetVehicleFloatParam, and in this example it is set with llSetVehicleVectorParam. A number of the vehicle parameters can be set this way, where calling llSetVehicleFloatParam(param, X) is equivalent to calling llSetVehicleVectorParam(param, <X, X, X>).

To actually turn the car, change the control event in the vehicle state so that the linear motor is turned on with the resident presses the Rotate Left or Rotate Right key, as shown in listing 8.7.

CHAPTER 8

MOVING
OBJECTS

SCRIPTING
VEHICLES

WORKING
WITH
PARTICLES

MANAGING
YOUR OBJECT'S
INVENTORY
WITH SCRIPTS

TUTORIAL:
BUILDING A
TIC-TAC-TOE
GAME

Listing 8.7: Vehicle Control Event with the Angular Motor

```
control(key from, integer level, integer edge)
    {
        integer pressed = (level & edge);
        vector velocity = ZERO_VECTOR;
        float speed = 15.0;

        vector turn = ZERO_VECTOR;
        float turnSpeed = PI;

        if (pressed & CONTROL_FWD)
        {
            velocity = <1.0, 0.0, 0.0>;
        }
        else if (pressed & CONTROL_BACK)
        {
            velocity = <-1.0, 0.0, 0.0>;
        }
        else if (pressed & CONTROL_ROT_LEFT)
        {
            turn = <0.0, 0.0, 1.0>;
        }
        else if (pressed & CONTROL_ROT_RIGHT)
        {
            turn = <0.0, 0.0, -1.0>;
        }
        if (velocity != ZERO_VECTOR)
        {
            velocity = velocity * speed;
            llSetVehicleVectorParam(VEHICLE_LINEAR_MOTOR_DIRECTION,
                velocity);
        }

        if (turn != ZERO_VECTOR)
        {
            turn = turn * turnSpeed;
            llSetVehicleVectorParam(VEHICLE_ANGULAR_MOTOR_DIRECTION,
                turn);
        }
    }
```

■ USING MOUSELOOK STEERING

It is fairly difficult to control a vehicle that explicitly sets the angular motor to a constant spin. Fortunately, there are vehicle parameters that allow a vehicle to be steered by mouselook to point the vehicle in the direction the avatar is looking. Setting the flag VEHICLE_FLAG_MOUSELOOK_STEER turns mouselook steering on. When mouselook steering is on, the angular motor is always on, trying to point the vehicle in the direction the avatar is looking, so the VEHICLE_ANGULAR_MOTOR_DECAY_ TIMESCALE setting has no effect. The VEHICLE_ANGULAR_MOTOR_TIMESCALE still has its usual effect, controlling the responsiveness of the angular motor.

Under mouselook steering, the meaning of the VEHICLE_ANGULAR_MOTOR_DIRECTION setting changes. It now specifies how quickly the vehicle will spin around each axis to reach the direction the avatar is looking. The farther away the x-axis of the vehicle is from the desired direction, the faster the vehicle will turn. A vehicle can be made to not turn in a given direction in response to mouselook by setting that component of its angular motor to 0. Thus a vehicle with an angular motor direction of <0.0, 1.0, 0.0> will rotate about its y-axis only in response to the avatar looking up and down, and will ignore left and right glances. On the other hand, a vehicle with mouselook steering enabled and an angular motor set to <0.0, 2.0, 1.0> will be twice as responsive to left-right steering as to up-down steering.

Since the avatar is sitting on the vehicle, when the vehicle rotates, the avatar's view will rotate too, so the angular motor will never align the vehicle's axes with the way the avatar is looking, and the vehicle will keep spinning unless the avatar looks back toward the center of the vehicle. Setting the flag VEHICLE_FLAG_CAMERA_DECOUPLED changes this behavior so that rotating the vehicle does not rotate the avatar's view, and the vehicle will come to be pointed at the thing the avatar is looking at rather than spinning in the direction the avatar is looking.

NOTE

> Scripts can use the function llForceMouselook to make a resident's viewer go into mouselook when the resident's avatar sits on the object. Unfortunately, the resident can leave mouselook at anytime.

To add mouselook steering to the car, remove the rotational controls from the vehicle's control event and change the vehicle setup function, reducing the timescale of the angular motor slightly, adding the mouselook flags, and setting the angular motor, as in Listing 8.8.

Listing 8.8: Steering with Mouselook

```
// set the vehicle parameters
setupVehicle()
{
    llSetStatus(STATUS_PHYSICS, TRUE);
    llSetVehicleType(VEHICLE_TYPE_CAR);

    // The vehicle will get up to full speed in 1 second
    llSetVehicleFloatParam(VEHICLE_LINEAR_MOTOR_TIMESCALE, 1.0);

    // The motor will become ineffective after 3 seconds.
    llSetVehicleFloatParam(VEHICLE_LINEAR_MOTOR_DECAY_TIMESCALE, 3.0);

    // The angular motor will quickly get up to speed
    llSetVehicleFloatParam(VEHICLE_ANGULAR_MOTOR_TIMESCALE, 0.75);

    // Turn off angular and linear deflection
    llSetVehicleFloatParam(VEHICLE_ANGULAR_DEFLECTION_EFFICIENCY, 0.0);
    llSetVehicleFloatParam(VEHICLE_LINEAR_DEFLECTION_EFFICIENCY, 0.0);

    // Set high linear friction in all directions except forward
    llSetVehicleVectorParam(VEHICLE_LINEAR_FRICTION_TIMESCALE,
        <5000.0, 1.0, 1.0>);

    // Set very high angular friction around all axes except z
    llSetVehicleVectorParam(VEHICLE_ANGULAR_FRICTION_TIMESCALE,
        <0.1, 0.1, 5000.0>);

    // Turn on mouselook steering and decouple the camera
    llSetVehicleFlags(VEHICLE_FLAG_MOUSELOOK_STEER |
        VEHICLE_FLAG_CAMERA_DECOUPLED);
```

CHAPTER 1
CHAPTER 2
CHAPTER 3
CHAPTER 4
CHAPTER 5
CHAPTER 6
CHAPTER 7
CHAPTER 8

CHAPTER 9
CHAPTER 10
CHAPTER 11
CHAPTER 12
CHAPTER 13
CHAPTER 14
APPENDICES
INDEX

CHAPTER 8

MOVING
OBJECTS

SCRIPTING
VEHICLES

WORKING
WITH
PARTICLES

MANAGING
YOUR OBJECT'S
INVENTORY
WITH SCRIPTS

TUTORIAL:
BUILDING A
TIC-TAC-TOE
GAME

```
    // Set the angular motor for mouselook steering, ignore
    // y-axis rotation
    llSetVehicleVectorParam(VEHICLE_ANGULAR_MOTOR_DIRECTION,
        <0.0, 0.0, 5.0>);
}
```

■ MAKING IT FUN

The vehicles described so far are suitable for going to the virtual grocery store or taking the virtual kids to virtual soccer. To make vehicles that skid, slide, bank, and roll, we need some more features.

■ FRICTION AND DEFLECTION

In addition to the angular and linear motors, some other parameters affect how a vehicle moves and turns.

Similar to the angular and linear motors that make a vehicle move, there are parameters for *angular and linear friction* that slow a vehicle down. In the previous car example, the VEHICLE_ LINEAR_FRICTION_TIMESCALE is set so that the vehicle has very high friction moving side to side and up and down, but easily moves back and forth. The VEHICLE_ANGULAR_FRICTION_TIMESCALE is set so that the vehicle easily turns around the z-axis (left to right) but does not like to rotate around the x and y axes.

Some real-world vehicles like to go in the direction they're pointing. Consider a car with its wheels pointed forward. Pushing on the back-right corner of the car will make it go forward even though the force being applied to the car is forward and to the left. This tendency to convert motion in a given direction into motion along a preferred axis of motion is known as *linear deflection*. The parameters VEHICLE_LINEAR_DEFLECTION_TIMESCALE and VEHICLE_LINEAR_ DEFLECTION_EFFICIENCY control linear deflection. Vehicles such as cars and boats have a fairly strong linear deflection, whereas hovercraft and spaceships have no linear deflection.

Other vehicles like to point in the direction they're going. A vehicle like an airplane, when moving, will tend to rotate until its nose is pointing in the direction of motion. This tendency to convert motion into rotation is known as *angular deflection*. Angular deflection is controlled by the parameters VEHICLE_ANGULAR_DEFLECTION_TIMESCALE and VEHICLE_ANGULAR_DEFLECTION_ EFFICIENCY.

TIP

When using deflection effects, it is important to not set the vehicle's friction in the "wrong" direction too high, or the vehicle will never be able to start moving or rotating in that direction, and the vehicle must be moving in the "wrong" direction to convert that motion into deflection in the "right" direction.

CHAPTER 1
CHAPTER 2
CHAPTER 3
CHAPTER 4
CHAPTER 5
CHAPTER 6
CHAPTER 7
CHAPTER 8

CHAPTER 9
CHAPTER 10
CHAPTER 11
CHAPTER 12
CHAPTER 13
CHAPTER 14
APPENDICES
INDEX

MORE INFO

UNDERSTANDING EFFICIENCIES AND TIMESCALES

Vehicle parameters that are *efficiencies* have a range between 0.0 (not efficient) and 1.0 (most efficient). They can be thought of as how well the vehicle does something. *Timescale* parameters are in seconds, and dictate how long the vehicle takes to do something. Setting a timescale to a very large value (for example, 10,000 seconds) often disables the behavior entirely.

For example, for a hovering vehicle, a low value for `VEHICLE_HOVER_EFFICIENCY` will mean that the vehicle is not very good at staying at its hover height; it will bounce around above and below that height. A high efficiency will mean the vehicle will stay close to hovering height. The `VEHICLE_HOVER_TIMESCALE` parameter sets how long the vehicle takes to get to the defined height.

High efficiencies and small timescales lead to quick movement while low efficiencies and big timescales lead to slower movement.

■ THE VERTICAL ATTRACTOR AND BANKING

The vertical attractor is a vehicle parameter that is used to keep the vehicle's z-axis pointing up. This is useful to prevent cars and boats from flipping over, and to prevent vehicles that are taller than they are wide from toppling onto their side. The vertical attractor parameters are `VEHICLE_VERTICAL_ATTRACTION_TIMESCALE` and `VEHICLE_VERTICAL_ATTRACTION_EFFICENCY`.

If the vertical attractor is active, then vehicle banking can be activated. Vehicles like motorcycles and airplanes don't turn by applying a rotation about the z-axis; they rotate about the x-axis (called *rolling*) and the physical properties of the vehicle cause it to turn. This turning behavior, called *banking*, can be simulated in *SL* vehicles by setting the `VEHICLE_BANKING_EFFICIENCY` and `VEHICLE_BANKING_TIMESCALE` float parameters.

Real-world banking vehicles usually can bank only if they are moving forward; however, in a virtual vehicle it is often desirable to "fake" a bit of banking, making the vehicle turn when standing still or moving slowly, to make it easier and more fun to control. The `VEHICLE_BANKING_MIX` parameter allows this. A banking mix of 0.0 is completely fake, meaning the vehicle will rotate only depending on its roll; a mix of 1.0 is completely realistic, so the vehicle turns proportionally to the roll and forward motion.

Vehicles that are steered by banking can be controlled by mouselook by setting the flag `VEHICLE_FLAG_MOUSELOOK_BANK`. The behavior of this flag is similar to `VEHICLE_FLAG_MOUSELOOK_STEER`, but instead of translating left-right motions of the avatar's view to rotation about the y-axis, it translates these motions into roll about the x-axis. Listing 8.9 creates a vehicle that moves a little like a motorcycle and uses banking to turn.

Listing 8.9: Crazy Motorcycle

```
// set the vehicle parameters
setupVehicle()
{
    llSetStatus(STATUS_PHYSICS, TRUE);
    llSetVehicleType(VEHICLE_TYPE_CAR);

    // The vehicle will get up to full speed in 1 second
    // and decay after 4
    llSetVehicleFloatParam(VEHICLE_LINEAR_MOTOR_TIMESCALE, 1.0);
    llSetVehicleFloatParam(VEHICLE_LINEAR_MOTOR_DECAY_TIMESCALE, 4.0);
```

CHAPTER 8

MOVING
OBJECTS

SCRIPTING
VEHICLES

WORKING
WITH
PARTICLES

MANAGING
YOUR OBJECT'S
INVENTORY
WITH SCRIPTS

TUTORIAL:
BUILDING A
TIC-TAC-TOE
GAME

```
        // The angular motor will start almost instantly and decay
        // quickly
        llSetVehicleFloatParam(VEHICLE_ANGULAR_MOTOR_TIMESCALE, 0.1);
        llSetVehicleFloatParam(VEHICLE_ANGULAR_MOTOR_DECAY_TIMESCALE,
            0.75);

        // no angular deflection, some linear deflection
        llSetVehicleFloatParam(VEHICLE_ANGULAR_DEFLECTION_EFFICIENCY, 0.0);
        llSetVehicleFloatParam(VEHICLE_LINEAR_DEFLECTION_EFFICIENCY, 0.5);

        // very little friction in x, lots in y and z
        llSetVehicleVectorParam(VEHICLE_LINEAR_FRICTION_TIMESCALE,
            <10.0, 2.0, 1.0>);

        // moderate angular friction
        llSetVehicleFloatParam(VEHICLE_ANGULAR_FRICTION_TIMESCALE, 4.0);

        // very strong quick vertical attractor
        llSetVehicleFloatParam(
            VEHICLE_VERTICAL_ATTRACTION_EFFICIENCY, 0.95);
        llSetVehicleFloatParam(
            VEHICLE_VERTICAL_ATTRACTION_TIMESCALE, 0.75);

        // strong banking
        llSetVehicleFloatParam(VEHICLE_BANKING_TIMESCALE, 1.0);
        llSetVehicleFloatParam(VEHICLE_BANKING_EFFICIENCY, 0.5);
        llSetVehicleFloatParam(VEHICLE_BANKING_MIX, 0.5);
}

// stop this object from being a vehicle
noVehicle()
{
    // Turn off physics and vehicle params
    llSetVehicleType(VEHICLE_TYPE_NONE);
    llSetStatus(STATUS_PHYSICS, FALSE);
    llSetRot(ZERO_ROTATION);
}

// give this prim an upside-down wedge shape
// and set it to about avatar size
setupObject()
{
    llSetPrimitiveParams([
    PRIM_TYPE,
        PRIM_TYPE_BOX,
        PRIM_HOLE_DEFAULT,
        <0.0, 1.0, 0.0>,
        0.0,
        <0.0, 0.0, 0.0>,
        <1.25, 2.0, 0.0>,
        <0.0, 0.0, 0.0>,
    PRIM_SIZE,
        <2.5, 0.5, 1>
        ]);
}
```

```
// default state, not a vehicle
default
{
    state_entry()
    {
        noVehicle();
        setupObject();

        // Set the location avatars will sit
        llSitTarget(<-1.0, 0.0, 0.5>, ZERO_ROTATION);

        // set the camera position and orientation
        llSetCameraEyeOffset(<-4.5, 0.0, 1.75>);
        llSetCameraAtOffset(<1.0, 0.0, 1.75>);

    }

    changed(integer change)
    {
        if (change & CHANGED_LINK)
        {
            if (llAvatarOnSitTarget() != NULL_KEY)
            {
                // someone is sitting on the object, request permission
                // to take controls
                llRequestPermissions(
                    llAvatarOnSitTarget(),
                    PERMISSION_TAKE_CONTROLS);
            }
        }
    }

    run_time_permissions(integer perm)
    {
        // the run time permissions have changed; if script can
        // take controls, do that and go to the vehicle state
        if (perm & PERMISSION_TAKE_CONTROLS)
        {
            llTakeControls(
                CONTROL_FWD | CONTROL_BACK |
                CONTROL_ROT_LEFT | CONTROL_ROT_RIGHT,
                TRUE, FALSE);
            state vehicle;
        }
    }
}

state vehicle
{
    state_entry()
    {
        setupVehicle();
    }
```

CHAPTER 8

MOVING
OBJECTS

SCRIPTING
VEHICLES

WORKING
WITH
PARTICLES

MANAGING
YOUR OBJECT'S
INVENTORY
WITH SCRIPTS

TUTORIAL:
BUILDING A
TIC-TAC-TOE
GAME

```
changed(integer change)
{
    // If the avatar sitting on this object gets up, stop
    // being a vehicle
    if (change & CHANGED_LINK)
    {
        if (llAvatarOnSitTarget() == NULL_KEY)
        {
            // no one is sitting on the object, stop
            // being a vehicle
            llReleaseControls();
            state default;
        }
    }
}

control(key from, integer level, integer edge)
{
    vector velocity = ZERO_VECTOR;
    float speed = 20.0;

    vector turn = ZERO_VECTOR;
    float turnSpeed = TWO_PI;

    if (level & CONTROL_FWD)
    {
        velocity = <1.0, 0.0, 0.0>;
    }
    else if (level & CONTROL_BACK)
    {
        velocity = <-0.3, 0.0, 0.0>;
    }
    if (velocity != ZERO_VECTOR)
    {
        velocity = velocity * speed;
        llSetVehicleVectorParam(
                VEHICLE_LINEAR_MOTOR_DIRECTION, velocity);
    }

    // to turn, at a lot of roll and a little rotation
    if (level & CONTROL_ROT_LEFT)
    {
        turn = <-1.0, 0.0, 0.25>;
    }
    else if (level & CONTROL_ROT_RIGHT)
    {
        turn = <1.0, 0.0, -0.25>;
    }
    if (turn != ZERO_VECTOR)
    {
        turn = turn * turnSpeed;
        llSetVehicleVectorParam(
            VEHICLE_ANGULAR_MOTOR_DIRECTION, turn);
    }
}
}
```

CHAPTER 1
CHAPTER 2
CHAPTER 3
CHAPTER 4
CHAPTER 5
CHAPTER 6
CHAPTER 7
CHAPTER 8

CHAPTER 9
CHAPTER 10
CHAPTER 11
CHAPTER 12
CHAPTER 13
CHAPTER 14
APPENDICES
INDEX

WORKING WITH PARTICLES

Particles are a client-side effect that allows an object to emit a lot of moving copies of an image. The images can change speed, size, and color, they can flow toward a target or spray out in all directions. Because particles are a client-side effect, they do not place a load on the region, but they can be hard on the viewer. Residents can limit the number of particles their viewer renders or disable particles entirely.

When an object has particles enabled, it is known as a *particle emitter*. Particles can be used to simulate explosions, fireworks, smoke, weather, and other effects. The image for the particles can be any texture, including the streaming media texture for the land parcel the emitter is on, allowing for almost limitless effects.

Residents will see the particles from a particle emitter if they can see the emitter. This means that if the emitter is a very small object and is clipped by the viewer, the particles will not be seen either, no matter how big the particles are.

Particles are enabled by calling the function `llParticleSystem`, which takes a list of parameters that define the particle system. Particles can be turned off by calling `llParticleSystem` with the empty list.

■ PARTICLE PATTERNS

Particles are emitted in one of four patterns, selected with the `PSYS_SRC_PATTERN` flag. The simplest pattern is `PSYS_SRC_PATTERN_DROP`. This creates particles at the center of the emitter with no initial velocity. With no other parameters, the particles do not move. An arbitrary acceleration can be applied to the particles with the `PSYS_SRC_ACCEL` flag, which takes a vector: the acceleration to apply (Listing 8.10).

Listing 8.10: Drop Particle Pattern

```
default
{
    state_entry()
    {
        // Create particles that fall at 9.8 meters per second, using
        // default values for particle texture, size and other values
        llParticleSystem([
            PSYS_SRC_PATTERN, PSYS_SRC_PATTERN_DROP,
            PSYS_SRC_ACCEL, <0.0, 0.0, -9.8>
            ]);
    }
}
```

`PSYS_SRC_PATTERN_ANGLE` will emit particles in a flat disc, in the emitter's z-y plane (a vertical circle, with the x-axis pointing out of the center). Particles can be emitted in a "pie slice" of the disc using the `PSYS_SRC_ANGLE_BEGIN` and `PSYS_SRC_ANGLE_END` parameters. Similar to sensors, the

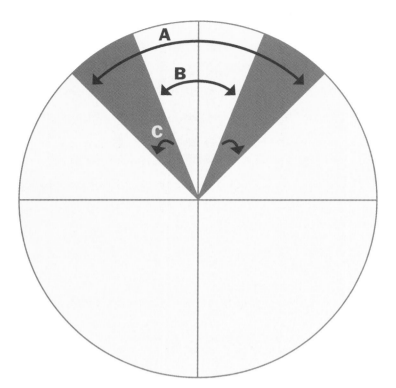

values for these parameters are half angles, and start from the positive z-axis. PSYS_SRC_ANGLE_END defines the slice where particles will be emitted, PSYS_SRC_ANGLE_START defines a slice out of that where particles will not be emitted. An end angle of pi radians, and a start angle of 0 will produce a complete disc (Figure 8.1). Listing 8.11 provides the details.

Figure 8.1: Particle angle parameter start and end

A: PSYS_SRC_ANGLE_END; B: PSYS_SRC_ANGLE_START; C: PARTICLES

Listing 8.11: Particle Angle Pattern

```
default
{
    state_entry()
    {
        // Create 2 wedges of particles using the angle pattern; use
        // more than the default number of particles with
        // PSYS_SRC_BURST_PART_COUNT to make the wedges more obvious
        llParticleSystem([
            PSYS_SRC_PATTERN, PSYS_SRC_PATTERN_ANGLE,
            PSYS_SRC_ANGLE_BEGIN, PI / 8.0,
            PSYS_SRC_ANGLE_END, PI / 4.0,
            PSYS_SRC_BURST_PART_COUNT, 500
            ]);
    }
}
```

PSYS_SRC_PATTERN_ANGLE_CONE is similar to PSYS_SRC_PATTERN_ANGLE, but in three dimensions, as if the angle pattern were spun around the z-axis. The particles are confined to a shape similar to a dimpled sphere, with the start dimple representing the end angle and the end dimple representing the start angle (weirdly enough). The PSYS_SRC_PATTERN_EXPLODE will fire out particles in all directions from the emitter.

BURST PARAMETERS

The PSYS_SRC_PATTERN_ANGLE, PSYS_SRC_PATTERN_ANGLE_CONE, and PSYS_SRC_PATTERN_EXPLODE particle patterns are modified by various "burst" parameters (Listing 8.12). PSYS_SRC_BURST_RATE specifies how often, in seconds, the emitter should emit a "puff" of particles; a burst rate of 0.0 emits particles constantly as fast as the viewer can render them. PSYS_SRC_BURST_PART_COUNT controls how many particles are emitted each burst. PSYS_SRC_BURST_SPEED_MIN and PSYS_SRC_BURST_SPEED_MAX give the range of initial speeds for particles in meters per second. Each particle is given an initial random speed in this range. PSYS_BURST_RADIUS specifies the distance from the center of the emitter at which particles will be created. Listing 8.12 creates a particle system that emits a burst of 50 particles every 3 seconds.

Listing 8.12: Using Particle Burst Parameters

```
default
{
    state_entry()
    {
        // Create a series of concentric expanding rings of particles
        llParticleSystem([
            PSYS_SRC_PATTERN, PSYS_SRC_PATTERN_ANGLE,

            // Emit particles in a complete circle
            PSYS_SRC_ANGLE_BEGIN, 0.0,
            PSYS_SRC_ANGLE_END, PI,

            // Make all the particles spread out at the same speed
            PSYS_SRC_BURST_SPEED_MIN, 0.3,
            PSYS_SRC_BURST_SPEED_MAX, 0.3,

            // Start the ring 1 meter from the emitter
            PSYS_SRC_BURST_RADIUS, 1.0,

            // Emit 50 particles every 3 seconds
            PSYS_SRC_BURST_PART_COUNT, 50,
            PSYS_SRC_BURST_RATE, 3.0
            ]);
    }
}
```

PARTICLE APPEARANCE

Particles have an initial color, size, and transparency value. Optionally, the particles can fade to different final values over the life of the individual particles. The options to have particles interpolate to different appearance values are set with flags in the PSYS_PART_FLAGS mask.

The initial color of particles is set with the PSYS_PART_START_COLOR setting; if the flag PSYS_PART_INTERP_COLOR_MASK flag is used then the final color is set with PSYS_PART_END_COLOR. Colors are vectors in the usual LSL fashion.

The initial transparency of particles is set with PSYS_PART_START_ALPHA. The final transparency value is set with PSYS_PART_END_ALPHA. Alpha values are floats from 0.0 to 1.0; 0.0 is fully transparent and 1.0 is fully opaque. Alpha fading is also enabled with the PSYS_PART_INTERP_COLOR_MASK. If you want to use color changing, but not alpha changing, or vice versa, specify the

CHAPTER 1
CHAPTER 2
CHAPTER 3
CHAPTER 4
CHAPTER 5
CHAPTER 6
CHAPTER 7
CHAPTER 8

CHAPTER 9
CHAPTER 10
CHAPTER 11
CHAPTER 12
CHAPTER 13
CHAPTER 14
APPENDICES
INDEX

CHAPTER 8

MOVING
OBJECTS

SCRIPTING
VEHICLES

WORKING
WITH
PARTICLES

MANAGING
YOUR OBJECT'S
INVENTORY
WITH SCRIPTS

TUTORIAL:
BUILDING A
TIC-TAC-TOE
GAME

same start and end values for the element you do not wish to change. Particles can only fade out (go from a higher alpha value to a lower one), not fade in. If the start alpha value is lower than the end alpha value, the particle will start at the end alpha value and not change.

The initial size of particles is set with PSYS_START_SCALE. If the PSYS_START_INERP_SCALE is set, PSYS_END_SCALE gives the final size of the particles. The size values are vectors, but since particles are two-dimensional images, the z-value of the vector is ignored.

Any texture can be used as a particle. The texture is set with PSYS_SRC_TEXTURE and the texture value is a string; it can be the name of a texture in the object's inventory or the key for a texture. Listing 8.13 demonstrates the color, alpha, size, scale, and texture particle parameters.

Listing 8.13: Using Particle Appearance Parameters

```
default
{
    state_entry()
    {
        // Create a fountain of particles that change color,
        // fade out, and get bigger.
        llParticleSystem( [
            // Create a narrow code of particles that shoot up
            // from the emitter
            PSYS_SRC_PATTERN, PSYS_SRC_PATTERN_ANGLE_CONE,
            PSYS_SRC_ANGLE_END, PI / 8.0,
            PSYS_SRC_BURST_SPEED_MIN, 2.0,
            PSYS_SRC_BURST_SPEED_MAX, 4.0,

            // Apply a downward acceleration to the particles so
            // they come back down again
            PSYS_SRC_ACCEL, <0.0, 0.0, -2.0>,

            // Turn on color and size interpolation
            PSYS_PART_FLAGS,
                PSYS_PART_INTERP_COLOR_MASK |
                PSYS_PART_INTERP_SCALE_MASK,

            // Set the start color to white and the end color to blue
            PSYS_PART_START_COLOR, <1.0, 1.0, 1.0>,
            PSYS_PART_END_COLOR, <0.0, 0.0, 1.0>,

            // Start at full opacity, fade to full transparency
            PSYS_PART_START_ALPHA, 1.0,
            PSYS_PART_END_ALPHA, 0.0,

            // Start out small, grow
            PSYS_PART_START_SCALE, <0.25, 0.25, 0.0>,
            PSYS_PART_END_SCALE, <2.0, 2.0, 0.0>,

            // Use the UUID of one of the Library textures,
            // Water Particle-Mist
            PSYS_SRC_TEXTURE, "dcab6cc4-172f-e30d-b1d0-f558446f20d4"
            ]);
    }
}
```

CHAPTER 1
CHAPTER 2
CHAPTER 3
CHAPTER 4
CHAPTER 5
CHAPTER 6
CHAPTER 7
CHAPTER 8

CHAPTER 9
CHAPTER 10
CHAPTER 11
CHAPTER 12
CHAPTER 13
CHAPTER 14
APPENDICES
INDEX

■ PARTICLE LIFETIME

The PSYS_SRC_MAX_AGE parameter sets the lifetime of the particle system; it indicates for how many seconds the emitter will produce particles once it comes into view. This can have some surprising effects. For example, if you place a call to llParticleSystem in a touch event that produces particles for two seconds, and a resident touches the object, then they will see the particles for two seconds. However, if another resident arrives sometime later and sees the emitter, they will then see the particles! Remember that particles can be turned off by passing the empty list, [], to llParticleSystem. The PSYS_PART_MAX_AGE parameter sets the lifetime, in seconds, of individual particles, up to a maximum of 30 seconds (Listing 8.14).

Listing 8.14: Setting the Particle System and Particle Lifetimes

```
default
{
    touch_start(integer total_number)
    {
        // Create a brief explosion of some long-lived particles
        llParticleSystem( [
            PSYS_SRC_PATTERN, PSYS_SRC_PATTERN_EXPLODE,
            PSYS_SRC_MAX_AGE, 2.0,
            PSYS_PART_MAX_AGE, 10.0
            ]);

        llSetTimerEvent(2.0);
    }
    timer()
    {
        // Turn the timer event off
        llSetTimerEvent(0.0);

        // Turn the particles off
        llParticleSystem([]);
    }
}
```

■ OTHER PARTICLE FLAGS

A few more flags that can be set in the PSYS_PART_FLAGS mask affect particle appearance and behavior. If PSYS_PART_BOUNCE_MASK is set, particles moving downward that get to the emitter's height will bounce back up. Setting PSYS_PART_EMISSIVE_MASK sets the particles to full brightness; otherwise they are subject to local lighting. PSYS_PART_WIND_MASK makes the particles subject to the region's wind.

PSYS_PART_FOLLOW_VEL_MASK makes particles rotate so that the top of the particle is pointing in the direction of movement. So, if the particle texture were an arrow pointing up, setting this flag would make the arrow always be pointing in the direction the particle is moving.

If PSYS_PART_FOLLOW_SRC_MASK is set, particles will stay in the same position relative to the emitter, so if the emitter is moving around, the particles will move around with it. If this flag is set, the PSYS_SRC_BURST_RADIUS setting is ignored. This is useful for effects that should be "stuck" to the source, such as glints or flames.

CHAPTER 8

MOVING
OBJECTS

SCRIPTING
VEHICLES

WORKING
WITH
PARTICLES

MANAGING
YOUR OBJECT'S
INVENTORY
WITH SCRIPTS

TUTORIAL:
BUILDING A
TIC-TAC-TOE
GAME

Setting PSYS_PART_TARGET_POS_MASK makes particles move toward an object or resident. The target is given with the PSYS_SRC_TARGET_KEY parameter, which takes the key of the target. If the target is out of range or the key is invalid (NULL_KEY), the particles will move toward the emitter. Particles will move toward the target so that they will get there at the end of their life. So if PSYS_PART_MAX_AGE is set to 10 seconds, the particles will move so that it takes 10 seconds to get from the source to the target.

OTHER PARTICLE PARAMETERS

PSYS_SRC_ACCEL applies a constant acceleration to the particles in an arbitrary direction. The acceleration is given as vector. This can be used to simulate gravity for particles or to make them move in any other direction.

PSYS_SRC_OMEGA applies a spin to the direction in which particles are emitted. This has no effect for PSYS_SRC_PATTERN_DROP and PSYS_SRC_PATTERN_EXPLODE patterns, but for the PSYS_SRC_PATTERN_ANGLE and PSYS_SRC_PATTERN_ANGLE_CONE patterns this setting rotates the z-axis of the emitter. This setting is given in a vector, with each component specifying the rotation in radians per second about each axis.

A PARTICLE EXAMPLE: SMOKE

Listing 8.15 uses long-lived, large, slow-moving particles to simulate thick smoke.

Listing 8.15: Smoke Particles

```
default
{
    state_entry()
    {
        llParticleSystem( [

            PSYS_SRC_PATTERN, PSYS_SRC_PATTERN_EXPLODE,
            PSYS_PART_FLAGS,
                PSYS_PART_INTERP_SCALE_MASK |
                PSYS_PART_INTERP_COLOR_MASK,

            // send out 25 particles a second
            PSYS_SRC_BURST_PART_COUNT, 5,
            PSYS_SRC_BURST_RATE, 0.2,

            // start out fairly transparent and fade out completely
            PSYS_PART_START_ALPHA, 0.4,
            PSYS_PART_END_ALPHA, 0.0,

            // go from small to large particles
            PSYS_PART_START_SCALE, <1.0, 1.0, 0.0>,
            PSYS_PART_END_SCALE, <10.0, 10.0, 0.0>,

            // puff out very slowly
            PSYS_SRC_BURST_SPEED_MAX, 0.25,
            PSYS_SRC_BURST_SPEED_MIN, 0.1,

            // push particles slightly up and in the y direction
            PSYS_SRC_ACCEL, <0.0, 0.01, 0.02>,
```

```
                PSYS_PART_MAX_AGE, 25.0,
                PSYS_SRC_TEXTURE, "5d6a12d4-8e49-c1a4-3bfb-5b8fc77fb598"

            ]);
        }
    }
```

CHAPTER 1
CHAPTER 2
CHAPTER 3
CHAPTER 4
CHAPTER 5
CHAPTER 6
CHAPTER 7
CHAPTER 8

MANAGING YOUR OBJECT'S INVENTORY WITH SCRIPTS

CHAPTER 9
CHAPTER 10
CHAPTER 11
CHAPTER 12
CHAPTER 13
CHAPTER 14
APPENDICES
INDEX

A script can manage the inventory of the object it is in. A script can use textures in the object's inventory on the sides of its object, can give items to residents, and can read the contents of notecards. Scripts get information about items by name. A script can get the names of all items in its object's inventory by calling llGetInventoryNumber to get the number of items, then getting each name by index number (Listing 8.16).

Listing 8.16: Enumerating Inventory Items

```
default
{
    touch_start(integer total_number)
    {
        integer nItems = llGetInventoryNumber(INVENTORY_ALL);
        integer x;
        for (x = 0; x < nItems; x++)
        {
            string name = llGetInventoryName(INVENTORY_ALL, x);
            llOwnerSay("Name: " + name);
            llOwnerSay("Creator: " +
                (string)llGetInventoryCreator(name));
            llOwnerSay("---");
        }
    }
}
```

llGetInventoryNumber can also be used to get the number of a given type of item in the object's inventory. There are constants for each Inventory type—for example, INVENTORY_OBJECT, INVENTORY_SCRIPT and INVENTORY_LANDMARK. There are functions to get information about most aspects of inventory items; in addition to llGetInventoryName and llGetInventoryCreator, there is llGetInventoryKey, which lets you get the UUID of the item, and llGetInventoryType, which returns a constant specifying the Inventory type—the same set of constants that llGetInventoryNumber takes. llGetInventoryPermMask can be used to get the item's permissions for its owner, for its group, for everyone, or for the object's next owner. The script can remove items from an object's inventory with llRemoveInventory.

If the owner of the object makes a change to the object's inventory, the change event will be raised with the change set to CHANGED_INVENTORY. If the script enables residents to add items to

CHAPTER 8

● MOVING
   OBJECTS

● SCRIPTING
   VEHICLES

● WORKING
   WITH
   PARTICLES

● MANAGING
   YOUR OBJECT'S
   INVENTORY
   WITH SCRIPTS

● TUTORIAL:
   BUILDING A
   TIC-TAC-TOE
   GAME

the object's inventory with llAllowInventoryDrop, then when the inventory is added to, a changed event will be raised with the change set to CHANGED_ALLOWED_DROP. Listing 8.17 demonstrates a script that accepts inventory drops from residents, but deletes all items in the object's inventory (except itself!) whenever anything is dropped in the object's inventory.

Listing 8.17: Allowing Inventory Drops, and Deleting Inventory Items

```
//delete all items in this object's inventory except this script
cleanUpInventory()
{
    list inventory;
    integer nItems = llGetInventoryNumber(INVENTORY_ALL);
    integer x;

    // note that since we will be deleting items from the Inventory,
    // item index numbers aren't reliable.
    //
    // First get all the names in a list, then delete using the list
    for (x = 0; x < nItems; x++)
    {
        inventory = inventory + [llGetInventoryName(INVENTORY_ALL, x)];
    }

    for (x = 0; x < llGetListLength(inventory); x++)
    {
        string item = llList2String(inventory, x);
        if (item != llGetScriptName())
        {
            llRemoveInventory(item);
        }
    }
}

default
{
    state_entry()
    {
        llAllowInventoryDrop(TRUE);
    }

    changed(integer change)
    {
        if (change & CHANGED_ALLOWED_DROP ||
            change & CHANGED_INVENTORY)
        {
            llSay(0, "Thanks, but I don't need any of those");
            cleanUpInventory();
        }
    }
}
```

■ REZZING OBJECTS

A script in an object with objects in its inventory can rez copies of those objects with the llRezObject function. Objects created with llRezObject are owned by owner of the script's object, and the owner must have permission to create objects in the land parcel that contains the rez location.

llRezObject takes the name of the inventory object to rez, a position at which to create the object, an initial velocity for the object, a rotation for the object, and an integer parameter. The velocity affects only rezzed objects that have physics enabled. The parameter argument to llRezObject is passed to the newly created object.

When a script successfully rezzes an object, the event object_rez is raised. The object_rez event receives a key, the ID of the newly created object. If the rezzed object has a script in it, the on_rez event is raised in that script. The on_rez event receives an integer, the parameter argument passed to llRezObject. The on_rez event is also raised when an object is rezzed from a resident's inventory, but the parameter to the on_rez event is always 0. Thus the parameter to the on_rez event can be used to by the object to determine if it has been rezzed by a resident or by a script. This is useful when you are creating temporary objects; when rezzed from a script and the on_rez parameter is whatever value you set in llRezObject, the object can set a short timer then call llDie when it expires, or do other volatile things. When the object is rezzed from your inventory and the on_rez parameter is 0, your script can enter a debugging mode, and not call llDie. This will allow you to work on the object without it disappearing on you.

Listing 8.18 shows a script that goes in an object that another script can rez. If its on_rez parameter is not 0, it sets a timer and the object will delete itself after 5 seconds. If its on_rez parameter is 0, it does nothing.

Listing 8.18: An Object That Dies on Rez

```
default
{
    state_entry()
    {
        // Enable physics for this object
        llSetStatus(STATUS_PHYSICS, TRUE);
    }

    on_rez(integer param)
    {
        if (param != 0)
        {
            llOwnerSay("Rezzed by a script, dying in 5 seconds");
            llSetTimerEvent(5.0);
        }
        else
        {
            llOwnerSay("Rezzed from resident inventory");
            // If this object was rezzed by a script, then taken in to
            // resident inventory before the timer expires, when it is
            // next rezzed, it will still have the timer event and will
            // die unless we remove the timer here
            llSetTimerEvent(0.0);
        }
    }

    timer()
    {
        llOwnerSay("Bye bye");
        llDie();
    }
}
```

CHAPTER 1
CHAPTER 2
CHAPTER 3
CHAPTER 4
CHAPTER 5
CHAPTER 6
CHAPTER 7
CHAPTER 8

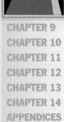

CHAPTER 9
CHAPTER 10
CHAPTER 11
CHAPTER 12
CHAPTER 13
CHAPTER 14
APPENDICES
INDEX

CHAPTER 8

Moving
Objects

Scripting
Vehicles

Working
with
Particles

Managing
Your Object's
Inventory
with Scripts

Tutorial:
Building a
Tic-Tac-Toe
Game

Listing 8.19 shows a script that rezzes an object. It creates the object one meter above its current position, with an initial velocity up and in the y-axis direction. When the object is rezzed and the `object_rez` event fires, the script announces the new object's key to its owner.

Listing 8.19: Rezzing an Object in Inventory

```
// Name of the object in inventory to rez
string objectName = "Thingy";

// Offset from this object to rez the new object at
vector vOffset = <0.0, 0.0, 1.0>;

// Initial velocity of the object
vector vVel = <0.0, 2.0, 4.0>;

default
{
    touch_start(integer total_number)
    {
        llRezObject(
            objectName,
            llGetPos() + vOffset,
            vVel,
            ZERO_ROTATION,
            1);
    }

    object_rez(key id)
    {
        llOwnerSay("Rezzed object, id is: " + (string)id);
    }
}
```

■ READING NOTECARDS

Scripts can access the content of notecards using `llGetGetNumberOfNotecardLines` and `llGetNotecardLine`. Both of these functions cause the `dataserver` event to be raised, when the data requested is ready for the script to read. `llGetNotecardLine` gets a maximum of 255 characters from the notecard line (Listing 8.20)

Listing 8.20: Read Each Line of a Notecard

```
string notecardName = "My Notecard";
integer currentLine = 0;

getNextLine()
{
    currentLine++;
    llGetNotecardLine(notecardName, currentLine);
}
```

```
default
{
    touch_start(integer total_num)
    {
        currentLine = 0;
        llOwnerSay("Attempting to read notecard: " + notecardName);
        getNextLine();
    }

    dataserver(key id, string data)
    {
        if (data == EOF)
        {
            llOwnerSay("done");
        }
        else
        {
            llOwnerSay((string)currentLine + ": " + data);
            getNextLine();
        }
    }
}
```

TUTORIAL: BUILDING A TIC-TAC-TOE GAME

Multiplayer games are some of the most interesting and popular content in *SL*. In this example we'll build a simple tic-tac-toe game from beginning to end. We'll build the individual game tiles and a central controller, then add some more features.

The game will be made of nine tiles and one controller prim (Listings 8.21 and 8.22). The game tiles will be cubes with an X side, an O side, and blank sides. To change a tile, we will rotate the cube. We'll start by developing the script to rotate one tile, then create a prim to use as the root of the game and a cube to use as the game tile. Then we'll link them so that the root is the parent and the tile is the child. The root will send link messages to the tile to tell it which face to show. Another way to implement this would be to use llSetLinkPrimitiveParams to set the rotation of each tile from the root prim.

Listing 8.21: Tic-Tac-Toe Tile, First Version

```
// linked message commands
integer CMD_SHOW_X = 1;
integer CMD_SHOW_O = 2;
integer CMD_SHOW_BLANK = 3;

// local rotatons to show faces, these will be initalized later
rotation SHOW_X_ROT = ZERO_ROTATION;
rotation SHOW_O_ROT = ZERO_ROTATION;
rotation SHOW_BLANK_ROT = ZERO_ROTATION;
```

CHAPTER 8

MOVING
OBJECTS

SCRIPTING
VEHICLES

WORKING
WITH
PARTICLES

MANAGING
YOUR OBJECT'S
INVENTORY
WITH SCRIPTS

TUTORIAL:
BUILDING A
TIC-TAC-TOE
GAME

```
// textures
key textureX = "69f794d3-e194-5090-367f-52c192b34059";
integer faceX = 2;
key textureO = "1f481f69-22ef-f104-89ec-5dea01be49d8";
integer faceO = 4;
key textureBlank = "8c77cf17-c87c-0311-8696-755cc26dc57e";

// calculate the rotations to show the different faces
initializeRotations()
{
    SHOW_X_ROT = llEuler2Rot(<0.0, 0 * DEG_TO_RAD, 0.0>);
    SHOW_O_ROT = llEuler2Rot(<0.0, 180 * DEG_TO_RAD, 0.0>);
    SHOW_BLANK_ROT = llEuler2Rot(<0.0, 270 * DEG_TO_RAD, 0.0>);
}

initializeTextures()
{
    llSetColor(<1.0, 1.0, 1.0>, ALL_SIDES);
    llSetTexture(textureBlank, ALL_SIDES);
    llSetTexture(textureX, faceX);
    llSetTexture(textureO, faceO);
}

showXFace()
{
    llSetLocalRot(SHOW_X_ROT);
}

showOFace()
{
    llSetLocalRot(SHOW_O_ROT);
}

showBlankFace()
{
    llSetLocalRot(SHOW_BLANK_ROT);
}

default
{
    state_entry()
    {
        initializeRotations();
        initializeTextures();
        showBlankFace();
    }

    on_rez(integer p)
    {
        llResetScript();
    }
```

CHAPTER 1
CHAPTER 2
CHAPTER 3
CHAPTER 4
CHAPTER 5
CHAPTER 6
CHAPTER 7
CHAPTER 8

CHAPTER 9
CHAPTER 10
CHAPTER 11
CHAPTER 12
CHAPTER 13
CHAPTER 14
APPENDICES
INDEX

```
link_message(integer sender, integer cmd, string s, key k)
{
    if (cmd == CMD_SHOW_X)
    {
        showXFace();
    }
    else if (cmd == CMD_SHOW_O)
    {
        showOFace();
    }
    else if (cmd == CMD_SHOW_BLANK)
    {
        showBlankFace();
    }
}
}
```

Listing 8.22: Tic-Tac-Toe Controller, First Version

```
// linked message commands
integer CMD_SHOW_X = 1;
integer CMD_SHOW_O = 2;
integer CMD_SHOW_BLANK = 3;

integer cmd = CMD_SHOW_BLANK;

default
{
    touch_start(integer total_number)
    {
        // for now, just flip the tile in response to touches
        cmd = (cmd + 1) % 3;
        llMessageLinked(LINK_ALL_OTHERS, cmd + 1, "", NULL_KEY);
    }
}
```

■ BUILDING THE BOARD

Now that we have a working tile (Figure 8.2), we can make a functional game. Create nine copies of the game tile and arrange them in a 3×3 grid along the global x- and y-axes. The next version of the controller script (Listing 8.23) will reset the game if the controller prim is touched. It will also keep track of whose turn it is and flip the tile that was touched.

Figure 8.2: Tic-tac-toe Version 1

Listing 8.23: Tic-Tac-Toe Controller, Second Version

```
// linked message commands
integer CMD_SHOW_X = 1;
integer CMD_SHOW_O = 2;
integer CMD_SHOW_BLANK = 3;

// Whose turn is it? 0 for O, 1 for X
integer whoseTurn = 0;

announceTurn()
{
    if (whoseTurn == 0)
    {
        llSay(0, "It's O's turn");
    }
    else
    {
        llSay(0, "It's X's turn");
    }
}

// set a game tile to X by its link number
setLinkToX(integer linkNum)
{
    llMessageLinked(linkNum, CMD_SHOW_X, "", NULL_KEY);
}

// set a game tile to O by its link number
setLinkToO(integer linkNum)
{
    llMessageLinked(linkNum, CMD_SHOW_O, "", NULL_KEY);
}

// completely reset the game
resetGame()
{
    llMessageLinked(LINK_ALL_OTHERS, CMD_SHOW_BLANK, "", NULL_KEY);
    whoseTurn = 0;
    announceTurn();
}

default
{
    state_entry()
    {
        resetGame();
    }

    touch_start(integer total_number)
    {
        if (llDetectedLinkNumber(0) == llGetLinkNumber())
        {
            // user touched the controller prim, reset the game
            resetGame();
        }
```

CHAPTER 1
CHAPTER 2
CHAPTER 3
CHAPTER 4
CHAPTER 5
CHAPTER 6
CHAPTER 7
CHAPTER 8

CHAPTER 9
CHAPTER 10
CHAPTER 11
CHAPTER 12
CHAPTER 13
CHAPTER 14
APPENDICES
INDEX

```
        else
        {
            if (whoseTurn == 0)
            {
                setLinkToO(llDetectedLinkNumber(0));
            }
            else
            {
                setLinkToX(llDetectedLinkNumber(0));
            }
            whoseTurn = !whoseTurn;
            announceTurn();
        }
    }
}
```

■ PLAYING BY THE RULES

The previous version has a few shortcomings. Since the controller doesn't keep track of which tiles have been flipped already, players can click on already-selected spaces to flip them again. In the next version (Figure 8.3), let's give the controller script a representation of the game. We'll store the game in a list of nine integers. A list position will be 0, 1, or 2 if the tile it represents is blank, X, or O, respectively. The list index of the tiles will be as follows:

```
0  1  2

3  4  5

6  7  8
```

Note that the link number of a prim is not the same as its tile number. The link number depends on the order in which the tiles were linked and can change if we add new prims to the link set (say, for example, decorative elements). We will also keep a list to map a tile number to its link number. In this list, the index will be the tile number and the value at that index will be the link number. We could hard-code this list, but link numbers are likely to change, so we will introduce a new link-message command that the controller will send to each tile to request its tile number. Each tile will have its tile number hard-coded in its script.

Figure 8.3 Tic-tac-toe, updated

MOVING
OBJECTS

SCRIPTING
VEHICLES

WORKING
WITH
PARTICLES

MANAGING
YOUR OBJECT'S
INVENTORY
WITH SCRIPTS

TUTORIAL:
BUILDING A
TIC-TAC-TOE
GAME

In each tile, we add these lines to the top of the script:

```
// This is different in each tile
integer myTileNumber = 6;


integer CMD_GET_TILE = 4;
```

And in the `link_message` event handler:

```
        else if (cmd == CMD_GET_TILE)
        {
            llMessageLinked(sender, myTileNumber, "", NULL_KEY);
        }
```

Unfortunately, now that the script in each tile is (slightly) different, if we want to change something in the tile script, we must remember to make this correction in every tile. It would be better to put the tile number in the object's name or in a notecard in the object's inventory, and have the script read that, and then the updated script could be placed in each tile without changes (Listing 8.24).

Listing 8.24: Tic-Tac-Toe Controller, Third Version

```
// linked message commands
integer CMD_SHOW_X = 1;
integer CMD_SHOW_O = 2;
integer CMD_SHOW_BLANK = 3;
integer CMD_GET_TILE = 4;

// This list maps tile numbers to link numbers.  It will be filled
// in as the child prims respond to CMD_GET_TILE
list tileToLink = [
0, 0, 0,
0, 0, 0,
0, 0, 0];

// The scripts representation of the board
integer BLANK = 0;
integer X = 1;
integer O = 2;
list board = [
BLANK, BLANK, BLANK,
BLANK, BLANK, BLANK,
BLANK, BLANK, BLANK
];

// Whose turn is it?
integer whoseTurn = X;
```

```
// Set the tile number to link mapping for this link
setLinkTile(integer link, integer tile)
{
    if (tile == 0)
    {
        tileToLink = [link] + llList2List(tileToLink, 1, 8);
    }
    else if (tile == 8)
    {
        tileToLink = llList2List(tileToLink, 0, 7) + [link];
    }
    else
    {
        tileToLink =
            llList2List(tileToLink, 0, tile - 1) +
            [link] +
            llList2List(tileToLink, tile + 1, 8);
    }
}

// Get the tile number of a link
integer getLinkToTile(integer link)
{
    return llListFindList(tileToLink, [link]);
}

// Get the link number of a tile
integer getTileToLink(integer tile)
{
    return llList2Integer(tileToLink, tile);
}


// What is the value of a tile, X, O or BLANK
integer getBoardAt(integer tile)
{
    return llList2Integer(board, tile);
}

// TRUE if tile is blank
integer tileIsBlank(integer tile)
{
    return getBoardAt(tile) == BLANK;
}

// Set the value of a tile in our representation of the board
setBoard(integer tile, integer player)
{
    if (tile == 0)
    {
        board = [player] + llList2List(board, 1, 8);
    }
    else if (tile == 8)
    {
        board = llList2List(board, 0, 7) + [player];
    }
```

CHAPTER 8

⬢ MOVING
OBJECTS

⬢ SCRIPTING
VEHICLES

⬢ WORKING
WITH
PARTICLES

⬢ MANAGING
YOUR OBJECT'S
INVENTORY
WITH SCRIPTS

⬢ TUTORIAL:
BUILDING A
TIC-TAC-TOE
GAME

```lsl
    else
    {
        board =
            llList2List(board, 0, tile - 1) +
            [player] +
            llList2List(board, tile + 1, 8);
    }
}

// set a game tile to X by its link number
setLinkToX(integer linkNum)
{
    llMessageLinked(linkNum, CMD_SHOW_X, "", NULL_KEY);
}

// set a game tile to O by its link number
setLinkToO(integer linkNum)
{
    llMessageLinked(linkNum, CMD_SHOW_O, "", NULL_KEY);
}

// Change a tile, send a link message to the tile and update the board
setTileTo(integer tile, integer player)
{
    setBoard(tile, player);
    if (player == X)
    {
        setLinkToX(getTileToLink(tile));
    }
    else
    {
        setLinkToO(getTileToLink(tile));
    }
}

// completely reset the game
resetGame()
{
    llMessageLinked(LINK_ALL_OTHERS, CMD_SHOW_BLANK, "", NULL_KEY);
    whoseTurn = X;
    board = [
    BLANK, BLANK, BLANK,
    BLANK, BLANK, BLANK,
    BLANK, BLANK, BLANK
    ];
}

announceTurn()
{
    if (whoseTurn == X)
    {
        llSay(0, "It's X's turn");
    }
    else
    {
        llSay(0, "It's O's turn");
    }
}
```

```
default
{
    state_entry()
    {
        // poll the tiles for their link numbers
        llMessageLinked(LINK_ALL_OTHERS, CMD_GET_TILE, "", NULL_KEY);
        resetGame();
        announceTurn();
    }

    link_message(integer sender, integer num, string s, key k)
    {
        // the only link message this script receives is link
        // number to tile mappings
        setLinkTile(sender, num);
    }

    touch_start(integer total_number)
    {
        if (llDetectedLinkNumber(0) == llGetLinkNumber())
        {
            // user touched the controller prim, reset the game
            resetGame();
        }
        else
        {
            integer tile = getLinkToTile(llDetectedLinkNumber(0));
            if (tile != -1)
            {
                if (tileIsBlank(tile))
                {
                    setTileTo(tile, whoseTurn);
                    if (whoseTurn == X)
                    {
                        whoseTurn = O;
                    }
                    else
                    {
                        whoseTurn = X;
                    }
                    announceTurn();
                }
            }
        }
    }
}
```

■ WINNER TAKE ALL

Now that the controller knows the state of the board, we can detect wins, losses, and draws
(Listing 8.25).

CHAPTER 8

MOVING
OBJECTS

SCRIPTING
VEHICLES

WORKING
WITH
PARTICLES

MANAGING
YOUR OBJECT'S
INVENTORY
WITH SCRIPTS

TUTORIAL:
BUILDING A
TIC-TAC-TOE
GAME

Listing 8.25: Tic Tac Toe Controller, Winner Detection

```
// Check the board to see if a player has won.  Return X if X has
// won, O if O has won, or BLANK if there is no winner
integer detectWinner()
{
    // Check diagonals
// the center tile must be used for a diagonal to win
    if (getBoardAt(4) != BLANK)
    {
        if (
            // top left to bottom right
            ((getBoardAt(0) == getBoardAt(4)) &&
             (getBoardAt(0) == getBoardAt(8))) ||
            // top right to bottom left
            ((getBoardAt(2) == getBoardAt(4)) &&
             (getBoardAt(2) == getBoardAt(6)))
          )
        {
            return getBoardAt(4);
        }
    }

    // check rows
    integer row;
    for (row = 0; row < 9; row = row + 3)
    {
        integer first = getBoardAt(0 + row);
        if (
            (first != BLANK) &&
            (first == getBoardAt(1 + row)) &&
            (first == getBoardAt(2 + row))
            )
            {
                return first;
            }
    }
    // check columns
    integer col;
    for (col = 0; col < 9; col = col + 3)
    {
        integer first = getBoardAt(0 + col);
        if (
            (first != BLANK) &&
            (first == getBoardAt(3 + col)) &&
            (first == getBoardAt(6 + col))
            )
            {
                return first;
            }
    }
    return BLANK;
}
```

```
// return TRUE if no one can win
// This only detects if the board is full.
integer detectDraw()
{
    return llListFindList(board, [BLANK]) == -1;
}
```

▪ CELEBRATING VICTORY

Finally, let's add some special effects. Create an object called Fireworks and add a script that, when rezzed by another script, shoots upward then creates a particle system as shown in Listing 8.26. Figure 8.4 shows the result.

Listing 8.26: Rezzed Fireworks

```
doParticles()
{
    // Create a burst of fireworks like particles with
    // a random color
    vector vColor = <llFrand(1.0), llFrand(1.0), llFrand(1.0)>;
    llParticleSystem( [
        PSYS_SRC_PATTERN, PSYS_SRC_PATTERN_EXPLODE,
        PSYS_SRC_BURST_RATE, 1.0,
        PSYS_SRC_BURST_PART_COUNT, 50,
        PSYS_SRC_MAX_AGE, 1.0,
        PSYS_SRC_ACCEL, <0.0, 0.0, -9.0>,
        PSYS_SRC_BURST_SPEED_MIN, 6.0,
        PSYS_SRC_BURST_SPEED_MAX, 7.0,
        PSYS_PART_EMISSIVE_MASK, 1,
        PSYS_PART_START_COLOR, vColor
        ]);
}

default
{
    state_entry()
    {
        // Turn on physics and phantom
        llSetStatus(STATUS_PHYSICS |STATUS_PHANTOM,
            TRUE);
        // make the object float
        llSetBuoyancy(1.0);
        // reset particle parameters
        llParticleSystem([]);
    }
```

```
on_rez(integer p)
{
    if (p != 0)
    {
        // rezzed from a script, apply an upwards impulse and
        // set a timer
        vector vImpulse = <
            llFrand(1.5) - 0.75,
            llFrand(1.5) - 0.75,
            llFrand(2.0) + 4.0>;
        llApplyImpulse(vImpulse, FALSE);
        llSetTimerEvent(1.0);
    }
    else
    {
        // rezed from resident inventory, turn off physics
        // and cancel the timer
        llSetStatus(STATUS_PHYSICS, FALSE);
        llSetTimerEvent(0.0);
    }
}
timer()
{
    // fire the particle effect, sleep for 1 second
    // then die
    doParticles();
    llSleep(1.0);
    llDie();
}
}
```

In the controller we add a function to rez a series of the fireworks objects as shown in Listing 8.27.

Listing 8.27: Launching Fireworks

```
// do winning effect
launchFireworks()
{
    integer x;
    // Name of the object in inventory to rez
    string objectName = "Fireworks";
    // Offset from this object to rez the new object at
    vector vOffset = <0.0, 0.0, 2.0>;
    for (x = 0; x < 10; x++)
    {
        llRezObject(
            objectName,
            llGetPos() + vOffset,
            ZERO_VECTOR,
            ZERO_ROTATION,
            1);
    }
}
```

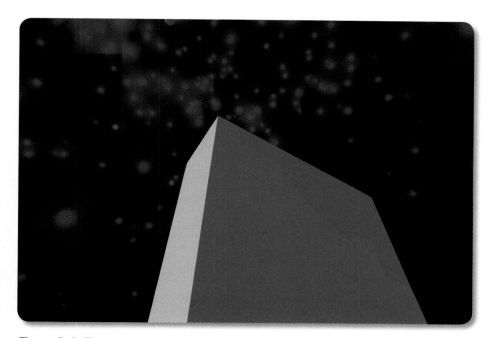

Figure 8.4: Fireworks

CHAPTER 9

OPTIMIZATION: CREATING A COMFORTABLE USER EXPERIENCE

Once you know how to use the *Second Life* tools to build things, you need to think about what to build and how to build it so that it's easy to use. Although *Second Life* is a lot like real life, there are differences in scale, perspective, and the way you get around and interact with the world. A designer almost always has to make *Second Life*–specific adjustments.

In this chapter, we'll discuss how to make your builds as accessible as possible and how to adjust the scale of your builds. You'll exercise your new skills in a tutorial on building a house in *Second Life*. Then we'll focus on designing friendly user interfaces for scripted objects.

CONTENTS

ENSURING ACCESSIBILITY

Figure 9.1: Unable to guess which glass pane is the door, one avatar attempts to drill his way out.

Everyone starts off in *Second Life* by bumping into things while flying, but a good design can make it easier—even for newbies—to use your build.

Unless you're purposely building a maze, make it easy for avatars to find their way around. Entrances and exits need to be obvious. From time to time, I have visited a build where I just couldn't tell which of the glass windows was really supposed to be a sliding door! (Figure 9.1 shows the consequences.) What's worse is feeling claustrophobic when you can't find an exit. Unless you have a specific reason to trap avatars, it's a good idea to add more than one exit to your building.

MORE INFO

SECOND LIFE AS A THEME PARK

Many people have compared *Second Life* to a 3D Web page, but I've always compared *Second Life* to a theme park. This has led to some very useful insights. When you enter a real-life theme park, you're going to see—or even be handed—a map. Information booths and other important locations are obviously marked. It's easy to follow broad, obvious pathways. But there's usually also some sort of transportation, like a train, that you can jump on for a quick tour around the entire place, usually with a recorded tour guide, or for a leisurely and fun way to get from one area to another. In *Second Life* you can include a big, dramatic, eye-catching thing to lure visitors to a specific attraction—theme-park designers call this a *wienie*. Walt Disney coined the term to describe leading theme-park guests with an eye-catching landmark as if they were being lured with a hot dog (or like a horse with a carrot). Channeling flying avatars where you want them is pretty tricky, but this always works.

If avatars are likely to approach your building by flying to it, make the entrance easy to spot from the air, and be sure that there's an adequate place to land near the door if avatars won't just swoop right in. You might also consider adding an entrance in the roof, or setting your roof to Phantom so avatars can pass through it. But remember: don't link that phantom roof or window to the rest of the building, or you'll fall through the floor when the whole link set goes phantom!

Additionally, make sure that walkways and flight paths are clear and wide enough for avatars to negotiate without being experts at controlling their movement. Even if you don't expect avatars to walk, paths or walkways can be a good way to indicate which way to go to find points of interest or entrances.

Stairs aren't required in *SL* because avatars can fly or teleport between levels of your build. But a lot of people do prefer to walk! Make sure the steps aren't too steep for avatars of average size to climb (see "Recommended Scale Changes" later in this chapter). Consider adding a script to your stairs to turn off the collision sound, so avatars that are a bit short won't go clunk-clunk-clunk-clunk all the way up. Or consider using a prim-saving ramp instead of a staircase—you can even texture it to look like stairs. Similarly, elevators look cool and they can be fun, but it's usually a lot more practical to fly straight up.

CHAPTER 1
CHAPTER 2
CHAPTER 3
CHAPTER 4
CHAPTER 5
CHAPTER 6
CHAPTER 7
CHAPTER 8
CHAPTER 9

CHAPTER 10
CHAPTER 11
CHAPTER 12
CHAPTER 13
CHAPTER 14
APPENDICES
INDEX

RESIDENTS SPEAK

TRICKS FOR NAVIGABLE SPACES

It seems that the more successful builds, while articulate in expression, also tend to simplify and open up the plan, making it obvious for the avatar to intuit his or her location within the overall build and to feel less disoriented. Intricate plans [provide] more places to go [but] also provide more places to get lost, and tend to rely heavily on signage to keep people moving in the right direction. This is especially evident in the design of many stores in *SL*, where it becomes quite an effort to hunt down an item that one is shopping for. I strive to keep it simple, giving each space its own unique characteristics rather than relying on rigidly symmetrical plans, and providing views to the outside landscape to aid in orientation with the surroundings. That said, for many residents mazes and dungeons are part of the fun in *SL* as they are with more-conventional video game experiences.

—Chip Poutine (aka Chad Oberg)

I'm flustered when I come to a skyscraper with many floors and I'm forced to enter on the ground floor and then use their teleporter (or elevator) to get to the fourth floor. Why can't I just fly up to a porch on the fourth floor?

—Troy McLuhan (aka Troy McConaghy)

I approach the layout very differently for a commercial build than I do for a private home. With a commercial build, I try to plan the layout from the perspective of a new customer—even taking the landing point of the parcel into account. I want it to be crystal clear where they have landed and where they are to go next—any guesswork on the part of the customer could lead them to leave the site and a potential sale is lost. With private homes, I approach the layout by defining unique spaces and the purpose of those spaces. Once I have the spaces defined, I play around with different layouts and try to make sure that the feel of the space is in line with the purpose. I like to cluster social spaces near each other and separate them away from the more-private spaces such as bedrooms.

—Juro Kothari

In later projects I've added invisible rails to keep avatars from falling off levels, and phantom windows to allow them to get in [easily].

—Scope Cleaver

SIMPLIFYING NAVIGATION

There are a lot of small, easy things you can do to make it simpler for people to find their way around your build. Some of these are even handy for quickly improving navigability of existing builds.

Landmark placement. When you create a landmark to help people find your building, be sure it lands them by an entrance.

Landing-point placement. You can use the Landing Point feature (in About Land) to set the position and orientation of an avatar teleporting via a landmark or Search, so that they'll arrive by the entrance (and facing it!).

Obvious teleporters. If your build includes *teleporters*—scripted objects that take avatars instantly from one point to another with just a click—make sure they are very obvious. People new to *Second Life* might not think of looking for them.

Furniture placement. Avatars are always pushed up when they stand. Be sure to test that avatars don't get stuck in a wall or ceiling when they stand up from a seat or when they try to fly out of your building.

Windows in tight spaces. If your build includes small spaces where an avatar's camera is likely to stick through the wall, consider adding a window so they can still see what they are doing.

Builds in the sky. Don't assume all of your visitors have flight-assist gadgets; if part of your build is located higher than avatars can normally fly, set up a teleporter.

Lighten up. If your build will be located in a place where it's sometimes (or always!) night, set signs to Full Bright. Consider adding some objects with the Light feature enabled if visibility is important in a certain area.

ADJUSTING BUILD SCALE

You probably remember what a difficult time you had getting around when you were new to *Second Life*—all the time you spent trying to get in through doorways, and the many collisions you had with buildings and other objects when flying. Part of this is because some builds in *Second Life* are designed for looks without enough attention to functionality, including a frequent disconnect between the scale of avatars and the things and places they use.

BIG AVATARS, SMALL WORLD

Figure 9.2: This door's obviously too small.

If you were to build a house exactly to real-life scale in *Second Life*, converting real-life feet or meters to meters in-world, you would probably run into problems like the one encountered by the tall avatar in Figure 9.2.

The default female avatar is about 6'1" and the default male is 6'7". Some other library avatars are even taller, like the Cybergoth Male, which is about 7'6" tall. There's no indication of this when you're new to *Second Life* and you're making modifications to personalize your shape. So, naturally, avatars tend to be pretty big. That makes a lot of normally scaled rooms, vehicles, and furniture a bit of a tight fit.

WHY AVATARS ARE TALL

The historical reason the 'middle of the sliders' avatar is taller than the average human is because our last non-modifiable avatar back in pre-alpha just happened to be that tall (a guy we called Primitar). Then we changed how the avatars looked without changing the physical representation of the avatar on the server, and their default size was scaled to match the collision model.

—Andrew Linden, posting on official *Second Life* forums, December 01, 2003

CAMERA PROBLEMS IN BUILDS

The *Second Life* camera can also make it necessary to design things a little bit differently from their real-life counterparts. Most *Second Life* residents do not use mouselook—a first-person view of the world. Instead, most people view the world from a default point a bit above and behind their avatar. This can pose problems. Figure 9.3 shows what you might see if your avatar entered a room with a low ceiling, and Figure 9.4 shows how the same room looks from another perspective. The left screenshot in Figure 9.3 was taken from my avatar's viewpoint—standing directly below the avatar with the striped slacks—with the camera in its default position. I'm seeing his feet standing up there on the next floor, instead of friends standing next to me. The right shot was taken with the camera view further out so you can see the entire scene, with the low ceiling over my avatar's head and my stripey friend above. *Second Life* residents call the problem illustrated in Figure 9.3 "getting your camera stuck in the ceiling."

Figure 9.3: (left) A case of "camera stuck in the ceiling," and (right) the camera pulled back to show the problematic layout

Similarly, you can get your camera stuck in the wall in a space that's too small. When building any sort of functional space in *Second Life*, consider the camera's dislocation from an avatar. Hallways, vehicle interiors, and even large event venues need to be designed with the camera view in mind. Figure 9.4 illustrates what happens when you put seats too close to a wall.

CHAPTER 9

Ensuring
Accessibility

Adjusting
Build Scale

Building
Design in
Practice

Tutorial:
Building a
House

Creating
Friendly
User
Interfaces

Figure 9.4: (left) A layout like real-life event seating, and (right) the camera "stuck in the wall"

RECOMMENDED SCALE CHANGES

By how much do we have to rescale our builds to avoid these problems? Good question. Avatars in *Second Life* vary in size, from giant mechas and dragons all the way down to *Tinies*—avatars of minimum size folded using animations to appear even smaller (and dressed in prim attachments to look like bunnies, warthogs, etc.). So the best you can do is build to suit a wide range of average-size and real-life-scale avatars. There are always going to be compromises.

Typically, ceilings need to be at least 3.5 meters high. A good rule of thumb is to increase scale to 1.25 to 1.5 times real-life size. If you plan to teleport people into a building, keep in mind that they'll appear a couple of feet above the ground. If this causes them to intersect with the ceiling, for example, *SL* will force them to bounce up to clear it, and they'll find themselves on the next floor or the roof. That makes it a good idea to go with the larger scale.

Make sure the doorway is as big as you can plausibly add to your structure. You wouldn't want to bring your friend to see your great new house, only to find he can't get through the door because his avatar is too tall or because he's new to *Second Life* and has a hard time lining up his avatar with the entrance.

WARNING

The Builders Tape Measure in the Second Life *Library gives suggested measurements, but they tend to be on the small side.*

Figure 9.5: This chair is a bit small for two of the three avatars, and the one on the right has his feet stuck in the floor.

Along with your buildings, you should consider up-sizing the furniture you'll put them in. First, you need to make sure that avatars are going to fit in their seats, and not have their feet stuck in the floor (like the far-right avatar in Figure 9.5).

Second, if you have scaled up the whole building, imagine how tiny real-life-scale furniture would look in there, and how cavernous and empty a normally furnished room would look. Of course, if your visitor's avatar was made to real-life scale, in your scaled-up seating they're going to feel a bit like Goldilocks in Papa Bear's chair, but at least almost everyone will be able to have a seat without sticking through it or the floor.

CHAPTER 1
CHAPTER 2
CHAPTER 3
CHAPTER 4
CHAPTER 5
CHAPTER 6
CHAPTER 7
CHAPTER 8
CHAPTER 9
CHAPTER 10
CHAPTER 11
CHAPTER 12
CHAPTER 13
CHAPTER 14
APPENDICES
INDEX

NOTE

You'll probably want to place furniture away from the walls; how far away depends on what sort of furnishings you have and what sort of animations might be built into them. This positioning keeps you from seeing the siding on the outside of the building instead of your friends because it keeps your camera from getting stuck in the wall.

Figure 9.6: These half-meter-high steps work great even for real-life-scale avatars, but Tinies will have to fly to the top.

Some of your visitors might not be human at all. It's nice to provide standing room for avatars that don't really fit in chairs, like dragons or Ents. You might also consider the needs of Tiny avatars, which often can't sit comfortably in normal furnishings (they have a different *sit offset*—they are placed differently from regular avatars in relation to objects on which they sit) or climb up stairs that work for average avatars (Figure 9.6). Half-meter-high steps will work great for most normal avatars, but if you really want to make it easy for everyone to access your build, use ramps instead.

Any time you build something in *Second Life*, have other people test your build. To be certain you haven't overlooked anything, invite some friends over to sit on your chairs, walk through your doorways, and generally make sure that everything works for them. Some of your testers should be new residents, because they have a lot more trouble getting around than an avatar at the advanced age of three months!

BUILDING DESIGN IN PRACTICE

Visiting good examples in-world is the best way to really understand the principles of functional *Second Life* building design. Here are some to check out, along with comments from their architects, some of the best in *Second Life*.

■ TEACHING CENTRE, BRITISHCOUNCIL ISLE (TEEN *SL*)

Figure 9.7: Teaching Centre (BritishCouncil Isle, 223,153,54)

This building's lounge is composed of comfy mismatched furniture casually scattered on the roof (Figure 9.7).

"The decision to have the recreational area on the roof came out of a number of factors. The building was shaping up with a very 'straight' feel to it and for a place to have fun I wanted something a little more funky and subversive. For a recreational area to actually be used it has to have very easy access so people can drop in and out without a

CHAPTER 9

- ENSURING ACCESSIBILITY

- ADJUSTING BUILD SCALE

- BUILDING DESIGN IN PRACTICE

- TUTORIAL: BUILDING A HOUSE

- CREATING FRIENDLY USER INTERFACES

commitment of time. Also it has to be seen to be in use, so that others will want to join what's going on there. Combined with the factor of space for people to rez objects, the roof seemed like the obvious solution."

—Art Laxness (aka Will Segerman)

CAPOZZI WINERY, CAPOZZI WINERY

Figure 9.8: Capozzi Winery (Capozzi Winery, 128,128,0)

It's easy to navigate the paths through the vineyard (Figure 9.8).

"Functional buildings in *SL* need to accommodate the airborne avatar with flight paths, landing perches, and alternate points of entry beyond those on the ground. Many great works of real-life architecture dwell quite a bit on the sequence of spaces and how they unfold as one moves through them. Personally, I strive to extend this sense of sequence and procession to the avian avatar in a more considered manner than merely cutting a hole in the roof, a commonly seen design strategy in *SL*. In fact, a preference is to design open-air structures wherever possible or at least limit the degree of overall enclosure as appropriate to the required functions."

—Chip Poutine (aka Chad Oberg)

NOTE

Chip's Virtual Suburbia blog at http://www.virtualsuburbia.com *is a great resource for information about "The Architecture of* Second Life, *reviewed on the fly."*

NASA COLAB HEADQUARTERS, NASA COLAB

Figure 9.9: NASA CoLab HQ (NASA CoLab, 244,111,23)

The offices in this building see a lot of practical use (Figure 9.9).

"The NASA CoLab building came out of dialogue with people wanting a meeting and convention center for NASA and various organizations that work with them. Using a simple 'space' theme and considering all the elements they wanted, I came up with a building that has met their needs, and will hopefully meet their needs in the future of their *Second Life* presence. The seven pods around the outer ring each represent the continents of the earth, the ring itself the circle of life, the globe in the center the planet itself, and the spire pointing to the heavens above symbolizes man's journey to the stars. The building has several access points, including hatches that one can fly into, making the building accessible on many different levels."

—DaVinci Doctorow (aka Barry Spencer II)

LITTLE REBEL DESIGNS, GALLINAS

Figure 9.10: Little Rebel Designs (Gallinas 142,98,58)

This shop features easy access through a wide-open roof (Figure 9.10).

"I think a very good example of a commercial build is the Little Rebel store I built for Jonquille Noir. She wanted a bright, airy store that had a strong visual theme to it, but would have a simplified layout to make it easier for the customers to find what they were looking for. The structure has a large entry area and a sculpted staircase leading to the second level, but the wings of the structure are very simple and modular, making expansion of the store easy."

—Juro Kothari

PRACTICAL MAGIC, SERENITE

Figure 9.11: Practical Magic (Serenite, 77,180,26)

This cottage's textures make it seem warm and earthy (Figure 9.11).

"Prim economy has always been a top priority for me, because I see it as every prim I save is a prim the homeowner can use to make it theirs with furniture and décor. I've found good texture work can rival prim-heavy builds. I've learned to rely on using my textures for depth over the prims themselves."

—Keith Extraordinaire

WELCOME TO UGS, UGS INNOVATION CONNECTION

Figure 9.12: Welcome to UGS (UGS Innovation Connection, 168,157,22)

Fresh, modern architecture invites exploration (Figure 9.12).

"While many corporate builds often feel sterile with approximately the same content, by using the architecture of the structure as a guiding piece of wayfinding, there is an improved connection with the build and the content in general. Also, by putting the landing point in the middle of the program for the various areas, the visitor is confronted with multiple easy options for circulation through the space, each leading to a differing procession through the build, giving a variety of subtly different experiences."

—Rez Menoptra (aka Jason Cerchie)

THE TELUS STORE, SHINDA

Figure 9.13: The Telus Store (Shinda, 149,67,21)

This deceptively simple-looking design projects a feel of pleasant order (Figure 9.13).

"The most important thing in terms of usability for a building is the way it presents its space to the avatar and the way it works around the limitations, like the camera, the precision, the difficulty of moving in general, and its good design in terms of how many people it's supposed to account for."

—Scope Cleaver

GRAND CENTRAL STATION, THE FUTURE

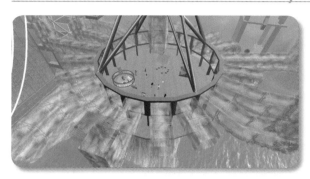

Figure 9.14: Grand Central Station (The Future, 130,200,64)

It's remarkably easy to navigate this build, despite all of its content (Figure 9.14).

"Grand Central Station in The Future was designed to be functional. It's a very open plan, with arriving avatars being able to fly out in any direction, as well as fitting in all of the transport-system geometry. Both the incoming funnel and the outgoing tubes had to be fit into the space while allowing flight paths in any direction."

—Seifert Surface
(aka Henry Segerman)

NOTE

Grand Central Station is the hub of Seifert's famous Transit Tube system, which shoots avatars to their destinations.

TUTORIAL: BUILDING A HOUSE

Now it's time to put your knowledge of accessibility and scale into practice. Let's walk through the process of building a functional structure in *Second Life*—a house.

CHAPTER 1
CHAPTER 2
CHAPTER 3
CHAPTER 4
CHAPTER 5
CHAPTER 6
CHAPTER 7
CHAPTER 8
CHAPTER 9

PLANNING THE HOUSE

Start out thinking about who the house is for and what sort of style they'll like. I'm going to build this house for myself, in the woods, so I want something with a look that will fit into a forest setting.

Also, think about where the house will eventually be placed. Will the ground be flat, or hilly? How much space do you have and how many prims can you spend?

I'm going to terraform a nice flat spot for this building, and I have a lot of space and free prims, but I don't want to go crazy, because I'll want to build other things on the parcel later.

Are there particular sorts of rooms you'll need? Some people want bathrooms, even if avatars don't really need them. Some people will want an office or multiple bedrooms.

I want a flexible, open floor plan because I have found I'll use the same building for different things over a long period of time. Also, I need a lot of open space because I like to build things in the house, especially furniture.

If possible, walk around the site where the build is going to be placed, and think about which way to orient the building. Partly, this is for getting good views out the windows. This is also so I can think about from what directions the building is likely to be approached, and where to put the doors.

Figure 9.15: Your model doesn't have to impress anyone but you.

Sometimes I make a sketch or, more often, a really rough scale model so I can see how my layout might work (Figure 9.15). In particular, because I'm pretty crummy at math, I spend some time considering the roofline and angle and how it's going to work. I don't necessarily stick strictly to this plan, but it gives me a general idea of where I'm headed. This sort of thing helps a lot if you are working with other people; it helps make sure all the different parts of the build fit together and harmonize.

I figure I'll build an open-plan lower floor, C-shaped, 30 meters across the back. There's going to be an upper floor over just the back part, 30×10. The two rooms in the front, 10×10 each, will have really high ceilings. This is going to be great for flying up and down between the levels. I'm not including stairs because we don't really need them. I might add a teleporter later, though, and I want to put phantom windows in the cupolas for easy access to the upper level.

BUILDING THE FOUNDATION

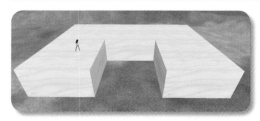

Figure 9.16: It starts with a foundation.

Actual construction starts with a foundation (Figure 9.16). You need a floor, and terraforming is not exact. If you're selling prefabs, in particular, this is a good idea because it will make it easier for your customers to place the house. I like to make a foundation around five meters high, which I can embed into the ground as far as possible so the building will look stable and supported, with no floaty corners.

CHAPTER 9

ENSURING
ACCESSIBILITY

ADJUSTING
BUILD SCALE

BUILDING
DESIGN IN
PRACTICE

TUTORIAL:
BUILDING A
HOUSE

CREATING
FRIENDLY
USER
INTERFACES

■ FRAMING AND FLOORING

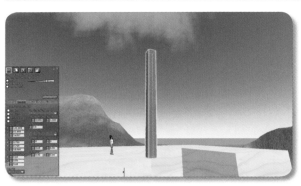

Figure 9.17: Raising the first post

This house will be constructed in a classic *Second Life* architectural style of posts and windows. Here's the first post, which I've textured already so it'll show up well (Figure 9.17).

This post is 10 meters high, which should allow plenty of room to put in two floors. I'll frame this building with posts just like this one, spaced 5 meters apart, except where I plan to put doors.

TIP

It can be really helpful to texture or tint parts of a build in progress. Some problems won't really show up until you have contrasting colors or textures on the prims. You can save yourself a lot of hassle if you catch this sort of thing early, before you have to revise a lot of your build to fix it.

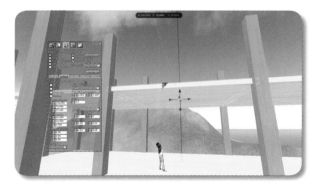

Figure 9.18: Building the upper floor

To put in the upper floor, I selected and Shift-copied the back three prims of the lower floor and dragged them straight up. Then I smushed them because they don't really need to be thick, and thinner prims will buy me a bit more headroom. This floor is 5.5 meters above the first floor—plenty high, but still low enough to feel cozy (Figure 9.18).

Now I put in some walls. If this were a shop, I might do this entirely with posts and windows, but in a house I like to feel a bit more closed up.

The lower and top wall pieces are a meter and a half high, and the middle one is about twice as high. I decided on this by standing my avatar next to the wall to see what looked and felt right to me, then I made it a bit higher, figuring most avatars are taller than my own. In Figure 9.19 you can see these walls, in a shot looking down one of the two-level-high front rooms, where I have tinted the floor to help make the perspective clear.

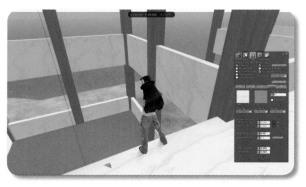

Figure 9.19: One of the front rooms

ADDING A DECK

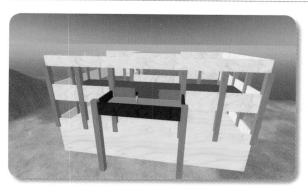

Figure 9.20: The deck

Something's been bothering me about this build. I planned for only one doorway. But I have found while working on the build that friends who come by like to swoop in the upper windows to enter the top floor, and I've been getting in and out the same way. So, I decided to add an entrance upstairs, with a nice deck that offers plenty of room for landing by the door (Figure 9.20).

In *Second Life* we don't need structural supports. But this is a fairly realistic-looking building, so I put supporting posts on the deck. When adding supports like this, it's easy to forget that they have to actually stick into the ground, especially when you're building a bit up in the air this way. Be sure to fly down and double-check.

CONSTRUCTING THE ROOF

Roofs give me a really hard time because I am mathematically challenged and I have this stubborn liking for interesting rooflines. Angles aren't the easiest thing to work out in *Second Life*. This one is pretty easy, as roofs go (Figure 9.21).

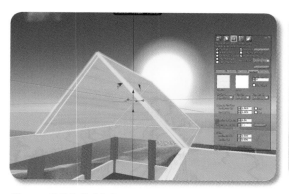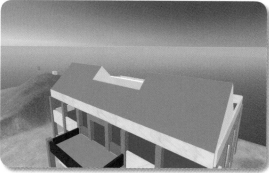

Figure 9.21 (left) One end of the roof and (right) the main part of the roof

I used a hollowed, cut 10-meter cube on either end, with a pair of flat prims that I have tilted and placed in between by eye. Some builders do things by the numbers, but I'm not one of them. I often build, and then, once things are roughly in place, I square things up by checking placement of the objects, rounding off the numbers, and making sure they work out.

The front two rooms have even simpler roofs: cubes, hollowed and tapered. I shift-dragged upward, to make two copies of the primary roof prim, untapered the lower one, and resized them a bit.

I wanted to pretty up the roofline to keep this house from just looking boxy. Plus, more headroom is always good. I modified a copy of the larger part of the roof in the back to make another cupola. Then I copied the cut triangle, squashed it horizontally, and made two copies for trim (Figure 9.22).

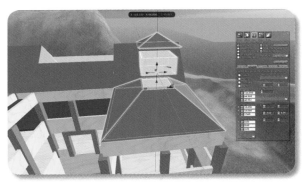

My original plan called for phantom windows in the cupolas, but I decided not to implement them. Once I had this built to scale, I decided the windows would be too small to allow easy access. Although it would be amusing to watch my friends bat against the windows like moths, for some reason they don't find this sort of thing so funny. So instead I have the entrance on the deck. This is much more obvious than the phantom cupola windows would have been, and it's easy to use.

Figure 9.22: Building a cupola

APPLYING TEXTURES

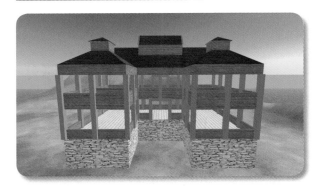

Figure 9.23: Textures snap this build into focus.

I wanted something woodsy, remember, so here I have used some wood siding, wood paneling on the ceilings, and a wood floor (Figure 9.23). To make the place seem cozy I wanted the ceiling to feel lower than it had to be functionally, so I didn't want a light-colored ceiling. On the other hand, I didn't want the space overall to feel tiny and I wanted some contrast, so I used a light-colored floor texture.

To keep the building from looking monochromatic and drab, I tinted the shingles a nice foresty green. Textures won't wrap correctly on those tapered cubes unless you remember to use planar mapping.

Although the foundation will be stuck in the ground, I slapped a stone texture on it. I might want to use this building somewhere else, where the ground isn't so flat.

TIP

Don't forget to check permissions on textures before you apply them. I think just about every builder has had the horrible experience of finishing a great build, then finding they are unable to transfer it because somewhere, some prim in the build has a texture without transfer permission!

■ SETTING THE HOUSE IN PLACE

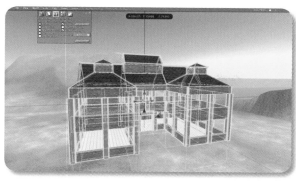

Now it's time to move the house into its resting place (Figure 9.24). This would be a really great time to grab a backup of the build. In fact, upon completing each step of this build, I drag-selected the entire build, took a copy, and then labeled it in my Inventory so I could tell later which version it was. This really paid off, because I messed up and accidentally deleted part of the build partway through!

Figure 9.24: Here I am moving the house to put the foundation into the ground.

■ DESIGNING WINDOWS

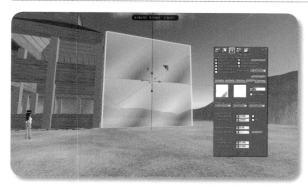

This looks nearly done, but prim windows will really make a difference. I whipped up a gradient texture in Photoshop and put it on a 10×10 prim. To make it tile so that it looks like four windows, I have increased the number of horizontal and vertical texture repeats and adjusted the offset (Figure 9.25).

Then I added a bit of transparency. This texture will work for a privacy-glass effect, though, if you set that transparency to zero and make the prim shiny. So with a simple alpha on/off script, you could have some nifty windows that could be clear or mirrored.

Figure 9.25: Creating windows

NOTE

One of the nice things about all of the windows in this design is that, even if your avatar stands close to the wall, you can still see inside with your camera outside the building.

■ INSTALLING DOORS

I've framed up and added huge double doors downstairs and up. These should accommodate smallish dragons, robots, and avatars on stilts or wearing towering hats.

These are modified freebie doors that open and close on touch, with sound effects. You'll notice the texture looks pretty well in scale to the building, but the door handles are larger and higher than would make sense for my avatar (which

Figure 9.26: Generous doors

is, real-life scale, about 5'5"). If I had put on handles realistically scaled and placed in relation to my avatar, they'd look pretty freaky on these giant doors!

■ LANDSCAPING

Figure 9.27: The finished house, with landscaping

Figure 9.27 shows the building in place. Landscaping makes a huge difference, even if it's nothing fancy. A building just doesn't look natural without it. Plus, landscaping helps direct visitors to the entrance. That's why I've put in some stepping stones.

NOTE

This build runs about 125 prims.

■ THE FINISHED BUILD

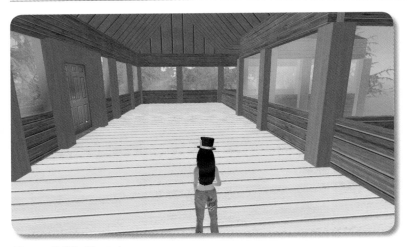

Figure 9.28: Upstairs

The interior feels pretty warm and open to me, and I think the ceiling height worked out really well (Figure 9.28).

The most interesting thing I discovered about this build during its first day of use? Everyone likes to land on and hang out on the deck, which wasn't even in the original plan!

RESIDENTS SPEAK

CHIP POUTINE (AKA CHAD OBERG) ON WHAT REALLY WORKS

Experience *Second Life*. Get out there and join in—chat, socialize, and participate. Research how avatars interact with each other in both your own builds and those completed by others. Ask questions and never assume that what works for buildings in the physical world is necessarily going to be successful in *Second Life*, especially when it comes to aspects of visual privacy. One related and often debated subject is the symbolic and functional aspects of doors in *SL*. Many have questioned putting doors on a store when they perhaps have more potential to keep people out rather than help them come in. Others reply that a door texture is a clear symbol, better telling people where they can enter and exit. Personally, I try to take cues from real-life structures such that people feel a sense of familiarity but then extend and transform the design to take advantage of the unique social, cultural, and climatic conditions of *Second Life*.

CREATING FRIENDLY USER INTERFACES

In *Second Life*, we interact with all sorts of gadgets. You tell your shoes what color you want them to be, a gadget automatically greets you and hands you a present when you arrive at a sim, you use a vendor to buy or sell things, a visitor counter tells you who stopped by when you weren't at your parcel, etc. There are a lot of different ways you can design things, and how smoothly they work has a huge impact on the user experience.

■ COMMON USER-INTERFACE PROBLEMS

Some user-interface problems are so common that most residents encounter them almost every day, in almost every build. These problems aren't very difficult for you to avoid!

Accidental purchases. The left-click default for an object can be changed using a pull-down menu in the Object Editor. This can be really useful, allowing someone to sit on a chair in one click instead of two, for example. But if this is set to make an avatar automatically purchase an object on left-click, you might get some irate IMs from people who've made accidental purchases. Consider avoiding one-click purchase settings in your build.

Hover tips toggled off. Sometimes new residents aren't aware that they can get information from an object by hovering their mouse over it or by editing it. If you want to make your build especially newbie-friendly, consider other ways of making this information available. For instance, if an object is to be clicked, make it look like a button.

Object spam. Objects that talk on channel 0—the open chat channel—can be very distracting, particularly if they shout. Think about who needs to hear the information, and try to get it to only them. Will a whisper do? Can you make this object communicate on a different channel? How about if the object sends an instant message instead?

Command spam. Some scripted gadgets want you to talk to them in open chat, which is distracting to those around you. Would it be better to talk to them on another channel or create a HUD that lets the user control the gadget graphically?

Forgettable commands. If your gadget is complicated and understands a lot of commands, you might have to dive into your Inventory to find its instruction notecard over and over again. Consider adding a simple Help command that will offer a reminder of the commands, or even use a different sort of interface, like script dialogs. Try to make commands short and memorable, and even user-configurable.

Inventory spam. Sometimes an object that automatically hands out Inventory will end up spamming people on the neighboring parcel. Be a good neighbor, and be sure to test this.

Floating text intrusion. Floating text is a quick and easy way to make a sign, but if the lines scale on the client side, they may grow so long that they'll stick through walls and objects. Consider adding line breaks.

Quick-scrolling chat. Sometimes a big block of chat or IM from an object scrolls by too fast, and having to open History to read it is a nuisance. It's a good idea to script some pauses between lines or use a different method of displaying text.

Unidentified chatting object. It's disconcerting when you can't tell what object is talking to you! Put some thought into what to name objects that communicate with residents.

Open listener lag. Objects that listen in open chat use up resources every time someone (or something!) speaks. You can reduce this by having your object listen on another channel, and only to certain people.

Slow-rezzing signs. Sign textures can take a long time to load, and it can be a drag waiting around for them. Some people might miss important information! Use the smallest texture you can, and think about other ways to get this info across when possible, to conserve texture resources.

RESIDENTS SPEAK

WHAT ARE THEY THINKING?

People in real-life buildings will read and follow signs. This is less true in *SL*.

—Seifert Surface (aka Henry Segerman)

Just do what I do—think like a newbie.

—CrystalShard Foo

Giant blocks of unformatted text. Big blocks of text are really hard to read in chat, and they're not a lot better on a notecard. Consider scripting an interface to open up an external web browser pointed to a web page where you can put your text.

Confusing script dialogs. Script dialogs are a great tool, but the buttons have a character limit on text, and can become abbreviated. Try setting them up as multiple-choice instead, labeled with letters or numbers.

Unreliable sounds. Scripted gadgets that play sound files in *SL* can be really nice for effect, but depending on how they are implemented, there might be a substantial delay before residents hear them, and sometimes they behave in various freaky ways (not playing at all or playing more than once). Don't depend on them for something really important. Sound can be an integral part of your creative arsenal, but loud, overly repetitive sounds can drive even the most patient avatar crazy.

No help with video. Streaming video is great, but for many residents it doesn't work or is disabled. To keep your event from being disrupted by cries of, "It won't play for me!" it's a great idea to have a source of help (a notecard or someone available to answer questions) obviously and immediately available.

HUD in the way. A lot of people really love HUDs (heads-up displays), and others hate them because they're distracting to look at and get in the way. Make HUDs as small as possible while leaving them readable and functional. If a HUD isn't intended to be in constant use, think about scripting it so that it can be made to disappear except for a small Restore button.

■ DESIGNING INTERFACES

Figure 9.29: This Click It! game has a very simple interface. The game gives feedback by firing happy and sad particles, with appropriate sound effects.

Second Life is a brilliant medium for social interaction, and it works especially well for simple visual user interfaces—point-and-click interfaces, things you talk to (or that talk to you), and things that give and take inventory. This makes *Second Life* wonderful for a sort of general environmental interactivity. Figure 9.29 shows a simple user interface for a game.

For example, a sensor notices your avatar nearby, so it gives you a cupcake and welcomes you to the sim. Or you can click on things that interest you and find that they tell you about themselves or give you an informative notecard. I find myself hiding clues and prizes under just about any rock or bush, often just for laughs, but also because it ensures that people will stick around and pay close attention. They certainly won't miss anything you actually label to indicate they should click it!

You can go pretty far with the script functions in *Second Life*, especially if you are not doggedly determined to avoid using external resources like servers, email, and linked web pages, and if you are flexible and focus on what *Second Life* does best. The key is to put a lot of thought into what you really need to accomplish, and in what way *Second Life* can be made to reach that goal—and be flexible about it!

RESIDENTS SPEAK

INTERFACE-DESIGN TIPS

I find simple physical analogies work best for user interfaces in *Second Life* . . . but that means you have to keep the interface simple. Think iPod rather than your TV's remote control. Some kind of feedback from the interface is really helpful too, but given the lag some people experience in-world, it is better if feedback augments the interface rather than being essential to it. It doesn't help much to hear a button click a couple of seconds after you touch it!

—Alexander Daguerre (aka Ian A. Young)

One of my favorite methods for inputting data into tools is by writing parameters into the object description field. It's fast and you can see what the parameters are and edit them all easily (particularly useful if the data needs to be typed in).

—Seifert Surface (aka Henry Segerman)

■ BRAINSTORMING

Suppose you want to hand out copies of a story you wrote. Seat your avatar in a thoughtful pose and brainstorm all the ways you might present your story to someone in *Second Life*. Your list might look like this:

- Type your story in Photoshop, import the textures, make a book of them, and sell it in a vendor.

- Drop your formatting, put your story on a bunch of nested notecards, and load it into a one-click notecard-giving box.

- Have an animated prim zebra tap dance as it reads your story in open chat or IM.

- Build a model of Times Square and scroll your story on a giant XY text billboard

- Build a teensy neon-colored scale model of Times Square and scroll your story as floating text.

- Put your story on a web page, which can be popped open by clicking a nifty sculpture in-world that contains a URL Loader script, or by using the Web tab of your avatar's profile.

- Script a gadget that will sense avatars nearby and ask for an email address. If the avatar types something that contains an @ sign, relay it to an outside server, which arranges to email the story as a `.doc` file

- Script a gadget that can be touched to get information about where to download a `.doc` file.

- Read the story aloud, chop it into 10-second `.wav` files, and use a script in-world to play them in order (if there isn't too much lag).

- Read the story aloud, record it, and stream it on your parcel.

- Broadcast a reading on an in-world radio station.

- Have a mixed-reality event where you give a reading in a café in real life and one just like it (but 1.5 times the size!) in *Second Life*.

RESIDENTS SPEAK

POINT AND CLICK

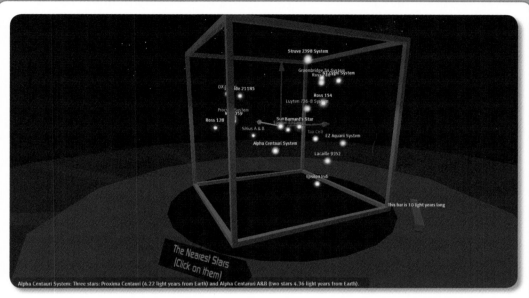

Alpha Centauri System: Three stars: Proxima Centauri (4.22 light years from Earth) and Alpha Centaruri A&B (two stars 4.36 light years from Earth).

I think the user interface on my exhibit The Nearest Stars is nice. It shows the 20 stars nearest the Earth (in 3D). Each star has its name floating above it as hover text. If you want to find out about that star, you just click on the star itself. It then glows brighter for a while and says a bit about itself. The brightened glow is so others can see which star you clicked. An alternative would have been to have signs all around with the name of each star on each sign, but then you would have to get the name of the star first and then use that to get the information about it from the associated sign. By clicking directly on a star, you don't have to pay any attention to the name.

—Troy McLuhan (aka Troy McConaghy)

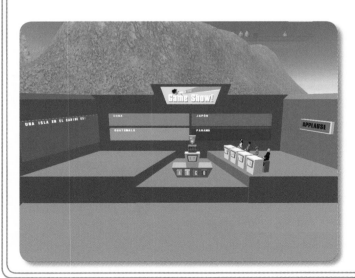

Button, button, who's got the button! We modeled a game show where contestants were asked a question and shown four possible answers on large display boards. The answers were color-coded to match the four buttons a player could press to choose their answer. That's how it works in real life. We discovered that in *SL*, players found it more natural to touch the correct answer up on the big board than to use separate buttons.

—Tracy Candour (aka Tracy Bialik)

DECIDING WHICH APPROACH IS BEST

Once you've thought up a bunch of possible interface types that might work—and some that are plain silly—how do you decide which is right for your project? Ask yourself some questions:

- How much time do you want to spend on this?
- What sort of resources can you commit to the project?
- What's the simplest thing that will work—particularly for your target audience?
- What approaches are sure to fail for technical or social reasons?
- Which of these approaches do you know how to do yourself?
- Do you already have some code you could repurpose for one of these approaches?
- Do you care about wowing people with special effects?
- How important to you is immersion?

TESTING YOUR UI

Once you've decided on an approach and implemented it, you'll need to test it to make sure it works properly. Test your interface, and test it again. Test it with an alt. Have experienced residents as well as newbies test it.

Round up as many testers as you can, and be ready to fix bugs and make changes. No matter how cool your UI design might be, if people find it confusing, it needs work.

INCLUDING INSTRUCTIONS AND DOCUMENTATION

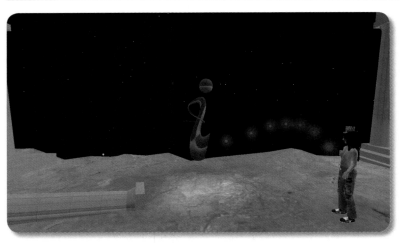

Figure 9.30: This sculpture targets random nearby avatars to interest them in clicking it.

Some gadgets are so simple that all you have to do is put them in place, and then people can touch them (Figure 9.30). A more complicated gadget might require a simple Help command that will make it list commands it knows. And then some scripted gadgets are so complex that they require documentation.

For example, Figure 9.31 depicts La Cocina de la Abuela, a game that helps people who are learning Spanish to practice their listening or reading skills. Players help the grandmother to find ingredients in her kitchen. When someone approaches this game machine, over the chair they'll notice floating text that tells the player (in Spanish) to sit down to play (Figure 9.32). Once they've followed that instruction, a script dialog offers the player a choice of difficulty levels and explains the game's backstory. From there, it's all point and click, audio feedback, and cool special effects, with a prize at the end. That's all the instruction the player needs, until the

Figure 9.31: I found the flour!

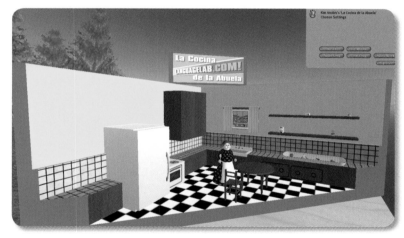

Figure 9.32: Script-dialog-driven controls for the game machine's owner

grandmother asks if the player would like to play another round.

However, this is a game my company built for a client. The client has to be able to deploy it. When they take it out of Inventory, it needs to be reset so it'll rez its moving parts and ingredients in the appropriate places and queue up the recipes and audio clips. Plus, it's configurable—the client can change out the dishes the grandmother prepares, the ingredients, the recipes for the various dishes, and the audio files. They can adjust the difficulty levels and decide if the machine should run in text mode, audio mode, or both. The client can change to what email addresses the game machine reports results. It's simple to play, but it isn't a simple gadget. That's why we included documentation and added a script-dialog-driven menu for the machine's owner to use for configuration.

Could we have gotten by without that menu, and let the client deal with everything manually? Sure. But it's important to make your interactive objects easy to use.

■ WEIGHING SIMPLICITY VS. REALISM

Common wisdom divides *Second Life* residents into two camps: *immersionists* and *platformists*. The former supposedly spend their entire second lives suspending disbelief and living in a fantasy world. The latter allegedly don't care at all about *Second Life* as a virtual world, and just view it as something similar to a web page or even a piece of graphics software. As someone with one foot planted solidly on each side of this divide, I think this is an oversimplified view that is bound to lead to unnecessary either-or decision making when designing things for *Second Life*.

How realistic you make your build or interface depends on your preferences, what you want to invest in making it work, and the actual purpose of the project. What aspect of this particular experience is most important to your end user? Are they living out a fantasy? Are they trying to learn something? Are they strictly about business?

RESIDENTS SPEAK

BALANCING FANTASY AND REALITY

When creating a functional build in *Second Life*, I think one of the most important things to keep in mind is that you have to find a balance between fantasy and reality. If you build something too realistic, people will be bored and take on a 'been there, done that' attitude. If your build is too whimsical, people will be put off and be hesitant to put it to use. I think architecture in *Second Life* should be something amazing that is impossible in, but also has its roots in, reality.

—DaVinci Doctorow (aka Barry Spencer II)

Don't get brain-locked by real life when you're modeling in *SL*. I wanted to make a kiosk that would show how large a build would be, by rezzing boundary markers to delineate the corners of the build. But an object can only rez other objects in a 10m radius, and these builds would be much larger than that. I had been thinking of the way a land surveyor would work by setting out markers. I was going to give up on my idea, due to the 10m limit, when I realized that I could rez the objects near the kiosk and tell *them* to move to the location. I gave each marker a timer as well, so it could clean itself up. The lesson is that objects can be smart in *SL*, even if they correspond to something dumb in real life, like an inanimate marker flag.

—Tracy Candour (aka Tracy Bialik)

Figure 9.33: People like their computers to talk to them.

Sometimes a realistic interface isn't very practical. For example, one of my clients wanted a way to do surveys in-world. We needed to offer a series of multiple-choice questions privately. Once again, I looked to good old script dialogs. The client wanted a fun build, though. Script dialogs, while functional, aren't what I'd call fun. The team brainstormed and came up with a computer with animated reels and blinking lights that spell out an invitation to take the survey (Figure 9.33). This isn't the sort of thing you encounter every day in real life, but it makes sense in a metaphorical way.

CHAPTER 1
CHAPTER 2
CHAPTER 3
CHAPTER 4
CHAPTER 5
CHAPTER 6
CHAPTER 7
CHAPTER 8
CHAPTER 9

CHAPTER 10
CHAPTER 11
CHAPTER 12
CHAPTER 13
CHAPTER 14
APPENDICES
INDEX

MORE INFO

COMBINING IN-WORLD AND EXTERNAL TOOLS IN *SECOND LIFE*

Some folks complain because *Second Life* doesn't have all the features they think it should have or because it doesn't do specific things well that they'd like to force it to do. It's as if you gave someone the most incredible Swiss Army knife ever designed, full of useful gadgets, and they complain because it does a pretty lousy job of jacking up their car or serving as a floatation device. *Second Life* is a powerful tool, but it isn't the right tool for every job. Sometimes you are better off letting folks access a web page in an external browser. Sometimes you should send documents or images or spreadsheets via old-fashioned email. That doesn't make *Second Life* lame—it's great at what it does. If you become frustrated because *Second Life* won't do what you want it to do, step back and consider whether there's a way to combine in-world and external tools to get better results.

Enchanted Palm Tree whispers: What do you mean, I'm not real?!

Figure 9.34: A friendly user interface

If I had to choose between function and realism, I'd choose function, because what good is a build you can't get around in or a gadget that's too confusing to use? But I don't think this is an either-or proposition. Even if you can't design something *literally* realistic, you can almost always come up with something that's *metaphorically* realistic enough.

Design something that functions well, and then imagine: What sort of face can I put on this to make it not only functionally user-friendly for avatars, but also just plain friendly for people (Figure 9.34)?

CHAPTER 10

TERRAFORMING

Almost everyone loves the outdoors, and everyone wants a good view when they look out the window. Plus, in *Second Life*, as in real life, builds depend on the lay of the land. Effective terraforming can make diverse builds into a cohesive whole, save you a lot of prims, channel traffic, and evoke a mood and a real sense of place.

In this chapter we'll discuss the tools used for terraforming and land management, the key considerations for effective *Second Life* landscape design, how to create features that involve both terraforming and objects, tips for how to set up your *Second Life* viewer and options like a terraforming pro, and some great info about terrain textures and height maps. Plus, you'll learn, step by step, how to create a landscape with a mountain trail. We're going to cover a lot of ground in this chapter—pun intended.

CONTENTS

CHAPTER 10

THE LAND
TOOLS

PLANNING
YOUR
LANDSCAPE

TUTORIAL:
CREATING A
MOUNTAIN
TRAIL

WORKING
WITH RAW
FILES

REGION
TERRAFORM-
ABILITY

THE LAND TOOLS

Second Life is divided into parts called *regions*. Most residents refer to a region as a *sim*—which is short for *simulator*. Each sim is 65,536 square meters in size (or 256 meters by 256 meters) and can support up to 15,000 objects.

Regions may be divided into smaller parcels. Some regions are part of the mainland. Others are detached from the mainland and cannot be reached by flying or walking. These are often called *private islands*. A resident's private islands (or just *islands*) together are called an *estate*.

The three main control panels you use to manage and modify land in *Second Life* are About Land, Region/Estate, and Edit Land (the terrain editor).

ABOUT LAND

The About Land control panel allows a property owner—or someone the property owner allows via group roles—to change settings for a parcel of land. To open About Land for the parcel on which your avatar is located, click the menu bar at the top of the screen where it shows the name of the region and parcel. You can also open About Land for this parcel, or others within range, using the pie menu. Right-click the ground and choose About Land. If it doesn't work, check to be sure you didn't accidentally click an object (maybe an invisible one) instead of the ground.

Let's look at the tabs on the About Land panel.

GENERAL

Figure 10.1: About Land, the General tab

The General tab on the About Land panel offers some basic information about this parcel (Figure 10.1).

Name: To change the parcel's name, type the new name in place of the old one. This change will take effect when you close the About Land console.

Description: Type a brief description of your parcel or what happens here, or some keywords. This text is used for your directory listing (more about that when we discuss the Options tab), and as the default text if you choose to add this parcel to your profile Picks tab (or of someone else adds it to theirs).

Owner: When you click the Info button, it'll open the parcel owner's profile, if it's an avatar. If the parcel is group-owned, the Info button opens Group Information.

CHAPTER 1
CHAPTER 2
CHAPTER 3
CHAPTER 4
CHAPTER 5
CHAPTER 6
CHAPTER 7
CHAPTER 8
CHAPTER 9
CHAPTER 10

CHAPTER 11
CHAPTER 12
CHAPTER 13
CHAPTER 14
APPENDICES
INDEX

> TIP
>
> *Only the parcel owner is able to set up—or, in some cases, use—a scripted object that affects parcel settings. So, if you want more than one person to be able to do this on a parcel, you need to make sure the parcel and object are both deeded to the same group, of which people who'll use the object are members. The most common reason you might do this would be to set up a radio or television object that controls streaming media on the parcel.*

Group: To set a group, click the Set button. This will open your Groups console, where you can select a group to which you belong. You can pick only one group, although you can change it later.

> TIP
>
> *Group-owned land gets a 10 percent tier bonus. In other words, if a group owns the land, it can hold 10 percent more land than an individual would for the same tier payment.*

Allow Deed to Group. This button allows you to transfer ownership of the parcel to the group. Check the box, then click the Deed button. Before you do this, take a careful look at the Group Information console to review who will have the ability to control the land, including the ability to sell it! This is not something you will be able to undo with a simple click of a button. The only way to reclaim the parcel deed will be to purchase the parcel from the group—if a group officer offers it for sale.

Also be sure that group members have contributed enough tier to maintain the parcel. Look at the Land tab on the Group Information console.

Owner Makes Contribution with Deed. When this is checked and you deed the parcel to the group, your tier will automatically be contributed to the group and applied to maintaining this parcel.

For Sale: If the land is for sale, this field will list the sale price and the name of any specific avatar for whom the sale has been set.

Sell Land: To set the parcel for sale, click this button. This opens the Sell Land window (Figure 10.2). Type the sale price and use the drop-down menu to choose whether to sell the parcel to anyone or to a specific avatar. So, for example, if you wanted to give a parcel to a friend, you could set it for sale specifically to them for L$1. This way, someone you don't know can't purchase it before your friend can hit the Buy Land button.

To sell the objects on the parcel along with the land itself, select the Yes, Sell Objects with Land radio button. Only transferable objects can be sold this way. To see what you'll be giving up, click Show Objects. This will highlight the objects so they're easy to spot.

WARNING

If you choose to sell objects with the land, be sure to keep backups and check the permissions on everything you're about to transfer. Some residents avoid using this feature, and instead transfer their builds manually.

CHAPTER 10

THE LAND
TOOLS

PLANNING
YOUR
LANDSCAPE

TUTORIAL:
CREATING A
MOUNTAIN
TRAIL

WORKING
WITH RAW
FILES

REGION
TERRAFORM-
ABILITY

Figure 10.2: The Sell Land window

There are no take-backs, do-overs, or eraseys when it comes to selling your parcel. Be sure you really do want to sell it, and that the price is set correctly. Some people even have scripted objects that watch for bargains, and they might snap up your land more quickly than you can change your mind!

Claimed: This indicates when the parcel was last claimed. This is not always an accurate measure of how long someone has held the land, though; it might have changed when two parcels were joined together, for example.

Area: This shows the size of the parcel, in square meters.

Traffic: This describes how much time visitors spend on the parcel, based on how many avatars visited it that day and the percentage of each visitor's in-world day spent on the parcel.

Buy Pass: Click this button if someone is charging admission to their parcel and you'd like to enter.

Reclaim Land: To reclaim a parcel on your estate that you have sold to another resident, click the Reclaim Land button.

Buy for Group: To purchase land for your group, click this button.

Abandon Land: To return a parcel to Linden Lab without receiving any payment, click this button. The Abandon Land button is clickable only when the option is available. Owners of private islands can't abandon their islands.

TIP

Before you abandon your land, consider the consequences. The only real benefit of using this feature is to avoid maintaining the land's tier fees, but if you were to list the land for sale for just a short period, someone would buy it. Even if you were to sell at a low price, you could recoup some or all of your investment.

COVENANT

The Covenant tab (Figure 10.3) displays the names of the parcel, estate, and estate owner to which the parcel belongs, as well as the covenant itself.

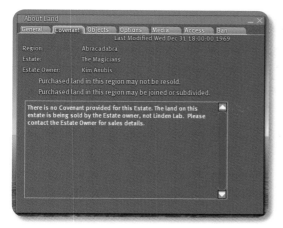

Covenants allow land owners to inform prospective land purchasers of the rules by which they'll have to abide as landowners within their estate. It's sort of like a Terms of Service statement. Land can't be resold on a private island if there's no covenant—people who buy parcels will have to abandon them if they don't want them any longer. If the estate owner does set the covenant using the Region/Estate console (which we'll discuss soon) it appears here.

Figure 10.3 The Covenant tab displays rules that the estate owner has set for parcel owners.

OBJECTS

Figure 10.4: You can use the Objects tab to highlight all objects belonging to a specific avatar.

The Objects tab (Figure 10.4) displays information about and helps you to manage the objects on your parcel.

Simulator Primitive Usage: This field shows the parcel owner's Simulator Primitive Usage data. Say you have two parcels in the same region, and one supports 20 primitives and the other supports 200. You would be able to put 20 on one and 200 on the other, or all 220 on one. You could get wild and crazy and put 110 on each. In other words, the number of prims you can use in a region is based on how much land you own in the entire region, and you can spend the prims wherever you like!

Primitives Parcel Supports: The number of objects—*primitives*—you can use on your parcel is tied to the parcel size. If you have 16 square meters of land (the smallest parcel allowed), it can have three objects—or *prims*—on it. For example, a 512-square-meter parcel normally supports 117 objects. An entire private island supports 15,000.

Primitives on Parcel: This indicates how many primitives are on the parcel.

Owned by Parcel Owner: This tells you how many prims on the parcel belong to the parcel owner.

Set to Group: This indicates how many prims on the parcel have been set or deeded to the group to which the parcel has been set or deeded.

CHAPTER 10

THE LAND
TOOLS

PLANNING
YOUR
LANDSCAPE

TUTORIAL:
CREATING A
MOUNTAIN
TRAIL

WORKING
WITH RAW
FILES

REGION
TERRAFORM-
ABILITY

Owned by Others: This shows how many prims are owned by people who neither own the land nor belong to the group to which the parcel has been set or deeded.

Selected / Sat Upon: This field indicates how many objects are currently being edited or used as seats.

To spot objects in these categories easily, click the appropriate Show button. Returning objects that belong to yourself, your group, or others is as easy as clicking the appropriate Return button.

TIP

When you use the Show button on the Objects tab, objects are highlighted. To make it even easier to spot highlighted objects in the region, you can "force the sun" and make it look like midnight. This affects only your own viewer, so you won't be turning out the lights for everyone else! Select World ▸ Force Sun ▸ Midnight. When you're done, select World ▸ Force Sun ▸ Return to Region Default.

Autoreturn Other Residents' Objects: Cleaning up stray prims left by visitors can be a time-consuming chore. Fortunately, *Second Life* allows you to automate it. In the box next to Autoreturn Other Residents' Objects, type a number corresponding to how many minutes you'd like to allow objects to remain on the parcel when they don't belong to you or to members of the group to which the parcel's set. The minimum is one minute. To turn off Autoreturn, type a zero in the box.

This tab also includes a list of names of residents who have objects on the parcel, and just how many objects each has left there. To highlight all of a person's objects on your parcel, find their name on the list and click it. To return just that person's objects, click the Return Objects button on the Object Owners line.

OPTIONS

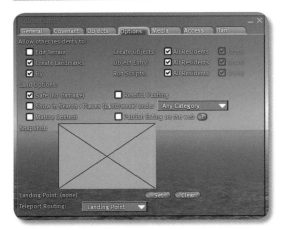

Figure 10.5: The Options tab offers you some control over what people do on your parcel.

The Options tab (Figure 10.5) offers tools to control what people are allowed to do on your parcel. It also allows you to make some arrangements to publicize your build.

Edit Terrain: This box, when checked, allows anyone to terraform here.

WARNING

If Edit Terrain is enabled on the Options tab, anyone can accidentally or maliciously edit your parcel's terraforming.

Create Landmarks: If you uncheck this box, no one can create a landmark on this parcel.

Fly: Uncheck this, and no one can start flying on this parcel. When they try, they'll jump without taking off, and they'll hear a distinctive sound effect. If avatars are already airborne when they arrive, though, they can still fly.

The next three parcel permissions come with a pair of boxes each. This means you can allow everyone to do these things, allow only members of the parcel's group to do them—if they're wearing their group tags—or not allow anyone do them.

Create Objects: Check this to control whether someone can create objects on your land or take something out of Inventory.

Object Entry: Check this to control whether someone's objects can enter your parcel from another parcel.

NOTE

Vehicles are not subject to Object Entry restrictions.

Run Scripts: To control whether someone can use scripted objects on your parcel, check this. This might not stop scripts that are already running when they arrive.

Safe: If you check this, no one will be damaged on your parcel. Otherwise, avatars can be hurt by weapons, by falling, by prims being dropped on their heads, etc. If an avatar is damaged enough, it will die. Fortunately, all that means is that the avatar is instantly teleported to their home point, damage-free and with their inventory intact. Whew!

MORE INFO

AN UNEXPECTED CONSEQUENCE OF AN OPTIONS SETTING

For a while I was fascinated with *Second Life* aviation, and I had a runway and a hangar and a collection of planes, and I flew everywhere instead of teleporting. But often, just as I was landing, I'd suddenly be teleported to my home point, right across the parcel! I thought it was some sort of bug. It took me the longest time to realize what was going on. My landings were more than a tad too hard. I was killing myself on impact on my damage-enabled parcel!

Show in Search > Places: This box allows you to list your parcel under the category of your choice so that other residents can find it using Search. Search will find your parcel based on its name, as well as keywords in the parcel description you fill in on the General tab. Search also displays that description, along with the image you set on the Options tab. This listing costs L$30 weekly.

Mature Content: Check this box to indicate your parcel contains mature content. Residents can restrict their Search so that it does not include parcels with mature content. You're responsible for using good judgment when you decide whether to check this box.

Restrict Pushing: `llPushObject` is a function that allows a scripted object to apply force to an object or avatar and move it. Check this box to disable this script function on your land. Why would you do this? Some residents might want to cause trouble by shooting you or visitors to your parcel with a *push gun*. This puts a stop to it. It also puts a stop to fun things, though, like trampolines, which also use the Push function.

CHAPTER 1
CHAPTER 2
CHAPTER 3
CHAPTER 4
CHAPTER 5
CHAPTER 6
CHAPTER 7
CHAPTER 8
CHAPTER 9
CHAPTER 10

CHAPTER 11
CHAPTER 12
CHAPTER 13
CHAPTER 14
APPENDICES
INDEX

CHAPTER 10

THE LAND
TOOLS

PLANNING
YOUR
LANDSCAPE

TUTORIAL:
CREATING A
MOUNTAIN
TRAIL

WORKING
WITH RAW
FILES

REGION
TERRAFORM-
ABILITY

Publish Listing on the Web: Check this box if you are willing to have your parcel description displayed on the *Second Life* web site.

Snapshot: Drag a snapshot of your parcel or another texture from your Inventory and drop it on the rectangle.

Landing Point: To set a landing point for avatars who teleport to your parcel, stand in the location facing the direction in which you would like new arrivals to face, then click the Set button.

Teleport Routing: Use this drop-down to select whether avatars can teleport only to the Landing Point, anywhere on the parcel, or nowhere on the parcel.

■ MEDIA

The Media tab (Figure 10.6) offers you an interface to control media on your parcel.

Figure 10.6: Choosing the media texture for a parcel

Restrict Spatialized Sound to This Parcel: Check this box to keep sounds generated on neighboring parcels from being heard on this one.

Music URL: Type the URL of a music stream here to play it on your parcel. This will take effect when you close the About Land tab.

Media Texture: Click the gray box to open the Pick: Texture window, then select one from the list. In Figure 10.6 we have chosen the *Default Media Texture from the Library. The texture you choose here will be replaced with your video stream. Enter the URL where the video stream you want to play is hosted.

Auto Scale Content: Check this box to have your video image automatically scaled to fit prims on which it appears. This can distort the image and make the stream run more slowly. For better results, make a video screen of the correct dimensions.

MORE INFO

MEDIA-TAB TIPS

You can use any texture you like for your Media texture. Consider using something that looks nice when people don't have streaming video enabled, such as your logo or even a texture with text explaining how to enable streaming video.

The Music URL and Media URL options can both be changed via script functions.

The Media Player object in your Library's Objects folder has a screen and scripted controls, ready to use with the *Default Media Texture.

ACCESS

Figure 10.7: The Access tab lets you control who can visit your parcel.

Use the Access (Figure 10.7) tab to allow avatars to enter your parcel when you have set access restrictions.

Group and **Avatars**: Check the Group box to grant access to members of the group to which the parcel is set, or check Avatars, click Add, and select to up to 300 specific avatars.

Sell Passes Allowing Temporary Access: If you restrict access to the parcel, the Sell Passes Allowing Temporary Access box will become functional. To sell passes, check the box then enter an admission price and the length of time a pass lasts.

TIP

A parcel owner can use scripted objects to control access settings.

BAN

The Ban tab (Figure 10.8) allows you to keep up to 300 specific avatars from entering your parcel. To do this, check Ban These Avatars, then the Add button to bring up the Choose Resident window. Highlight the avatar's name and click Select. Use the same process to remove an avatar from the list, but click the Remove button instead of Add. In Figure 10.8, you can see the abusive instant message I received from that litterer TheGreat Gandini. I checked the Ban These Avatars box, clicked the Add button, typed the miscreant's name in the box in the Choose Resident window, highlighted his name, and clicked Select. If he takes back the threat to saw my car in half, I might highlight his name in the Ban These Avatars list and choose Remove. Maybe.

CHAPTER 1
CHAPTER 2
CHAPTER 3
CHAPTER 4
CHAPTER 5
CHAPTER 6
CHAPTER 7
CHAPTER 8
CHAPTER 9
CHAPTER 10

CHAPTER 11
CHAPTER 12
CHAPTER 13
CHAPTER 14
APPENDICES
INDEX

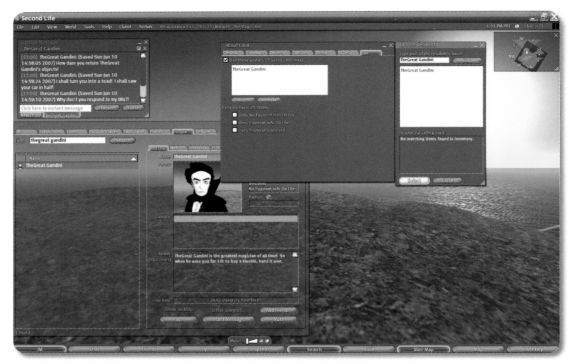

Figure 10.8: Here's an example of how to ban an avatar from your parcel.

You can also restrict access based on residents' payment status by checking the Deny by Payment Status boxes:

Deny No Payment Info on File

Deny Payment Info on File

Deny Payment Info Used

To freeze or eject an avatar from your land, right-click them and choose the appropriate option from the pie menu.

Residents not allowed access to a parcel will not be able to approach lower than 50 meters above the ground. Residents banned from a parcel will not be able to approach lower than 768 meters.

■ USING THE REGION/ESTATE WINDOW

The Region/Estate window offers tools for managing private islands. Some of the settings on this tab will affect all of the regions that are part of the estate.

◼ REGION

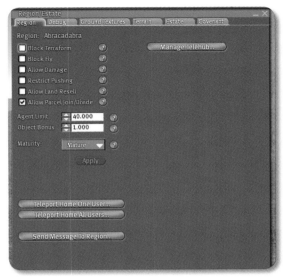

CHAPTER 1
CHAPTER 2
CHAPTER 3
CHAPTER 4
CHAPTER 5
CHAPTER 6
CHAPTER 7
CHAPTER 8
CHAPTER 9
CHAPTER 10
CHAPTER 11
CHAPTER 12
CHAPTER 13
CHAPTER 14
APPENDICES
INDEX

The Region tab (Figure 10.9) gives you access to settings that control your sim or one you are allowed to manage.

> **Block Terraform**, **Block Fly**, **Allow Damage**, and **Restrict Pushing**: Check this to override the settings on parcels. When unchecked, these can be set individually on each parcel using About Land.
>
> **Allow Land Resell** and **Allow Parcel Join/Divide**: Checking these will change these settings for all parcels on the island.
>
> **Agent Limit**: Use this control to raise or lower the number of avatars allowed in the region at once. The default is 40. Region performance is affected by the number of avatars in it; you might hear complaints about "lag" if too many avatars visit at once!

Figure 10.9: The Region tab

Object Bonus: Use this control to increase the number of objects each square meter of your sim is allowed to support. So a 512-square-meter parcel with an object bonus of 2 could have 234 prims on it instead of 117! But this doesn't increase the number of prims you can use on the entire island— that's always 15,000 total.

Maturity: Use this drop-down to switch the region's rating between PG and Mature.

Teleport Home One User: Click this to bring up the Choose Resident window, where you can select a name.

Teleport Home All Users: To send home everyone in the region, click this button.

Send Message to Region: To send a message to every avatar in the region, click this button. This opens a window in which to type your message (Figure 10.10). Everyone in the sim will see it in a blue pop-up in the corner of their screen.

Figure 10.10 Using the Send Message to Region button

Manage Telehub: Click this to open a window, shown in Figure 10.11, that you can use to turn objects into Telehubs or to disconnect them. Once an object has been turned into a Telehub, you can move it, and the Telehub will move with it. You can also create multiple spawn points to keep avatars from stacking up when they arrive. The prims you use to set the spawn points can be removed once the points are saved.

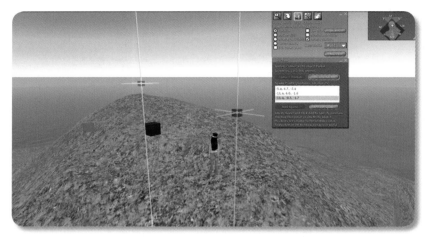

Figure 10.11 The yellow beacon marks the Telehub and the orange beacon marks a spawn point

DEBUG

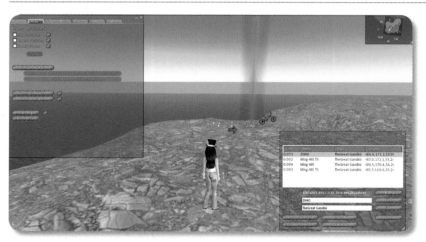

The Debug tab (Figure 10.12) offers tools for troubleshooting resource-hogging objects and scripts.

Disable Scripts: Check this to turn off all scripts in the region.

Disable Collisions: Check this to stop physical-object collision in a region.

Figure 10.12: Using the Top Scripts window from the Debug tab to set a beacon on litter

Disable Physics: Check this to turn off physics in the region—including avatar movement!

Get Top Colliders and **Get Top Scripts**: Click one of these to open a window that will list objects that are putting a load on the region. You can use this window, shown in Figure 10.12, to set a beacon on these objects to find them or return them.

Region Restart: Click this to force the region to restart in two minutes.

Cancel Restart: Click this within two minutes if you decide not to restart your region.

GROUND TEXTURES

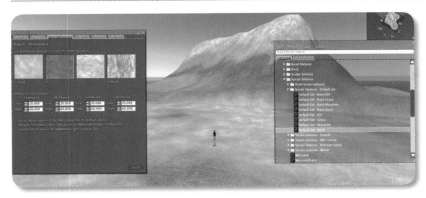

Figure 10.13: The Ground Textures tab has controls for setting terrain textures and ranges.

The Ground Textures tab (Figure 10.13) is used for setting the terrain textures on a private island. It isn't as complicated as it looks!

There are four texture levels, and this window lists them, with a picture of the lowest on the left and the highest on the right. You just drag textures from inventory and drop them on the rectangles shown in Figure 10.13. They'll blend into each other where they meet. The textures have to be 512×512 pixels in 24-bit TGA format. You can find a good selection in the Library ▸ Textures folder.

The texture heights can be adjusted in each corner of the sim; the heights will automatically average out in its center. So, for example, changing the numbers for Southwest can make a dramatic change to how high or low various textures appear on the southwest corner of the sim, with gradually less impact toward the center of the sim, and none on the other corners.

The Low settings adjust the maximum height of Texture 1 in each corner; the High numbers set the minimum height of Texture 4 in each corner; 2 and 3 fill in between these. So if you set Texture 1 at 10 meters and Texture 4 at 60 feet, everything from an altitude of 0 to 10 would be dirt, then you'd have a band of grass halfway from there to 60 meters, then that brownish rock up to 60 meters, and gray rock at the top. Once you have all of this set, click Apply.

RESIDENTS SPEAK

KEITH EXTRAORDINAIRE ON CREATING LANDSCAPE TEXTURES

Creating textures for a sim takes a bit of forethought. Sims tile four layers of 512×512 textures, the elevation of the land determining which textures will render where. In order for this to come off well, the textures must be perfectly seamless, appropriately in scale with the size they will render, and also be able to blend into one another in an attractive way. Also, using extremely detailed textures for the terrain will render poorly, giving off an annoying pixel flicker as your camera moves, so a slightly less sharp image is much better to use than a crisp one. Avoid creating anything in which the repeats will become extremely apparent.

TIP

You don't have to use four different terrain textures, and you don't have to stick to natural textures. You can even terraform the ground flat and use a texture like wood flooring or kitchen tile.

CHAPTER 1
CHAPTER 2
CHAPTER 3
CHAPTER 4
CHAPTER 5
CHAPTER 6
CHAPTER 7
CHAPTER 8
CHAPTER 9
CHAPTER 10

CHAPTER 11
CHAPTER 12
CHAPTER 13
CHAPTER 14
APPENDICES
INDEX

TERRAIN

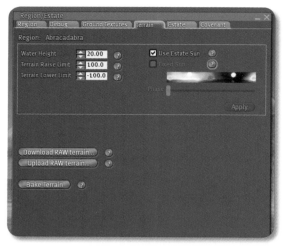

Figure 10.14: The Terrain tab offers some powerful tools.

The tools on the Terrain tab (Figure 10.14) offer you the ability to make some big changes to the region, as well as to make a backup of your terraforming.

Water Height: Change this setting to adjust at what height water will be rendered in the region. It will look freaky if you set it higher or lower than 20 meters, though, because that is where it's set on all the water around private islands and by most landowners.

Terrain Raise Limit and **Terrain Lower Limit**: Change this setting to choose by how much terraforming on the sim may vary.

Bake Terrain: To set the current terrain as the default, click this. Now when you use the Revert Land tool, this is the terrain to which you'll revert.

Use Estate Sun: Check this to make the day/night cycle match throughout all of the regions in the estate. If you uncheck this, you can set this region's time of day independently.

Download RAW Terrain: Click this to export your terrain for backup or modification outside of *Second Life*.

Upload RAW Terrain: Click this to import terrain you have modified or created outside of *Second Life*. We'll discuss RAW files further on in this chapter.

TIP

If you want a dark and murky effect, consider putting your build underwater!

RESIDENTS SPEAK

TONY BECKETT ON ESTATE MANAGEMENT

- A sim is 256m×256m—but the grid is 4m×4m squares.
- Ground textures come in from the corners.
- If being attacked by griefers, always remember no one dies in SL.
- Private estates can be rolled back.
- Work with people you trust and respect.

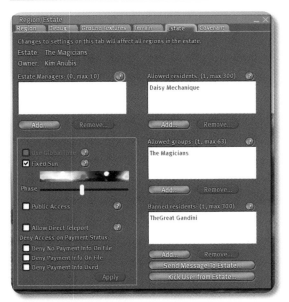

Figure 10.15: The Estate tab offers tools that affect multiple regions.

This tab (Figure 10.15) lists the name of the estate to which this region belongs and the name of the estate's owner, plus offers tools that affect the entire estate, especially avatar access.

Estate Managers: Click the Add button to bring up a window you can use to add names of other residents you want to have the ability to use most of your Region/Estate controls. Estate managers can't deed land or access About Land, but they can request rollbacks. Use the Remove button if you decide to take away these abilities.

Use Global Time: Check this box to keep the region's day/night cycle in sync with the mainland.

Fixed Sun: Check this box to keep the sun from moving.

Phase: Use this slider to set the time of day when you have checked the Fixed Sun box.

Public Access: Check this box to allow all residents to visit the estate, except those who have been specifically banned.

Allow Direct Teleport: Check this to allow avatars to teleport directly to any point. However, if they teleport to a parcel with Landing Point routing set on About Land, they'll arrive at the parcel's landing point. You can also disable Direct Teleport and set up a Telehub.

Deny Access on Payment Status: Use the check boxes to block visits to the estate from avatars on the basis of aspects of their *Second Life* billing history.

Allowed Residents: Click Add or Remove to bring up a window that will allow you to choose avatars that will be allowed in the estate when you have restricted access, or to take them off the list.

Allowed Groups: Click Add or Remove to bring up a window that will allow you to choose groups that will be allowed in the estate when you have restricted access, or to take them off the list.

Banned Residents: Click Add or Remove to bring up a window that will allow you to ban specific avatars from visiting your estate, or to take them off the list.

Send Message to Estate: This works like the Send Message to Region button, but sends the message to all avatars in the estate.

Kick User from Estate: Use this button to open a window to use to select a specific avatar to kick from the estate.

THE LAND
TOOLS

PLANNING
YOUR
LANDSCAPE

TUTORIAL:
CREATING A
MOUNTAIN
TRAIL

WORKING
WITH RAW
FILES

REGION
TERRAFORM-
ABILITY

COVENANT

Figure 10.16: Use the Covenant tab to post an agreement for your tenants.

This tab lists the name of the region, estate, and estate owner (Figure 10.16). Use this tab to post the rules for your island, which will appear in the Covenant tab on About Land on each parcel. You have to set a covenant if you want to allow people who buy land to resell it, and even if that isn't something you want to do, you might want to post other things here, such as "keep out" or messages to friends.

To change the covenant, type it on a notecard and then drag it from Inventory onto this tab. You can also use the Reset button if you own the region, but not if you are an estate manager. Estate managers can drop a notecard here and set parcels for sale, but the estate owner can reclaim the land.

EDIT LAND

Figure 10.17: Two ways to open Edit Land

Edit Land gives you access to the in-world tools you use to terraform in *Second Life*. To open it, right-click your land and select Edit Terrain from the pie menu, or press the button to open this on the same tool you use to edit prims, or even find the Terrain Edit tool on the Tools menu (Figure 10.17).

Select Land: From the drop-down menu you can choose to select Small, Medium, or Large squares of terrain to edit. The tool will appear as a square of white dots hovering over the land. If you want to edit a larger area, click the Select Land radio button, and then click and drag to select an area (Figure 10.18).

The other radio buttons, pictured in Figure 10.18, switch between the different ways in which you can modify the terrain, directly or by using Select Land to choose an area and clicking Apply to Selection.

Flatten Land: Each click makes the land flatter, with a target of being perfectly flat, and will match the altitude of the center of the selected area.

Figure 10.18: Edit Land controls

Raise Land: Each click increases the altitude of this piece of land.

Lower Land: Each click decreases the altitude of this piece of land.

Smooth Land: Each click smoothes this piece of land, with a target altitude at the center of the selected area. So if the center of the land you select is 50m high, the target altitude will be 50m.

Roughen Land: Each click makes the land more uneven, adding bumps and hollows.

Revert Land: Each click makes the terrain more and more like the baked terrain height map.

Show Owners: Click the Show Owners check box to put a colored overlay on the ground to indicate who owns it:

- *Red: Owned by others*

- *Green: Your land*

- *Aqua: Land owned by a group of which you're a member*

- *Gray: Public land*

- *Purple: Land in the auction system*

Buy Land: Click this to purchase the land.

Abandon Land. Click this button to give up the parcel. You can't undo this, and you will not get a refund for the land.

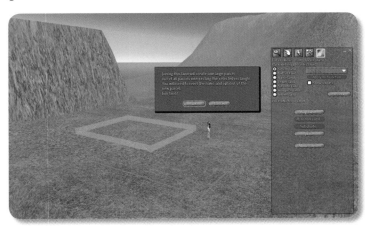

Figure 10.19: Joining two parcels

Subdivide. Select a piece of land, then click this button to make the land a new parcel—provided this option is allowed by the estate owner!

Join: To combine parcels (if allowed on the estate), click and drag to select an area that includes at least part of each one, then click the Join button (Figure 10.19).

CHAPTER 10

The Land
Tools

Planning
Your
Landscape

Tutorial:
Creating a
Mountain
Trail

Working
with RAW
Files

Region
Terraform-
ability

WARNING

If you divide a parcel with the intent of transferring part of it to someone else, look at the Objects tab on About Land to make sure the number of objects on each parcel can actually be supported by that parcel, rather than only as part of the simulator total. Otherwise, part of the build might be returned to their owners!

FROM LINDEN LAB

Eric Linden (aka Eric Call) on Terraforming Dos and Don'ts

Don't create extreme slopes (textures will smear and look bad).

Perfection is imperfect: leaving some bumps and "noise" in your terrain is more realistic than completely flat land.

Use caution when using the Apply to Selection button: a smoothing algorithm extends the effect of your work beyond the land you've selected.

The Smooth Land control is a powerful tool when you need to blend between simulators or parcels having different elevations.

Always "bake" the land when your work is done to establish a revision point.

According to Eric, the most common terraforming mistakes are as follows:

Accidentally burying existing content

Not understanding that the Land Editor bases its edits on a reference point at the center of the selected area, regardless of the selection size

Over-working the terrain: not knowing when to stop.

RESIDENTS SPEAK

Hayduke Ebisu (aka Josh Knauer) on Terraforming Dos and Don'ts

Come up with an overall concept that applies to the entire sim.

Find photos of real-life (or illustrations of imaginary) places that evoke the concept.

Sketch it out on paper in two dimensional form (i.e., from above), but to scale.

Make sure you can actually fit everything you want to do within the sim.

Share your sketch/concept with others by writing up a short description of your concept along with your sketch.

Revise your sketch based on the feedback you get that you agree with.

Learn how to manipulate RAW terrain files within Photoshop.

- Start experimenting with the RAW file to implement some of the concepts you have sketched, upload and pray.

- Be prepared to tweak and iterate through many revisions in Photoshop; save every single one as a separate RAW file so you can revert!

- Finally, add finishing touches using the *Second Life* terraforming tools.

  Hayduke points out the following mistakes to avoid:

- Trying to do it all using the manual terraforming tools.

- Not incorporating enough vertical height into the landscape . . . flat is boring!

- Not having enough roughness. Too many builds in *Second Life* are always rounded and even looking. Nature is messy. Mimic it!

- Use the various channels within the RAW file . . . experiment!

- Most designers always try to create the perfect masterpiece on the first go-around. Great design comes from lots and lots of iterative steps along the way.

- SCALE! Most terraformers in *SL* forget about the scale of what they are trying to build. If you are creating a sim that is supposed to mimic or evoke something from nature, make sure you think about the average height of avatars, of the trees or foliage you are going to want to place in the environment, and then make your terraforming scale to an appropriate size. Far too often, mountains and other features in *SL* are way too small.

PLANNING YOUR LANDSCAPE

It's fun to play with the terraforming tools and controls available in *Second Life*, and you're probably ready to fly right to your parcel and get started. But planning and preparation help a lot in creating a landscape that's not just special-looking, but that also does a great job of meeting functional goals.

■ CHOOSING A LOCATION

What might be the perfect parcel for your project might be totally unworkable for someone else's, and some parcels might not suit your needs at all. If you can, take the time to choose a parcel that suits your plans, and you'll have a much easier and fun time terraforming it . . . with far better results.

Mainland or private island? Your terraforming options are far more limited on the mainland. On most mainland sims, you can terraform plus or minus four meters, but some you can't terraform at all, and others allow plus or minus 100 meters. As well, on the mainland, you can't use the Region/Estate tools. However, the mainland does have foot (or flyby) traffic and Linden infrastructure, like roads and Infohubs.

Lay of the land: If you decide you want a mainland parcel, you'll typically be able to raise or lower the land by only four meters. Will you be able to get the results you want from the parcel you're considering? It's hard to tell if, for example, a low-lying island is at its natural

CHAPTER 10

THE LAND
TOOLS

PLANNING
YOUR
LANDSCAPE

TUTORIAL:
CREATING A
MOUNTAIN
TRAIL

WORKING
WITH RAW
FILES

REGION
TERRAFORM-
ABILITY

height, or if a previous owner raised it and it's already at its maximum. Ask the seller to show you, or try chatting with the neighbors.

PG or Mature? Estate owners can decide, but if you're a renter, choose land in a region with the rating you require.

Private island or Openspaces? Sometimes called *void regions* (because Linden Lab used them to fill in former voids on the mainland map), Openspaces are purchased only in blocks of four, and must be linked to your existing estate. They're the same size as normal sims, but you get four for the price of one. The catch? They also have the same computing power as one normal private island, and you can put only 1,875 objects on each Openspace. They're great if you want to create large areas for sailing or landscapes, but not for general use.

Own or rent? You have more control if you own land—you can't access the option to manage RAW terrain files unless you actually own an estate. However, if the owner has made you an estate manager, you can do just about everything else.

Neighborhood and covenant: Some neighborhoods are a lot nicer than others, and some are pricier. Some look like the result of an explosion at the junkyard. Sometimes neighbors have a formal or loose agreement to stick to a certain style or theme. Unless there's a covenant, though, the only thing you can count on is change.

Neighboring parcels and sims: Be sure to consider the water height, terrain height, and terrain texture of the neighboring parcel or sim. It can look pretty freaky if these change abruptly.

MORE INFO

WHAT DO YOU DO IF YOUR NEIGHBOR DECIDES TO LEAVE A 15-METER-HIGH STACK OF TOILETS IN THEIR DOORYARD?

- Offer to purchase their dooryard and plant trees instead
- Plant trees on your side of the property line
- Terraform a hill between your build and their junk
- Build a wall—it's convenient and neighborly to set it phantom and clear on their side
- Create or buy screens with scenery you would rather see, like hills and trees
- Orient your build so you look out at a different view

■ SETTING UP YOUR VIEWER

Once you have your land, you're almost ready to start terraforming. Here are a few tips on how to tweak your *Second Life* viewer and options like a master landscape artist.

Ditch your HUD: You need to look at the big picture when terraforming, so clear away clutter that blocks part of your view by minimizing or removing HUDs.

Resize the client: You want a big view, so run *Second Life* in full-screen mode if you can, or in a very big window. If you have a widescreen monitor, take advantage of it. However, if you are running full-screen on a widescreen monitor, resize the window from time to time to check how your landscape will look to others with regular monitors.

Day or night: Landscapes, more than anything else in *Second Life*, appear very different at different times of day. World ▸ Force Sun lets you make a client-side change to the apparent time of day, or you can use the Region/Estate controls.

Show property lines: Select View ▸ Property lines (or Ctrl+Alt+Shift+P) to see the edges of the parcel. These show up even better at night, so I often force midnight when I am checking them.

Draw distance: The default distance you can see is 128 meters, which lets you see only halfway across a flat sim. Select Edit ▸ Preferences ▸ Graphics ▸ Draw Distance and try increasing and decreasing it. Longer distances mean your client has to draw more objects, which means slower performance, so you will have to find a happy medium. Always be sure to check how your finished terrain looks at the standard 128-meter draw distance, and the minimum 64 meters, too.

Increase detail: To increase or decrease the detail level at which your terrain and Linden Library plants are rendered, select Edit ▸ Preferences ▸ Graphics Detail and then use the Tree Mesh Detail slider and the Terrain Detail radio button.

Disable camera constraints: You can zoom way out if you select Client ▸ Disable Camera Constraints (Figure 10.20). If you don't see Client as an option, type Ctrl+Alt+Shift+D to add it to the menu. This is really handy to check how the terrain you are standing on and working on looks from a distance without having to walk away.

Figure 10.20: Disabling camera constraints

Clouds in the way? Prims stuck underground? You can stop your viewer from drawing clouds (Figure 10.21), the ground, avatars, and more. For example, to see underground, select Client ▸ Rendering ▸ Types ▸ Surface Patch.

CHAPTER 10

THE LAND
TOOLS

PLANNING
YOUR
LANDSCAPE

TUTORIAL:
CREATING A
MOUNTAIN
TRAIL

WORKING
WITH RAW
FILES

REGION
TERRAFORM-
ABILITY

Figure 10.21: Stopping clouds from being rendered

Minimap: The Minimap (View ▸ Minimap) helps you to see just where you are in your terrain, and shows you textures, water, the cardinal directions, and locations of objects. Your objects are shown in aqua blue, and the rest are dark gray.

Walking or flying? Some visitors will want to walk, and others will fly. You need to see things from both points of view, so you can't do all your terraforming from in the air. Walking back and forth to check things is time-consuming. Ctrl+R will make your avatar run instead of walking; press it again to revert. It might be a good idea to buy a flight-assist gadget or a jet pack, too.

■ LANDSCAPE DESIGN

You probably have an idea of what sort of landscape you want to create—you might even have sketches or photographs. A lot of real-life landscape-design concepts apply in *Second Life*. However, unless you are planning to create a tiny jewel of a walled garden or own multiple sims, you will probably have to adjust your vision to make it work in *Second Life*.

Perspective: Perspective isn't quite accurate in *Second Life* and sims are small (and avatars are large!). So it's a good idea to limit how many features you include in your landscape. Sometimes you have to make features larger or smaller, closer or farther apart, than they would be in real life in order to give a natural effect.

Neighbors or the edge of the world: You might have immediate neighbors or the edge of the estate—or even the world—right next to your build. It might be necessary to rearrange your layout to camouflage this!

Replace buildings: Think about when you can use terrain instead of buildings. Terrain doesn't cost any prims. How can you use terraforming to divide spaces and make them private? Take a look at some traditional Japanese or formal European gardens for ideas about creating outdoor garden "rooms."

Drive traffic: Terraforming can drive traffic where you want it. Tempting paths that wind off to an unseen area lure visitors to seek adventure. You can also turn off the ability to fly and create obstacles from forbidding terrain or deep water. In theme park-design, a big, eye-catching feature that draws traffic is called a *wienie*—try this in *Second Life*. Remember that residents tend to follow pathways, roads, and waterways.

RESIDENTS SPEAK

CHAPTER 1
CHAPTER 2
CHAPTER 3
CHAPTER 4
CHAPTER 5
CHAPTER 6
CHAPTER 7
CHAPTER 8
CHAPTER 9
CHAPTER 10

CHAPTER 11
CHAPTER 12
CHAPTER 13
CHAPTER 14
APPENDICES
INDEX

KEITH EXTRAORDINAIRE WITH SIM-DESIGN TIPS

- Don't just duplicate the mainland. You bought a sim to not be on the mainland, so be different.

- Pick a theme. The sims with the most impact have some unifying element throughout.

- Don't put it all at the hub. If your visitors all port to a hub, don't cram that area full of stuff. Give them a chance to rez first.

- Make reasons for your visitors to want to hang around and to come back for another visit.

- Make reasons for folks to want to explore—add a few secrets to be discovered.

- Be conscious of lag. Remember that laggy neighbor that made you leave the mainland and buy the island in the first place? Don't go nuts with lag-producing objects just because you can. A laggy sim is not a fun place to be.

- Don't make your builds too big. I've been to many place that, just because they have the space, they build *huge*. Don't get caught it this trap. A huge, spread-out build takes far more prims to fill than a modest-sized one, will always feel empty, and those 15,000 prims will get used up fast on an estate. Build smarter and smaller.

- Don't forget empty spaces. Not every inch has to be something. Create neutral zones between your focal points.

- Traffic is a goal of many a sim owner, whether it is for a business, or just to share your *SL* dream. Think of ways to attract and then retain visitors. You don't need a 24-hour-a-day club or camping chairs to do it. Not all *SL* users want to dance all night. Think outside the club box. Give out unique free stuff, have unusual spots to visit, make quiet areas to hang out to encourage folks to linger.

- Most important, love your land. If this is just a business to you, then that's fine, but for most this is a passion first, job second, so listen to your inner muse. Don't forgo your *SL* dreams to make a quick buck. Clubs and casinos are a dime a dozen—make something that is uniquely your own vision.

COMBINING TERRAFORMING AND PRIMS

Some landscape features can't be created with terraforming alone. For these, you will have to use a combination of terraforming and prims.

CHAPTER 10

THE LAND
TOOLS

PLANNING
YOUR
LANDSCAPE

TUTORIAL:
CREATING A
MOUNTAIN
TRAIL

WORKING
WITH RAW
FILES

REGION
TERRAFORM-
ABILITY

CAVES

You can't really dig a tunnel, basement, or cave in *Second Life*. You can, however, dig a trench or a really big hole, then roof over the top with prims (Figure 10.22). Creating realistic ground from prims is a special art. One way to make it a lot easier is to build your cave in a location where the ground texture isn't in transition, so it's easier to match the texture with roof prims.

Figure 10.22: The Magicians Enchanted Mine Ride at Emerce Een 13, 172, 31 includes a good example of prims and terraforming used together to create a tunnel.

WATERFALLS

Water features above the Linden water table and moving water (like a waterfall) have to be built from prims or particles (Figure 10.23). Here are a few tips:

- Look for the Waterfall Textures folder in the Library—it contains water textures and some cool scripts, too.

- Check the Scripts section of the Library for texture animation scripts to make your water texture move.

- Make the water prims at least somewhat transparent.

Figure 10.23: This waterfall is located at Strong Angel 157, 219, 27. Prim stone keeps the ground from showing through the biggest drop.

- Water isn't really blue; it reflects the color of whatever is around it. Take a look around your water and consider what color to tint it.

- Rocks make the waterfall. Don't despair if your water prims won't go just where you want them. Terraform and use rocks to hide the edges.

- If you add a script to play a sound loop, think carefully about the volume and how long it will take before you get really sick of it.

- Unless the terrain texture is rock, it might not look right showing through the water; consider lining your waterfall with rock-textured prims.

CLIFFS AND GROUND

When you back up from a terrain feature, you'll see it changes—simplifies a bit. Things are drawn in less detail when you are far from them. This can be a real problem with features that combine terraforming and prims, especially cliffs and prim ground (Figure 10.24). Always check the view from a distance and see if you want to embed some extra rock under the ground to make sure it will still look OK from a distance.

Figure 10.24: The Dover Cliffs at BritishCouncil Isle 211, 14, 21 (in Teen SL) combine terraforming, prim rock, prim grass, and prim seabed, and are scripted to crumble if avatars get too close to the edge.

BUILDINGS

Landscapes can be settings for buildings, or buildings can decorate your landscape. It's best when it goes both ways, and it's important to keep buildings scaled correctly to suit the landscape. The structure on the mountaintop in Figure 10.25 looks far from the village, and decorates the mountaintop.

Figure 10.25: The castle on the mountain looks very small when viewed from the village at BritishCouncil Isle 96, 101, 37 (Teen SL).

Viewed from the other side of the mountain, we can see this is actually a really big castle (Figure 10.26). It's built into a big step terraformed into the side of the mountain. This hides its bulk from view so the massive structure won't dwarf the village. Also, because the core of the building is terrain, it saves a lot of prims.

Figure 10.26: The castle's true size is visible from BritishCouncil Isle 67, 226, 61 (Teen SL).

CHAPTER 10

THE LAND
TOOLS

PLANNING
YOUR
LANDSCAPE

TUTORIAL:
CREATING A
MOUNTAIN
TRAIL

WORKING
WITH RAW
FILES

REGION
TERRAFORM-
ABILITY

TUTORIAL: CREATING A MOUNTAIN TRAIL

In the next part of this chapter you will learn to create a mountain trail, including the mountain itself and a land mass to support it, along with a prim trail and more.

■ PLANNING

Once you have your viewer's options and settings set for working on the landscape, take a walk around the land you're about to terraform and think about your preferences and requirements. We're starting out with a newly delivered private island, which arrived with the default Island 1 terrain.

We are going to terraform a mountain, of course, and a larger landmass to support it. And with the mountain, we need foothills, because the trail will have to rise gradually. At the top of the mountain we'll have snow. At the bottom, let's have something more summery, though.

Let's raise the mountain toward one corner of this island, with the landing point near the corner farthest from it, so there will be a dramatic view—think Matterhorn—when people arrive . . . and a long trail. We'll put the mountain on the west side of the island so the sun will set behind it, and the mountain won't block out the view of the moon from the rest of the island.

■ SETTING TERRAIN TEXTURES

1. Start by opening the Edit Land tools. Right-click the ground and choose Edit Terrain.

2. Drag-select a square of land about 30 or 40 meters on a side. Click Apply to Selection repeatedly until you have a tower of land that's at least 70 meters high. This should be high enough to show all four terrain texture levels. We do this so we will be able check how the textures we choose blend where they meet.

3. Select World ▸ Region/Estate and then open the Ground Textures tab.

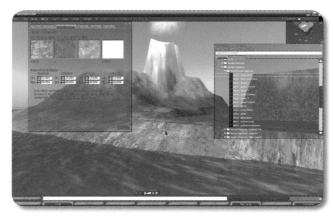

Figure 10.27: Using the Region/Estate console to set terrain textures

4. Open your Inventory and go to Library ▸ Textures ▸ Terrain Textures ▸ Atoll Terrain Textures. Drag the Atoll - Blue Coral texture from Inventory onto the (Low) texture square in the Ground Textures tab. For the second texture, use NW Coastal - Grass - Clumpy from the NW Coastal folder. For the third texture, use Islands - Rock from the Terrain Textures - Islands folder. For the fourth texture, use Primitive Islands - Snow 2 from the Terrain Textures - Winter folder. You can see how this looks in Figure 10.27.

Next we're going to make sure the lowest texture won't extend too far inland.

5. Under Texture Elevation Ranges, set the Low range to 15 meters at all four corners. Set the High range to 60 meters at all corners.

Now we can see how the textures look where they blend. These are not our final settings for the terrain textures, but they will be good to work with. We'll finalize our choices and adjust the heights if necessary once we have the land shaped roughly how we want it. Right now, the lower elevations have a look that is probably too arid to blend with what looks like heavy snow. However, the snow texture is probably a good choice. This particular texture is more tolerant than most of being stretched, which is important for steep terrain. Also, it looks especially dramatic at a distance—just what we want for our mountaintop. We're hoping for a gee-whiz reaction when visitors first see it, followed by a hike up the trail!

■ RAISING THE MOUNTAIN

1. Open Edit Land again, then drag-select a big square of land, like the one in Figure 10.28.

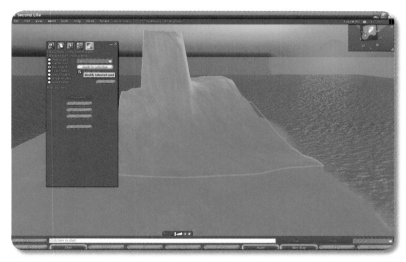

Figure 10.28: The selected area is the base of our mountain. The terrain is green because Show Owners is checked.

2. Click the Raise Land radio button.

3. Click Apply to Selection three or four times. This is the base of your mountain. We're shooting for something about a quarter of the size of the sim, but this doesn't have to be exact.

4. Now drag-select another, smaller area of land on top of the first and apply Raise Land to it three or four times (Figure 10.29). You will end up with nasty sheer cliffs and weird points. That doesn't matter at this stage. What does matter is the general placement and shape of the raised land. You want it to be highest in the middle, stepped down at the sides, with the most gradual slope running toward the landing point—where the yellow avatar beacon shows on the minimap in Figure 10.28, also the location of the colored boxes in Figure 10.31.

CHAPTER 10

THE LAND
TOOLS

PLANNING
YOUR
LANDSCAPE

TUTORIAL:
CREATING A
MOUNTAIN
TRAIL

WORKING
WITH RAW
FILES

REGION
TERRAFORM-
ABILITY

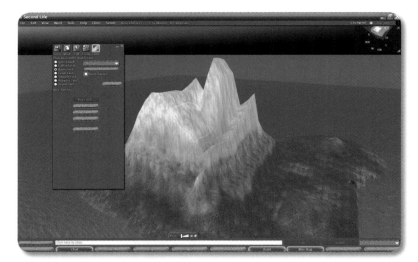

Figure 10.29: Adding height to the mountain

5. We want a few foothills around the mountain so the increase in elevation won't look unnaturally abrupt, and so that we will have a gradual slope for the trail. Select a few squares of land at the base of the mountain, about the size of those in Figure 10.30, and raise them.

Figure 10.30: Raising a foothill

6. Next we'll smooth the mountain just a bit to get a better idea of how it will look when it's done. Select a very large section of the mountain and foothills, like the one in Figure 10.31. Click the Smooth Land radio button and then click Apply to Selection two or three times. If you apply it too many times, you will flatten the mountain, so use this sparingly now.

Figure 10.31: Smoothing the mountain

■ CREATING THE COASTLINE AND AN ISLAND

1. Select and raise sections of land at the edges of the existing island to extend the landmass. We'll leave water all the way around the edge of the sim for boating, and around a small island in the northeast corner.

2. Select smaller squares of land to raise at the shoreline, about the size of the one shown in Figure 10.32. Don't be neat about this—make sure they extend different distances into the water.

Figure 10.32: Creating the coast of an island

3. Select a square of land along the coast, including some that is underwater, then apply Smooth Land until the land slopes naturally into the water. Do this along the entire coastline, including the small island.

FINALIZING THE TERRAIN TEXTURES

1. The mountain needs to be taller—we'll want it to reach up near the clouds. But we don't want the snow to extend down too far. Open World ▸ Region/Estate ▸ Ground Textures and increase the High texture to 80 meters at all corners.

2. Now that we have the island roughly in shape, we can see that the Low texture still extends far inland. Lower it to 12 meters at all corners.

3. Now would be a good time to swap out the terrain textures, if you would like to try something different. Figure 10.33 shows some alternate textures for the two lowest levels of the terrain. To create something like the Low texture, open Library ▸ Textures ▸ Terrain Textures ▸ Terrain Textures - Islands - Rock. Then select File ▸ Save Texture As and save the texture to your hard drive. Now you can modify the texture with your own graphics software, then upload it to *Second Life*.

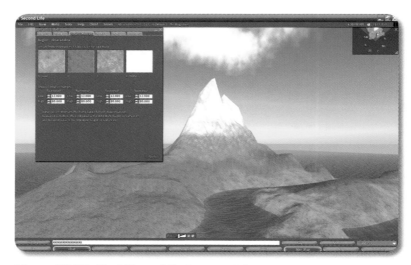

Figure 10.33: Final Ground Textures settings

The red dirt texture, reminiscent of the southeastern United States, goes well with very green grass—it also gives a nice color to the water in this sim. We went to Library ▸ Textures ▸ Terrain Textures ▸ Atoll Terrain Textures, exported Atoll - Moss, made it greener in Photoshop, then uploaded it to *Second Life*. It is used as the second-lowest terrain texture, or the second from the left on the Ground Textures tab.

The third texture is NW Coastal - Rock, from Library ▸ Textures ▸ Terrain Textures ▸ Terrain Textures - NW Coastal. It blends well with the snow at the top of the mountain, which we haven't changed. It also looks reddish in the cracks of the rock, which goes well with the red dirt.

SHAPING THE MOUNTAIN

Mountains have ridges that run down to the foothills. We'll create those now.

1. Open Edit Land. Where you find a steep drop-off, especially in the lower-two-thirds of the mountain, drag-select from the top of it, and past it onto a foothill or to the coastline.

2. Click the Raise Land radio button and choose Apply to Selection two or three times (Figure 10.34).

Figure 10.34: Roughing in a realistic slope on the mountain

3. Drag-select again, starting at about the same point, but take in a little more land around it.

4. Click the Smooth Land radio button then Apply to Selection however many times it takes until the upper part of the land you raised in the previous step has been lowered to about where it started (Figure 10.35).

Figure 10.35: Smoothing the slope on the mountain

CHAPTER 10

THE LAND
TOOLS

PLANNING
YOUR
LANDSCAPE

TUTORIAL:
CREATING A
MOUNTAIN
TRAIL

WORKING
WITH RAW
FILES

REGION
TERRAFORM-
ABILITY

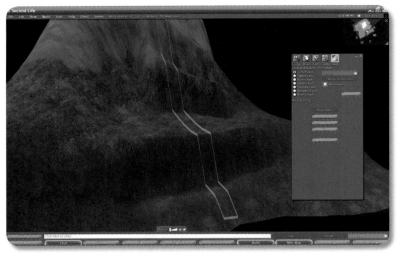

Do those two steps, in vertical strips of various widths, all the way around the mountain, creating ridges (Figure 10.36).

Figure 10.36 The strips of land selected to create ridges should vary in size

5. Drag-select horizontally across the bottom one-quarter to one-third of the mountain, in big sections, and apply the Smooth Land tool. Don't overdo this—use no more than one or two applications on each section. We don't want to completely lose the ruggedness of the landscape or to lower the mountain too much.

6. On the south side of the mountain, select and raise a rectangle of land like that shown in Figure 10.37. Leave a low valley between it and the main bulk of the mountain. This is going to be a pass where we will put the trail (Figure 10.38).

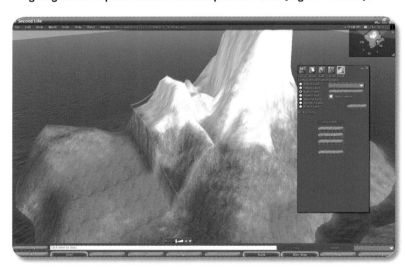

Figure 10.37: Raising a foothill and leaving a valley for a trail

Figure 10.38: View along planned route of the trail, including the pass

CREATING THE TRAIL BED

1. Select short sections of the pass—about 10 meters long and the width of a broad sidewalk. Apply Lower Land, Flatten Land, and then Smooth Land, just one to three times each, in that order (Figure 10.39).

Figure 10.39: Creating the path through the pass

2. Walk up and down the path you have created to check how steep it is.

3. Repeat steps 1 and 2 until this section of path through the pass is walkable.

4. Select another 10 meters of the pass and repeat steps 1 through 3.

5. If necessary, smooth the foothills near the path to get rid of unnatural-looking cliffs and to create a smooth slope down to the path (Figure 10.40).

Figure 10.40: Smoothing the foothill beside the path

You want the trail to be entirely obvious without any signs, so leave the sides fairly steep (Figure 10.41).

Figure 10.41: The finished trail bed through the pass

6. Do the same thing on the west side of the mountain to extend the path uphill, as shown in Figure 10.42.

Figure 10.42: Extending the trail bed on the west side of the mountain

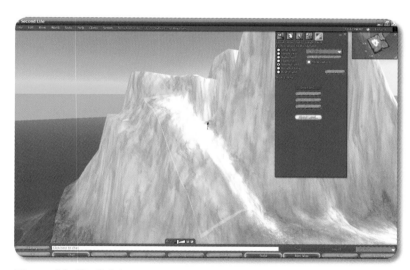

Figure 10.43: Raising some land to the west of the trail bed

You'll probably need to raise some of the land to the west of this part of the trail, as you did on the south side of the lower part of the trail (Figure 10.43.).

7. **If the mountaintop isn't already high enough, select it and raise it to about 90 meters. Your trail bed might be pretty steep toward the end to make it up this high, but avatars will still be able to walk up it.**

At the top of the mountain we want to create an area for a winter wonderland, very different from the land below. We don't want anything large we build up here to ruin the perspective trick we're going to use for the view from below.

8. **Raise the east side of the mountaintop in a wall, as shown in Figure 10.45, to block the view from the land below. This terraformed wall needs to be at least 20 meters thick to be sure it will show even if it's rendered more simply when viewed from far away.**

CHAPTER 10

THE LAND
TOOLS

PLANNING
YOUR
LANDSCAPE

TUTORIAL:
CREATING A
MOUNTAIN
TRAIL

WORKING
WITH RAW
FILES

REGION
TERRAFORM-
ABILITY

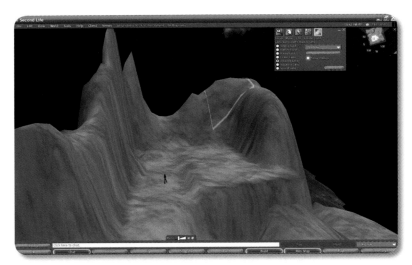

Figure 10.44: Terraforming a wall on the east side of the mountain peak

9. Select and raise squares of mountaintop land of decreasing sizes, similar to the way you built the mountain base. This will create terraces so you can climb up to the front wall of the mountain and admire the view of the land below (Figure 10.45).

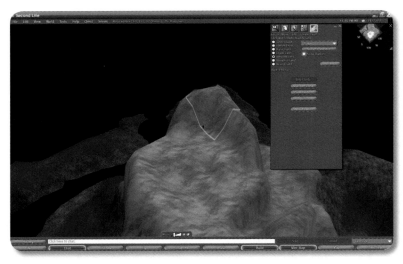

Figure 10.45: Terracing the mountaintop

■ LAYING THE TRAIL

1. Click the Build button to open the Object Editor, then click on the ground to create a cube. Then switch to Edit mode and make your cube 10×5×10 meters.

2. Click the Texture tab and apply the same texture you used for the lowest terrain. In this case, we are using the modified red dirt texture. If your lowest terrain texture doesn't look right for a trail—maybe you're still using Atoll - Blue Coral—instead use the rock texture from the second-highest terrain texture level.

3. Place the prim so one end of it is where you want your trail to begin and orient it so that it lines up roughly from there to the mountain pass. This doesn't have to be exact! A trail that winds a little actually looks better.

4. Click the Rotate radio button. Now tilt the prim so it's at approximately the same angle as the land, pointed uphill.

5. Click the Position radio button. Drag the prim until it's just barely under the ground.

6. Click the Land tab on the Object Editor—the one with the bulldozer. Using the Small selection setting and the Lower tool, tap your left mouse button over the prim. Do this just enough to clear the grass from the middle of it, leaving the edges of the prim covered. If you lower the land too much, switch to the Raise tool to fix it, then try again

7. Shift-drag the prim toward the mountain to make a copy and line it up roughly with the first, as shown in Figure 10.46. If necessary, rotate the new prim to adjust the slope to roughly match the ground. You will probably have to position this prim higher. Repeat steps 4 through 6.

CHAPTER 1
CHAPTER 2
CHAPTER 3
CHAPTER 4
CHAPTER 5
CHAPTER 6
CHAPTER 7
CHAPTER 8
CHAPTER 9
CHAPTER 10

CHAPTER 11
CHAPTER 12
CHAPTER 13
CHAPTER 14
APPENDICES
INDEX

Figure 10.46: The outline of one of the trail prims shows through the ground in Edit mode.

8. Keep adding prims this way. If the flat prim doesn't work out because you get to some land that's just too curved, especially around the area where grass is giving way to rock, use a curved prim. Change one of your dirt prims into a cylinder (Figure 10.47) or a sphere. To make the mountain seem farther away from the start of the trail than it really is, make the trail narrower as you go.

CHAPTER 10

🔹 THE LAND
TOOLS

🔹 PLANNING
YOUR
LANDSCAPE

🔹 TUTORIAL:
CREATING A
MOUNTAIN
TRAIL

🔹 WORKING
WITH RAW
FILES

🔹 REGION
TERRAFORM-
ABILITY

Figure 10.47: Using a cylinder to extend the trail

The dirt path needs to run up the trail only until you get past the grassy terrain texture and onto rock. The exact point where the terrain textures switch will change depending on the time of day, so you may want to look at your trail during different times of day to check this out.

9. Now we'll need a few boulders. It's usually a safe bet to echo similar shapes throughout a landscape (Figure 10.48). Create a prim, then apply the rock texture you are using for the terrain, so it will match.

Figure 10.48: The boulder echoes the mountain's shape

10. Taper the top of the prim about 60 or 70 percent on both the x- and y-axis. If you like, add a few degrees of Sheer and up to maybe 20 percent Twist on one axis. You can also cut and hollow this—every boulder on the island will be a copy of this one, modified slightly. Experiment and see what looks good! Resize at will.

11. Place small boulders, mostly embedded in the ground, to hide any gaps or uneven joins between the trail prims. They're useful in other ways, too. You can stack them up where

the rocky top of a hill looks too smooth, or use them as footings for bridge supports. Invariably you will find you have left a few sheer drops you forgot to smooth, but sometimes cliffs make sense, except that they are grassy. You can get a good effect by facing them with boulders (Figure 10.49).

CHAPTER 1
CHAPTER 2
CHAPTER 3
CHAPTER 4
CHAPTER 5
CHAPTER 6
CHAPTER 7
CHAPTER 8
CHAPTER 9
CHAPTER 10

CHAPTER 11
CHAPTER 12
CHAPTER 13
CHAPTER 14
APPENDICES
INDEX

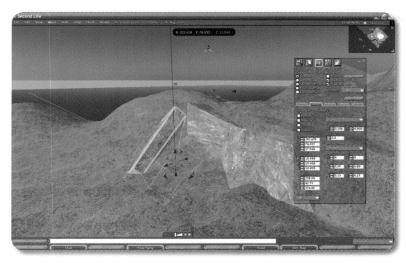

Figure 10.49: Facing a small cliff with boulders

■ PLANTING TREES

Trees will bring this landscape to life and help us to create an optical illusion.

1. To start, click **Build** to open the Object Editor.

2. Open Library ▸ Objects ▸ Trees, Plants and Grasses and take out a Cypress Tree 1 and place it near the start of the trail.

Figure 10.50: Tilting a tree away from the trail

It's important to make sure we don't obscure too much of the view of the trail up the mountain. This means you will have to tilt trees near the trail away from it and keep them a bit small (Figure 10.50).

3. Shift-drag the first tree to make copies, but be sure to resize some of them slightly or turn them a little bit so they don't look exactly alike.

CHAPTER 10

● THE LAND
  TOOLS

● PLANNING
  YOUR
  LANDSCAPE

● TUTORIAL:
  CREATING A
  MOUNTAIN
  TRAIL

● WORKING
  WITH RAW
  FILES

● REGION
  TERRAFORM-
  ABILITY

4. Resize one of the trees so that it's about eight or nine meters high and plant them all over the grassy part of the island, but no higher!

5. Trees tend to arch out over water unless strong prevailing winds have stopped them from doing it, so tilt those you place near water. Tilt trees away from boulders or other terrain features—think about which way a tree would reach to get more sun (Figure 10.51).

Figure 10.51: Trees arch out over the water.

Higher up, we'll use trees better suited to rocky, drier soil and colder weather—pine trees.

6. Go back to the Library and take out a Pine Tree - Ponderosa. This band of trees should start around the level where the grass begins to blend with rock, and end short of the snow line (Figure 10.52).

Figure 10.52: Here's a band of pine trees above the larger cypresses

We want to make sure the trees we use at this altitude are smaller than the trees lower down the mountain, and these are conveniently the right size already. Like making the trail narrower higher up the mountain, this contributes to an optical illusion we are building called *forced perspective*. Viewed from the landing point, the tinier the trees are, the bigger and farther away the mountain will seem. The pointy mountaintop helps with this, too.

7. Open the Library and take out a Winter Pine Tree 1. These are snowy, and smaller than the Ponderosa pines. Place these in a band starting just at the snow line and ending where the terrain gets steep (Figure 10.53).

Figure 10.53: Snowy pines along the trail

8. Now take Winter Pine Tree 2 from the Library and scatter a few at the top of the mountain. These are the smallest, snowiest pines in the Library. Don't place them where they'll be seen when someone standing at the base of the mountain looks up. As small as they are, they are still big enough to ruin the illusion of how large this mountain peak really is. Also, because the terrain is rendered in a simplified way at a distance, they might appear to be floating in the air! It's OK to use them all the way to the top of the mountain in the back, where there's no long view (Figure 10.54).

Figure 10.54: Placing trees on the mountaintop

CHAPTER 10

The Land
Tools

Planning
Your
Landscape

Tutorial:
Creating a
Mountain
Trail

Working
with RAW
Files

Region
Terraform-
ability

9. Fly to the farthest point from the mountain, or just move your camera out to be sure that none of your trees are floating in the air, and adjust them if necessary (Figure 10.55).

Figure 10.55: Checking tree placement from a distance

ADDING FINISHING TOUCHES

There are a lot of little touches you can add to make a landscape seem real. Here are some suggestions for things you might want to use for this landscape.

- Scripted particle generators that make snow at the top of the mountain (Figure 10.56).

Figure 10.56: Placing particle snow at the top of the mountain

- A bridge across the river—which probably means terraforming the riverbanks up to the right height and putting in some boulders for footings (Figure 10.57).

Figure 10.57: A little covered bridge

💬 Grasses and flowers. In Figure 10.58 you can see we used a Fern and Grass - Tall 2 from the Library.

💬 Scripted objects that play environmental sound effects

Time for a hike!

Figure 10.58: Hiking up the new trail

WORKING WITH RAW FILES

Second Life terrain can be exported, imported, and developed in outside editing tools. The format of the file you export or import has a .raw extension, which is why it's called a RAW file.

IMPORTING TERRAIN

It's easy to export your terrain. Just go to the Terrain tab on the Region/Estate console and click the Download RAW Terrain button. Be sure to name it something you will recognize! The Upload RAW Terrain button is just as easy to use if your file is in the correct format and has a name without spaces.

CREATING YOUR OWN RAW FILES

The easiest way to start working with RAW terrain files is to export one from your sim, then open it up and modify it. You can open it in a program like Photoshop. When it prompts you, tell it the image is 256×256 pixels with 13 channels.

TIP

If you're a Mac user and want to try out an outside editor for your terrain, check out Backhoe by Zarf Vantongerloo: `http://secondlife.com/devdown/detail.php?pid=00000012`

Each of the channels stores information about a different aspect of the region. Information is represented by shades of gray, or values of 0 (black) to 255 (white).

When creating the file, you can make it arbitrary dimensions, as long as it is divisible by 256 pixels. Consider including the dimensions in the name of the file. Also, remember not to include spaces in the file name.

In the past all 13 channels of a RAW file were used in the terraforming process. Although all 13 must still be included, only 3 of them are still useful today.

Channel 1 (red) is the Height Field data. This grayscale map represents the height of the terrain in meters. Black is 0 meters high. White is 255 meters high. The height of the terrain is further modified by values in Channel 2.

Channel 2 (green) is the Height Multiply Factor data. This grayscale map is used as a multiplier to scale the heights specified in Channel 1. The formula it uses is complicated; here are some examples from the *Second Life* Knowledge Base of effects of values in this channel:

CHAPTER 1
CHAPTER 2
CHAPTER 3
CHAPTER 4
CHAPTER 5
CHAPTER 6
CHAPTER 7
CHAPTER 8
CHAPTER 9
CHAPTER 10

CHAPTER 11
CHAPTER 12
CHAPTER 13
CHAPTER 14
APPENDICES
INDEX

32: Divides pixel values by 4. The resultant elevations will be ¼ of the original.

64: Divides pixel values by 2. The resultant elevations will be ½ of the original.

128: No effect.

255: Multiplies pixel values by 2. The resultant elevations will be twice that of the original.

Channel 3 (blue) represents the Water Height of the sim. The water height can't vary in different parts of a sim, so you should fill this channel with one value of gray. The Height Multiply Factor doesn't apply to this data, so the maximum water height is 255m.

REGION TERRAFORMABILITY

Private islands have terraforming limits of ± 100m from their last baked level. Most mainland regions are terraformable by ± 4m of their original shape. The regions listed here are exceptions:

Avalon: ± 20m

Garmisch: ± 14m

The following regions can't be terraformed at all:

Barcola

Brown

Grignano

Miramare

Sistiana

The following regions can be terraformed ± 40m:

Aqua

Argent

Bisque

Blue

Bonifacio

Cayman

Chartreuse

Clara

Clementina

Clyde

Crimson

DaBoom

DarkWood

De Haro

Dore

Federal

Freelon

Gibson

Gray

Green

Hawthorne

Immaculate

Indigo

Jessie

Kissling

LiasonLand

Lusk

Magenta

Maroon

Mauve

Minna

Mocha

Natoma

Olive

Periwinkle

Perry

Plum

Purple

Ritch

Rose

Sage

Shipley

Taber

Umber

Varney

Welsh

Zoe

CHAPTER 11

ANIMATIONS: BREATHING LIFE INTO AVATARS

Avatars in *Second Life* would seem drab and lifeless if you couldn't jump for joy, hug a good friend, or dance a merry jig. Fortunately, all of this and much more is possible using animations. In general, an animation is a set of instructions that cause an avatar to change the position in which it appears. These instructions may include a sequence of poses to give the illusion of motion, such as walking, dancing, or sorting a stamp collection.

You can find many useful animations in-world for free or for a small fee, but when you really want to express the nuance of your own particular personality, there is no better way than to create an animation of your own. In this chapter we will show you how to make poses and animations to give your avatar a whole new dimension of life.

CONTENTS

CHAPTER 11

- UNDERSTAND-
  ING ANIMATION
  BASICS

- CHOOSING
  AND USING
  ANIMATION
  TOOLS

- CREATING
  ANIMATIONS

- TUTORIAL:
  MAKING A
  DANCE
  ANIMATION

UNDERSTANDING ANIMATION BASICS

In common *SL* parlance, an *animation* uses a sequence of related stances to produce the appearance of movement. You would use animations to make your avatar run, jump, or dance. A *pose* places an avatar in a static stance which technically makes poses a subset of animations. Poses are great when you want your avatar to model for photographs, or perhaps take a nap.

RESIDENTS SPEAK

FRANCIS CHUNG ON PROACTIVE ANIMATIONS

Second Life's animations are intended to be proactive, not reactive. For example, putting your arm out for a handshake is quite simple. Having your hand shaken by another player would (for the most part) be impossible to do well.

Creating poses and animations, even in their most basic forms, is a relatively advanced topic. They require the use of third-party software, so the final effect cannot be viewed during creation—unlike building with primitives. There are a few fundamental concepts to cover before we dig into the specifics. These concepts apply to all the applicable software products equally.

■ FIRST FRAME

Second Life uses the first frame of any pose or animation for reference location. Ideally, the first-frame figure will have all joints at zero rotation (legs straight, arms out, and head forward, as in Figure 11.1); while essential to the inner workings of animations, this frame's posture will never actually be shown in-world.

Figure 11.1: An avatar with all joints at zero rotation.

HIPS

The hips are the center of the figure. The position and orientation of the animated movement is all relative to the hip joint of the *Second Life* skeleton. If you want to move the whole body, you have to move the figure's hips relative to the first frame's hip position.

NOTE

Second Life will also determine whether a joint should be animated based on whether it ever changes from the first frame.

SCALING

Figure 11.2: While the sit may have looked fine in the animation software, Aimee's avatar is sized such that she appears to be hovering over the wall rather than sitting on it.

Your avatar in *Second Life* is extremely customizable; there is a very strong chance that it has different proportions than the figure in the animation software that you are using. For this reason, even if you place the figure's hands (for example) in an exact location, they may not—and probably will not—appear in the same location when you play the animation in-world. Sitting positions are also affected (Figure 11.2). An avatar may appear to be sunken or hovering while sitting; this difference is caused by avatar leg length.

KEY FRAMES

One possible way to animate an avatar would be similar to creating a cartoon flipbook or using stop-motion animation. This would involve positioning the avatar hundreds or even thousands of times for every single tiny change in position until finally, after weeks of hard work, we have a few seconds of finished animation.

Fortunately, thanks to key-frame animation, we don't have to go through that painful process. If you want your avatar to raise its hand, you need only set a handful of frames that define where the hand starts and ends, and perhaps one or two positions in the middle. These special frames, called *key frames*, are then used by *Second Life* to do all the hard work for you. *SL* will automatically fill in all the poses between the key frames so the animation looks like one smooth continuous motion.

The best placements of key frames are the second frame (remember that the first frame is a reference!), the last frame, and each turning point (point of maximum rotation) for every body part. For a static pose, only two frames are needed: the reference (first) frame, and the second frame, which defines the pose.

CHAPTER 11

UNDERSTAND-
ING ANIMATION
BASICS

CHOOSING
AND USING
ANIMATION
TOOLS

CREATING
ANIMATIONS

TUTORIAL:
MAKING A
DANCE
ANIMATION

ANIMATION SPEED

For most software, the default speed is 30 frames per second (fps). That is, it takes one second do go through 30 frames of animation. More animation frames between key frames means a more gradual transition between the two positions. The actual amount of time between them is determined by the animation speed.

CHOOSING AND USING ANIMATION TOOLS

Second Life does not contain a built-in animation editor. However, several programs can produce the type of file that *Second Life* uses for avatar animations. The two programs that will be discussed in depth here are Poser and QAvimator.

Regardless of the software used to produce the animation, there is only one file format that *Second Life* will accept: Biovision Hierarchy (.BVH). This file type is not the most common, but all of the programs covered here can employ it.

POSER

Poser (http://www.e-frontier.com/go/poser) is an extremely powerful and full-featured rendering engine and character-animation suite. It is a fabulous program, even given the hefty price tag. There is an extraordinary number of Poser tutorials on the Web, and the full range of possibilities is well beyond the scope of this book. For the purpose of *Second Life*, only a small fraction of the software's ability is used.

WARNING

Poser 7 is the current release. If you get an older release, especially Poser 6, make sure that you have all the available updates. Several releases have had known problems with exporting to the .BVH format.

SETTING UP AND CHOOSING THE RIGHT MODEL

In this section you'll learn how to get the little odds and ends set up in Poser so you will be ready to start creating animations. We've assumed that you own a copy of Poser and have installed it according to the manufacturer's instructions. Most of the work we will be doing will take place under the Pose tab.

Your starting avatar: One model included in Poser works with *Second Life*: Poser 2 Lo Default Guy. To retrieve this figure, open the pallet on the right; if it's not already open, you should see a small handle to click and open it. Click the Figures tab. If you are not already in the Poser 2 Lo folder, click the folder name (directly beneath the figures label) and find Figures/Poser 1-4/Poser 2 Lo. Scroll down, and select Default Guy (Figure 11.3). Alternately, Linden Labs has developed a Poser model for use by residents. You can locate it at http://secondlife.com/community/avatar.php. Now you can close the pallet by clicking on its handle.

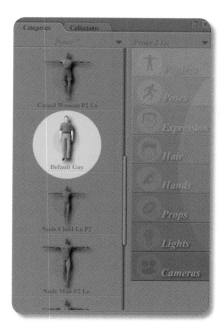

Figure 11.3: The Default Guy figure packaged with Poser is compatible with Second Life animations.

Parameter dials: You can move or rotate the body part selected on the model (and listed at the top of the window) by using these dials or by clicking the Value text, and entering digits directly. If the parameter dials are not visible, go to Windows ▸ Parameter Dials.

Animation palette: This allows you to add and edit key frames for each body part. From here you can also play the animation and alter its interpolations. If the animation palette is not visible, go to Windows ▸ Animation Palette.

Other settings: Now you can see the three main windows: the preview (centered on the posing figure), the parameter dials, and the animation palette. We just have a few more odds and ends to set up. Under the Figure menu, uncheck Genitalia (if it's checked) and check Lock Hand Parts; *Second Life* does not recognize these features so it's best to disable them. Next, choose Edit ▸ General Preferences. Choose Centimeters as display units instead of Feet in the Interface tab (SL uses metric measurements). Finally, select Launch to Previous State in the Launch Behavior section and press OK. This final step ensures you won't have to go through this setup every time you wish to use Poser. Now when you start Poser, your windows and options will be configured just as you left them.

CHAPTER 1
CHAPTER 2
CHAPTER 3
CHAPTER 4
CHAPTER 5
CHAPTER 6
CHAPTER 7
CHAPTER 8
CHAPTER 9
CHAPTER 10
CHAPTER 11

CHAPTER 12
CHAPTER 13
CHAPTER 14
APPENDICES
INDEX

◼ MANIPULATING THE FIGURE

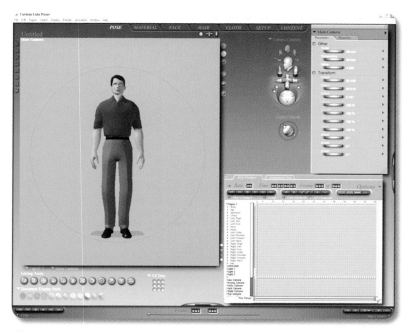

Figure 11.4: Poser with the default guy, ready to create **Second Life** animations.

Now that Poser is all set up (Figure 11.4), we are ready to dig in. In this section you will learn how to set key frames and move model parts by their joints.

CREATING KEY FRAMES

Let's start by looking at the animation palette. On the left side you will find a list of all the parts of the figure with obvious names such as Head and Right Foot. The chart view to the right displays all of the key frames in green for each part with respect to time. The further to the right you go, the later in the animation sequence the key frame appears.

CHAPTER 11

UNDERSTAND-
ING ANIMATION
BASICS

CHOOSING
AND USING
ANIMATION
TOOLS

CREATING
ANIMATIONS

TUTORIAL:
MAKING A
DANCE
ANIMATION

Notice all parts have a green block for frame number one. You can add a key frame for any part and for any point in time by clicking the appropriate block and pressing the + (plus) button. Likewise, you can delete key frames by pressing the – (minus) button.

POSITIONING THE MODEL

In Poser you have three options for moving joints, and each can result in the same effects; it is just a matter of preference.

Direct manipulation: Poser allows you to move individual body parts by clicking and dragging them in the preview window. In this mode you are able to adjust position, rotation, and twist by using the round buttons just above the window labeled Editing Tools. While this method may lack precision, it's a quick and fun way to see how the animation model works.

Parameter dials: The dial window provides more-exact control over each body part. Once you select a body part by clicking it on the preview model or selecting it in the animation palette, you can drag the dials left or right to alter the figure's body-part rotation or position. There are also dials for body-part scale and size, although they have no effect on a *Second Life* animation.

Number entry: Next to each dial is a number. Clicking on one of these numbers will allow direct text entry. This is most useful when you already know the Twist, Side-Side, and Bend value you want for the body part.

NOTE

Changes to faces and hands in Poser will not have any effect on the Second Life *pose you create with the animation file. Unfortunately, the only way to change the hand or face morph in* Second Life *is through the settings on the upload dialog.*

Inverse kinematics lets the person editing a Poser figure set up a reverse relationship in which the feet and hips determine the position of the legs—so with inverse kinematics turned on for the legs, the feet will stay put as the rest of the body moves. You can move the feet individually with the Move/Translate tool, and the legs will bend appropriately. This is very useful when you want to keep the figure's feet on the ground or its hands against the wall. You can turn inverse kinematics off (individually, for each leg and arm) by going to Figure ▸ Use Inverse Kinematics if the behavior is undesirable for the frame on which you are working.

Another useful (but occasionally unwanted) tool is the Use Limits option located under Figure ▸ Use Limit. This prevents your model's body parts from extending or rotating beyond human capability.

Figure 11.5: The bottom of the Poser user Interface displays the frame you are currently on, the total number of frames, and a slider for quick navigation.

At the bottom of the Poser window there is a small yellow triangle on a slider line (Figure 11.5). This represents the position of the frame that you are currently viewing within the animation. Above this line are two boxes; one contains the number of the current frame, and the second is the total number of frames that the animation contains. Either of these boxes can be clicked for direct editing. Editing the first box will skip you directly to the specified frame number; editing the second box will change the total number of frames in the animation. Clicking on a frame number in the animation palette will also skip to that frame number.

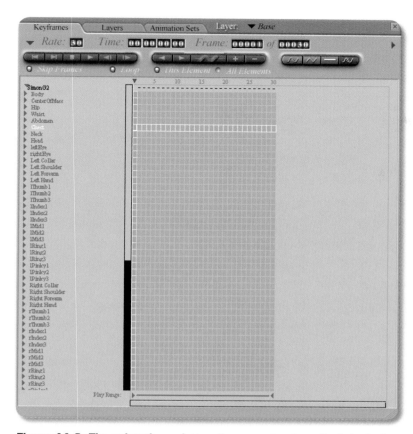

Figure 11.6: The animation palette allows you to view all of the body parts and the key frames (in green) associated with them.

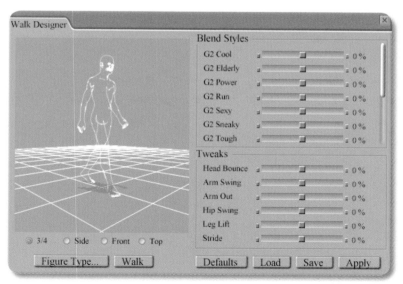

Figure 11.7: The Walk Designer palette allows you to create different walks by using blend and tweak sliders.

You can adjust the frame rate by setting the Rate value located on the upper-left side of the animation palette. The default setting is 30 frames per second, which is fine for most *Second Life* projects.

You will see Play Range in green on the bottom of the animation palette. It's helpful to tweak the range from the second frame to the end of the animation to view your animation without the first-frame pose. Any loop that you use here will have to be implemented in the *Second Life* Upload Animation dialog. Fortunately, that's easy to do if you know the number of frames prior to the loop, and the number afterward (and can convert them to percentage of total frames).

Key frames in Poser are noted on the animation palette by green squares (Figure 11.6). The grid layout tells you which body part(s) form the key frame (on the left of the palette), and the frame number in which it occurs (at the top of the palette). You can always click and drag these green boxes anywhere you choose if you feel they're placed incorrectly.

Finally, Poser 5 and later versions include a very powerful tool called Walk Designer (Figure 11.7). Ctrl+Shift+W opens the Walk Designer palette, which allows you to move any of 13 "blend style" and six "tweak" sliders to produce a unique and personalized walk animation.

CHAPTER 11

⬦ UNDERSTAND-
ING ANIMATION
BASICS

⬦ CHOOSING
AND USING
ANIMATION
TOOLS

⬦ CREATING
ANIMATIONS

⬦ TUTORIAL:
MAKING A
DANCE
ANIMATION

INTERPOLATION

Interpolation is a mathematical tool used to determine smooth motion between key frames. Poser has four styles of interpolation, accessible in the upper-right section of the animation palette.

Spline: This form of interpolation uses a curve to determine the rate at which each body part moves. It is considered the most realistic type of motion.

Linear: This style of interpolation moves body parts at a constant rate. This is sometimes preferred, especially for lateral motion.

Constant: This will prevent body parts from moving at all during the selected frames (or between key frames if only one frame is selected).

Break: This selection will stop the interpolation at a midway point—the frame you have selected. It is sometimes useful when you want to change the direction of motion on a specific body part or to isolate a specific frame (usually the first frame). If used indiscriminately, though, it can cause jerky, incongruous motion.

SAVING YOUR ANIMATION

To save your file in a format that *Second Life* can use, choose File ▶ Export ▶ BVH Motion. This brings up a dialog asking, "Do you want Poser to attempt to scale this motion capture data automatically or leave it unmodified?" Choose Scale Automatically.

When you want to open a .BVH file, choose File ▶ Import ▶ BVH Motion. Poser will ask about scaling (as it does when you save), but will also ask what axis the arms are aligned on; select X-Axis.

■ QAVIMATOR

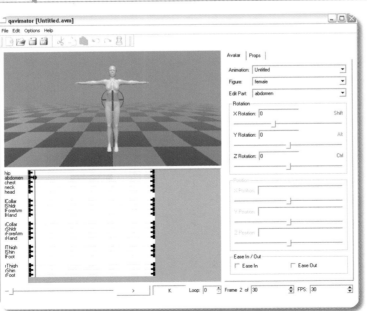

QAvimator (Figure 11.8 and www.qavimator.org) is a program developed by *Second Life* residents for the specific use of developing in-world animations. Because of its intended function, it doesn't have all the extras that Poser contains, but it is capable of doing everything necessary to develop your own animations—for free!

Most of the features and concepts used for animations in Poser are also used in QAvimator. The primary differences between using QAvimator and Poser for *Second Life* are as follows:

Figure 11.8: QAvimator is a free alternative to Poser for creating Second Life animations.

- No direct manipulation. You cannot drag a body part to position it; you must use the sliders or number entry.

- No hand or face morphs. This isn't a problem, since *Second Life* can't use them.

- Linear interpolation only. QAvimator does not use splines, but it can break or pause the linear interpolation. This is the program's greatest weakness; to create a smooth, humanlike motion without splines, each frame has to be carefully and individually manipulated.

- Model choice. Your only choices are Male and Female, but since gender information isn't included in the file, it makes no difference to the final animation.

- The first frame is automatically set to zero offsets and rotations, is uneditable, and is delinked from the second frame's motion .Therefore you don't have to set aside the first frame as you do in Poser.

- While the program does have a setting for the location of a loop's start, there is no setting for a loop's end. If you wish to test a loop, QAvimator will start at the designated frame and continue to the last frame, then loop back to the designated frame.

CHAPTER 1
CHAPTER 2
CHAPTER 3
CHAPTER 4
CHAPTER 5
CHAPTER 6
CHAPTER 7
CHAPTER 8
CHAPTER 9
CHAPTER 10
CHAPTER 11

■ OTHER ANIMATION PROGRAMS

The following are some other common animation editors for *Second Life*:

- Blender (www.blender.org): A powerful modeling and rendering tool that includes highly flexible skeleton and animation tools. While this application is free, the learning curve and unnecessary features may make Blender a bit daunting for users who only wish to produce animations.

- SLAT (http://sourceforge.net/projects/free-bvh-editor): Short for *Second Life* Animation Tool, this barebones tool is free, and it's quick and easy to get started.

- Maya (http://usa.autodesk.com/adsk/servlet/index?siteID=123112&id= 7635018): A professional modeling and rendering tool that includes animation capabilities. This product is difficult to learn and is priced for professional movie production. Most people consider it too expensive for the average *Second Life* animator.

MORE INFO

CONSIDERING MOTION CAPTURE?

If you have a big budget for your animation project, you might consider renting some time at a motion-capture studio. Motion capture (MOCAP for short) records motion information directly from a special suit that is worn by the subject of the animation. A dancer can dance, a kung fu master can fight, or a model can strut her stuff. All of their motion can be captured and imported into *Second Life*.

CREATING ANIMATIONS

Right-clicking the animation name in your Inventory and selecting Open from the context menu will produce a dialog box with the animation name, a field for a description of the animation, and two buttons: Play in World and Play Locally. Play Locally will let you see the animation but it will not be visible to other users. This is useful if the animation is really something you don't want others to see your avatar doing, such as snogging. Play in World will cause the users within visual range to see your avatar perform the animation. Double-clicking an animation name in your Inventory list has the same effect as Play in World.

LOOPING

For any animation in *Second Life*, it is possible to define a sequence of frames that *loop*, meaning they are repeated indefinitely. The most common use of this feature is to produce static poses. A pose-only animation contains two frames. The first is the reference frame; the second is repeated, keeping the avatar in that pose.

A more professional look includes adding entry and exit animations. For example, if you wanted a custom ground-sit animation, you could use the first 100 frames (roughly 3 seconds) to make the figure kneel down and get into the seated position, then a few frames of being seated (that will be repeated), then another 100 or so frames of getting back up. When the animation is triggered in *Second Life*, the avatar will perform the sitting action and remain seated until the animation is stopped, at which point the standing-up portion of the animation will be executed.

For some animations, like typing or dancing, repeated sets of motions are desired. Fortunately, a loop can be of any size (up to the length of the animation). You could define the looping points (during upload to *Second Life*) to include any portion of your animation. Looping can sometimes be difficult to accomplish gracefully. If the figure isn't in the same position at the end of the loop as at the beginning of the loop, when the animation is played, the avatar will "jump" from one position to the other each loop, giving a very discontinuous motion.

RESIDENTS SPEAK

LAUNA FAUNA ON SMOOTH MOTION

It is very important for a figure not to be rigid. Never use a one-frame animation. Always include a little body sway or hand movement or leg swing—anything to prevent your avatar from looking like a statue.

SETTING PRIORITIES

Each animation is given a priority. Priorities range from 0 to 4 (with 4 being the highest). Higher priorities will override lower ones; when two animations have the same priority, animations started later override prior ones.

The default animations (the ones built into the *Second Life* client) are always present. To prevent them from triggering, your animation must have a higher priority than theirs. An animation's priority is set once—during upload—and it affects the entire animation, including each body part controlled by the animation.

While it may seem wise to use priority 4 for any animation to avoid problems, there are conditions where you need lower priorities. For instance, if you wanted a custom sitting position where your avatar's arms rest lazily on the back of a bench but move to the typing position while you are entering text, you want to choose a priority equal to or higher than the sitting animation's priority (2), but lower than the typing animation's priority (3). For a full list of default animation priorities, check the Secondlife.com knowledge base.

■ COMBINING ANIMATIONS

It is possible, and even preferred occasionally, to animate separate body parts with different animations. This method is sometimes necessary when the default animation priorities conflict with your desired effect.

For example, if you're producing a desk work animation, you might want to include talking on the phone, typing on a keyboard, writing on paper, reading a book, and berating an intern. While you could produce each of these activities as a separate animation and script each to turn on and off at the appropriate time, there is a more elegant solution. You could produce one animation for the seated position (legs and hips only), and a separate set of animations for the torso and arms. This way, you never have to worry about the seated-position height or the avatar sliding around on the chair when changing animations. It also allows for default animations to take control of the upper body while the avatar remains seated (if no upper-body animations are running).

■ UPLOADING

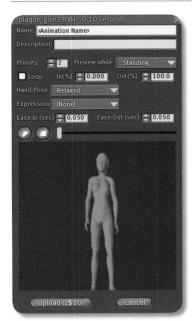

Figure 11.9: The Second Life animation upload screen allows you to preview your animation before committing to the upload.

As mentioned before, *Second Life* will accept only animations of the file type .BVH. Furthermore, the upload utility limits the length of animations to 900 frames; as noted before, looping can extend this. You should also know that when uploading an animation, *Second Life* runs some optimization algorithms that can eliminate minor or subtle movements.

To upload an animation you've created, click the File drop-down menu in the *Second Life* viewer, select Upload Animation (it'll cost you L$10), and choose the file that you want to upload. The dialog window in Figure 11.9 will appear. The parts of the window are detailed here.

Name: This is the name your animation will have in your Inventory. This field defaults to the file name.

Description: Like any other item, animations have a field for brief notes.

Priority: Select the priority for this animation (0 to 4; default is 2).

Preview While: You can select several default poses to make sure your animation looks correct while playing. This setting will not affect the final animation, just the previewer. This is useful for checking if all body parts have an animation associated with them. Normally you will want Standing selected unless you plan on playing the animation simultaneously with a different, default animation.

CHAPTER 1
CHAPTER 2
CHAPTER 3
CHAPTER 4
CHAPTER 5
CHAPTER 6
CHAPTER 7
CHAPTER 8
CHAPTER 9
CHAPTER 10
CHAPTER 11

CHAPTER 12
CHAPTER 13
CHAPTER 14
APPENDICES
INDEX

Loop: When the box is checked, the animation will loop. This is useful when you want a set of motions to be repeated (like a dance), or when you want one position in the animation to be static until the animation is stopped (like a pose).

In(%) and Out(%): You can select the range in which you want to loop your animation. While the input is a percentage, the upload utility will round to the nearest whole frame. If you have an exact frame on which you want to begin or end the loop, you may have to break out a calculator. Otherwise, you can watch the previewer for an approximation. In any loop, you don't want to include the first frame; the animation will try to jump to the T-pose (the default pose where your avatar stands with arms stretched outward to the side like a big letter T) every loop. For example, a simple two-frame pose would use an In% (start of loop) of 51% (beginning of the second frame) and an Out% (end of loop) of 100% (end of the second frame).

Hand Pose: You can add one of several hand morphs to your animation with this selection. Hand poses last for only a few seconds, so using Relaxed (the default) for any looping animation is recommended.

Expression: Like hand poses, you can add one of several facial morphs to your animation with this selection. Like hand poses, facial expressions last for only a few seconds.

Ease In (sec) & Ease Out (sec): You can delay the start of your animation. When you choose Ease In, the animation will move smoothly from the avatar's current position to the first frame of the animation during delay. Ease Out does the same at the end of an animation. So if you create a stationary pose and set any value here, you can get the animation to move into the pose and then release smoothly when the pose is ended.

Previewer: This part of the dialog shows how your animation will look when played in-world. To zoom in or out, click and drag up or down on the screen. If you drag left or right, the camera turns around the figure. Hold **Ctrl+Shift+Alt** and drag to make the camera move in any direction.

There are also control buttons to play and stop the previewer. You can play your animation in the pose screen to make sure it looks correct before uploading.

WARNING

The previewer features the Ruth (default) body shape, so it may not tell you if limb positions will be correct for your avatar.

Upload (L$10) and Cancel: When you have selected the value you want for each field, you can select Upload (L$10) to send the animation to your Inventory. If you find an error while using the previewer, use the Cancel button to cancel the upload, and correct the error without being charged the upload fee.

RESIDENTS SPEAK

IUMI CLINE ON THE BENEFITS OF UPLOADING ANIMATIONS

Upload to make sure all the joints and body-part angles look correct on your avatar from every direction. Having [an animation] uploaded also allows you to get feedback and opinions from in-world friends.

■ USING GESTURES

CHAPTER 1
CHAPTER 2
CHAPTER 3
CHAPTER 4
CHAPTER 5
CHAPTER 6
CHAPTER 7
CHAPTER 8
CHAPTER 9
CHAPTER 10
CHAPTER 11

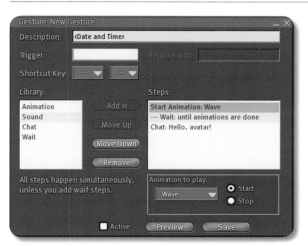

Figure 11.10: Gestures allow you to combine animations, sounds, and chat messages that will trigger when you enter certain words in chat or press predefined hotkeys.

Now that you have your animation loaded into *Second Life*, there are several things you can do with it. First and most common is including it in a gesture.

Gestures are a combination of animations, lines of chat, and sound files. In some software this might be called a *macro*, but *Second Life* is avatar-centered, so it uses a more familiar name. For instance, you could combine a bow animation, send "Domo arigato" to chat, and play a little Japanese theme music to form a simple gesture that can be easily triggered.

Because animations have a 30-second limit, a gesture can be used to string together multiple animations to produce a single motion that can continue past the time limit without looping. There is no limit to how long you can string multiple animations together. To create a new gesture, open your Inventory, right-click on the folder where you want the gesture to be stored, and select New Gesture from the context menu. This will create a gesture named (not surprisingly) New Gesture. To edit this item, right-click on it and select Open from the context menu. You will see a dialog box (Figure 11.10) with the following fields:

Description: As with any item in *Second Life*, this field can hold a short note about the item.

Trigger: The trigger is the chat text that will begin the gesture. Most triggers begin with a forward slash (/) to prevent starting the typing animation, but it can be any text.

Replace With: Whatever you type in this box will replace the trigger text.

Shortcut Key: You can define a shortcut to your gesture, triggering it by pressing one of the function keys (F2 to F12), or Control or Shift plus a function key. These choices are defined by the two Shortcut Key pull-downs.

Library: These are the types of task that a gesture can perform. The choices include Animation, Sound, Chat, and Wait. You can choose any number of these tasks for your gesture and place them in any order. For example, you might play three animations followed by a sound and two chat messages.

Steps: A gesture is a series of tasks. This window contains information about what tasks are to be performed, and in what order. The following controls allow you to change the steps in the gesture.

> **Add and Remove**: If you have selected a task from the library, the Add button will place a generic task of that type in the Steps window (which can then be modified). If you have selected a task from the steps window, the Remove button will delete that task.

> **Move Up and Move Down**: These buttons allow you to impose the order in which tasks in the Steps window will be performed. To use them, select a task in the Steps window and then use the buttons to move the task into place.

Modification Box: Depending on what task is selected in the Steps window, the title of this box changes, along with they types of modification you may use:

CHAPTER 11

UNDERSTAND-
ING ANIMATION
BASICS

CHOOSING
AND USING
ANIMATION
TOOLS

CREATING
ANIMATIONS

TUTORIAL:
MAKING A
DANCE
ANIMATION

💠 *Animation to play gives options for the animation name and for whether you want to issue a start or stop for that animation. Usually you'll want just a starting order issued (so the animation will play until it's ended). In the case of looping animations, you will need to include a stop order.*

NOTE

Animations are selectable for use in a gesture only if you have full permissions.

💠 *Sound to Play gives you the option to select from the audio files in your Inventory for which you have full permissions.*

💠 *Chat to Say provides a blank line where you can place text for your avatar to say.*

💠 *Wait gives the option to wait until all animations are complete, or to wait for the number of seconds you specify.*

Active: If you check the Active check box the gesture will then be triggered whenever you enter the appropriate trigger, such as a chat message or a hotkey. Deactivated gestures will not be triggered except by the Preview button. Note that activating or deactivating a gesture is saved automatically and independently from the Save button. Active gestures with triggers are also accessible from the Gestures menu on the right side of the chat bar.

Preview: Pressing this button will play the gesture in-world, where you (and other avatars) can see and hear it to ensure it is working as you intend.

Save: This button will save the changes you have made to the gesture.

There is a memory limitation on gestures, but it is (in general) far more than what's necessary. A very complex gesture can last for several minutes and be choreographed for nearly any purpose.

MORE INFO

SCRIPTING ANIMATIONS

Employing a script to control animations is one of the most widely used features in *Second Life*. Here we'll discuss the most common methods of combining scripts and animations. The scripting section of this book may assist you in creating your own. Gestures cannot be triggered directly from a script.

The main problem with using an animation to interact with an object that is not one of your attachments (be it another avatar, a set of prims, or worse—particles) is that animations are not scalable. You need to know your location and the precise location of the target before you trigger the animation. In fact, this type of animated interaction is so difficult that having the position information is recommended before you even make the animation.

Each prim can have only one scripted *sit target*. A sit target is not necessarily literally sitting; it may be a standing pose or a lying-down pose, or it may even be in motion. Without a script, as many avatars as will fit can sit upon a flat surface, but curved surfaces will often reject anyone trying to sit on them.

Here are some typical uses for scripted animations.

 Pose balls are spheres scripted to play a specific animation. Typically these are sitting positions, although they are used for sexual animations often enough to be directly associated with them. Some people like the use of pose balls because they are simple to use (often including hovering text describing the animation) for those who can't determine where on a chair to sit. Other people believe they're ugly and distracting from the furniture's design. They may also be considered lazy or wasteful because they require less modification work than an integral pose—at the cost of an extra prim per seated position.

- *Integral poses* are scripts included in a prim of a build (such as a piece of furniture or a dance floor) that trigger an animation or pose when clicked. This style of scripted animation has the advantage of being transparent to the viewer, at the cost of being less obvious to the user.

- *Animation overriders* (AOs) are attachments that replace (or override) the default animations. These animations usually include a mixture of standing poses, walking, sitting, and swimming animations, and several others. These scripts tend to be somewhat complicated. Fortunately, there are many available for sale or even for free (like Francis Chung's Wet Icon AO). Replacing these animations gives your avatar an enormous feeling of personalization—especially if you create your own AOs.

- It is possible through scripting to produce more-complex animations. *Multipart animations*, which are those that last longer than 30 seconds, require several different poses, or body parts animated separately that can be stitched together with scripts. Furthermore, interactive animations between avatars—like hugs and kisses—can be produced. The two main difficulties of interactive animations are aligning the avatars and accounting for their height differences.

One limitation of *Second Life*'s streaming technology is that it prevents unconditional, absolute timing between gestures and sounds. That is to say, they may be triggered at the same time, but because most sound files are significantly larger than animation files and because of varying download speeds, it is not possible to guarantee that any specific avatar will hear a sound at a specific time after it is triggered (for instance, if you tell an animation and a sound to start at exactly 9 o'clock, they won't start at that exact time if they aren't fully loaded). However, this effect can be minimized through scripting; `llPreloadSound` is a scripting command that will cause the audio file to be sent to nearby avatars and stored in their cache. With the audio file already received, it is much more likely that an animation and a sound will play simultaneously, as you intended.

TUTORIAL: MAKING A DANCE ANIMATION

Are you happy with what you have learned? If so, express your joy by dancing! This tutorial will guide you step-by-step through creating a complex animation—in this case, a dance. Because Poser has many advantages over the other programs that can produce an animation, this tutorial uses Poser. However, it can be translated to QAvimator with one exception: intermediate frames should be adjusted by hand to produce more fluid, lifelike motions than simple linear interpolation provides.

CHAPTER 11

 UNDERSTAND-
  ING ANIMATION
  BASICS

 CHOOSING
  AND USING
  ANIMATION
  TOOLS

 CREATING
  ANIMATIONS

 TUTORIAL:
  MAKING A
  DANCE
  ANIMATION

The Hokey Pokey has seven distinct steps that we will mimic in our animation:

 You put your *body part* in

 You put your *body part* out

 You put your *body part* in

 And you shake it all about.

 You do the Hokey Pokey

 And you turn yourself around

 That's what it's all about!

■ LAYING THE GROUNDWORK

1. Open Poser and make sure your selected model is in the previewer.

2. We want an animation length of about 30 seconds (maximum length). At 30 frames per second, that's a total of 900 frames. This high number may seem daunting, but a great number of these frames will be filled automatically. Change the number of frames at the bottom of the screen to 900.

3. Move to frame 2 and make that it's a key frame. Push the Play Range arrow so your loop begins at the second frame.

4. Frame 2 is our starting position. We will use *Second Life*'s Ease In feature so that an animated "get into position" sequence is unnecessary.

Figure 11.11: He may look grumpy, but he was born to do the Hokey Pokey.

5. For our starting position, we want a relaxed pose with the arms to the side, and the knees slightly bent (Figure 11.11).

   a. Drag the model's feet out to about shoulder width, using the Pull tool.

   b. Switch to the Twist tool and level the soles of the model's feet with the floor.

   c. Make sure inverse kinematics are on for the legs and off for the arms.

   d. Switch to the rotate tool, select the right shoulder, and rotate it down until it looks like it's in a comfortable position.

   e. With the Pull tool, move the hips down slightly so the knees bend.

6. Now we want to the figure to bob up and down with the music. For this, we will simply bend the knees a little and then come back to our frame-2 position. Because humans usually pause at a comfortable position, we will include this behavior. We will assume the beat repeats evenly every second, so we will use 30 frames.

    a. Highlight frame 2 and copy it (Ctrl+C).

    b. Select frame 13 and paste the copy.

    c. Repeat step b for frames 25 and 31.

    d. To isolate the remainder of the animation from the first frame, break the spline at the second frame.

    e. Because we want a brief pause at the top of the figure's motion, select frames 26 though 30 and make them Constant.

    f. Select frame 13 again, and using the Move tool drag the hips down (along the y-axis) a small amount. Remember that inverse kinematics should still be on, keeping the feet in place.

    g. Now that we have one cycle of up-down-up completed, we can select frames 2 through 31 (30 frames total) and paste them one after the other, filling the entire animation (900 frames).

■ ANIMATING THE DANCE

At this point we have 30 seconds' worth of a figure performing shallow squats. Now we want to include the song's body-part motions. There are seven steps for each body part. Each step will include two of our squat loops (30 frames). We want also include one loop of pause before every body-part rhyme. This makes 18 seconds per rhyme. Those of you who are mathematically inclined may notice that 18 goes into 900 evenly—which is great—but even if it did not, we would continue on and crop the unused frames when we completed the other motions. Because of the time constraint imposed by animation maximum length, we will do only the right arm and the left arm.

1. We're going to skip the first 60 frames and allow it to be a simple squat-only animation. The end of the third squat is at frame 83. If we alter this frame and allow it to change from the beginning of the squat, we will have a single smooth motion. Alter frame 83 so that the right arm is extended and ready to be put "in."

Generally, people will use a small amount of motion on several body parts to produce the overall motion desired.

2. Twist the abdomen about slightly, and the chest double the amount used for the abdomen.

3. Rotate the right collar forward and the shoulder upward until the hand is about bust-high.

4. Twist the upper arm, lower arm, and hand until the hand is somewhat parallel with the ground.

5. Rotate the lower arm until the hand seems centered on the body.

6. People counter-balance themselves, so we want to bring the left arm back some. Rotate the left collar and left shoulder back until it seems that the elbow-spine-elbow alignment is roughly straight.

7. Adjust the forearm and hand of the left arm so they seem comfortable with the upper arm.

8. Go back to frame 71 so we can make the midpoint of this section meld with the two ends.

▪ YOU PUT YOUR RIGHT ARM IN

Figure 11.12: Our Default guy puts his right arm in.

1. At this point we should have brought our arm up, ready to "put it in" as the song commands (Figure 11.12).

2. To bring the body to more natural "decision points" rather than using a single smooth motion, there are several changes that should be made to the posture in this frame. The left collar should roll back slightly. The right arm should be in a pulled back and up, with the hand only slightly in front of the body and at chest height. The chest and abdomen should be nearly parallel with the hips.

3. Next, we leave the arm "in" for one cycle.

4. Select all of frame 83 in the animation pallet (white outline around the green dots), and copy it.

5. Select the beginning for the next cycle (frame 89), and paste. Repeat for frame 112 (the end of this same cycle).

6. Because the constant section between cycles was formed with the right arm down, we need to resample it. To do this, select the section (frames 84 through 88) in the animation pallet, delete it (using the Delete button on your keyboard), then reapply constant interpolation.

7. The midpoint of this cycle also has the arms down. To correct this, we need to change the arm (collar, shoulder, forearm, and hand), abdomen, chest, and neck positions. We can copy and paste this information from frame 89, one body-part key at a time.

▪ YOU PUT YOUR RIGHT ARM OUT

Now, it's time to take the arm out. The remainder of the right-arm section will be largely copying and pasting frames that have already been made—with a few adjustments.

1. We want to make sure the arm doesn't have discontinuous motion between cycles. Copy the end of the cycle (frame 112) and paste it into the beginning of the next cycle (frame 118). Delete and re-constant the intervening frames (113 to 117), as we have done before.

2. We made a midpoint frame for this motion earlier (while putting the arm "in"). This position should be duplicated as the midpoint of taking the arm back "out." This can be done easily by copying frame 70 and pasting it to frame 129.

3. A person would know that the next step is to put the arm back in, so we won't drop the figure's hand all the way to its side. Paste only the arm positions from frame 70 into frame 141. (As a small time-saver, you could copy and paste all of frame 70, then paste just the hip location from 129). The arm is still not very relaxed though; rotate the right collar down a little, and twist the right shoulder in.

4. To leave the arm out for a cycle, copy frame 141 into the beginning, middle, and end of the next cycle (frames 147, 158, and 170). Then delete and re-constant the frames between these cycles. At the midpoint of this cycle, we want the figure to squat again, so we copy the hip position from frame 129 and paste it in frame 158.

■ You Put Your Right Arm In

It's time to put the right hand back in. This will be the reverse of taking it out.

1. Copy from frame 141 to 176, from 129 to 187, and from 118 to 199.

2. To maintain the hand at the "in" position, simply copy and paste into another three frames: from 112 to 205 and 228, and from 100 to 216.

3. Delete the between-cycle frames (171 through 175 and 200 through 204) and make them constant again.

■ You Shake It All About

Shaking it all about will use two cycles. This example produces a fairly leisurely shake; you may want to alter it to your taste.

1. Copy from frame 199 and paste to frames 234, 245, 257, 263, 274, and 286. Paste the hips from frame 216 through 245 and 274.

2. Delete the between-cycle frames (229 through 233) and make them constant again.

3. For the between-cycle frames during the shake (258 through 262), just delete the constant frames and leave them splined.

4. Adjust the twist and rotations of the shoulder, forearm, and hand to various positions in frames 245, 257, 263, and 274 to simulate shaking the hand "all about." These key frames can also be dragged to different positions to give timing variations; but remember to keep the hip keys where they are so the squats don't get mistimed. Also, more key frames can be included to increase the number of hand-motion direction changes.

■ You Do the Hokey Pokey

The next cycle brings the arm back in, and prepares the figure for the Hokey Pokey. By the end of this cycle, the hand should be near the body, at shoulder level, with palms facing out.

1. We will base this motion on the reverse of taking the arm out. So, copy frames 286 through 292, 129 through 303, and 141 through 315.

2. On frame 315, rotate the right shoulder and forearm to bring the arm up to position, and then give the left arm a symmetric position.

3. Frame 303 is the midpoint of this cycle. The arms need to be positioned to indicate this motion. Fortunately, the pose we copied into this frame already has the right arm in an appropriate position. Adjust the left arm to a symmetric position.

4. Re-constant the section between cycles as before.

CHAPTER 11

UNDERSTAND-
ING ANIMATION
BASICS

CHOOSING
AND USING
ANIMATION
TOOLS

CREATING
ANIMATIONS

TUTORIAL:
MAKING A
DANCE
ANIMATION

AND YOU TURN YOURSELF AROUND

For "turn yourself around," we will use three cycles (frames 321 through 402).

1. To define the ends of this section of animation, copy frame 315 and paste it to frame 321 and frame 402.

2. Because we don't want the figure squatting during this phase of the animation, delete the keys between the two ends of the animation (frames 322 through 401).

3. Now we have 80 frames for a full turn. For simplicity, we will use eight steps to turn around (10 frames each). This makes the timing for steps during this phase obvious. First we will create the key frames of the turn by rotating the hips 1/8 of a turn (to the figure's left) every 10 frames. Twist the neck to keep the head facing roughly in the same direction as the hips. Having inverse kinematics off during this step should make it a little easier.

4. Animating the steps is a bit more intricate. Turning consists of a forward step and a reverse step.

   a. The forward step places the right foot toe-in and in front of the left foot. Remember that the figure's body needs to be balanced over the nonmoving foot. Some hip rotation is necessary to make the leg motion look natural, which requires abdomen and chest rotation to keep the body somewhat vertical.

   b. The reverse step places the left foot toe-out and behind the right foot. For this step, the hip needs to be rotated in the opposite direction.

   c. We'll include midstep motions next to keep the figure from simply sliding its feet along the floor.

5. The Hokey Pokey includes an alternating hands-up movement (Figure 11.13). This motion is mostly performed by rotating the collar upward; however this needs to be balanced by rotating the shoulder and the forearm inward. To make the figure appear coordinated, this motion should be completed at the same time as each footstep.

6. This combination of step and hand motion will be performed four times. We will copy and paste the first set of leg and arm key frames frames 322 through 342) to the remainder of this section (frames 343 through 402).

Figure 11.13: The hands-up portion of the Hokey Pokey

7. Complete a quarter-turn animation for the Hokey Pokey, paste it to the remainder of the section, and turn the whole body at each key frame. This will require the use of linear interpolation (for the "body" in this section) to avoid a rapid unwinding appearance to the spline.

■ THAT'S WHAT IT'S ALL ABOUT!

The final step is a basic clapping motion—centered on a pause between the next two cycles of the animation.

1. As before, copy the first frame of this section from the last frame of the previous section.

2. Alter the midcycle frame to have the arms at a comfortable position alongside the body, but bent at the elbows with the hands in front of the chest. Copy this key frame to the mid position of the next cycle.

3. The final frame of this cycle should have the hands together. Some hand overlap is necessary to make *Second Life* avatar hands meet. Twisting the shoulders inward and rotating the hands outward accomplishes this.

4. After clapping, the arms should return to the figure's side. This can be done simply, since we have already produced this pose: copy it from frame 25.

5. This clap is a little slow. We can make it faster by dragging the midcycle key frames toward the between-cycle pause until it appears to be the speed you want.

The second half of this animation (the left arm) should be much simpler, because of one powerful tool available in Poser.

6. First, copy frames 31 through 465 and paste them beginning at frame 466. Now there are two "right arm in" animations.

7. To convert the second half to the left arm, select each key frame from 495 through 750, then for each key frame select the Figure menu, then Symmetry ▸ Swap Right and Left. Because the motion will be mirrored with a mathematic algorithm, the "shake it all about" section may require close scrutiny and some re-adjustment to make it look less artificial. Movements that look natural right-handed may not look suitable when left-handed, so just used your judgment.

TIP

Go through the process outlined in step 4 in the "Preparing the Animation for Upload" section before previewing the animation.

■ PREPARING THE ANIMATION FOR UPLOAD

Cropping the unused portions of the animation is critical to your ability to upload the animation easily.

1. Remove extra frames from the end of the animation by determining the last useful frame and altering the number of frames in the whole animation to that number. For this example this step is not necessary because we used exactly 900 frames.

2. Delete any changes to hair, ground, or camera positions.

CHAPTER 1
CHAPTER 2
CHAPTER 3
CHAPTER 4
CHAPTER 5
CHAPTER 6
CHAPTER 7
CHAPTER 8
CHAPTER 9
CHAPTER 10
CHAPTER 11

CHAPTER 12
CHAPTER 13
CHAPTER 14
APPENDICES
INDEX

Potentially the most important step in producing any animation is the final step: mussing up. The introduction of small, manual changes at many (or most) key frames prevents the overall feel of the animation being too automated or mechanical.

3. Simply select a key frame and very slightly change a few body-part locations, then move on to the next key frame.

During the process of creating an animation, the between-key-frame positions will often look mangled. This effect is common and shouldn't cause concern. Once your key frames look acceptable and you've removed the excess frames, this can be repaired.

Figure 11.14: When the work is done you can upload your dance in Second Life for all to enjoy.

4. It is often wise to go back and delete each group of frames between key frames. This will force the spline to be recalculated. For this animation, each of the between-cycle constant sections should be deleted and made constant again.

5. If you play the animation now and see that the spline has determined very unrealistic motion, make sure Figure ▸ Use Limits is checked. If it isn't, check it and use Animation ▸ Resample Key Frames (the analyze curvature method). This should correct most problems.

6. Upload the animation for all to enjoy (Figure 11.14) and include it in a gesture if desired.

TIP

Possibly a better option for doing the whole dance would be to produce one animation for each body part and script them together. In this way, the order of the body parts could be shuffled. If you are interested in developing a complete set of animations, some common body parts to animate are arms, legs, chest, head, and tail.

You may have noticed that in this example, many imprecise terms were used. Making an animation is more artwork and "eyeballing" than technical or mathematic composition. As stated earlier, the most challenging part of creating a high-quality animation is producing movements that mimic human motion. This requires an artistic intuition and at least some study of the human form.

Having created your first animation and having a fair idea of how animations can be used, you should be capable of producing more-advanced, interactive builds and a more-polished, personalized experience in *Second Life.*

CHAPTER 12

PERFORMANCE AND FIGHTING THE LAG MONSTER

Once people discover the unbridled power of *Second Life* to realize their visions and dreams, there is a temptation to go hog wild. They may create homes in which the details of every panel, every nook, and every molding is built with a complex array of prims. A preponderance of textures of the highest detail and resolution might be used to decorate every surface. Scripts may fill every object, causing them to play a din of music, animate objects, and fill the scene with a flurry of motion and activity. However, when visitors find themselves nearly immobilized by the resulting drop in performance, it becomes clear—*Second Life* builds require balance!

In this chapter we'll look at the crippling performance degradation that can make your *Second Life* experience feel like a stroll through a swimming pool filled with molasses. We will identify the different kinds of lag and discuss ways in which you can maximize the performance of your build while minimizing the sacrifices necessary to give your visitors a smooth, responsive experience.

CONTENTS

■ DIFFERENT
SPECIES
OF LAG

■ CREATING
EFFICIENT
BUILDS

RESIDENTS SPEAK

CATHERINE OMEGA ON WRAPPING YOUR HEAD AROUND *SL's* MECHANICS

Wrapping one's head around the mechanics of *Second Life* often requires us to step back and stop thinking of *Second Life* as a "world," but rather as a client and a server, as well as the processes that exist on both. Without delving into the source code itself, fully understanding those processes can be very difficult.

The *Second Life* server doesn't simulate space; it just processes data that is interpreted into 3D space by the client, just as a website isn't stored as the visual page you see in your browser, but rather as a collection of graphics and text files that are downloaded from the server to your computer.

If you're used to the idea of *Second Life* as a world, it can be hard to remember that when you're "in" *Second Life*, there's no "there" there.

DIFFERENT SPECIES OF LAG

To fight the lag monster, it's important to understand it. While many new users are hoping to find a silver bullet to end all of their lag problems, the actual source of a performance problem can vary, and in many cases it can be a combination of problems. In this section you'll learn to differentiate and identify the three different kinds of lag: network lag, client side lag, and server lag.

■ NETWORK LAG

Second Life is constantly streaming data to and from your computer. If for whatever reason something hinders the stream between the *Second Life* server and a user's computer, the user is going to experience performance problems. Network lag normally manifests itself with the following symptoms:

- 🔹 **Avatars experience the "rubber band" effect, where they appear to walk normally in the direction you want to go, but periodically snap back to a previous position.**

- 🔹 **Avatars experience a delay in reaction. For example, you may hold down the W key to walk forward and nothing happens until five seconds later. Your avatar will then overshoot its destination.**

- 🔹 **When you're editing and positioning objects, they randomly snap back to their original positions.**

- 🔹 **When you're interacting with objects by clicking on them, the object may register your click multiple times or not at all.**

- 🔹 **Text messages are delayed or duplicate messages appear.**

Another way to determine if the lag you are experiencing is due to your network is to look at packet loss. Data is streamed across the Internet from one computer to another in the form of little

Figure 12.1: The statistics bar provides you with information about how many packets you are losing, as well as the bandwidth you are using.

Figure 12.2: Second Life's About window provides a tally of your packet loss since you logged in.

CHAPTER 1
CHAPTER 2
CHAPTER 3
CHAPTER 4
CHAPTER 5
CHAPTER 6
CHAPTER 7
CHAPTER 8
CHAPTER 9
CHAPTER 10
CHAPTER 11
CHAPTER 12

CHAPTER 13
CHAPTER 14
APPENDICES
INDEX

chunks called *packets*. If a packet is somehow damaged or lost in transit, another copy is quickly sent before anybody ever notices a problem. However, if network issues cause a large number of packets to become lost and resent, the result is a degradation in performance. You can view the percentage of packets being lost in the communication between your computer and the *Second Life* server by looking at the Packet Loss indicator on the statistics bar (Figure 12.1) by going to View ▸ Statistics Bar or pressing Control+Shift+1. You can find a mini version of the packet-loss information on the upper-right corner of the *Second Life* window and you can view the total packet loss since the time you logged in by going to Help ▸ About Second Life (Figure 12.2). A steady packet loss of more than 5 percent is a strong indication of network problems.

Network lag is rarely caused by anything related to a *Second Life* build, so there is little you can do as a content creator to alleviate this problem for your visitors. If a visitor experiences network lag, you can offer them the following suggestions:

- If on a wireless connection, plug directly into a network instead.

- Close any network-intensive applications such as BitTorrent, streaming music, or large FTP transfers.

- Make sure their computer network drivers and BIOS are up-to-date.

- Get a better Internet connection.

■ CLIENT LAG

Client lag is the kind of lag that exists entirely on your visitor's machines. Here are some of the typical symptoms of client lag:

- When you zoom your camera around, it goes very slowly, almost halting at every frame like a slideshow.

- Performance becomes worse when you point your camera at certain builds or avatars, but is alleviated when you look in another direction with fewer complex builds.

- When you type text messages, there is a delay for individual characters to appear on the chat line (not to be confused with the delay after hitting Enter, which is a symptom of network lag).

You can also diagnose client lag using the FPS meter at the top of the statistics bar. FPS stands for *frames per second* and represents the number of times each second *Second Life* is redrawing the scene you are currently viewing. FPS values below 15 are considered slow and may result in a frustrating *SL* experience, while FPS values above 60 are considered exceptional and are ideal for fast-paced gaming. You will likely notice a change in FPS as you zoom your camera around. Focusing on highly detailed or complex builds (like Figure 12.3) will cause low FPS values, while focusing on empty sky (Figure 12.4) will result in very high FPS values.

DIFFERENT
SPECIES
OF LAG

CREATING
EFFICIENT
BUILDS

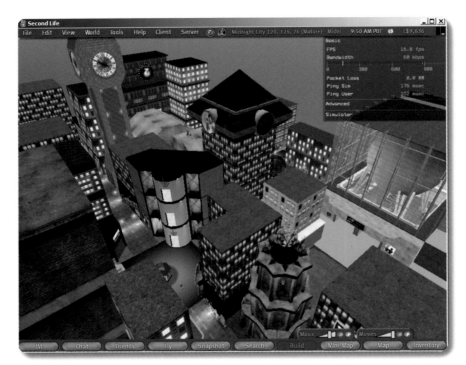

Figure 12.3: Viewing a build as enormous and complex as Midnight City in its entirety can cause a lowered FPS value (in this case 16.8 FPS).

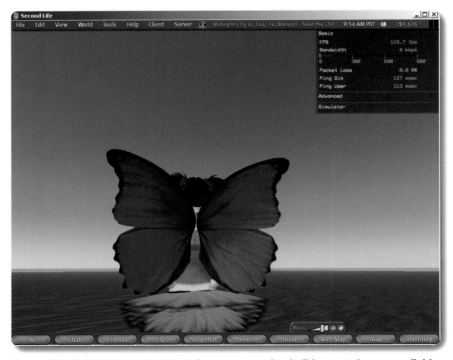

Figure 12.4: Staring out to sea where no complex builds come into your field of vision can give you an exceptional FPS value (119.7 FPS here)

There are two causes of client lag and low FPS values: builds that are generally too complex and demanding on visitors' computers, and visitors' computers that are old or are poor performers. Here are a few computer-related causes of client lag:

- Inadequate RAM. *Second Life* stores a lot of data in your computer's memory. If that memory is insufficient, your computer will write that data to your hard drive, allowing it to load new data into memory. This is called *swapping* and it's a very slow process. By purchasing more ram, your computer can keep more data in memory for easy access, which means less swapping and better performance.

- Inadequate CPU. *Second Life* does a lot of data decompression that places a heavy load on your CPU (as opposed to putting the load on your video card as many video games do), causing a loss in performance. Upgrading the CPU will help alleviate this kind of lag.

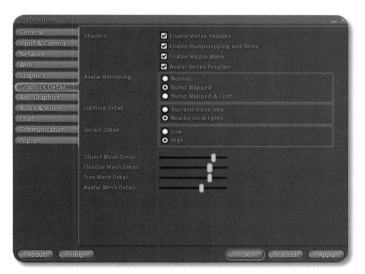

Figure 12.5: The Graphics Detail tab of Edit ▸ Preferences provides fine control over what the client does and does not render.

- Inadequate video card. *Second Life* performs real-time rendering, including shading, shadowing, and lighting. These tasks place a heavy load on a system's video card, and some older cards are simply not up to the task. A newer video card can do wonders for your system's performance.

- Graphics settings are too high. Even a great computer can choke on *Second Life* if you place all the settings at the maximum. If you go to Edit ▸ Preferences you will find a variety of graphics settings on the Graphics, Graphics Detail (Figure 12.5), and Advanced Graphics tabs. Try reducing some of these settings until your performance increases to a comfortable level.

Of course, the responsibility of reducing client lag doesn't fall entirely on your visitors. By making your builds efficient you reduce the load your visitors' computers must endure and you allow them the opportunity to enjoy your work without having to shell out the big bucks for a pimped-out new machine! We will go into detail about making your builds more efficient in the next section, "Creating Efficient Builds," but for now, here are some tips to reduce client lag:

- Avoid overusing complex prims. Prims such as tori contain much more geometry data than, say, a box. Some client computers can slow down significantly when a large number of these prims come into view.

- Be frugal with textures. *Second Life* servers will compress your build's images before sending them to a visitor's computer. Their computers will then have to decompress the data, which places a load on their CPUs and contributes to lag. Even once your visitors have all the texture data decompressed on their systems, their troubles are not over. If those textures are numerous and very large, their systems will likely be unable to keep all that data in RAM. This means the data will cause swapping, which creates more lag. Keeping textures and texture resolution to the minimum required for the build helps minimize this problem.

- Be careful of client-side scripts. While most scripts function on the server side, some scripting features, such as particle systems, are executed on the client side. If these client-side features are not written properly, they can impact client performance.

CHAPTER 1
CHAPTER 2
CHAPTER 3
CHAPTER 4
CHAPTER 5
CHAPTER 6
CHAPTER 7
CHAPTER 8
CHAPTER 9
CHAPTER 10
CHAPTER 11
CHAPTER 12

CHAPTER 13
CHAPTER 14
APPENDICES
INDEX

CHAPTER 12

DIFFERENT
SPECIES
OF LAG

CREATING
EFFICIENT
BUILDS

■ SERVER LAG

The final type of lag is server lag. *Second Life* servers keep track of everything that is going on in any given region. This includes tasks such as running server-side scripts and resolving the outcome of collisions between physical objects and avatars. When these tasks become numerous enough to overload the server, you are likely to see these symptoms:

- Avatars are slow to respond, similar to client lag response times.

- Attachments are slow to load and appear on your avatar.

- Scripts are slow to respond to events or don't respond at all.

- Physical objects and vehicles function slowly.

- The region restarts.

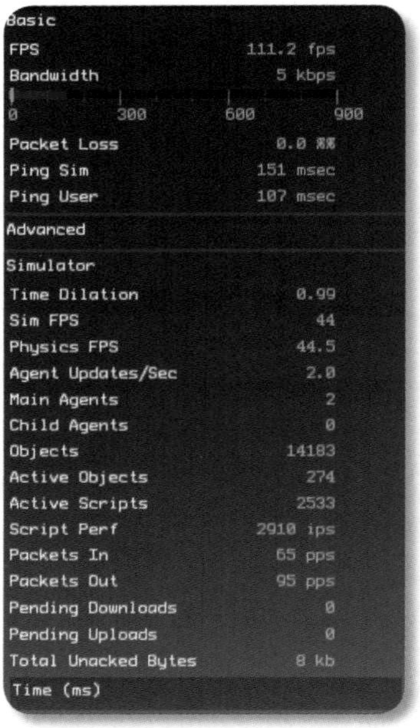

Basic	
FPS	111.2 fps
Bandwidth	5 kbps
0 300 600 900	
Packet Loss	0.0 %%
Ping Sim	151 msec
Ping User	107 msec
Advanced	
Simulator	
Time Dilation	0.99
Sim FPS	44
Physics FPS	44.5
Agent Updates/Sec	2.0
Main Agents	2
Child Agents	0
Objects	14183
Active Objects	274
Active Scripts	2533
Script Perf	2910 ips
Packets In	65 pps
Packets Out	95 pps
Pending Downloads	0
Pending Uploads	0
Total Unacked Bytes	8 kb
Time (ms)	

Figure 12.6: The statistics bar displays time dilation, sim FPS, and physics FPS, all of which are useful for diagnosing server lag.

You can also diagnose client lag using the statistics bar (Figure 12.6). One of the most effective indications of server lag is *time dilation*. This is a value between 0 and 1 that represents the degree to which the server is able to complete operations in a timely fashion. Values of 1.0 or 0.99 means the server is processing and completing tasks close to real time. Values below 0.80 mean the region is experiencing difficulty keeping up with the high volume of tasks it must complete. It therefore gets behind and cannot complete the tasks in real time. Time dilation values below 0.20 are indicative of problems that make functioning in the region unpleasant, difficult, and in some cases impossible.

Sim FPS is another indicator of server performance. This number represents the number of frames per second the sim is executing. A value of 45, the maximum, indicates a healthy sim that is able to handle the tasks it has been given. Lower sim frame rates may result in a reduction in the amount of execution time scripts are given, and that will cause performance problems. Just below the Sim FPS value you have Physics FPS, which works exactly the same way, but it measures the frames per second for physical interactions, such as balls bouncing and people flying into buildings.

Server lag can be alleviated by cutting back on the physical objects floating around the region. You should also reduce the number of scripts that perform costly tasks, such as public-channel listeners and tight loops (loops that go off and execute instructions multiple times per second.)

NOTE

When dealing with performance, you may be tempted to say "Enough of your infernal vagaries—tell me what size to make my textures so that I can end lag forever!" Unfortunately, there is no universal solution. A tremendous number of variables blend together to create a resulting level of lag. Builds that are problematic to some are high performers to others. Some releases of Second Life *may see improved performance in some features and reduced performance in others. The dividing line between laggy and non-laggy builds is blurry. We can't give you a formula that will give you a high-performance build. All we can do is tell you what kind of things increase or decrease lag, and let you decide when you are satisfied with your build's performance.*

CHAPTER 1
CHAPTER 2
CHAPTER 3
CHAPTER 4
CHAPTER 5
CHAPTER 6
CHAPTER 7
CHAPTER 8
CHAPTER 9
CHAPTER 10
CHAPTER 11
CHAPTER 12

CREATING EFFICIENT BUILDS

Now that we've uncovered the mystery behind lag, let's go into detail as to how to combat it. In this section we will discuss how to make builds more efficient without sacrificing aesthetics or function.

■ EXAMINING PRIM COMPLEXITY

It should not come as a surprise that the more complex the geometry of your builds, the more client-side lag your visitors will have to endure. It may, however, be difficult to determine exactly which prims are causing all the trouble. Let's take a closer look at the prim family and see for ourselves.

1. Rez one of each prim type: a box, a prism, a cylinder, a sphere, a torus, a tube, and a ring.

2. Go to Client ▸ Rendering ▸ Wireframe or simply press Control+Shift+R. The world should now look like a big wireframe to you (Figure 12.7).

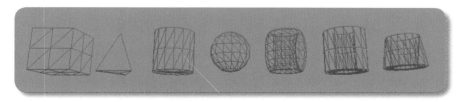

Figure 12.7: Wireframe mode reveals how prims are made up of triangular polygons.

3. Examine the box. You will notice it is made up of numerous little triangles, or *polygons*.

4. Zoom in and out from the box. Notice how the object will have fewer polygons when you zoom out and more when you zoom in. Your eyes are not fooling you! Polygons will actually disappear when you zoom out, and they will reappear when you zoom in to examine the object in greater detail.

5. Go to Edit ▸ Preferences ▸ Graphics Detail and set the Object Mesh Detail slider to the far right.

6. Zoom in and out on the box. You notice the box is now made up of more polygons.

7. Set the Object Mesh Detail slider to the far left and reexamine the box. You can see the box has fewer polygons.

This example is intended to help you understand the complexity of dealing with the performance issues associated with build geometry. The more polygons, the greater the performance hit. But the actual number of polygons will vary from client to client depending on how closely the *Second Life* user is examining the build and what graphics settings they are currently using.

8. Now try adding a Hollow value of 50 to the box. By adding complexity to the box, we have also added more polygons.

9. Set the Hollow value back to 0.

10. Set the Twist value to B = 10. The box twists but this doesn't change the complexity of the box!

11. Carefully watch the polygons on one side of the box while you slowly increase the Twist to B = 180. *Second Life* will periodically add more polygons to accommodate the added complexity of your twisted box shape (Figure 12.8).

Figure 12.8: As we increase the Twist value on this box, more and more polygons are added to accommodate the increase in complexity.

12. Now examine the other prims and compare the number of polygons. The complexity seems to rise from prisms, to boxes, to cylinders, to tubes, to rings, to tori.

13. Carefully watch the torus as you slowly increase the Revolutions value to 4.00.

14. Add a Hollow value of 50.0 and examine the effect on the polygons (Figure 12.9).

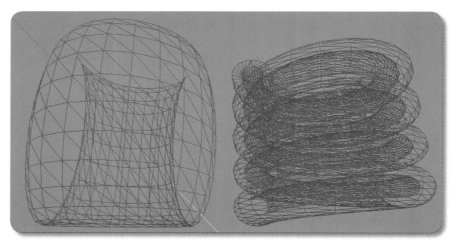

Figure 12.9: Add revolutions and Hollow to a torus—you will see just how complex a prim can get.

15. Now count all the polygons. Just kidding!

Hopefully this demonstration has impressed upon you the importance of being mindful of prim complexity. Used wisely, complex prims are a powerful tool that can add striking realism to any build. But when overused you may find that your builds tax your visitors' systems to the point where things run far too slowly to enjoy.

■ UTILIZING TEXTURES TO REDUCE PRIM USE

CHAPTER 1
CHAPTER 2
CHAPTER 3
CHAPTER 4
CHAPTER 5
CHAPTER 6
CHAPTER 7
CHAPTER 8
CHAPTER 9
CHAPTER 10
CHAPTER 11
CHAPTER 12

CHAPTER 13
CHAPTER 14
APPENDICES
INDEX

Now that we've sufficiently frightened you away from wasteful overuse of prims, you may be wondering how you can make up for all the beautiful detail we've denied you. The answer is textures.

Imagine building your dream house and wanting to create a wooden rail around the back patio. You could use three prims for the horizontal rails and about 30 prims on each side for the vertical supports, giving you a 93-prim rail. As you may guess, this horrible waste of prims can be alleviated by simply using one prim on each side that is textured with the vertical supports. The overall effect is just as attractive at a fraction of the prim costs.

You should always be on the prowl for where a small, well-placed texture can save you on prims. Sometimes windows look just as good when they're made up of textures rather than real openings in the walls, and moldings drawn directly onto a wall can look just as nice as (if not better than) a prim version.

TIP

A Prim-Saving Workaround! Here's a little trick for using textures to reduce prims. Let's say you are using prims to create a complex effect, perhaps a dizzying array buttons, levers, and dials for a spaceship control console, as shown in the left image here. That console uses 146 prims. Once you decide that it would have been better to use a texture rather than wasting all those prims, simply take a snapshot of the control console, crop it to an acceptable size in Photoshop, and apply that snapshot texture to your control console in lieu of the prims. The visual result, shown in the right image, is nearly identical but requires only one prim!

■ OPTIMIZING TEXTURE USE

You may now think that you have the secret to fighting lag: simply use textures everywhere and use as few prims as possible. However, textures cause their share of lag too. Large, numerous textures take time to download to visitors' computers, decompressing lots of textures puts a load on their CPUs, and having an excessive number of textures to load into RAM could cause swapping, all of which result in lag. The answer is to use textures wisely and sparingly. Here are a few simple techniques you can use to get the most out of your textures.

CHAPTER 12

DIFFERENT
SPECIES
OF LAG

CREATING
EFFICIENT
BUILDS

Use the lowest resolution possible. Most builders attempting to put their best foot forward may believe "bigger is better" when selecting the resolution for their textures. On close inspection, 1024×1024-pixel textures will always look better than 512×512 or 256×256 pixel textures. The question is how many people will subject the object in question to close inspection. Admittedly, if you are hanging a virtual Mona Lisa in your virtual gallery, people are likely to zoom in on the painting to enjoy the vivid detail. But how many people will zoom in on the beautifully textured velvet rope in front of it?

The trick is to use precious few high-resolution images for the central focus of your build, while allowing all the ancillary details to be served by the lowest-resolution textures that you can get away with. Not only will this help the performance of your build, but it will draw your visitors' eyes to those details that are important while the rest of the build sits in the periphery to add ambiance.

Reuse textures as much as possible. In an ideal world you could have a unique texture for every prim, each with tiny variations in character and flavor. But in *Second Life* this kind of build would consume an enormous amount of resources and make the user experience very unpleasant.

Instead, try to make your textures with reusability in mind. For example, if you were building the interior of a hotel, you might consider blurring the room number on each finely paneled wooden door so you could use the same door texture for every room. When creating the hotel lobby, you could use parts of the door texture to create wood-paneled walls simply by adjusting the repeats and offsets to hide the room number and door knob. In fact, you could use this technique to panel any wooded portions of the hotel. When you get very good at texture reuse, you find that you can create very complex and beautiful builds with just a handful of textures.

Figure 12.10: Rather than load several textures individually, consider combining them onto one single texture sheet, then use repeats and offsets to display the correct portion of the sheet.

Use texture sheets. Normally textures come complete with additional data in hidden headers. If you have, say, 16 textures in a build, each at 256×256 pixels, your visitors have to download those textures along with the 16 headers that go with them. One way sneak in a little extra performance is to combine those textures in one large 1024×1024-pixel *texture sheet*. When you apply this texture to a prim surface, you simply adjust the offset and repeats so that only the relevant portion of the image is showing (Figure 12.10).

This technique is not always going to be the best solution. If you need a repeating texture, you cannot use a texture sheet because those repeats would end up displaying the neighboring textures on the sheet. Additionally, you should employ texture sheets only when all of the textures will be used in close proximity to each other. This way you aren't forced to wait for a 1024×1024 pixel texture to load up for a small detail in front of you when the rest of the textures in the sheet appear in another region altogether.

Precache your textures. When visitors arrive at a new build, the texture data will begin to load and parts of the build will appear one section at a time. But sometimes it may be important for textures to appear instantly, such as when you are doing a virtual slideshow presentation and you wish for each slide to load immediately so you can discuss it.

One trick you can use, called *precaching*, takes advantage of the fact that textures do not need a line of sight to be loaded on a client's system. Simply being in proximity to the texture causes it to be quietly loaded onto your system, making it instantly available when it later appears in view. To capitalize on this effect, consider hiding prims that feature all the needed textures in locations where visitors will likely be loitering. For example, you could hide such prims under the stage where a slideshow presentation is being given such that most of the audience will already have most of the slide textures downloaded before you ever get to the part of the speech associated with those slides.

RESIDENTS SPEAK

AARON EDELWEISS ON EFFICIENT SCRIPTING

The Second Life *engine gives residents access to powerful features that bring this virtual world to life. But like prims and textures, these features should be used carefully with attention to the performance impact you may be making on the region. Here are some suggestions by SL old-timer and scripting expert Aaron Edelweiss.*

Improving script performance is mostly a matter of avoiding function calls that require a large overhead, rather than avoiding large numbers of operations. Outside of *Second Life* the number of operations you try to do is usually an important factor in how much of a load your program puts on the hardware. In *Second Life* the number of operations a single script can execute is pretty effectively throttled, so it's the type of operations which matter. For instance, an infinite loop that is just doing math or parsing a string or a list will be throttled fairly effectively by the script engine. That same loop causing the object to change position will cause an update to be pushed out to all connected clients, and the scene graph to be updated. That's a much more expensive procedure than finding the third letter of each string in a list.

A basic rule of thumb is anything that does not have to be synchronized between multiple external clients or internal threads/systems is easier to process. Visual updates to objects including texture changes, shape changes, or position changes are an example of something that has to be synchronized between multiple clients and affects multiple subsystems on the server. Chatting text (not listening) is just a push operation into a queue and is not *expensive* [or performance-intensive]. Math or basic logic operations are internal to the script engine, map fairly directly to low-level operations, and are can be easily throttled so they are not expensive operations. Physical calculations are math-heavy and time-sensitive and also have to be synchronized between clients, so they are an example of an expensive operation. Listen [events] have also historically caused heavy server load because each text message being queued up will trigger an event handler for each listener within the region and/or regions next to the region where the text originated. It can cause a lot of code to be executing all at once, which can avalanche into a large overhead. Just because your script didn't hear anything doesn't mean the listen event wasn't fired behind the scenes, which is why people don't realize it's doing as much work as it is.

Some things, like listen [events], are counter-intuitive as to how much overhead they will take. An idle script takes processing time because it must be polled by the script scheduler, regardless of what the script is actually doing. It's a tiny hit per script, but 15,000 idle scripts doing nothing at all is just as effective at bringing a region to its knees as a physics engine deep think [a collision state so complex that the *Second Life* engine could take hours to resolve it]. Vehicles, objects that have called `llSetVehicleType` with a flag other than `VEHICLE_TYPE_NONE`, require lots of processing time even when they're not being used, because they are being polled [which means the server is constantly checking it for activity]. You can call

CHAPTER 1
CHAPTER 2
CHAPTER 3
CHAPTER 4
CHAPTER 5
CHAPTER 6
CHAPTER 7
CHAPTER 8
CHAPTER 9
CHAPTER 10
CHAPTER 11
CHAPTER 12

CHAPTER 13
CHAPTER 14
APPENDICES
INDEX

CHAPTER 12

DIFFERENT
SPECIES
OF LAG

CREATING
EFFICIENT
BUILDS

that function with the "type none" option to stop the polling and reduce the vehicle's overhead when it's not being used.

Some things that take less overhead than you might think are flexible prims, `llTargetOmega`, texture animations, and particles. The reason they are low-overhead is that they don't have to be processed by the server and they are not synchronized between clients. To the server it's just one burst of information and then each connected client can take care of itself. The downside is that not everybody is guaranteed to see the same thing on their screen where those are concerned. Some of those operations also cause a lot of work for each client in updating the image on your screen, like particles. That can cause a low visual frame rate for individuals while not causing a heavy workload for the server. Timers [see Chapter 6, "Getting Your Feet Wet with Scripting"] are also pretty low-overhead by themselves, but they get a bad name because they are frequently used to execute high-overhead operations repeatedly.

There are a lot of LSL functions, and it's fairly difficult to quantify which ones are "bad" because a lot of the time it depends on where and how they're being used. Things that start with `llGet` are usually pretty safe. Those functions are usually just moving some memory around rather than changing or processing something. Things that start with `llRequest` may cause network load, but probably not too much processing load. `llSet` usually means a hard update to the world but will be okay if you're not doing it repetitively, like in a timer firing every 0.1 seconds.

Another rule of thumb is that when at all possible, [you should] combine scripts, combine listens, and combine timers so that you are using as few as possible. It might be easier to have every primitive in your object listen, but it's better to have one listen and then tell the other prims [what they heard] via link message. It might be easier to have four scripts so you can have four timers. But it's better to have one script with a timer you are using to do four different things.

ACTION! CREATING MACHINIMA

Simply put, *machinima* is the art of using video games to produce movies. The whole thing started out for fun when users used third-party video-capture applications to record their gaming sessions and later added humorous dialogue and music. Games like *Halo*, *Quake*, and *Half-Life* were popular for this application but it wasn't until platforms that allowed user-created content and interactive scripting came about that machinima became a powerful commercial tool.

Using *Second Life*, you can create practically any kind of movie you can imagine. The powerful building tools allow you to create almost infinite kinds of props, sets, and models. The scripting capabilities allow for unlimited effects such as doors that glide open on the bridge of a spaceship, blasters and machine guns, airplanes that swoop down upon a target, or sea creatures that swim off into the distance. Avatars can be customized to create your dream cast of movie stars, from a beautiful heroine to a killer robot, and by using custom animations you can bring life to any character.

CONTENTS

CHAPTER 13

RECOMMENDED
TOOLS

FILMING
TECHNIQUES

A TOUR OF
THE SOLAR
SYSTEM

RECOMMENDED TOOLS

Making movies in real life requires a variety of tools, including cameras, lighting, boom microphones, and of course director's chairs. Since machinima is virtual, you won't have to worry about most of this stuff, but you will need to keep a variety of important tools in your toolbox to help with the movie-production process.

■ CAPTURING FOOTAGE

Second Life comes complete with a video-capture feature located under File ▸ Start/Stop Movie to Disk (Control+Shift+A), which allows you to record and save movies to disk. Most Machinimists, however, prefer to use a third-party application known as Fraps (www.fraps.com) because of its ease of use, performance, and additional features such as the frame rate display.

■ POST-PRODUCTION EDITING

When you have all of your footage, you will need video-editing software to put the clips together and mix in the sound and music. I highly recommend Final Cut Pro and Adobe Premiere for most of your video editing. If you're willing to pay a little more, Adobe After Effects can be used for editing but also comes with powerful tools for creating special effects and compositing.

■ CAMERA CONTROLS

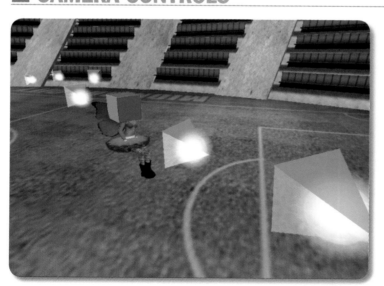

Some of the best camera tools you can find for your movie production can be found right inside of *Second Life*. Alt-Zoom Studios (http://www.alt-zoom.com/), for example, has produced an invaluable tool called the Alt-zoom camera (Figure 13.1) to overcome the jerky motion that results in filming with your mouse. If you need mouse smoothness in a pinch, you can also simply turn on *Second Life's* Mouse Smoothing feature by going to Client ▸ Mouse Smoothing.

Figure 13.1: The Alt-zoom camera allows you to place waypoints along a path. By wearing the special Alt-zoom camera prim on your head, you can ride along the waypoints in mouselook mode, which makes you essentially a camera on smooth rails.

■ THE JOYSTICK FLYCAM

CHAPTER 1
CHAPTER 2
CHAPTER 3
CHAPTER 4
CHAPTER 5
CHAPTER 6
CHAPTER 7
CHAPTER 8
CHAPTER 9
CHAPTER 10
CHAPTER 11
CHAPTER 12
CHAPTER 13

CHAPTER 14
APPENDICES
INDEX

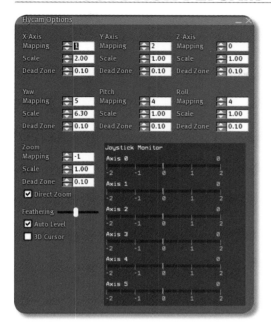

Figure 13.2: The joystick flycam feature gives you fine control over how your control inputs will behave—perfect for controlling a camera during filming.

Second Life recently introduced a powerful tool called the joystick flycam (Figure 13.2; accessible from Client ▸ Joystick Flycam) that allows you to control your camera using a joystick or 3D mouse (such as the one at www.3dconnexion.com/products/3aaa.php). This feature provides you with fine control over how your camera will respond to control inputs. The flycam's Options window is broken down into the seven kinds of available motion:

X-Axis: Slide side to side.

Y-Axis: Slide up and down.

Z-Axis: Slide forward and back.

Yaw: Turn left and right.

Pitch: Turn up and down.

Roll: Bank clockwise or counterclockwise.

Zoom: Zoom in or out.

Each type of movement can be programmed with the following values:

Mapping: This value determines which of the joystick axes will be mapped to which movement characteristics.

Scale: This value sets the sensitivity. Positive and negative values are permitted.

Dead Zone: This sets the threshold before *Second Life* reacts to joystick input. This is handy for avoiding drift.

Direct Zoom: Checking this option will cause any zoom inputs to narrow or widen the field of vision.

Feathering: This option changes the perceived weight of the camera. Moving the Feathering slider to the right will make camera motions very rigid and precise. Moving it to the left will make camera motions fluid but sluggish.

Auto Level: Checking this box will provide stability of the vertical axis so the camera will tend to stay rightside up.

3D Cursor: Certain devices communicate inputs as cursor positions (which are absolute x,y positions, like with drawing tablets) rather than push values (which don't care about your x,y position, such as joysticks). Checking 3D Cursor will allow the flycam to correctly interpret these inputs.

To help you get a feel for the force being transmitted by your joystick, the Flycam Options window includes a joystick monitor with a graphical display that represents the various joystick inputs.

CHAPTER 13

RECOMMENDED
TOOLS

FILMING
TECHNIQUES

A TOUR OF
THE SOLAR
SYSTEM

FILMING TECHNIQUES

Now that you have your software and equipment, it's time to ready for some filming. In this section we will discuss the setup and filming of your virtual movie.

SETTING UP

Unless you're making a *Second Life* tutorial, you should turn off the user interface. (Control+Alt+1 toggles the UI on and off.) Next you should decide on the resolution you will be using. I recommend using twice your target resolution. So if you want the final product to be 320×240 you should film in a resolution of 640×480. This will ensure high-quality output during the editing process, and in some cases it may give you a buffer that allows you to zoom into areas without making the scene appear pixelated. You can change your resolution by going to Edit ▶ Preferences ▶ Graphics ▶ Display Resolution when you are operating in full-screen mode, or simply resize your *Second Life* window if you are in windowed mode.

To improve your frame rate while filming, I recommend closing down all nonessential applications on your system—especially processes that run constantly, such as streaming music. Also close any applications that may surprise you in the middle of an important scene with a pop-up. ("You have mail!")

Finally, make sure you have enough hard-drive space to capture the uncompressed video while filming. These uncompressed movie files can easily grow to tens and even hundreds of megabytes during filming, and nothing will ruin a perfect shot like a "Low Disk Space" error.

CHOOSING A LOCATION

Figure 13.3: The draw distance on the left is set to 512 meters. This provides beautiful detail of the city, but the subject is lost in complexity. On the right the image is reduced to 64 meters, which fogs out distant detail and makes the subject easier to see.

Making movies in *Second Life* is astonishingly similar to making them in real life. For example, a director may have to choose between filming on a set, on location, or perhaps even against a blue screen so that a setting can be added later.

When filming on location, your biggest consideration will be low frame rate. Most public locations will be filled with numerous extraneous builds and bystanders who may not be important to your shot but may very well reduce your frame rate. To alleviate this problem, try reducing your draw distance (Edit ▶ Preferences ▶ Graphics ▶ Draw Distance) such that your subject is clearly rendered but objects outside of the scene are not (Figure 13.3).

You should also fine-tune your graphics detail sliders (Edit ► Preferences ► Graphics ► Graphics Details) so that unseen or unimportant elements are rendered at the lowest quality while important features are rendered at the highest quality. For example, if you are filming a battle scene between giant robots with no avatars in the scene, you should reduce Avatar Mesh Detail to the minimum but raise Object Mesh Detail to a setting that looks best. This will prevent nearby avatars behind the scenes from reducing your frame rate while your prim-based subjects will look great.

Filming on a set is where your production starts to really resemble one in Hollywood. Just as buildings in a real-life Western movie sets are actually thin facades to keep production costs down, sets in *Second Life* should feature only those details that will appear in the movie. Unnecessary textures and prims may reduce your frame rate, so avoid them when possible. There is no need, for example, to create an elaborate exterior for a loft apartment if the exterior will never be seen in your final production.

TIP

The Second Life *client will suffer a performance hit from objects on the other side of your set wall, even if those objects are not visible! A good technique to prevent unnecessary lag is to place your set on the edge of a region bordering a void region such that you have nothing behind your facade except empty sea.*

■ CINEMATOGRAPHY

The basic composition of every shot will vary depending on what you are trying to convey, but a few basic rules will help you create exciting scenes and communicate the right mood to the viewer. Let's start with basic composition and camera shots.

The rule of thirds: This states that you should imagine your scene divided into nine squares like a tic-tac-toe board. You then arrange the shot so that important features appear on the intersection of the lines and transitions run along the lines. For example, the eyes of a portrait subject could be placed at the two upper intersections of the grid while the horizon falls along one of the horizontal lines, as in Figure 13.4.

Figure 13.4: The rule of thirds is a useful way to visualize a shot to get the best aesthetics.

CHAPTER 1
CHAPTER 2
CHAPTER 3
CHAPTER 4
CHAPTER 5
CHAPTER 6
CHAPTER 7
CHAPTER 8
CHAPTER 9
CHAPTER 10
CHAPTER 11
CHAPTER 12
CHAPTER 13

CHAPTER 14
APPENDICES
INDEX

Figure 13.5: A long shot helps your audience understand where your characters are in the setting.

Figure 13.6: Close-up shots help establish mood.

Figure 13.7: High-angle shots can make the subject look small or imply that they are gazing on something enormous.

The long shot: This shows the subject in its entirety and can be useful for communicating to the audience where a character or object fits into the setting (Figure 13.5). A lone wanderer walking across a desert or an action hero seen surrounded by his opponents are great scenes for a long shot.

The medium shot: Medium shots focus the audience's attention entirely on the subject of the scene. Sometimes the subject will not fit entirely in the scene, so focus can be placed on the most important areas. For example, medium shots are good to show characters in a movie talking to you or slow-dancing with each other. Their upper bodies are the focus while their legs are often left out of the shot.

The close-up: Close-ups focus on a small part of the subject. For inanimate objects this shot can convey detail, such as the writing on a tomb wall or a red self-destruct signal on a space station. The face is normally the focus of human close-ups, which are used to give the audience a sense of intimacy and a feeling for the character's internal process (Figure 13.6).

High-angle shot: In this shot the camera hovers above the subjects, looking down at them, usually from about a 45-degree angle. This shot is ideal for making the subjects look small and for communicating a sense of awe toward something off-camera (Figure 13.7). You might use this shot to show characters watching a spaceship depart. (Goodbye, E.T.!)

Low-angle shot: In this shot the camera is located below the subject and angles upward at around 45 degrees to give the subject a powerful presence.

Canted angle: Sometimes referred to as the *Batman* angle, a reference to its extensive use in the 1960s television series, this shot communicates a sense of instability by having the camera tilted to the side. Consider using the canted angle when your subjects are on a ship that is sinking or when they're perched precariously atop an unfinished skyscraper. This angle can also convey psychological instability for characters, such as a spy who has just been drugged or a villain who is criminally insane.

One final word about filming: most scenes will be expensive and time-consuming to set up. You have to deploy the sets, reserve land, get your actors together in the same location and be ready to go, and so on. This means that reshooting a scene can be very costly. You'd be wise to film much more footage than you ever expect to use. You should film shots in different perspectives and under different lighting conditions so you will have many options during the editing phase of the moviemaking process. It's not uncommon for more footage to end up on the cutting-room floor than in the movie.

FROM LINDEN LAB

 ### ERIC LINDEN ON MAKING THE MOST OF MACHINIMA

- Familiarize yourself with basic cinematography. There are proven methods for shooting scenes, and when they are ignored the flow and rhythm of the movie is broken and you lose your audience.

- Try to keep elements out of your frame if they aren't lending something to either the environment or the story. This will also help improve performance.

- Always leave enough padding at the beginning and end of your capture. This extra bit of footage is very helpful when you edit.

- Keeping the rules of cinematography in mind, try to get as many different angles on the action as you can. Again, this helps tremendously when you edit.

- I always capture larger than my intended output. This way, when I edit and recompress for final output I can maintain more clarity in the footage (degradation is minimized).

- Have a good script, and follow it. It's too easy to get lost in images and motion, and having a formula to follow will help you make sure you get all the necessary footage and expedite the process.

- For dynamic shots, use a joystick or 3D mouse rather than scripted cameras: their resolution in *Second Life* is wonderful, and you'll have *far* greater control over what your camera is doing.

- Find movies or commercials that are done in a style you like, and mimic them the best you can. Copying camera moves and cinematic style is a great way to get wonderful footage and to learn how the pros do it!

A TOUR OF THE SOLAR SYSTEM

Rather than a tutorial like the ones found in other chapters, this chapter concludes with an excerpt from an article I wrote for James Wagner Au's New World Notes in March 2006. The article details the steps taken to produce an educational movie about our solar system. This article will take you through a step-by-step example of creating your own movie in *Second Life*.

THE MAKING OF THE SOLAR SYSTEM

Anybody who hasn't been hiding under a prim for the last year knows that machinima is what the cool kids in gaming are doing these days. If you haven't heard of machinima, I recommend you buy a pair of trendy sunglasses, have 8×10 glossies taken of your avatar, and tell your agent to call machinima. com. Machinima is the growing art of using online gaming environments to produce movies. Like most budding technologies, early machinima productions suffered from an acute case of self-awe by featuring movie plots along the lines of "Everybody look! You can make a movie with this platform!" But the honeymoon is over and it's time to find substance in our love of virtual movie making. Enter Aimee Weber's tour of the solar system.

The idea behind the tour of the solar system was to use machinima techniques to produce an educational film on a shoelace budget. While conventional techniques for making a computer-generated educational film could cost thousands of dollars, I was able to create a highly informative video for little more than travel expenses to Pluto. Kidding! My producer said I had to wait until off-season if I wanted to get anywhere near the Kuiper belt.

SCREENPLAY

The process began with a screenplay, which is essentially dialogue combined with cinematic direction. Like any blueprint, this simple document provides an early opportunity to iron out potential problems before they become labor-intensive to fix later in production. I timed myself as I read the narration aloud to make sure the pacing would be comfortable for my audience. If a scene felt drawn out or hurried, I rewrote it until it felt natural.

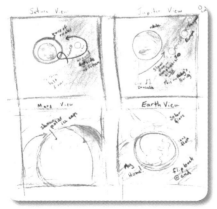

Figure 13.8: Storyboards help you plan your shot.

STORYBOARDING

I then sketched a rough storyboard (Figure 13.8) to provide direction for filming. Storyboards are helpful because they allow me to visualize the aesthetics and composition. Borrowing techniques from George Lucas, I decided the best way to captivate my audience was to zoom them around the planets as if they were in a fast-moving spaceship. This motion became a useful tool to instill a sense of planetary size in my audience. For example, by zooming quickly around the planet Pluto my audience got a feeling that it was a small, easily navigated planet. On the other hand, by slowly panning around Jupiter I gave the audience a feeling that this celestial body was a massive force to be reckoned with.

Figure 13.9: Just as it is in real-life movie making, virtual sets are rarely actual size. In this movie the planet Earth was slightly bigger than an avatar's head.

SET BUILDING

"In the beginning . . ." Ironically, it did take me about six days to create the solar system. I started by enclosing an enormous portion of the sim with a star field backdrop (Figure 13.9). I then created the sun, each planet, and all major moons. Many of the moons were not even mentioned in the movie, but if you look closely you can see some of them loitering in orbit. One scene featuring the planet Saturn (which I would call the "money shot" were this phrase not already in use by some other kinds of movies) included several thousand primitive rocks of various sizes scattered around an enormous model of the gaseous planet. I enjoyed filming this scene the most because the size of the debris was small enough to allow my camera to zoom by them very quickly.

FILMING

You know those home movies taken by our parents during our childhood birthday parties? The movies that, given the tumultuous shaking and jarring of the camera, *must* have occurred during an earthquake? Well that is what machinima looks like when you attempt to control the camera with the mouse. To glide serenely from planet to planet in my movie, I used the Alt-zoom camera created by BuhBuhCuh Fairchild. The process basically involved setting waypoints along the path of the intended journey, and then "riding" a camera as you zoom smoothly from waypoint to waypoint. Fraps is then used to capture this glorious footage.

POST-PRODUCTION

To make a good machinima movie, you will need to be familiar with some post-production editing software. I'm fond of Adobe After Effects; however, Premiere is also a popular product for the job. You should be familiar with a technique known as keyframing, which allows smooth transitions from one effect to the next. For example, I used keyframing to wipe smoothly from one planet scene to the next, and to fade between songs on the soundtrack. It was in After Effects that I edited, assembled, and coordinated the footage, music, and narration for the movie. The final result is the polished, Academy Award hopeful now available on the Alt-Zoom website.

FUTURE OF MACHINIMA IN EDUCATION

I'm hoping I fired the first shot in a revolution for virtual education. Educational movies utilizing 3D computer-generated imagery are no longer six-figure productions. On a tight budget publishers can provide movies about molecular models on a CD in the back of college text books, they can allow students to visit the ruins of the Colosseum (or a brand new coliseum!) or take a ride through the internal-combustion engine. We are limited by our imagination, not our coffers. I think Galileo Galilei put it best when he said "The sun is a mass of incandescent gas, a gigantic nuclear furnace." Well it was either Galileo or '90s pop sensation They Might Be Giants; it's all rather sketchy for me, but I *do* know that Constantinople got the works, and it's nobody's business but the Turks.

CHAPTER 14

CREATING AN AIRPLANE

Now it's time to put together many of the skills you've learned. In this chapter we'll build and texture an airplane, and then we'll add scripts to make it fly, plus animations to seat the pilot and passengers, and some special effects.

Barnes Boutique

eTc...

FASHIONABLY DEAD

CONTENTS

CHAPTER 14

- DESIGN
  CONSIDER-
  ATIONS

- MODELING
  THE PLANE

- TEXTURING
  THE PLANE

- CREATING THE
  ANIMATIONS

- LINKING
  THE PRIMS

- SCRIPTING
  THE PRIMS

DESIGN CONSIDERATIONS

Most vehicles in *Second Life* rely on the in-world physics engine. But the physics system won't allow us to enable physics for link sets composed of more than 31 objects—and avatars seated on the vehicle count as linked objects. That means in order to build a three-seat plane, we have to either set it as physical before avatars are seated, or use 28 prims or fewer.

The plane has to be balanced well atop its landing gear, or else it will fall over on the runway when physics are enabled. Plus, we want a cockpit large enough for our passengers—and the plane should look cool!

Some time online looking at photos of airplanes turned up something that adapts well to being modeled within our prim limits. Since it's a real plane, we know the general design is stable. Our plane will be based very loosely on a Viperjet MKII.

Just as the model is dictated in part by the script requirements, some of the scripting is suggested by the model. We're building a jet, so it makes sense to include an appropriate particle effect and sound effect, and we'll need to come up with a way to raise the landing gear for an aerodynamic look.

■ PREPARING YOUR WORK AREA

We'll need a work area where you are allowed to build objects and run scripts. It should be able to support at least the plane's 28 prims in addition to those already there, of course, but you'll probably want more available, in case you want to keep copies of parts in-world or need to rez an extra box to test something. You'll also need enough space in which to build the plane. Our model will be about 17.5 meters wide by 14 meters long, plus you need space around it to rez more prims. And, of course, you'll want to find a runway—or at least a level area—for test flights!

■ BUILDING A SIMPLE RUNWAY

If you have the space and available prims, you might find it helpful and inspiring to build a runway on which to build your plane.

1. **Rez a box and stretch it to 10×10×10m.**

2. **Now perform a path cut of B 0.125 and E 0.625.**

3. **Rotate it so X = 270, Y = 0, Z = 90.**

4. **Rotate the textures 90 degrees.**

5. **Drag the box downward so just the top is sticking up from the ground.**

6. **Apply whatever texture you would like on the sides of the runway that stick up from the ground.**

7. **Go to Inventory ▸ Library ▸ Textures ▸ Road Textures and choose one with markings.**

8. **Apply this texture to the top of the box, which has two surfaces because it was cut—you'll have to apply the texture twice.**

9. Select the surface that has the yellow stripe at the edge of the runway instead of down the middle, and check Vertical Flip.

10. Shift-drag to copy this runway segment to lengthen your runway as much as you like.

MODELING THE PLANE

Modeling objects in *Second Life* isn't always an exact art. Many things are done by eye. In the course of modeling the plane, we're going to keep that in mind, and sometimes we won't measure things at all! At the same time, we're going to reinforce some good work habits and learn a few useful workflow tricks.

■ BUILDING THE FUSELAGE

1. To begin building the fuselage, rez a cylinder. If you are building this on a runway, it might be convenient to put the cylinder right in the center of it. This prim will be the parent of just about every prim in our plane.

2. Rotate the cylinder 90 degrees on the x-axis.

3. Now resize it so that it is 1.5×1.5×1.5m.

4. Drag it upward so it is about a meter off the ground—this doesn't have to be exact. The idea is to be able to add more prims under it later, and to be able to look at the underside of the plane. You might even find it easier if you raise the plane higher.

5. Shift-drag the cylinder along the plane's y-axis to copy it.

6. Resize the new prim so that it is 3.5m along the z-axis.

Figure 14.1: Here's how the first two prims fit together.

7. Butt the new prim up against the first, as shown in Figure 14.1.

8. Taper this prim to 1.00 on both axes.

9. Top-shear to –0.50 on the y-axis. This is the nose of the plane.

10. Next, select the original prim again and Shift-drag it in the opposite direction this time—still along the y-axis—to make another copy. Do this twice.

CHAPTER 14

● Design
  Consider-
  ations

● Modeling
  the Plane

● Texturing
  the Plane

● Creating the
  Animations

● Linking
  the Prims

● Scripting
  the Prims

11. Now resize the last prim you created so that it is 5.5m on its z-axis.

12. Taper this prim –0.45 on both axes. This is the tail end of the fuselage.

13. Now select the second-to-last prim you created and resize it so that it is 3m on its z-axis.

14. Rotate this prim 45 degrees on the z-axis.

15. Path-cut it B 0.25.

15. Hollow it 80 percent. This is the plane's cabin.

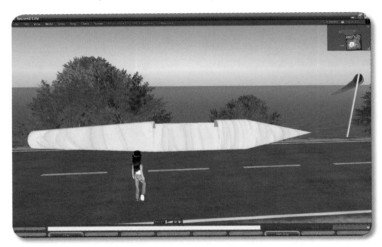

Figure 14.2: The fuselage

16. Now butt the prims together so that you have something that looks like the fuselage in Figure 14.2.

17. Select all four prims and then right-click and select Take Copy. This way, you'll have a backup in case something goes wrong in the next step. Find the backup in your Inventory and rename it Wizard Jet in Progress 1.

■ CREATING THE COCKPIT

1. Now select the cylinder prim with the cutout—the cabin—and Shift-drag it upward.

2. Change the new prim's Z rotation to 270.

3. Next make E Path Cut .75

4. Set Hollow to 95.

5. Resize the prim on the x-axis so it is 1.0m.

6. Shift-drag it along the y-axis, toward the pointy end of the fuselage, to make a copy.

7. Change this new prim's rotation to 270, 0, 0.

8. Next change Path Cut B to 0.5.

9. Change the prim's size to 1, 1.5, 3.

9. Finally, change the Building Block Type to Sphere.

10. Shift-drag this prim along the y-axis toward the blunt end of the plane to create a new prim.

11. Now rotate this new prim to 90, 0, 180.

12. Change the size on the z-axis to 3.5.

13. Set this prim's hollow to 0.

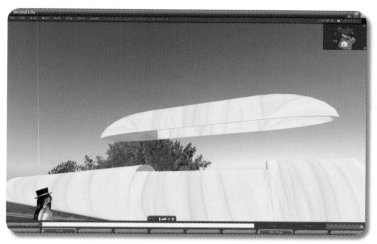

Figure 14.3: This is how the cockpit should look.

14. These three prims will form our cockpit. Leaving the center prim in place, butt the two end prims up against it on the y-axis so it looks like Figure 14.3.

15. Select the three new prims, as well as the fuselage, and take a copy of it all into Inventory. Rename it Wizard Jet in Progress 2.

ADDING THE WINGS

1. Create a box next to your fuselage. Placement isn't important yet.

2. Resize the box to 6×8×0.05m.

3. Next, rotate it 90 degrees on the z-axis.

4. Set Path Cut E to 0.50. This is the first wing.

5. Shift-drag this prim along the x-axis—perpendicular to the fuselage—to make a copy.

6. Change its rotation to 180, 0, 270.

8. Select both of the wings and lift them so they are just a bit higher than the bottom of the fuselage, but not poking through to the inside of the hollow cylinder.

9. Position them so the leading edges are just a little behind the pointy nose prim.

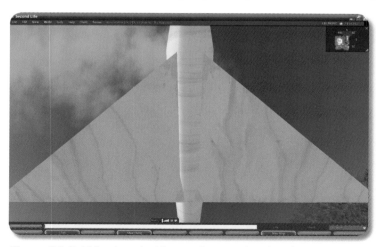

Figure 14.4: This shot, looking up from under the plane, shows how the wings should be aligned with the fuselage.

10. Now, with just one of the wings selected, move it perpendicular to the cabin so that its edge is just barely embedded in the fuselage, as shown in Figure 14.4. This doesn't have to be exact; it just has to look OK!

11. Do the same thing with the other wing.

12. Select all of the plane prims you have so far and take a copy into inventory. Name it Wizard Jet in Progress 3.

RESIDENTS SPEAK

MODELING TIPS

◈ Start building on integer alignments / orthogonal boundaries whenever possible.

◈ Link stuff into large chunks if you have to move it. *Especially* if you need to move it over a sim boundary.

◈ If you're building, say, a llama, do a fast survey and peek at what other people have done in the general field of llama construction. No, I'm not saying "steal other people's ideas"—just that looking at what other people have done, and how they've done it, can be inspirational for you.

◈ Try to make stuff that's different from anything else in *SL*.

◈ Learn to solicit and deal with constructive criticism. This can be hard: ya gotta be thick-skinned and open-minded. It helps to build up a circle of critics that you know and trust: anybody can say 'that sucks!'—but a true critic will tell you *how* it sucks (that's why it's *constructive* criticism). I hate hearing 'oh, that looks great!'—if people won't tell me what's bad, I can't make it better!

—Jessica Qin

◈ Whenever possible, build to the nearest meter or tenth of a meter. This prevents rounding errors as the user's camera moves away from the object, thus reducing pixelation and artifacting. It also makes aligning textures a whole lot easier.

—Hiro Pendragon (aka Ron T. Blechner)

■ ADDING THE INTAKES

A jet plane needs to suck air into its engine. This means we need to build intakes.

1. **To start, create a box.**

2. **Resize it so that it is 0.5×0.75×5m.**

3. **Now rotate the prim 90 degrees on the x-axis.**

4. **Hollow it 60 percent.**

5. **Now taper the prim –1.0 on the x-axis and –0.45 on the y-axis.**

6. **Set the Top Shear to .50 on the x-axis. This is the first intake.**

7. **Next, Shift-drag the intake along its x-axis, to make a copy.**

8. **Rotate the copy 180 degrees on its z-axis.**

9. **Now select both intakes and lift them so that they are resting on top of the wings.**

10. **Move them along the y-axis until their fronts are about a half a meter back from the end of the cockpit cutout, as you can see in Figure 14.5.**

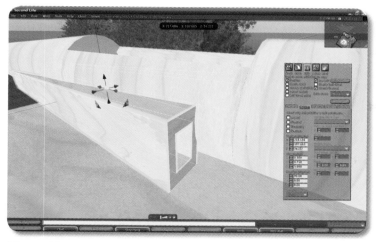

Figure 14.5: This is how the intakes should be placed.

11. Now select one prim at a time and move it along its x-axis to lay it along the side of the plane, so the long, flat sides are against the fuselage, as they are in Figure 14.5. Just a bit of this prim should be embedded in the fuselage.

12. Time to make a backup! Select all of the plane prims and take a copy into inventory. Name this Wizard Jet in Progress 4.

TIP

If you're building by eye instead of exactly to the grid, you can always rez a prim and make it the right length to use for a quick measurement.

▮ ATTACHING THE LANDING GEAR

We're going to space the wheels well apart to make sure our plane will be stable and easy to handle during takeoffs and landings.

1. Select the first prim we rezzed (the cylinder just in front of the cockpit) and Shift-drag it along the y-axis to make a copy.

2. Change its Building Block Type to Sphere.

3. Shift-drag the new sphere upwards, on the z-axis, to make a copy of it.

4. Reselect your first sphere.

5. Resize this prim to 0.25×0.5×0.5m.

6. Change the rotation to 0 on the x-axis.

7. Now dimple the sphere to 0.25 and 0.75. Now we have a wheel.

8. Select the second sphere.

9. Change its Building Block Type to Ring.

10. Resize it to 1×0.35×0.685

11. Change its rotation to 270, 0, 90.

CHAPTER 14

- DESIGN
  CONSIDER-
  ATIONS

- MODELING
  THE PLANE

- TEXTURING
  THE PLANE

- CREATING THE
  ANIMATIONS

- LINKING
  THE PRIMS

- SCRIPTING
  THE PRIMS

Figure 14.6: Here's how the housing should fit over the wheel.

Figure 14.7: Here's how the rear landing gear assembly fits on the fuselage.

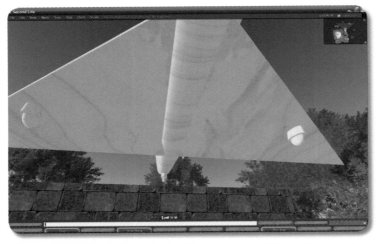

Figure 14.8: Here's how the landing gear should look from under the plane.

12. Adjust this prim's hole size to 0.35 on the x-axis and 0.15 on the y-axis. This is the wheel housing.

13. Move it down on the z-axis until it partially covers your dimpled wheel, as shown in Figure 14.6.

14. Select both the wheel and the housing and move them down on the z-axis so they are lower than the bottom of the plane.

15. Keeping both selected, move them along the y-axis to the back of the plane until they are about a half a meter from the end of the fuselage.

16. Drag the whole assembly upward on the z-axis until the housing is just barely embedded in the fuselage, as shown in Figure 14.7.

17. Now we'll add two more wheels. Shift-drag the assembly on the x-axis to make a copy. Do this twice.

18. Select all the pieces of the two newly copied assemblies.

19. Move them on the y-axis until they are about even with the center of the cockpit.

CHAPTER 1
CHAPTER 2
CHAPTER 3
CHAPTER 4
CHAPTER 5
CHAPTER 6
CHAPTER 7
CHAPTER 8
CHAPTER 9
CHAPTER 10
CHAPTER 11
CHAPTER 12
CHAPTER 13
CHAPTER 14

APPENDICES
INDEX

20. Now we'll select just one of the assemblies and move it toward the tip of the wing—on the x-axis—until it is just a little bit behind the wing's leading edge. Do the same with the other assembly. These should end up roughly 7 meters apart.

21. Select all the prims of both assemblies—four total. Move them downward on the z-axis until the tops of the housings are just barely embedded in the underside of the wings (Figure 14.8).

22. By now you know the drill: select all 17 airplane prims and take a backup. Name this one Wizard Jet in Progress 5.

■ ADDING INSTRUMENTATION

You won't really need instrumentation to fly the plane—you'll use your keyboard. But the plane sure would look funny without a control panel and a steering yoke.

1. First, let's select that first cylinder we rezzed. Shift-drag it along the y-axis, toward the nose of the plane, to make a copy.

2. Shift-drag the newly created prim upward, along the x-axis, to make a copy of it.

3. Now select the first of the new prims you just created.

4. Resize it to 1×0.6×0.25.

5. Rotate this prim to 112.5, 0, 180.

6. Now Path Cut B 0.5.

7. Next, set the Top Shear on the y-axis to –0.15. This is the control panel.

8. Move the control panel on the y-axis back into the plane, so that it is protruding through the original cylinder, into the cabin area.

Figure 14.9: This is the correct placement for the control panel.

9. Move the control panel up on the z-axis until it is placed as shown in Figure 14.9.

10. Next, we'll build the steering yoke. Select the cylinder you created in step 2 of this instrumentation-building process.

11. Shift-drag it downward, on the z-axis, to copy it.

12. Now resize this new prim to 0.10×0.10×1 m.

13. Change the rotation on the x-axis to 315.

14. Now, taper the prim –0.45 on both axes.

15. Next select the prim above this one.

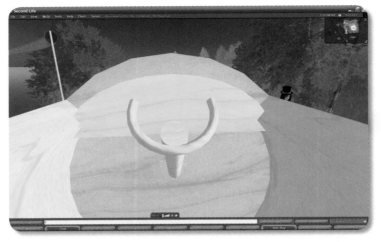

Figure 14.10: Here's how the two parts of the steering yoke line up.

Figure 14.11: This is the correct placement for the steering yoke.

16. Change the Building Block Type to Torus.

17. Resize the prim to 0.35×0.35×0.35.

18. Now change the rotation to 0, 270, 225.

19. Path-cut the torus 0.2 and 0.8.

20. Change the Hole Size to 0.10 on both axes.

21. Next move the prim downward on the z-axis so it's close to the prim below it.

22. Now move it on the y-axis to line up the prims as shown in Figure 14.10.

23. Select both prims and move them along the y-axis, into the cabin of the plane, so that it's placed so that the steering yoke extends about a half a meter from the control panel as shown in Figure 14.11. This doesn't have to be exact—it is something you can adjust to fit your avatar later.

24. Now take a copy of the current iteration of the plane and name it Wizard Jet in Progress 6.

■ PUTTING IN SEATS

We're going to build seats for a pilot and two passengers.

1. First, Shift-drag that original prim yet again, on the y-axis, toward the front of the plane, to make a copy.

2. Change the new prim's Building Block Type to Box.

3. Resize it to 1×0.5×0.5m.

4. Set the rotation to 0, 270, 180.

5. Path-cut the box E 0.5.

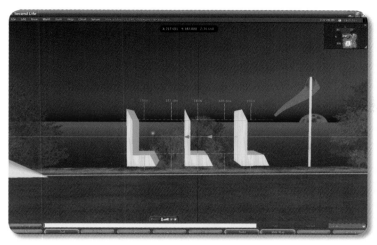

Figure 14.12: Here's how the seats should be spaced.

Figure 14.13: Correct placement of the seats

6. Hollow the prim 60 percent. Now we have a seat with a backswept, speedy look.

7. Shift-drag the seat along the y-axis to make a copy. Do this twice.

8. Space the seats about a meter apart, as shown in Figure 14.12.

9. Now select all three seats and move them on the y-axis into the cabin of the plane, so that the back seat is against the rear wall.

10. Next, raise the seats on the z-axis until they are about a half a meter above the floor of the cabin. This doesn't have to be exact (Figure 14.13). Seat height is another thing you can adjust later to fit your avatar or your favorite passengers, if you like.

11. Now take a backup of the plane and name it Wizard Jet in Progress 7.

■ ATTACHING A TAIL

A plane isn't stable without a tail, and it would look funny, too.

1. First, select the original cylinder prim and Shift-drag it along the y-axis to make a copy.

2. Next, change that prim's Building Block Type to Box.

3. Resize the prim to 5×0.05×1.5m.

4. Taper it to 0.55 on the x-axis.

5. Shift-drag this prim upward on the z-axis to make a copy.

6. Resize the new prim to 3×0.05×1.5.

7. Now set its rotation to 0, 0.70, 90.

8. Path-cut the prim B 0.75.

9. Change the Taper setting on the x-axis to 0.75.

10. Move this tail piece on the y-axis so it is above the wheel at the rear of the plane.

11. Now raise it on the z-axis until its lower edge is barely embedded in the top of the fuselage.

12. Select the other tail prim.

13. Move it on the y-axis so it is lined up more or less under the first tail piece.

14. Lower this prim on the z-axis until it is about a third of the way up from the bottom of the fuselage, as shown in Figure 14.14. Now our plane has a tail.

15. Take a copy of the plane and name it Wizard Jet in Progress 8!

Figure 14.14: Correct placement of the two parts of the tail

■ BUILDING THE JET EXHAUST ASSEMBLY

A jet plane calls for jet exhaust. Now we'll model the prims, and later we'll add a particle flame.

1. Select the original prim that started this whole project and Shift-drag three copies of it along the y-axis, to the rear of the plane.

2. Select the middle one of the three prims you have just created.

3. Resize this prim to 0.5 m in all directions.

4. Hollow it 60 percent.

5. Taper it –0.30 on both axes. Looks like nozzle, doesn't it?

6. Next, select the prim you created in step 1 that is closest to the plane.

7. Change its Building Block Type to Torus.

8. Resize the torus to 0.5×0.825×0.825m.

9. Set its rotation to 0, 0, 270.

10. Set Profile Cut B 0.75.

11. Now select the last of the prims you created in step 1.

12. Change its Building Block Type to Sphere.

13. Resize the prim to 0.25m in all directions.

Figure 14.15: The jet assembly

14. Set its rotation to 0, 0, 270.

15. Hollow it 90 percent.

16. Dimple the sphere E 0.5.

17. Now butt the torus up against the rear of the fuselage.

18. Next move the nozzle up against the torus.

19. Move the sphere on the y-axis until it is mostly inside of the hollow cylinder, as shown in Figure 14.15.

CHAPTER 1
CHAPTER 2
CHAPTER 3
CHAPTER 4
CHAPTER 5
CHAPTER 6
CHAPTER 7
CHAPTER 8
CHAPTER 9
CHAPTER 10
CHAPTER 11
CHAPTER 12
CHAPTER 13
CHAPTER 14

APPENDICES
INDEX

20. We're finished building the model, which means that first prim we rezzed won't be needed as a source of copies. Hollow it 80 percent so the pilot will have a place for their legs! Yes, the cockpit is still hanging above the plane. But we'll be making adjustments in the cabin, so let's leave it for now.

21. Take a backup of the plane model and name it Wizard Jet in Progress 9. Make sure you get all 28 prims.

TEXTURING THE PLANE

In this section we're going to create a simple texture from scratch for the fuselage and wings, reuse an old texture, scavenge on the Web for a public-domain photo to use for another texture, and then mine the Library for more resources. We could have applied some of these textures during the modeling phase of this build, but that might have been a bit more confusing to explain! Let's start texturing.

■ MAKING IT SHINY

1. First, select the entire plane.

2. Click the Texture tab.

3. Click the Blank button, then set Shininess to Low. Doesn't the plane seem less flat-looking now?

ADDING STRIPES

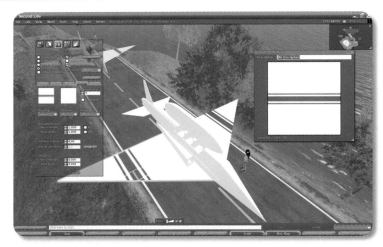

Figure 14.16: We've just applied stripes to the wings.

1. Now we're going to create and upload our texture. It should be a 128×128-pixel .bmp file. The background is white, with three horizontal lines across the center of it in the foreground, as shown in the Texture box in Figure 14.16. (If you don't like red, you can try something else!)

2. Drag the new stripe texture from Inventory and drop it on the top surface of each wing. The result will look like the plane in Figure 14.16.

3. On the Texture tab, click the Select Texture radio button. Holding the Shift key, select the top surfaces of the wings and change the Vertical Repeats per Face to 1.75. Deselect the wings. Pretty spiffy!

4. Now we'll put stripes on the fuselage. Holding the Shift key, click on the exterior of all of the fuselage prims except the pointed nose prim.

5. Drag the stripe texture from Inventory to the Texture tab, so it textures the exterior of those three prims—keep these surfaces selected.

6. Change the Texture Rotation to 90.

7. Change the Vertical Repeats per Face to 2.

8. Now select only the exterior of the cabin prim—the one with the cutout.

9. Change the texture's Vertical Offset to 0.75. You can see how the stripes should look in Figure 14.17.

TEXTURING WINDOWS AND METAL

1. Next we'll repurpose the black-and-white gradient texture we used for the windows of the house in Chapter 9, "Optimization: Creating a Comfortable User Experience." It's also 128×128 pixels.

2. Click the Position radio button.

3. Select both the front and the middle cockpit prims—not the one toward the tail of the plane.

4. Next, drag a free Clear texture from your inventory onto the Texture tab to apply it to all sides of these two prims. This will help hide the join in the window. (You can find a transparent texture in a box of freebies—try YadNi's Junkyard or the Stillman Bazaar.)

5. Now click the Select Texture radio button.

6. Holding the Shift key, select both the exterior and interior of both prims, but not the edges.

7. Drag the gradient texture onto the Texture tab.

8. Still maintaining the same selection, set the Transparency to 50. Aha—glass!

9. Click the Position radio button again.

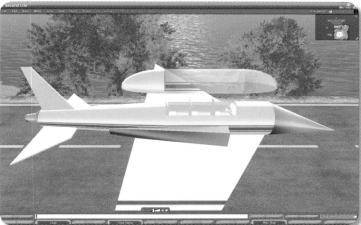
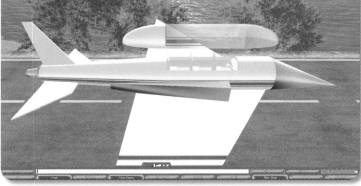

Figure 14.17: Here's how the plane looks so far.

10. Holding the Shift key, select the pointed nose cone, both intakes, and the three pieces of the jet assembly.

11. Drag the gradient texture onto the Texture tab.

12. Set Shininess to Medium. It's the same texture, but now it looks like metal (Figure 14.17).

■ TEXTURING THE WHEELS

1. We want to add even more nice shiny metal to the plane. Select all three wheels.

2. Drag the gradient texture onto the Texture tab.

3. Color the wheels light gray.

4. Set the wheels' Shininess to Medium.

5. That's great for the hubcaps, but not for the tires. Click the Select Texture radio button.

6. Holding the Shift key, select the outside of each wheel—the undimpled part.

7. Set Shininess to None.

8. Color this part of the wheels a very dark gray, about as dark as the background of the Object Editor. Now we have tires (Figure 14.18)!

Figure 14.18: The wheels are textured now.

■ TEXTURING INTERIOR SURFACES

1. If you haven't by now, take a copy of the plane and label it Wizard Jet in Progress 10. We're about halfway through the texturing process.

Figure 14.19: Coloring the exhaust nozzle.

2. Click the Position radio button and select the sphere piece of the jet assembly. Color it black, as shown in Figure 14.19.

3. Click the Select Texture radio button. Select the inside of the intakes and color those surfaces black. Better that it seems too dark to see inside the intakes than make it really obvious that our plane doesn't have any sort of working parts in there!

4. Let's use this trick again. Select the hollow interior of that first prim we created when we started building the plane and color it black.

■ TEXTURING THE STEERING YOKE

1. Click the Position button, then Select both of the pieces of the steering yoke. We want to make this into metal.

Figure 14.20: Here's how the steering yoke should look.

2. Apply the gradient texture to these.

3. Keeping these two prims selected, set Shininess to Medium.

4. Select only the handles—the torus—and color this prim black.

5. Click the Select Texture radio button, then Select the top of the cylinder and color it red, as shown in Figure 14.20. Why? Because it looks cool! If you don't like red, pick something else.

■ TEXTURING THE CONTROL PANEL

1. Next we'll texture the control panel with photo-sourced material—a photo of a real airplane control panel. Using our favorite search engine, we looked for an image that was in the public domain so we can use it however we like. The one we finally chose came from the U.S. Coast Guard's site (this image is included on the CD included with this book). We uploaded it and put it on the control-panel prim to see how it looked, then went back and cropped it and blocked out some of the dials that would have been cut in half at the lower edge of the prim. Then we uploaded it.

2. Select the control-panel prim in the front of the cockpit.

3. Color this prim black.

CHAPTER 1
CHAPTER 2
CHAPTER 3
CHAPTER 4
CHAPTER 5
CHAPTER 6
CHAPTER 7
CHAPTER 8
CHAPTER 9
CHAPTER 10
CHAPTER 11
CHAPTER 12
CHAPTER 13
CHAPTER 14

Figure 14.21: The control panel

4. Click the Select Texture radio button and color the front of the prim white.

5. Now drag the cropped photo texture onto the face of the prim.

6. Set the Repeats per Face to 1.1 and 1.3.

7. Set the Vertical Offset to –0.15. That looks pretty good (Figure 14.21)!

8. Take a copy of the plane. This is Wizard Jet in Progress 11.

■ COMPLETING THE CABIN TEXTURING

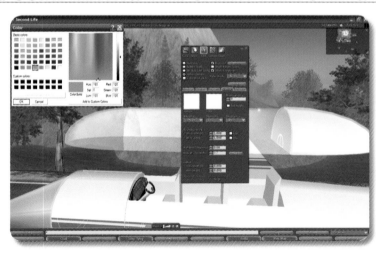

Figure 14.22: Texturing the interior of the cabin

1. Next, click Select Texture and Select the inside edge of the prim right above the control panel. Holding the Shift key, also select the inside of the cockpit prim closest to the tail of the plane, as shown in Figure 14.22.

2. Color these surfaces a medium gray.

3. Now select the interior surface of the cabin prim, as well as the interior end of the back piece of the fuselage. It's time to put in some carpet.

4. Set their Shininess to None.

5. Go to Library ▸ Textures and drag the Gray Mat texture onto the Texture tab.

6. Now select only the interior surface of the cabin prim and set the Repeats per Face to 5×5.

7. Select only the interior of the fuselage piece at the rear of the cabin and set the Repeats per Face to 1×2.5.

■ TEXTURING THE SEATS

Figure 14.23: The completed cabin texturing

1. Next well texture the seats. Turn off the Select Texture radio button.

2. Select all three seats.

3. Set Shininess to None.

4. Go to Library ▸ Textures and drag the Rubber texture onto the Texture tab.

5. Set the Repeats per Face to 2 horizontally and vertically. Hey—it's upholstery!

6. Click the Select Texture radio button.

7. Select the outside edges of the seats.

8. Apply the gradient texture.

9. Set these surfaces' Shininess to Medium (Figure 14.23).

10. Take a copy of the plane and label it Wizard Jet in Progress 12.

RESIDENTS SPEAK

BUILDING WITH A TEAM

Project management is project management is project management. There is nothing special in *Second Life* project management: the same factors will make or break a project. Careful planning, modularity, clear objectives, clearly defined roles, effective communications within the project team and with the client. The only difference that I can see between a *Second Life* project and other IT projects done by distributed teams is that in *Second Life* you can actually drop in the workplace and see if they are actually working—but if you *have* to do that maybe you did not choose your people well.

—Giulio Perhaps (aka Giulio Prisco)

Build with permissions set ahead of time, and as you Shift-copy, it stores permissions. This is extremely helpful if you are working with teammates who are likely to pester you later for a permissive copy of your work. If building on someone else's land, and the parcel is set to only Group can build, it will force you to keep your group tag on, thus eliminating your fear of, "Uh-oh; it's time to turn on Autoreturn, and I didn't make everything in group!"

—Hiro Pendragon (aka Ron T. Blechner)

CHAPTER 1
CHAPTER 2
CHAPTER 3
CHAPTER 4
CHAPTER 5
CHAPTER 6
CHAPTER 7
CHAPTER 8
CHAPTER 9
CHAPTER 10
CHAPTER 11
CHAPTER 12
CHAPTER 13
CHAPTER 14

CREATING THE ANIMATIONS

We've used Avimator (`http://avimator.com`) to make two simple one-frame animations, one for the pilot and one for passengers.

The pilot is posed with arms extended to grip the steering yoke, with legs apart so they don't intersect it. The pilot's legs are extended somewhat so the pilot's knees don't poke into the bottom of the control panel if we seat a long-legged pilot.

The passenger is posed with legs bent sharply so they won't stick into the seat in front of them. Additionally, we've kept the passenger's arms pretty close to the torso so they won't poke into the walls of the cabin.

Now we'll upload the pilot animation.

Figure 14.24: Uploading the pilot's animation

Figure 14.25: Testing the pilot's animation

1. Go to File ▸ Upload Animation, then locate pilot1 on our hard drive and open it.

2. Set the Priority to 4—we want to make sure we don't wave to a friend or something and put a hand through the glass of the cockpit.

3. Check the Loop box.

4. Select the Fist Hand Pose so we can grip the steering yoke.

5. Choose to Preview While Sitting.

6. Play the preview and see if this is about right, then click the Upload button (Figure 14.24)

Next we test this animation.

1. Rez a box or chair and seat your avatar on it.

2. Locate pilot1 in Inventory ▸ Animations.

3. Play the animation.

4. Open the Object Editor and move the chair so that your avatar is in the plane's passenger seat. How does it look? Is it about like Figure 14.25?

If your avatar's hands don't rest on the steering yoke, you have a choice: revise your animation and upload it, or move the steering yoke or even the seats. At this point it would be a better idea to revise the animation unless the only adjustments to the yoke are along the y- or z-axis. What if there's no way to fix this by revising the animation or moving the yoke—if the yoke would end up placed in a way that doesn't make sense? Then you might resort to moving the seat.

TIP

It's a good idea to keep all of the seats at the same height—select them all and raise or lower them together. Also keep in mind that if you move the pilot's seat back, the passengers might be squashed!

It took us two tries to get the passenger animation right, so we called it passenger2. Upload it next. All the preview settings are the same as they were for pilot1, except the Hand Pose is Relaxed. Test the passenger animation in both of the passenger seats, the same way we tested pilot1.

LINKING THE PRIMS

Now that we're done adjusting things in the cabin, we can put the cockpit in place. First, select and link the cockpit prims. Then move the cockpit down until it's in position—the bottom edges of it should barely touch the cut edges of the cabin cylinder.

Now we'll link the rest of the plane.

1. Select the entire plane—all 28 prims. Check the General tab on the Object Editor to be sure.

2. Holding down the Shift key, click on the three parts of the jet exhaust assembly so they aren't highlighted. Their link order is important, so we'll take care of that separately.

3. Link the objects that are selected. Deselect them.

4. Now, holding down the Shift key, select the jet exhaust assembly in this order: the cut torus closest to the fuselage, then the tapered cylinder, and then the black sphere. It's important to do this in order, as you'll see later, when we add scripts to the plane.

5. Link the jet exhaust assembly, then deselect it.

6. Select the rest of the plane.

7. Holding the Shift key, also select the jet assembly.

8. Link all of the prims. The black sphere prim at the very back of the plane should be the parent prim of the link set, as shown in Figure 14.26.

9. Take a copy of the plane and label it Wizard Jet in Progress 13.

Figure 14.26: Linking the completed plane model

CHAPTER 1
CHAPTER 2
CHAPTER 3
CHAPTER 4
CHAPTER 5
CHAPTER 6
CHAPTER 7
CHAPTER 8
CHAPTER 9
CHAPTER 10
CHAPTER 11
CHAPTER 12
CHAPTER 13
CHAPTER 14

APPENDICES
INDEX

RESIDENTS SPEAK

LINKING PRIMS

Sometimes *Second Life* doesn't want to let you link your objects together and complains they are 'too far apart.' Realize that they measure from center of the object's bounding box, which isn't always the same thing as the shape. Also, sometimes you can delink a full set of prims, and then relink them all at once, and that tricky last prim that was not linking will link properly.

—Hiro Pendragon (aka Ron T. Blechner)

SCRIPTING THE PLANE

Scripting doesn't happen in a vacuum. We repurpose and modify existing scripts, build on existing scripts, or piece together snippets of code. Most scripts in *Second Life* are not created from scratch. This plane isn't going to be an exception. In this section, we're going to repurpose and revise existing scripts to make this plane fly and to seat avatars, as well as to control the sound effects, particle effects, and landing gear.

■ DEVELOPING THE VEHICLE SCRIPT

Now it's time to make our plane fly! Instead of trying to reinvent the wheel—or the wing—we're going to modify an existing script: Andrew Linden's Simple Airplane Script Example. Before we start, though, let's think a little bit about just how we want this script to behave.

NOTE

Andrew Linden's Simple Airplane Script Example can be found at `http://forums.secondlife.com/showthread.php?t=7134`. This Second Life Forums thread also includes discussion of the script, and some modified versions of it posted by Second Life residents.

■ DESIGNING THE VEHICLE SCRIPT

A lot of vehicles in *Second Life* are pretty hard to drive, which has caused some residents to think that vehicles just don't work in *Second Life*. This problem is due, in large part, to the same root cause that usually leads to other complaints about *Second Life*: it isn't real life, and sometimes trying to re-create real life too exactly won't yield very functional results.

First let's think about an average *Second Life* resident. They probably just want to have fun flying this plane—this doesn't have to be an accurate flight simulator, and no one is going to be studying gauges. They don't want to learn a lot of complicated commands . . . a very simple interface is called for so it doesn't get in the way of the fun or pose a steep learning curve.

Similarly, our probable pilots may well have average or slower Net connections and computers, so objects and textures take a while to load for them and they might complain of "lag." This means if the plane moves too fast or responds too quickly, these pilots will end up *augering in*, as pilots put it—crashing (Figure 14.27). Let's make sure our plane doesn't accelerate too quickly or corner too suddenly.

Figure 14.27: Augering in: what we don't want the plane to do!

It would be no fun to fly over an empty wasteland because the plane moves faster than buildings and other things can load! Vehicles in *Second Life* aren't really for transportation (we can fly without them, or teleport)—they're toys. This plane doesn't need to go fast. Plus, if the plane doesn't move too quickly, we can cross simulator borders without being disconnected.

Residents have to answer instant messages, talk to passengers, answer the phone, etc. Let's try to make the plane behave in a docile way if the pilot's attention wanders for a few seconds. Heck, they might want to just admire the view!

All that said, we want the plane to be fun to fly, so it should still behave like a flying vehicle rather than like a prim that's being dragged with the Object Editor. Let's make sure it banks and swoops.

On top of these things, our vehicle script is going to have to seat the pilot and do a jet special effect with sound and particles.

CHAPTER 1
CHAPTER 2
CHAPTER 3
CHAPTER 4
CHAPTER 5
CHAPTER 6
CHAPTER 7
CHAPTER 8
CHAPTER 9
CHAPTER 10
CHAPTER 11
CHAPTER 12
CHAPTER 13
CHAPTER 14

APPENDICES
INDEX

MORE INFO

HANG GLIDERS AND THE WIZARD JET

To test if a glider was properly tuned, my real-life hang gliding instructor would attach a bag of potatoes to it and throw it off the top of the tallest mountain in the area. It had to glide safely from the top of mountain to the landing area, without any input from a pilot. This is how we want the Wizard Jet to handle!

RESIDENTS SPEAK

SCRIPTING TIPS

Comment your code!

—Seifert Surface (aka Henry Segerman)

Link order of prims shouldn't matter for your scripts; write your internal communications in a way that they only respond when a certain integer/string/key/command is passed along. This way you can link and delink prims without worry. When writing a script, test early, test often. I do it a lot by adding: `if(DEBUG)llOwnerSay(somevalue);` on lots of places to makes sure the script enters/leaves certain loops or to verify values. **DEBUG** is here a global integer set to **TRUE**. This way you can easily turn your debug message off by setting it to **FALSE**, or easily remove them with the search function.

—Frans Charming (aka Jeroen Frans)

■ MODIFYING THE VEHICLE SCRIPT

First we make a copy of the script we're going to modify, in case we need to back up from a mistake or we want to use the original script for something else. Then we open it and get started.

Andrew Linden's script begins with some comments.

```
// simple airplane script example


// assumes that the root primitive is oriented such that its
// local x-axis points toward the nose of the plane, and its
// local z-axis points toward the top
```

That's to make sure that the plane's forward motion isn't perpendicular to the plane model, and so that the plane won't fly upside down.

```
// control flags that we set later
integer gAngularControls = 0;
integer gLinearControls = 0;
```

Angular means turning and Linear means the direction of travel.

```
// we keep track of angular history for more responsive turns
integer gOldAngularLevel = 0;


// the linear motor uses an accumulator model rather than keeping track
// of the linear control level history
vector gLinearMotor = <0, 0, 0>;


default
```

Now we're going to make our first change to Andrew's script. We want to reset this script when the plane is taken from inventory. This way, if it has been given to a new owner it will recognize them instead of the previous owner—more about this in a bit. Also, if the plane is taken into inventory while in operation, this shuts down the "engine" when it's rezzed. Although it might be funny if the plane takes off by itself, it could be inconvenient!

```
{
on_rez(integer start_param)
    {
        llResetScript();
    }
}
```

We don't have to make changes to the next part of the script, which defines some things we'll want the script to recognize right away.

```
state_entry()
{
llSetSitText("Fly");
llCollisionSound("", 0.0);
```

The first function in this part of the script, llSetSitText, changes the pie menu that comes up when you right-click the plane, so it says *Fly* instead of *Sit*. The second, llCollisionSound, turns off the sound the plane makes when it drags along the ground—the wheels don't really roll, and that collision sound gets annoying quickly.

```
// the sit and camera placement is very shape dependent
// so modify these to suit your vehicle
llSitTarget(<8.46381,0.0,-0.10174>, ZERO_ROTATION);
```

When you select Fly from the pie menu, the script will seat you in the plane, and that placement is determined by this line of code. The first `llSitTarget` variable sets how far from the prim containing this script your avatar is placed. `ZERO_ROTATION` means that the avatar is not rotated in relation to that prim. We've already checked out the offset and rotation and entered the correct variables, but you might want to fine-tune them when you test-fly the plane.

We're not going to change the following variables, which take control of your avatar's camera when your avatar is seated in the plane. If we didn't have these functions here, you wouldn't see much more than a close-up view of the plane. It'll be more fun to be able to watch our aerobatic maneuvers. And it'll be a lot easier to land if we can see the runway!

```
llSetCameraEyeOffset(<-10.0, 0.0, 2.0>);
llSetCameraAtOffset(<3.0, 0.0, 1.0>);
```

This next function, `llSetVehicleType`, tells our vehicle just what sort of behavior we want it to mimic:

```
llSetVehicleType(VEHICLE_TYPE_AIRPLANE);
```

We're not going to change the next part of the code. `EFFICIENCY` is the vehicle's tendency to move in this way, and `TIMESCALE` is how quickly it does it. The plane doesn't want to veer off course.

```
// weak angular deflection
llSetVehicleFloatParam(VEHICLE_ANGULAR_DEFLECTION_EFFICIENCY, 0.1);
llSetVehicleFloatParam(VEHICLE_ANGULAR_DEFLECTION_TIMESCALE, 1.0);
```

The plane wants to go in a straight line, which is achieved with the following code:

```
// strong linear deflection
llSetVehicleFloatParam(VEHICLE_LINEAR_DEFLECTION_EFFICIENCY, 1.0);
llSetVehicleFloatParam(VEHICLE_LINEAR_DEFLECTION_TIMESCALE, 0.2);
```

The next functions set how the plane responds to the throttle. The `TIMESCALE` variable sets how long it takes the plane to get to its maximum speed. The `DECAY` variable sets how long it will take for it the motor to wind back down.

```
// somewhat responsive linear motor
llSetVehicleFloatParam(VEHICLE_LINEAR_MOTOR_TIMESCALE, 0.5);
llSetVehicleFloatParam(VEHICLE_NEAR_MOTOR_DECAY_TIMESCALE, 20);
```

```
// somewhat responsive angular motor, but with 3 second decay timescale

llSetVehicleFloatParam(VEHICLE_ANGULAR_MOTOR_TIMESCALE, 0.5);

llSetVehicleFloatParam(VEHICLE_ANGULAR_MOTOR_DECAY_TIMESCALE, 3);
```

Now we're going to make another modification to the code. Friction slows down moving objects. Remember when we discussed keeping the plane docile if the pilot isn't actively steering it every second? This script originally called for extremely low friction, which meant that a pilot had to be very attentive and quick on the controls. Once we got up to speed, we weren't stopping. This made landings, especially, pretty rough, and the plane had a tendency to skitter off the runway as soon as we were seated. So, we're going to decrease the linear friction from 1000 across the board to 1.0.

We're also going to decrease the angular friction in turns, but not as radically. We want the plane to be easy to handle, but we still want a swoopy feel. We've left the final angular friction variable higher than the others, for diving.

```
llSetVehicleVectorParam(VEHICLE_LINEAR_FRICTION_TIMESCALE, <1.0, 1.0,
    1.0>);

llSetVehicleVectorParam(VEHICLE_ANGULAR_FRICTION_TIMESCALE, <10.0, 10.0,
    100.0>);
```

We're not changing the next two variables, which control how efficient the vehicle is at righting itself and how quickly it does so. We want to be able to bank and even do loops and rolls, so let's leave these alone.

```
llSetVehicleFloatParam(VEHICLE_VERTICAL_ATTRACTION_EFFICIENCY, 0.25);
    // almost wobbly

llSetVehicleFloatParam(VEHICLE_VERTICAL_ATTRACTION_TIMESCALE, 1.5);
    // mediocre response
```

The next three lines control how the plane banks. We increased the banking efficiency a tad because we wanted to bank into turns more tightly:

```
llSetVehicleFloatParam(VEHICLE_BANKING_EFFICIENCY, 0.7);
```

Conversely, we increased the time it takes the plane to reach its peak banking efficiency. We want it to be forgiving so we don't end up suddenly snapping into a spin around one wingtip:

```
llSetVehicleFloatParam(VEHICLE_BANKING_TIMESCALE, 0.5);
```

We won't change the next variable, because it makes our plane more agile when flying than it is on the ground, which is realistic:

```
llSetVehicleFloatParam(VEHICLE_BANKING_MIX, 0.95); // more banking when
    moving
```

We're going to leave the next block of code commented out because we have a runway made of prims:

```
// hover can be better than sliding along the ground during takeoff and
    landing
// but it only works over the terrain (not objects)
//llSetVehicleFloatParam(VEHICLE_HOVER_HEIGHT, 3.0);
//llSetVehicleFloatParam(VEHICLE_HOVER_EFFICIENCY, 0.5);
//llSetVehicleFloatParam(VEHICLE_HOVER_TIMESCALE, 2.0);
//llSetVehicleFlags(VEHICLE_FLAG_HOVER_UP_ONLY);
```

We'll leave the next variable alone, too:

```
// non-zero buoyancy helps the airplane stay up
// set to zero if you don't want this crutch
llSetVehicleFloatParam(VEHICLE_BUOYANCY, 0.2);
```

Let's also leave the following definitions alone, which will be used when the plane takes over the pilot's keyboard controls:

```
// define these here for convenience later
gAngularControls = CONTROL_RIGHT | CONTROL_LEFT | CONTROL_ROT_RIGHT
| CONTROL_ROT_LEFT | CONTROL_DOWN | CONTROL_UP;
gLinearControls = CONTROL_FWD | CONTROL_BACK;
```

However, we're commenting out the next function, which would make the plane into a physical object. We don't like to leave objects physical when it isn't necessary, since physical objects put load on the region and they tend to drift away, be pushed around, etc. We'll set the plane to physical elsewhere in the script.

```
//llSetStatus(STATUS_PHYSICS, TRUE);
}
```

As we discussed at the beginning of this chapter, the physics engine will recognize avatars seated on the vehicle as linked objects. The script takes advantage of this here. It recognizes that the pilot has been seated when the number of prims in the link set changes. Then it checks if the avatar sitting on the vehicle is the owner of the plane:

CHAPTER 14

🔹 DESIGN
   CONSIDER-
   ATIONS

🔹 MODELING
   THE PLANE

🔹 TEXTURING
   THE PLANE

🔹 CREATING THE
   ANIMATIONS

🔹 LINKING
   THE PRIMS

🔹 SCRIPTING
   THE PRIMS

```
changed(integer change)

{

if (change & CHANGED_LINK)

{

key agent = llAvatarOnSitTarget();

if (agent)

{

if (agent != llGetOwner())
```

Remember when we added a reset to the start of the script? That was to make sure the plane wouldn't be erroneously comparing the person seated on it to the previous owner instead of the current one. We don't want anyone swiping our nifty airplane, so when someone who isn't the owner tries to pilot it, the plane tells them off. Then it throws them up into the air!

```
{

// only the owner can use this vehicle

llSay(0, "You aren't the owner");

llUnSit(agent);

llPushObject(agent, <0,0,10>, ZERO_VECTOR, FALSE);

}
```

However, if the avatar on the plane is the owner, they're allowed to stay on the plane. The script resets the linear motor so it doesn't take off with the throttle open:

```
else

{

// clear linear motor on successful sit

gLinearMotor = <0, 0, 0>;

llSetVehicleVectorParam(VEHICLE_LINEAR_MOTOR_DIRECTION, gLinearMotor);
```

Now we'll make another change to the script. Earlier we commented out the line that set the plane as physical. We'll put it back here. This means that once the pilot's aboard, the plane will be affected by the physics engine.

```
llSetStatus(STATUS_PHYSICS, TRUE);
```

Later in the script, there's a pair of functions corresponding to the pair shown next. The former are intended to serve as brakes when there's no pilot aboard, by increasing the plane's friction. But because we're recoding this the plane won't even be physical then, so it won't need brakes. We'll comment these out.

```
//llSetVehicleFloatParam(VEHICLE_LINEAR_FRICTION_TIMESCALE, 1000.0);

//llSetVehicleFloatParam(VEHICLE_ANGULAR_FRICTION_TIMESCALE, 1000.0);
```

Here the script gets permission to animate the pilot and to take over their controls:

```
llRequestPermissions(agent, PERMISSION_TRIGGER_ANIMATION | PERMISSION_
TAKE_CONTROLS);
}
}
```

When the pilot stands, we want to stop the vehicle.

```
else
{
// stop the motors
gLinearMotor = <0, 0, 0>;
llSetVehicleVectorParam(VEHICLE_LINEAR_MOTOR_DIRECTION, gLinearMotor);
llSetVehicleVectorParam(VEHICLE_ANGULAR_MOTOR_DIRECTION, gLinearMotor);
```

Here's the other half of the friction braking we talked about, commented out. We've commented the physics back in:

```
// use friction to stop the vehicle rather than pinning it in place
llSetStatus(STATUS_PHYSICS, FALSE);
//llSetVehicleFloatParam(VEHICLE_LINEAR_FRICTION_TIMESCALE, 1.0);
//llSetVehicleFloatParam(VEHICLE_ANGULAR_FRICTION_TIMESCALE, 1.0);
```

Now the script allows the controls to work on the pilot's avatar instead of on the plane:

```
// driver is getting up
llReleaseControls();
```

We'll make a minor modification here—we'll add the name of our pilot's sit pose so that once the pilot is unseated they'll no longer be animated:

```
llStopAnimation("pilot1");
```

We're going to have another script in the plane that generates a particle effect. It needs to know whether the plane's motor is running. So we'll add a message here to tell it the pilot's gotten off the plane and the motor's off:

CHAPTER 1
CHAPTER 2
CHAPTER 3
CHAPTER 4
CHAPTER 5
CHAPTER 6
CHAPTER 7
CHAPTER 8
CHAPTER 9
CHAPTER 10
CHAPTER 11
CHAPTER 12
CHAPTER 13
CHAPTER 14

APPENDICES
INDEX

```
llMessageLinked(LINK_SET, 0, "unseated", "");
```

We'll be adding a looping sound as part of our jet-engine effect. This function stops it:

```
llStopSound();
}
}
}
```

We need `run_time_permissions` to take over the pilot's animation and controls:

```
run_time_permissions(integer perm)
{
if (perm)
```

We'll add the name of our pilot's sit pose here:

```
{
llStartAnimation("pilot1");
```

And turn on our sound loop here:

```
llLoopSound("jet",1.0);
```

Here's our message to the other script in the plane, telling it to turn on the particle effect:

```
llMessageLinked(LINK_SET, 0, "seated", "");
```

We don't need to make any more changes to the code, which takes the pilot's controls so your keyboard controls the plane instead of your avatar controlling it.

```
llTakeControls(gAngularControls | gLinearControls, TRUE, FALSE);
}
}

control(key id, integer level, integer edge)
{
```

```
// only change linear motor if one of the linear controls are pressed
vector motor;
integer motor_changed = level & gLinearControls;
if (motor_changed)
{
if(level & CONTROL_FWD)
{
if (gLinearMotor.x < 0)
{
gLinearMotor.x = 0;
}
else if (gLinearMotor.x < 30)
{
gLinearMotor.x += 5;
}
motor_changed = TRUE;
}
if(level & CONTROL_BACK)
{
if (gLinearMotor.x > 0)
{
gLinearMotor.x = 0;
}
else if (gLinearMotor.x > -30)
{
gLinearMotor.x -= 5;
};
motor_changed = TRUE;
}
llSetVehicleVectorParam(VEHICLE_LINEAR_MOTOR_DIRECTION, gLinearMotor);
}
```

CHAPTER 14

DESIGN
CONSIDER-
ATIONS

MODELING
THE PLANE

TEXTURING
THE PLANE

CREATING THE
ANIMATIONS

LINKING
THE PRIMS

SCRIPTING
THE PRIMS

```
// only change angular motor if the angular levels have changed
motor_changed = (edge & gOldAngularLevel) + (level & gAngularControls);
if (motor_changed)
{
motor = <0,0,0>;
if(level & (CONTROL_RIGHT|CONTROL_ROT_RIGHT))
{
// add roll component ==> triggers banking behavior
motor.x += 10;
}
if(level & (CONTROL_LEFT|CONTROL_ROT_LEFT))
{
motor.x -= 10;
}
if(level & (CONTROL_UP))
{
// add pitch component ==> causes vehicle lift nose (in local frame)
motor.y -= 8;
}
if(level & (CONTROL_DOWN))
{
motor.y += 8;
}
llSetVehicleVectorParam(VEHICLE_ANGULAR_MOTOR_DIRECTION, motor);
}
// store the angular level history for the next control callback
gOldAngularLevel = level & gAngularControls;
}
}
```

Once we've finished modifying the script, we'll save it then rename it Wizard Jet Script 1.0.

TESTING THE VEHICLE SCRIPT

This script has to be placed in the plane's parent prim. You may be wondering why we've chosen this particular prim as our parent instead of the pilot's seat,. This prim had the correct rotation! Plus, although we might adjust the seat's location, we're not likely to move this prim.

Find Wizard Jet Script 1.0 in Inventory, then drag it onto the plane model and drop it. It'll end up in the parent prim by default. Let's get ready to fly!

We talked about a simple user interface, right? This plane's controls are about as easy as those you use to control your avatar. The left and right arrows turn the plane. The up arrow opens the throttle. The down arrow opens the throttle in *reverse*. Press the up and down arrows together to slow the plane, or even stop it when you land. Page Up raises the plane's nose, and Page Down points it downward. (Because we want this to be intuitive for people used to the behavior of Page Up and Page Down in *Second Life*, rather than in flight-simulator software, we haven't reversed the function of these two keys.)

In real life a jet doesn't fly in reverse. Fortunately, this isn't real life, so you and your plane will be perfectly fine if you crash into a mountain—unless you crash on a damage-enabled parcel! Also, you can *reverse* to get the plane's nose out of the ravine or the street in which it's stuck, and resume your flight.

Start with your plane on a level, fairly flat surface. Right-click it and choose Fly. If you notice a script error (like the one in Figure 14.28), don't worry about it—we'll be taking care of that in a moment. But right now you have a jet to fly—go have some fun!

■ TWEAKING THE SIT OFFSET

Take a look at your avatar's position in the plane. Are you on the seat, with your hands on the steering yoke? If not, fix it by adjusting the first set of variables in the line of code near the top of the script that says:

```
llSitTarget(<8.46381,0.0,-0.10174>, ZERO_ROTATION);
```

Be sure to save a backup copy of your plane once it's set up correctly.

■ ADDING AUDIO

Figure 14.28: This script error indicates we haven't yet added our sound clip.

Now let's take care of that pesky script error (Figure 14.28)! This popped up because the vehicle script was looking for a sound clip named *jet* and couldn't find it. That's because we still need to add it. It has to be placed in the same prim as the vehicle script.

During our adventures in *Second Life* we picked up an appropriate-sounding freebie sound clip that was created by Cory Linden. Hooray for recycling! We'll drag the sound clip from inventory and drop it onto the plane, and by default it'll end up in the parent prim, right next to the vehicle script.

When you get into the plane now, instead of getting a script error you'll hear a jet-engine noise, which will stop when you stand up.

CHAPTER 1
CHAPTER 2
CHAPTER 3
CHAPTER 4
CHAPTER 5
CHAPTER 6
CHAPTER 7
CHAPTER 8
CHAPTER 9
CHAPTER 10
CHAPTER 11
CHAPTER 12
CHAPTER 13
CHAPTER 14

APPENDICES
INDEX

■ SETTING UP THE PASSENGER SEATS

We need to add two scripts to the plane to seat and animate passengers. For this we're going to use a plain old sit script that we found for free.

■ MODIFYING SIT SCRIPTS

This code looks familiar! In fact, it contains a lot of the same functions we used in Wizard Jet Script 1.0.

PASSENGER 1

This script contains the same functions Wizard Jet Script 1.0 used for detecting when avatars sit or get up, to request permission to animate the avatar, to trigger the animation and stop it, and to set the sit target. This script just has them in a different order. To adapt it to use in our plane, we simply need to add the name of our passenger animation and the variables for the sit target. The sit offset is the `vector` and the rotation variables are located in the line with the actual `llSitTarget` function.

```
//Put the name of your animation here
string Pose = "passenger2";


key agentKey = NULL_KEY;
integer permissionResult = FALSE;
vector sittingPosition = <0.00086, 0.30649, 6.78241>;


init()
{
    llSitTarget(sittingPosition,<-0.49998, -0.49998, -0.50002, 0.50002>);
}


default
{
    state_entry()
    {
        init();
    }


    on_rez(integer times)
    {
        llResetScript();
    }
```

```
    changed(integer change)
    {
        if (change & CHANGED_LINK)
        {
            key agent = llAvatarOnSitTarget();
            if ( agentKey == NULL_KEY && agent != NULL_KEY )
            {
                agentKey = agent;
                llRequestPermissions(agentKey, PERMISSION_TRIGGER_
                    ANIMATION);
            }
            else if ( agentKey != NULL_KEY && agent == NULL_KEY)
            {
                if (permissionResult)
                {
                    llStopAnimation(Pose);
                }
                llResetScript();
            }
        }
    }
    run_time_permissions(integer value)
    {
        if (value == PERMISSION_TRIGGER_ANIMATION)
        {
            permissionResult = TRUE;
            llStopAnimation("sit");
            llStartAnimation(Pose);
        }
    }
}
```

Save the script and name it Sit Script with Pose, Passenger 1.

Now copy that script and change the vector:

CHAPTER 14

DESIGN
CONSIDER-
ATIONS

MODELING
THE PLANE

TEXTURING
THE PLANE

CREATING THE
ANIMATIONS

LINKING
THE PRIMS

SCRIPTING
THE PRIMS

```
vector sittingPosition = <5.71283, 0.00108, -0.09571>;
```

And the rotation:

```
llSitTarget (sittingPosition,<-0.00000, 0.00003, -0.00000, 1.00000>);
```

Save this script and name it Sit Script with Pose, Passenger 2.

ADDING THE PASSENGER SIT SCRIPTS AND ANIMATION

Now we'll add the passenger scripts and animation to the plane. Here's why the link order of the jet exhaust assembly was so important. The first avatar who sits on the plane will be seated in relation to the last prim added to the link set—the parent prim, which contains our vehicle script, Wizard Jet 1.0. The next avatar who sits on the plane will sit on the second-to-last linked prim that contains a sit script. The third will be seated in the third-to-last prim that contains a sit script. If there isn't a sit script, then the avatar will either not find a seat, or will be placed on that prim . . . probably pretty awkwardly.

So, it's important to have the prims in the correct order and to add the passenger script with the correct offset to each one. Here's how:

1. **Open the Object Editor and click the Edit Linked Parts radio button.**

2. **Select the tapered cylinder piece of the jet exhaust assembly—the nozzle-shaped part right next to the parent prim.**

Figure 14.29: Adding the sit script and animation to the third-to-last prim in the link set

3. **Drag Sit Script with Pose, Passenger 1 into the Contents tab of this prim.**

4. **Drag the passenger2 animation into the Contents tab.**

5. **Select the cut torus piece of the jet exhaust assembly, and put Sit Script with Pose, Passenger 2 into its Contents, as well as a copy of the passenger2 animation, as shown in Figure 14.29.**

6. **Make a backup and label it!**

CHAPTER 1
CHAPTER 2
CHAPTER 3
CHAPTER 4
CHAPTER 5
CHAPTER 6
CHAPTER 7
CHAPTER 8
CHAPTER 9
CHAPTER 10
CHAPTER 11
CHAPTER 12
CHAPTER 13
CHAPTER 14

APPENDICES
INDEX

■ TESTING AND ADJUSTING THE PASSENGER SIT SCRIPTS

Now it's time to test the plane. Round up a couple of friends. You have to be the first to sit in the plane, because if someone else tries to pilot it, they'll be ejected. Once you're seated, tell your friends to right-click the plane and select Fly. Check if your friends' avatars are placed correctly, and adjust the vector of the sit targets if necessary. Then take your friends for a ride!

■ ADDING A PARTICLE EFFECT

To go with our jet sound, we want a flame to shoot from the plane's exhaust (Figure 14.30). We'll use particles to get this effect, and to do that we'll modify a particle script The Magicians used for an entirely different project. It was based largely on a free particle script written by Jopsy Pendragon, the most famous particle artist in *Second Life*.

Figure 14.30: Trying out the particle effect

TIP

Want to learn more about particles? Visit Jopsy Pendragon's Particle Laboratory, Teal 180,74,21. There you'll find free example scripts, as well as a particle-scripting tutorial with examples that illustrate and explain every aspect of particle scripting in Second Life.

The script starts out by calling a particle system, then it sets a lot of flags and variables that control how the particles look.

```
do_particles()

{

      llParticleSystem( [

            // Appearance Settings
```

The next two lines set the size the particles are when they appear, and then the size they'll be at the end of their life. We want these particles to start out pretty small, then we want them to grow. They should lengthen as they extend from the exhaust:

```
    PSYS_PART_START_SCALE,(vector) <.25,.5,.5>,
// Start Size, (minimum .04, max 10.0?)

    PSYS_PART_END_SCALE,(vector) <1.75,.25,.25>,
// End Size,  requires *_INTERP_SCALE_MASK
```

The next two lines control the color of the particles. They'll start out blue and gradually shift to cyan at the end of their life span:

```
    PSYS_PART_START_COLOR,(vector) <0,0,1>,
// Start Color, (RGB, 0 to 1)

    PSYS_PART_END_COLOR,(vector) <0,1,1>,
// EndColor, requires *_INTERP_COLOR_MASK
```

Now we set the transparency of the particles. We want them to remain opaque, so both of these values are set to 1:

```
    PSYS_PART_START_ALPHA,(float) 1,
// startAlpha (0 to 1),

    PSYS_PART_END_ALPHA,(float) 1,
// endAlpha (0 to 1)
```

The next line is commented out. If we wanted the particles to have a texture different from the default, we'd put its name here and add the texture to the Contents of the prim that holds this script.

```
// PSYS_SRC_TEXTURE,(string) "coloredsmoke",
// name of a 'texture' in emitters inventory
```

Now we'll set the particle flow. As the comment in the following snippet points out, we don't want to flood the place with excessive particles. Particles are generated client-side, so they wouldn't affect the region's performance; however, they could affect the performance client-side.

First we set the number of particles per burst. We don't need very many at once. We certainly won't be in danger of exceeding the limit Jopsy suggests in his comment below. On the other hand, we don't want a very long delay between bursts, or else our flame will sputter:

```
// Flow Settings, keep (age/rate)*count well below 4096 !!!

    PSYS_SRC_BURST_PART_COUNT,(integer) 10,
// # of particles per burst

    PSYS_SRC_BURST_RATE,(float) .2,
// delay between bursts
```

Our particles don't have to last very long, so we'll set their age to a second and a half:

```
    PSYS_PART_MAX_AGE,(float) 1.5,
// how long particles live
```

And we don't want the emitter to turn itself off here. We're going to arrange for that later in the script, and change the next variable here to zero:

```
        PSYS_SRC_MAX_AGE,(float) 0.0,
// turns emitter off after 15 minutes. (0.0 = never)
```

Now we set the variables that control where our particles appear. First we choose a pattern—drop, in this case. We don't want variation in our particles' starting and ending locations:

```
        // Placement Settings

    PSYS_SRC_PATTERN, PSYS_SRC_PATTERN_DROP,

        // _PATTERN can be: *_EXPLODE, *_DROP, *_ANGLE, *ANGLE_CONE
or *_ANGLE_CONE_EMPTY
```

We don't need to change the next few settings.

```
    PSYS_SRC_BURST_RADIUS,(float) 1.0,
// How far from emitter new particles start,

    PSYS_SRC_INNERANGLE,(float) 10.5,
// aka 'spread' (0 to 2*PI),

    PSYS_SRC_OUTERANGLE,(float) 0.0,
// aka 'tilt' (0(up), PI(down) to 2*PI),

    PSYS_SRC_OMEGA,(vector) <1,1,0>,
// how much to rotate around x,y,z per burst,
```

Now we tell our particles how fast to go on each axis. This will make our flame travel perpendicular to the plane:

```
        // Movement Settings

    PSYS_SRC_ACCEL,(vector) <0,.7,0>,
// aka gravity or push, ie <0,0,-1.0> = down
```

We are going to vary the speed at which particles move when they first come out of the prim—before we add push. The next two variables set the range:

```
    PSYS_SRC_BURST_SPEED_MIN,(float) 0.0,
// Minimum velocity for new particles

    PSYS_SRC_BURST_SPEED_MAX,(float) 0.2,
// Maximum velocity for new particles
```

We'll leave this next bit commented out. This code was set to target the particle generator's owner—the particles would have traveled toward that avatar. This could be modified to target another avatar, or even a specific named object:

CHAPTER 1
CHAPTER 2
CHAPTER 3
CHAPTER 4
CHAPTER 5
CHAPTER 6
CHAPTER 7
CHAPTER 8
CHAPTER 9
CHAPTER 10
CHAPTER 11
CHAPTER 12
CHAPTER 13
CHAPTER 14

APPENDICES
INDEX

```
                    //PSYS_SRC_TARGET_KEY,(key) llGetOwner(),
                    // key of a target, requires *_TARGET_POS_MASK

                    // for *_TARGET try llGetKey(), or llGetOwner(), or
               llDetectedKey(0) even. :)
```

Now we set some of the flags that enable various types of particle behavior. We want the jet flame to glow, but bouncing up doesn't make sense:

```
                    PSYS_PART_FLAGS,
            // Remove the leading // from the options you want enabled:

                    PSYS_PART_EMISSIVE_MASK |
            // particles glow

                    //PSYS_PART_BOUNCE_MASK |
            // particles bounce up from emitter's 'Z' altitude
```

This flame is too powerful to be blown by the wind or to change direction! We will comment out the next two flags to keep the particles from being blown around by the wind or changing direction.

```
                    //PSYS_PART_WIND_MASK |
            // particles get blown around by wind

                    //PSYS_PART_FOLLOW_VELOCITY_MASK |
            // particles rotate towards where they're going
```

The next flag is particularly interesting to us right now. We have enabled this flag because we want the flame to always appear to be coming from the jet exhaust. However, we could have an interesting effect here if we didn't enable this—our plane would leave a trail of particles.

```
                    PSYS_PART_FOLLOW_SRC_MASK |
            // particles move as the emitter moves
```

The next two flags, PSYS_PART_INTERP_COLOR_MASK and PSYS_PART_INTERP_SCALE_MASK, must be set so we can make the particles shift their color and size. We don't need them to target anyone or anything, so we will comment out PSYS_PART_TARGET_POS_MASK:

```
                    PSYS_PART_INTERP_COLOR_MASK |
            // particles change color depending on *_END_COLOR

                    PSYS_PART_INTERP_SCALE_MASK |
            // particles change size using *_END_SCALE

                    //PSYS_PART_TARGET_POS_MASK |
            // particles home on *_TARGET key

                0 // Unless you understand binary arithmetic, leave this 0 here.
            :)

                ] );

        }
```

Now we have defined our particles. The next part of the script turns the particles on and off. Seifert Surface (aka Henry Segerman) replaced the original touch-start with code that turns the script on and off when told to by another script. In this case, we have modified it to listen to the link messages from Wizard Jet Script 1.0.

The first function sets the particle generator to do nothing when it rezzes.

```
default
{
    on_rez(integer param)
    {
        llParticleSystem([]); //starts off
    }
```

The next line of the script listens for link messages. If it gets the `seated` message, it starts the particle effect we defined in the first part of the script. If it hears the `unseated` message, it starts an empty particle system—it turns off the flame effect.

```
    link_message(integer sender_num, integer num,
        string message, key id)
    {
        if( message == "seated" )
        {
            do_particles();
        }
        if( message == "unseated" )
        {
            llParticleSystem([]);
        }
    }
}
```

Save this script and name it Blue Jet Flame, linkmessage.

Next, drag it from Inventory and drop it onto the jet. It will end up in the Contents of the parent prim. The next time you hop into the Wizard, the effect will start, and it will stop when you stand up.

NOTE

Particle effects look the same from any angle. That means the flame won't look the same in relation to the jet exhaust assembly all the time. It still looks cool, though. If it bugs you, you can make the jet leave a trail instead, or comment out the PSYS_PART_INTERP_SCALE_MASK *tag so the particles won't change size.*

RESIDENTS SPEAK

JOPSY PENDRAGON WITH PARTICLE TIPS

◆ One of the best ways to really make amazing particle effects is to use two or three emitters instead of just one! This requires one prim per particle effect, of course. A candle could have three parts: a flame effect, a glow effect, and a smoke effect. My favorite, for things that move, is mixing effects that use FOLLOW_SRC (like a glow) with effects that don't (like a trail of sparkles).

◆ The most common mistake I see people make with particles is using too many, often because they want to fill a space with very tiny particles. It is almost always better to use fewer and slightly larger particles. Using more than one 'greedy' particle emitter will result in other particle effects looking very sparse and weak.

◆ With water, quite often a combination of llSetTextureAnim() and particles works far better than just one or the other. llTargetOmega() is also a useful attribute to experiment with. All three, particles, texture animation, and object omega rotation, are processed on the client . . . and cause no extra lag for scripts or the sim, making them outstanding for permanent displays!

◆ If you have an object with a compound particle effect, read up on using llMessageLinked() and link_message() in the scripting wiki [http://www.lslwiki. net/]. Using one script as a controller, telling the other scripts to turn their particles on or off with linked messages, is fast, secure, and fairly simple once you have an example to work from.

◆ Particle *ANGLES* can be confusing at first, and take more practice to master than most of the particle options. Angle values are given in radians . . . and if you've forgotten all the trigonometry you learned in high school don't panic; you can use degrees to, (i.e., 45, 90, 180) and multiply it by DEG_TO_RAD instead of trying to guess at values from zero to pi.

◆ Particle *TARGETS* cause people the most grief, and is the only part of particles that require some advanced knowledge of the LSL programming language and what 'asset UUID keys' are in *Second Life*. Some functions can be used to grab keys, like llGetOwner() or llGetKey(), but they are very limited in usefulness. The best way to grab a key is different, depending on whether the target is linked to the emitter, or in another attachment, or somewhere nearby. At the moment, there are four different methods demonstrated in Teal's Particle Laboratory with free sample scripts for you to study!

■ CODING THE LANDING GEAR

The Wizard's landing gear is fairly low-profile, but the jet will look a lot more aerodynamic if we can raise it after takeoff. We'll use two scripts to do this because we're going to have a listener in our code, and listeners are resource hogs. So one script will do the listening, and then it'll tell copies of the other script what to do via link messages.

CHAPTER 1
CHAPTER 2
CHAPTER 3
CHAPTER 4
CHAPTER 5
CHAPTER 6
CHAPTER 7
CHAPTER 8
CHAPTER 9
CHAPTER 10
CHAPTER 11
CHAPTER 12
CHAPTER 13
CHAPTER 14

■ THE PARENT SCRIPT

This is the script with the listener. We considered other interfaces for telling the plane to raise and lower the gear, but this one is practical to do in a hurry as you approach the runway. Touch-start is easy to activate by accident, and a HUD would block our view!

We start off by resetting the script when the plane is rezzed, so that it will check if it has a new owner:

```
default
{
on_rez(integer start_param)
    {
        llResetScript();
    }
state_entry()
    {
        key owner = llGetOwner();
```

Here we arrange for the plane to remind the owner of the commands it recognizes:

```
        llOwnerSay("To raise/lower gear say 'gear up' or 'gear down.'");
```

We've set things up so the plane listens only to what its owner says, which reduces its impact on script resources in the region. We have left it to listen to open chat, though, because we want to keep the command short enough to type quickly during final approach. We thought about making the commands just *up* and *down*, but we already have an object listening for those common words, and we don't want a conflict!

```
        llListen(0,"",owner,"");
    }
```

When the script hears the owner say *gear up*, it sends the rest of the link set the message up (Figure 14.31). When it hears the owner say *gear down* . . . well, you know (Figure 14.32):

Figure 14.31: Gear down

Figure 14.32: Gear up

CHAPTER 14

DESIGN
CONSIDER-
ATIONS

MODELING
THE PLANE

TEXTURING
THE PLANE

CREATING THE
ANIMATIONS

LINKING
THE PRIMS

SCRIPTING
THE PRIMS

```
    listen( integer channel, string name, key id, string message )

    {

        if( message == "gear up" )

        {

            llMessageLinked(LINK_SET,0,"up","");

        }

        if( message == "gear down" )

        {

            llMessageLinked(LINK_SET,0,"down","");


        }

    }

}
```

Save this script and name it Gear Controller. Then drag it from Inventory and onto the plane so it will end up in the parent prim.

THE GEAR CHILD SCRIPT

This script controls transparency. But first it listens for a link message telling it what to do:

```
default

{

    state_entry()

    {
    }

            link_message(integer sender_num, integer num, string
message, key id)
```

If the message is *down*, then the gear becomes opaque.

```
    {

        if( message == "down" )

        {

            llSetAlpha(1,ALL_SIDES);

        }
```

If the message is *up*, the gear becomes invisible.

```
if( message == "up" )
{
    llSetAlpha(0,ALL_SIDES);
}
}


}
```

Save the script and name it Gear Child.

RESIDENTS SPEAK

HIRO PENDRAGON WITH A SCRIPTING TIP

Sometimes it is a lot easier to prescript an object and Shift-copy than to drag and drop a script into each one.

INSTALLING THE GEAR CHILD SCRIPTS

Now we put copies of the Gear Child script into each of the plane's wheels. We're also going to put copies into the wheel housings so nothing will mess up our plane's clean-looking lines while in flight. It's not real life, so we don't have to play by real-life rules. However, if it bothers you that the wheels disappear into thin air, don't add the Gear Child to the housings, and imagine the wheels nestled safely in them while aloft.

1. **Open the Object Editor and click the Edit Linked Parts radio button.**

2. **Select each wheel and drop a copy of Gear Child into its Contents.**

3. **If you believe in magic, do the same thing to the wheel housings, but skip this step if you're a hard-nosed realist!**

4. **Take a copy of your plane and label it Wizard Jet 1.0.**

Now your plane talks to you when you rez it, reminding you—and only you—of the commands to control the gear. No chat spam. And, of course, you have the power to control your landing gear. And the power to create a really cool plane (Figure 14.33)!

Figure 14.33: Victory lap

APPENDICES

SUPPLEMENTAL INFO

In the following section you'll find a number of useful extras, including links to online resources, a glossary of common *Second Life* terms, the details of *Second Life*'s community standards, and information related to the contents of the CD that comes with this book.

경회루 慶會樓
Gyeonghoeru

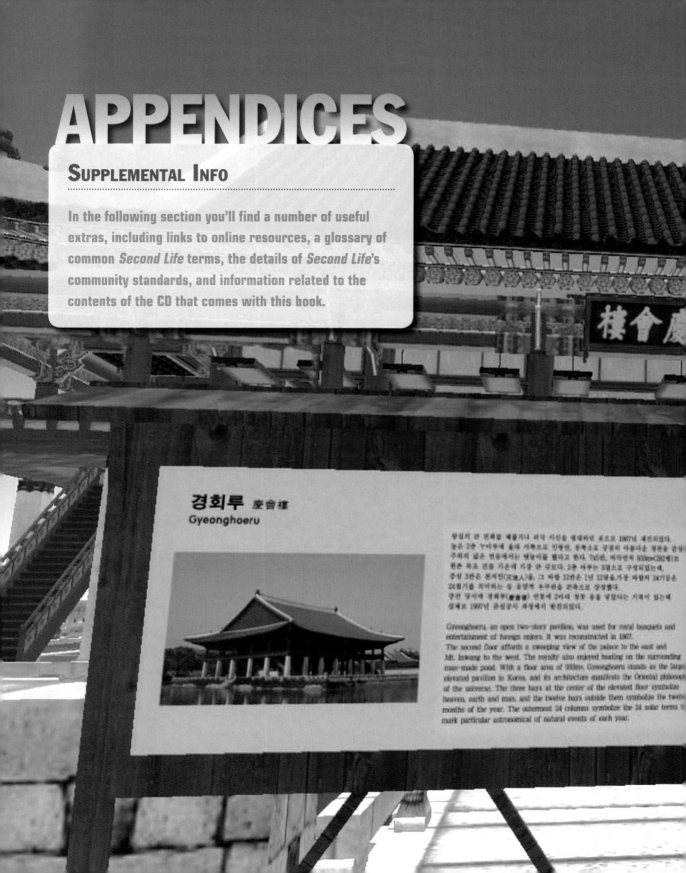

Gyeonghoeru, an open two-story pavilion, was used for royal banquets and entertainment of foreign envoys. It was reconstructed in 1867.

The second floor affords a sweeping view of the palace to the east and Mt. Inwang to the west. The royalty also enjoyed boating on the surrounding man-made pond. With a floor area of 903m², Gyeonghoeru stands as the largest elevated pavilion in Korea, and its architecture manifests the Oriental philosophy of the universe. The three bays at the center of the elevated floor symbolize heaven, earth and man, and the twelve bays outside them symbolize the twelve months of the year. The outermost 24 columns symbolize the 24 solar terms to mark particular astronomical of natural events of each year.

CONTENTS

APPENDIX A: RESOURCES

■ GENERAL RESOURCES

Second Life **Resource Matrix**. This is a list of useful Linden Lab links as well as resident-driven links targeted mostly at content creators.

    http://secondlife.com/developers/resources/matrix.php

Second Life **content creation forum**. This is the official place to ask questions, discuss problems, trade tips, and share ideas about content creation in *Second Life*.

    http://forums.secondlife.com/forumdisplay.php?f=294

Video Tutorials. This page provides links to a wide variety of content creation video tutorials.

    http://wiki.secondlife.com/wiki/Video_Tutorials

SLuniverse Knowledge Base. This site run by famed *Second Life*r, Cristiano Midnight, and offers helpful tutorials along with user feedback.

    http://www.sluniverse.com/kb/

SLTutorials. This website provides a place for users to submit and browse *Second Life* tutorials on different subjects.

    http://www.sltutorials.net/

■ BUILDING RESOURCES

SL Building. SL Building provides basic building tutorials along with video.

    http://www.slbuilding.com

Squidoo. This multiplatform site features a fairly comprehensive collection of *Second Life* tutorial links and videos.

    http://www.squidoo.com/Second-Life-Building/

■ SCRIPTING RESOURCES

LSL Portal. This wiki contains technical descriptions of all LSL features.

    http://wiki.secondlife.com/wiki/LSL_Portal

LSL Wiki. Much like the LSL portal, this wiki contains technical descriptions of all LSL features. This is a good place to go for alternative descriptions of LSL features to supplement the official *Second Life* Wiki.

```
http://lslwiki.net/
```

Kan-Ed. The LSL tutorial here explains some basics of LSL scripting, including particles, physics, texture animation, and more.

```
http://www.kan-ed.org/second-life/using-LSL.html
```

LSL Library. This section of the *Second Life* Wiki features a sizable collection of complete *Second Life* scripts available for your own personal use.

```
http://wiki.secondlife.com/wiki/Category:LSL_Library
```

Shill. This site provides information about external LSL editors and resources for creating scripts off-line.

```
http://adammarker.org/shill/
```

■ THIRD-PARTY TOOLS

Texture Maker. A handy tool for simulating materials, shading, and tiled textures.

```
http://www.texturemaker.com
```

Adobe. Creator of essential third-party tools such as Photoshop, Illustrator, After Effects, and Premiere.

```
http://www.adobe.com/
```

Corel. Creator of powerful graphics tools such as CorelDRAW and Paint Shop Pro.

```
http://www.corel.com/
```

Fraps. The preferred video-capture tool for *Second Life* machinimists.

```
http://www.fraps.com/
```

APPENDICES

APPENDIX A:
RESOURCES

APPENDIX B:
GLOSSARY

APPENDIX C:
SL
COMMUNITY
STANDARDS
AND
INTELLECTUAL
PROPERTY
RIGHTS

APPENDIX D:
ABOUT THE
COMPANION
CD

APPENDIX B: GLOSSARY

alpha Textures with invisible layers created using 32-bit TGA files.

Alt-zoom A technique for looking around without moving your avatar by holding Alt and left-clicking an object.

Autoreturn A feature on the About Land panel that can be set to return objects to their owners after a configurable time limit.

avatar Your personal manifestation within *Second Life*. Anthropomorphic by default, avatars can take any number of forms, shapes, and sizes.

building by the numbers A method of building where prim sizes and positions are mathematically calculated to ensure the highest precision and reduce gaps or overlaps.

Bumpiness An object state where a special texture (a bump map) is used to emulate shadowing to add a sense of depth to the object surface.

camera Term to describe your point of view in relation to your avatar. By default your camera sits about three meters behind and slightly above your avatar's head.

client The portion of the *Second Life* software that resides on the end user's computer and communicates with the *Second Life* servers.

composite textures Textures created by combining image elements from multiple other sources.

content Any objects, clothing, animations, sounds, textures, terrain modification, scripts, or notecards inside *Second Life*.

Copy An object state where the owner is permitted to make copies of the item.

covenant Terms of service offered by region owners to parcel purchasers.

dimple A cone shape cut from the poles of a sphere around its vertical axis.

estate One or more regions owned by an avatar, managed via the Region/Estate panel.

floating text Also known as hovertext, this is text that appears above a prim.

frames per second (FPS) A measure of performance calculated by taking the number of times a scene is rendered or "drawn" each second.

Full Bright An object state where a prim is not subject to the local lighting and shadowing and instead shines at full luminosity.

grid A collection of sims through which a resident can access any other sim that is also part of that grid. Multiple grids exist, including the Main grid and the Teen grid.

heads-up display (HUD) An attachment worn by an avatar at a special attachment point. It is viewable only by the wearer.

hovertext See *floating text*.

hub Short for Telehub.

lag A reduction in game performance caused by network problems, client machine problems, or server problems.

landmark An inventory item that stores location information. Landmarks are frequently given to others to make it easier for them to find locations.

Library A folder in Inventory that contains assets provided by Linden Lab.

linearly extruded prims Prims that are made up of a basic two-dimensional start shape and a basic two-dimensional end shape. A path is then interpolated between the two shapes. Boxes, prisms, and cylinders are linearly extruded prims.

link set A group of prims that are linked together.

Locked An object state that makes it impossible to edit or move until unlocked.

Level of Detail (LOD) A characteristic of the *Second Life* engine where objects lose detail when viewed from a distance.

LSL Linden Scripting Language.

machinima The process of using *Second Life* or other gaming platforms to create movies.

megaprim A prim that is larger than the 10-meter limitation created using a hack by Gene Replacement (AKA Plastic Duck).

Modifiable (Mod) An object state where the owner of the object is permitted to modify it.

mouselook A mode in which the camera is positioned to see through the avatar's eyes. The M key toggles mouselook mode on and off.

object A prim or a linked collection of prims.

openspaces Regions that support only 1,875 prims. Purchased in blocks of four and required to be attached to a private island, one block costs the same as a regular island.

parcel A piece of virtual land; part of a region.

permissions (perms) May refer to object permission settings (see *privileges*) or to parcel or Region/Estate permission settings.

Phantom An object state that permits avatars and other objects to move freely through it.

photosourcing Creating textures from photos.

Physical An object state that causes the object to behave like a physical object, including falling due to gravity, bouncing, and pushing other physical objects.

Polygons The basic two-dimensional shape that makes up the sides of *Second Life* prims.

primitive (prim) The most basic building blocks for all *Second Life* objects. Prims come in the form of boxes, prisms, cylinders, tori, rings, tubes, and spheres.

prim attachments Any prims or objects intended to be attached to the avatar as a clothing accessory or body part.

prim limit The number of primitives supported by a parcel or region.

prim torture Common phrase to describe the practice of contorting prims in unusual ways.

private island A region owned by a resident, not attached to the mainland.

privileges (privs) A word that describes the combination of Modify, Copy, and Transfer settings on an object. (For example, "Could you send me a copy with full privs?" would mean the resident would like a copy of the object that permits him to modify, copy, and transfer it freely.)

radially extruded prims Prims that are made up of a basic two-dimensional shapes rotated around a central axis. Spheres, tori, rings, and tubes are radially extruded prims.

rez The act of bringing a prim or object into existence.

region An area of virtual land that can be managed via the Region/Estate panel. Commonly called a sim.

root prim A prim that carries the characteristics of a linked set.

shadow prim A prim that hosts a texture in the shape of a shadow that can be used in combination with other objects to create the illusion of shadowing.

Shift-drag (or Shift-copy) Technique of copying an object, link set, or group of objects by dragging them while holding down the Shift key.

Shininess An object state where the surface of a prim takes on a reflective quality.

simulator (or sim) A sim is a 256-square-meter block of land. Sims can be further divided into *parcels* of various shapes and sizes.

slider clothing Clothing created using textures applied to avatar modification layers.

APPENDICES

APPENDIX A:
RESOURCES

APPENDIX B:
GLOSSARY

APPENDIX C:
SL
COMMUNITY
STANDARDS
AND
INTELLECTUAL
PROPERTY
RIGHTS

APPENDIX D:
ABOUT THE
COMPANION
CD

SLURL Short for *Second Life* URL, this string can be entered into most Internet browsers to allow users to locate and teleport to a *Second Life* location.

Telehub Target set by a region owner for avatars arriving via teleporting. May also refer to a building or other structure built around this point, or the parcel in which it is located.

teleport (TP) This is the method of moving instantly from point to point by using the *Second Life* map.

Teleporter (AKA Sit Hack Teleporter) A scripted object that an avatar touches to be sent nearly instantly to a set location.

Temporary (Temp) An object state that will cause the object to disappear shortly after being rezzed.

texture An image applied to the side of a prim.

tinting Changing the texture color on one or more sides of a prim.

tiny prim A prim that is made smaller than the 0.010 meter limit using cuts, hollows, and other techniques.

Transfer (Trans) An object state where the owner is permitted to transfer the item to another user.

void regions See *openspaces*.

WASD The most popular keyboard configuration used for movement in 3D worlds. W moves forward, A moves left, D moves right, and S moves backward.

ZMGWTFBBQ An expression of shock or surprise.

CHAPTER 1
CHAPTER 2
CHAPTER 3
CHAPTER 4
CHAPTER 5
CHAPTER 6
CHAPTER 7
CHAPTER 8
CHAPTER 9
CHAPTER 10
CHAPTER 11
CHAPTER 12
CHAPTER 13
CHAPTER 14
APPENDICES
INDEX

APPENDIX C: *SL* COMMUNITY STANDARDS AND INTELLECTUAL PROPERTY RIGHTS

It's important to know *Second Life*'s community standards and excellent intellectual property policies. Here they are, and you can visit `http://secondlife.com/corporate/cs.php` to get the latest community standards and see Section 3.2 of the Terms of Service (`http://secondlife.com/corporate/tos.php`) for up-to-date intellectual property information.

■ COMMUNITY STANDARDS

Welcome to *Second Life*.

We hope you'll have a richly rewarding experience, filled with creativity, self expression, and fun.

The goals of the Community Standards are simple: treat each other with respect and without harassment, adhere to local standards as indicated by simulator ratings, and refrain from any hate activity which slurs a real-world individual or real-world community.

Within *Second Life*, we want to support Residents in shaping their specific experiences and making their own choices.

The Community Standards sets out six behaviors, the "**Big Six**", that will result in suspension or, with repeated violations, expulsion from the *Second Life* Community.

All *Second Life* Community Standards apply to all areas of *Second Life*, the *Second Life* Forums, and the *Second Life* Website.

1. **Intolerance:** Combating intolerance is a cornerstone of *Second Life*'s Community Standards. Actions that marginalize, belittle, or defame individuals or groups inhibit the satisfying exchange of ideas and diminish the *Second Life* community as whole. The use of derogatory or demeaning language or images in reference to another Resident's race, ethnicity, gender, religion, or sexual orientation is never allowed in *Second Life*.

2. **Harassment:** Given the myriad capabilities of *Second Life*, harassment can take many forms. Communicating or behaving in a manner which is offensively coarse, intimidating or threatening, constitutes unwelcome sexual advances or requests for sexual favors, or is otherwise likely to cause annoyance or alarm is Harassment.

3. **Assault:** Most areas in *Second Life* are identified as Safe. Assault in *Second Life* means: shooting, pushing, or shoving another Resident in a Safe Area (see Global Standards below); creating or using scripted objects which singularly or persistently target another Resident in a manner which prevents their enjoyment of *Second Life*.

4. **Disclosure:** Residents are entitled to a reasonable level of privacy with regard to their Second Lives. Sharing personal information about a fellow Resident—including gender, religion, age, marital status, race, sexual preference, and real-world location beyond what is provided by the Resident in the First Life page of their Resident profile is a violation of that Resident's privacy. Remotely monitoring conversations, posting conversation logs, or sharing conversation logs without consent are all prohibited in *Second Life* and on the *Second Life* Forums.

APPENDICES

APPENDIX A:
RESOURCES

APPENDIX B:
GLOSSARY

APPENDIX C:
SL
COMMUNITY
STANDARDS
AND
INTELLECTUAL
PROPERTY
RIGHTS

APPENDIX D:
ABOUT THE
COMPANION
CD

5. **Indecency:** *Second Life* is an adult community, but Mature material is not necessarily appropriate in all areas (see Global Standards below). Content, communication, or behavior which involves intense language or expletives, nudity or sexual content, the depiction of sex or violence, or anything else broadly offensive must be contained within private land in areas rated Mature (M). Names of Residents, objects, places and groups are broadly viewable in *Second Life* directories and on the *Second Life* website, and must adhere to PG guidelines.

6. **Disturbing the Peace:** Every Resident has a right to live their *Second Life*. Disrupting scheduled events, repeated transmission of undesired advertising content, the use of repetitive sounds, following or self-spawning items, or other objects that intentionally slow server performance or inhibit another Resident's ability to enjoy *Second Life* are examples of Disturbing the Peace.

■ POLICIES AND POLICING

GLOBAL STANDARDS, LOCAL RATINGS

All areas of *Second Life*, including the www.secondlife.com website and the *Second Life* Forums, adhere to the same Community Standards. Locations within *Second Life* are noted as Safe or Unsafe and rated Mature (M) or non-Mature (PG), and behavior must conform to the local ratings. Any unrated area of *Second Life* or the *Second Life* website should be considered non-Mature (PG).

WARNING, SUSPENSION, BANISHMENT

Second Life is a complex society, and it can take some time for new Residents to gain a full understanding of local customs and mores. Generally, violations of the Community Standards will first result in a Warning, followed by Suspension and eventual Banishment from *Second Life*. In-World Representatives, called Liaisons, may occasionally address disciplinary problems with a temporary removal from *Second Life*.

GLOBAL ATTACKS

Objects, scripts, or actions which broadly interfere with or disrupt the *Second Life* community, the *Second Life* servers or other systems related to *Second Life* will not be tolerated in any form. We will hold you responsible for any actions you take, or that are taken by objects or scripts that belong to you. Sandboxes are available for testing objects and scripts that have components that may be unmanageable or whose behavior you may not be able to predict. If you chose to use a script that substantially disrupts the operation of *Second Life*, disciplinary actions will result in a minimum two-week suspension, the possible loss of in-world inventory, and a review of your account for probable expulsion from *Second Life*.

ALTERNATE ACCOUNTS

While Residents may choose to play *Second Life* with more than one account, specifically or consistently using an alternate account to harass other Residents or violate the Community Standards is not acceptable. Alternate accounts are generally treated as separate from a Resident's principal account, but misuse of alternate accounts can and will result in disciplinary action on the principal account.

BUYER BEWARE

Linden Lab does not exercise editorial control over the content of *Second Life*, and will make no specific efforts to review the textures, objects, sounds or other content created within *Second Life*. Additionally, Linden Lab does not certify or endorse the operation of in-world games, vending machines, or retail locations; refunds must be requested from the owners of these objects.

CHAPTER 1
CHAPTER 2
CHAPTER 3
CHAPTER 4
CHAPTER 5
CHAPTER 6
CHAPTER 7
CHAPTER 8
CHAPTER 9
CHAPTER 10
CHAPTER 11
CHAPTER 12
CHAPTER 13
CHAPTER 14
APPENDICES

INDEX

REPORTING ABUSE

Residents should report violations of the Community Standards using the Abuse Reporter tool located under the Help menu in the in-world tool bar. Every Abuse Report is individually investigated, and the identity of the reporter is kept strictly confidential. If you need immediate assistance, in-world Liaisons may be available to help. Look for Residents with the last name Linden.

■ INTELLECTUAL PROPERTY

You retain copyright and other intellectual property rights with respect to Content you create in *Second Life*, to the extent that you have such rights under applicable law. However, you must make certain representations and warranties, and provide certain license rights, forbearances and indemnification, to Linden Lab and to other users of *Second Life*.

Users of the Service can create Content on Linden Lab's servers in various forms. Linden Lab acknowledges and agrees that, subject to the terms and conditions of this Agreement, you will retain any and all applicable copyright and other intellectual property rights with respect to any Content you create using the Service, to the extent you have such rights under applicable law.

MORE INFO

WHAT ARE IP RIGHTS?

A thumbnail version of the *Second Life* intellectual property is (quoting from `http://secondlife.com/whatis/ip_rights.php`): Linden Lab's Terms of Service agreement recognizes Residents' right to retain full intellectual property protection for the digital content they create in *Second Life*, including avatar characters, clothing, scripts, textures, objects, and designs. This right is enforceable and applicable both in-world and offline, both for non-profit and commercial ventures. You create it, you own it—and it's yours to do with as you please.

Notwithstanding the foregoing, you understand and agree that by submitting your Content to any area of the service, you automatically grant (and you represent and warrant that you have the right to grant) to Linden Lab: (a) a royalty-free, worldwide, fully paid-up, perpetual, irrevocable, non-exclusive right and license to (i) use, reproduce and distribute your Content within the Service as permitted by you through your interactions on the Service, and (ii) use and reproduce (and to authorize third parties to use and reproduce) any of your Content in any or all media for marketing and/or promotional purposes in connection with the Service, provided that in the event that your Content appears publicly in material under the control of Linden Lab, and you provide written notice to Linden Lab of your desire to discontinue the distribution of such Content in such material (with sufficient specificity to allow Linden Lab, in its sole discretion, to identify the relevant Content and materials), Linden Lab will make commercially reasonable efforts to cease its distribution of such Content following the receipt of such notice, although Linden Lab cannot provide any assurances regarding materials produced or distributed prior to the receipt of such notice; (b) the perpetual and irrevocable right to delete any or all of your Content from Linden Lab's servers and from the Service, whether intentionally or unintentionally, and for any reason or no reason, without any liability of any kind to you or any other party; and (c) a royalty- free, fully paid-up, perpetual, irrevocable, non-exclusive right and license to copy, analyze and use any of your Content as Linden Lab may deem necessary or desirable for purposes of debugging, testing and/or providing support services in connection with the Service. Further, you agree to grant to Linden Lab a royalty-free, worldwide, fully paid-up, perpetual, irrevocable, non-exclusive, sublicensable right and license to exercise the copyright, publicity, and database rights you have in your account information, including any data or other information generated by your account activity, in any media now known or not currently known, in accordance with our privacy policy as set forth below, including the incorporation by reference of terms posted at `http://secondlife.com/corporate/privacy.php`.

APPENDICES

APPENDIX A:
RESOURCES

APPENDIX B:
GLOSSARY

APPENDIX C:
SL
COMMUNITY
STANDARDS
AND
INTELLECTUAL
PROPERTY
RIGHTS

APPENDIX D:
ABOUT THE
COMPANION
CD

You also understand and agree that by submitting your Content to any area of the Service, you automatically grant (or you warrant that the owner of such Content has expressly granted) to Linden Lab and to all other users of the Service a non-exclusive, worldwide, fully paid-up, transferable, irrevocable, royalty-free and perpetual License, under any and all patent rights you may have or obtain with respect to your Content, to use your Content for all purposes within the Service. You further agree that you will not make any claims against Linden Lab or against other users of the Service based on any allegations that any activities by either of the foregoing within the Service infringe your (or anyone else's) patent rights.

You further understand and agree that: (i) you are solely responsible for understanding all copyright, patent, trademark, trade secret and other intellectual property or other laws that may apply to your Content hereunder; (ii) you are solely responsible for, and Linden Lab will have no liability in connection with, the legal consequences of any actions or failures to act on your part while using the Service, including without limitation any legal consequences relating to your intellectual property rights; and (iii) Linden Lab's acknowledgement hereunder of your intellectual property rights in your Content does not constitute a legal opinion or legal advice, but is intended solely as an expression of Linden Lab's intention not to require users of the Service to forego certain intellectual property rights with respect to Content they create using the Service, subject to the terms of this Agreement.

CHAPTER 1
CHAPTER 2
CHAPTER 3
CHAPTER 4
CHAPTER 5
CHAPTER 6
CHAPTER 7
CHAPTER 8
CHAPTER 9
CHAPTER 10
CHAPTER 11
CHAPTER 12
CHAPTER 13
CHAPTER 14
APPENDICES
INDEX

APPENDIX D: ABOUT THE COMPANION CD

■ WHAT YOU'LL FIND ON THE CD

The following sections are arranged by category and provide a summary of the software and other goodies you'll find on the CD. If you need help with installing the items provided on the CD, refer to the installation instructions in the "Using the CD" section of this appendix.

Some programs on the CD might fall into one of these categories:

Shareware programs are fully functional, free, trial versions of copyrighted programs. If you like particular programs, register with their authors for a nominal fee and receive licenses, enhanced versions, and technical support.

Freeware programs are free, copyrighted games, applications, and utilities. You can copy them to as many computers as you like—for free—but they offer no technical support.

GNU software is governed by its own license, which is included inside the folder of the GNU software. There are no restrictions on distribution of GNU software. See the GNU license at the root of the CD for more details.

Trial, *demo*, or *evaluation* versions of software are usually limited either by time or functionality (such as not letting you save a project after you create it).

■ AIRPLANE TUTORIAL FILES

Here you'll find all the files you need to complete Chapter 14's tutorial.

■ SCRIPTS

Check out all the scripts from Chapters 6–8. We've also included a popular vehicle script from Linden Lab and a couple from Jopsy Pendragon: his very well-commented basic particle script as well as his "Scrubber," which is a great tool for cleaning many of the persistent and annoying attributes that only scripts can set or reset. Visit Jopsy's Particle Lab at `http://slurl.com/secondlife/Teal/200/50/21/`. Hop in the balloon when you get there and you'll be on your way.

■ TEMPLATES AND TOOLS

Here you'll find a collection of templates and software to aid all *Second Life* content creators.

- The avatar texturing templates by Chip Midnight and another set by Linden Lab will help you create beautiful clothing and skins. Use them with the avatar mannequin in the disc's "Animation Resources" section and get more info on Chip's templates at `http://goodies.onrez.com/shop/chipmidnight/`.

- You'll also find Vince Invincible's Avimator (`http://avimator.com/`) and the follow-on port Qavimator (`http://www.qavimator.org`), excellent open source tools for easily creating avatar animations. Use them with the templates in the "Animation Resources" section of the disc.

APPENDICES

APPENDIX A:
RESOURCES

APPENDIX B:
GLOSSARY

APPENDIX C:
SL
COMMUNITY
STANDARDS
AND
INTELLECTUAL
PROPERTY
RIGHTS

APPENDIX D:
ABOUT THE
COMPANION
CD

- Backhoe (http://www.notabene-sl.com/Backhoe/), by Zarf Vantongerloo, is a region terrain editor. Even if you don't own an island yet, you can experiment with the RAW terrain files Linden Lab has provided.

- Finally, check out Sweet Vitriol's (http://www.sweetvitriol.com) cool *Second Life* Status Widget, which shows all kinds of useful information (friends, visitors, fps, etc.).

ANIMATION RESOURCES

Get the avatar mannequin and more than 100 great sample animations.

TEXTURES

Here you'll find tons of textures created by Linden Lab and Aimee Weber: everything from floors and walls to clothing and cloth. You'll also find cool shadow overlays.

MACHINIMA

We've included a sampling of great resident-created video. Check out:

- *Lip Flap*, by David Laundra (a.k.a., Kronos Kirkorian): http://kronostv.com

- *Watch the World(s)* and *Better Life*, by Robbie Dingo: http://digitaldouble.blogspot.com/

- *Battle for Truth: The Birth of Stephen Eagleman* (a.k.a. *Stephen Colbert's Dream*) and *Second Life: Get One* by Silver and Goldie: http://silverandgoldie.com

- *Tale from Midnight City* by Trace Sanderson (a.k.a., *Lainy Voom and Tracechops*): tracesanderson@hotmail.com

- *Silver Bells & Golden Spurs*, by Eric Call: http://ericcallmedia.com

GUIDES

Here you'll find some additional resources for your content-creating pleasure, including a great building demonstration video as well as Robbie Dingo's *Suzanne's Guitar* video so you can see how fast the pros operate. There's also more information on the Linden Scripting Language, machinima, and a region terraformability list.

■ SYSTEM REQUIREMENTS

Make sure that your computer meets the minimum system requirements shown in the following list. If your computer doesn't match up to these requirements, you may have problems using the software and files on the companion CD. For the latest and greatest information, please refer to the ReadMe file located at the root of the CD-ROM.

- A PC running Microsoft Windows 2000 (service pack 4) or Windows XP (service pack 2)

- A Macintosh running Apple OS X 10.3.9 or better

- A CD-ROM drive

■ USING THE CD

To install the items from the CD to your hard drive, follow these steps.

1. Insert the CD into your computer's CD-ROM drive. The license agreement appears.

NOTE

*Windows users: The interface won't launch if you have autorun disabled. In that case, click Start
▸ Run (for Windows Vista, Start ▸ All Programs ▸ Accessories ▸ Run). In the dialog box that
appears, type* D:\Start.exe. *(Replace D with the proper letter if your CD drive uses a different
letter. If you don't know the letter, see how your CD drive is listed under My Computer.) Click OK.*

*Mac users: The CD icon will appear on your desktop; double-click the icon to open the CD,
and double-click the Start icon.*

**2. Read through the license agreement and then click the Accept button if you want to use
the CD.**

The CD interface appears. The interface allows you to access the content with just one or
two clicks.

■ TROUBLESHOOTING

Wiley has attempted to provide programs that work on most computers with the minimum system
requirements. Alas, your computer may differ, and some programs may not work properly for
some reason.

The two likeliest problems are that you don't have enough memory (RAM) for the programs
you want to use, or you have other programs running that are affecting installation or running of a
program. If you get an error message such as "Not enough memory" or "Setup cannot continue," try
one or more of the following suggestions and then try using the software again:

- **Turn off any antivirus software running on your computer.** Installation programs
  sometimes mimic virus activity and may make your computer incorrectly believe that it's
  being infected by a virus.

- **Close all running programs.** The more programs you have running, the less memory is
  available to other programs. Installation programs typically update files and programs, so
  if you keep other programs running, installation may not work properly.

- **Have your local computer store add more RAM to your computer.** This is, admittedly, a
  drastic and somewhat expensive step. However, adding more memory can really help the
  speed of your computer and allow more programs to run at the same time.

■ CUSTOMER CARE

If you have trouble with the book's companion CD-ROM, please call the Wiley Product Technical
Support phone number at (800) 762-2974. Outside the United States, call +1(317) 572-3994.
You can also contact Wiley Product Technical Support at http://sybex.custhelp.com. John Wiley
& Sons will provide technical support only for installation and other general quality-control items.
For technical support on the applications themselves, consult the program's vendor or author.

To place additional orders or to request information about other Wiley products, please call
(877) 762-2974.

Note to the Reader:
Throughout this index **boldfaced** page numbers indicate primary discussions of a topic. *Italicized* page numbers indicate illustrations.

CHAPTER 1
CHAPTER 2
CHAPTER 3
CHAPTER 4
CHAPTER 5
CHAPTER 6
CHAPTER 7
CHAPTER 8
CHAPTER 9
CHAPTER 10
CHAPTER 11
CHAPTER 12
CHAPTER 13
CHAPTER 14
APPENDICES
INDEX

CHAPTER 1
CHAPTER 2
CHAPTER 3
CHAPTER 4
CHAPTER 5
CHAPTER 6
CHAPTER 7
CHAPTER 8
CHAPTER 9
CHAPTER 10
CHAPTER 11
CHAPTER 12
CHAPTER 13
CHAPTER 14
APPENDICES
INDEX

CHAPTER 1
CHAPTER 2
CHAPTER 3
CHAPTER 4
CHAPTER 5
CHAPTER 6
CHAPTER 7
CHAPTER 8
CHAPTER 9
CHAPTER 10
CHAPTER 11
CHAPTER 12
CHAPTER 13
CHAPTER 14
APPENDICES
INDEX

CHAPTER 1
CHAPTER 2
CHAPTER 3
CHAPTER 4
CHAPTER 5
CHAPTER 6
CHAPTER 7
CHAPTER 8
CHAPTER 9
CHAPTER 10
CHAPTER 11
CHAPTER 12
CHAPTER 13
CHAPTER 14
APPENDICES
INDEX

CHAPTER 1
CHAPTER 2
CHAPTER 3
CHAPTER 4
CHAPTER 5
CHAPTER 6
CHAPTER 7
CHAPTER 8
CHAPTER 9
CHAPTER 10
CHAPTER 11
CHAPTER 12
CHAPTER 13
CHAPTER 14
APPENDICES
INDEX

Get down to business.

Business is flourishing in Second Life, and many savvy residents are earning real-world money selling their virtual goods. This full-color guide has everything you need to set up shop in Second Life, including an overview of the SL economy, top traits of successful in-world businesses, and great ideas on planning, starting, and running a wide range of businesses in the metaverse.

978-0-470-17914-7